Policy Issues
for Business

Policy Issues for Business: A Reader

This book – *Policy Issues for Business: A Reader* – is one of a series of three readers which constitute the main teaching texts of the Open University course Business Behaviour in a Changing World (B300). The other titles are *Decision Making for Business: A Reader*, edited by Graeme Salaman and *Strategy for Business: A Reader*, edited by Mariana Mazzucato.

This course is one of three core courses which are compulsory elements in the Open University's BA in Business Studies. In addition to the compulsory courses, students who intend to gain this degree also study courses which include topics such as Economics, Organizational Change, Design and Innovation, Quantitative Methods.

Business Behaviour in a Changing World (B300) is innovative in terms of the breadth of material studied. The course covers decision-making, strategy and policy from a variety of different theoretical stances supplemented by a range of empirical findings. In this way B300 provides a synthesis of each of the fields while at the same time considering the important linkages betweeen them.

As with all Open University courses, students are not only supplied with teaching texts; they also receive comprehensive guidance on how to study and work through these texts. In the case of B300, this guidance is contained in three Study Guides which are supplied to students separately. These guides explain the choice of readings, identify key points and guide the students' work and understanding. A core feature of the guides is an explicit focus on the identification, development, deployment and testing of a series of business graduate skills. These include study skills, cognitive skills of analysis and assessment, IT and numeracy.

Each student is allocated a local tutor and is encouraged to participate in a strategically integrated set of tutorials which are held during the course.

Details of this and other Open University courses can be obtained from the Course Reservation Centre, PO Box 724, The Open University, Milton Keynes MK7 6ZS, United Kingdom. Tel.: +44 (0)1908 653231, e-mail: ces-gen@open.ac.uk. Alternatively, you may visit the Open University website at http://www.open.ac.uk where you can learn more about the wide range of courses and packs offered at all levels by the Open University.

For information about the purchase of Open University course components, contact Open University Worldwide Ltd, The Berrill Building, Walton Hall, Milton Keynes MK7 6AA, United Kingdom. Tel.: +44 (0)1908 858785; fax: +44 (0)1908 858787; e-mail: ouwenq@open.ac.uk; website: http://www.ouw.co.uk.

Policy Issues
for Business

A READER

EDITED BY VIVEK SUNEJA

SAGE Publications
London · Thousand Oaks · New Delhi
www.sagepub.co.uk

in association with

www.open.ac.uk

First published 2002

SAGE Publications Ltd
6 Bonhill Street
London EC2A 4PU

SAGE Publications Inc
2455 Teller Road
Thousand Oaks, California 91320

SAGE Publications India Pvt Ltd
32, M-Block Market
Greater Kailash – I
New Delhi 110 048

British Library Cataloguing in Publication data

A catalogue record for this book is available from the British Library

ISBN 0–7619–7414–8
ISBN 0–7619–7415–6(pbk)

Library of Congress control number available

Typeset by SIVA Math Setters, Chennai, India
Printed in Great Britain by The Alden Press, Oxford

The importance and influence of business in the modern world has been widely recognized. For us as citizens, consumers, employees, managers, voters and so on, understandings how firms, and indeed all forms of organization work, is therefore of direct relevance. The way that businesses conduct themselves affects us all. As a consequence it is vital for us to understand how they make decisions, for example to invest in some products or services rather than others. The variety of factors that are taken into account, the way in which conclusions are reached, all help us get to grips with these sorts of issues. This involves developing an understanding of how decisions in organizations are made. We also should understand the strategies that businesses pursue, the development of their core competencies as well as how organizations innovate. Finally, the range of policy issues from regulation of competition to environment and the developing world provide a rich contextual seam within which strategies and decisions are made in a world where the norm is change.

This book is one in a series of three readers which bring together classic and seminal materials, many of them summaries and reviews, which are designed to achieve the teaching objectives of the Open University course Business Behaviour in a Changing World (B300) – a core course in the Open University's BA in Business Studies. The volumes are organized in an innovative way around three important themes: decision-making, strategy and policy. The volumes have been designed to supply a selection of articles, theoretical and empirical, in each of these areas. They are supported by study guides so that together they allow the identification, development, deployment and practice of a range of skills required by the Business Studies courses in general. Therefore while they constitute the core teaching resources of this Open University course, the volumes would also make admirable selections for any course concerned with these areas. They are not intended to be cutting edge or fashionable. They are designed as a resource for anyone seeking an understanding of the changing nature of organizations and of the world of business.

Each of these volumes has been edited by members of the course team. But in a very real sense they are collective products of the course team as a whole. That is why all the members of the course team deserve recognition and acknowledgement for their contribution to the course and to these collections.

Contents

ACKNOWLEDGEMENTS

Chapter 1: *The New Republic* for 'The Insider' by J. Stiglitz © J. Stiglitz, 17 April, 2000.

Chapter 2: *The New Republic* for 'Stiglitz vs. The IMF: Another View' by R. Dornbusch © R. Dornbusch, April 2000.

Chapter 3: Simon & Schuster, Inc., for an extract from *Economics Explained* by Robert L. Heilbroner and Lester C. Thurow. Copyright ©1982, 1987 by Robert L. Heilbroner and Lester C. Thurow.

Chapter 4: Edward Elgar Publishing Limited for an extract from *Culture, Social Norms and Economics* by Mark Casson © Mark Casson, 1997.

Chapter 5: Oxford University Press for an extract from *The Economics of the European Union, 2nd Edition* by M.J. Artis and Normal Lee © D. Young and S. Metcalfe, 1997.

Chapter 6: *Harvard Journal of Law and Public Policy* for 'Externalities in Open Economy Antitrust and their Implications for International Competition Policy' by A. Sykes, Vol 23, Issue 1 © *Harvard Journal of Law and Public Policy*, 1999.

Chapter 7: MCB University Press for 'Science Policy and Technology Policy in a Competitive Economy' by J.S. Metcalfe © *International Journal of Social Economics*, Vol 24, No 7/8/9.

Chapter 8: Oxford University Press for C. Freeman, 'The National System of Innovation in Historical Perspective', *Cambridge Journal of Economics*, 1995, Vol 19, No 1.

Chapter 9: *Harvard Business Review* for an extract from 'The Competitive Advantage of Nations' by M. Porter, March–April, 1990. Copyright © 1990 by the Harvard Business School Publishing Corporation. All rights reserved.

Chapter 10: Oxford University Press, India for an extract from *Trade and Industrialization* by Deepak Nayyar © S. Lall, 1997.

Chapter 11: Oxford University Press for P. Krugman, 'Making Sense of the Competitiveness Debate', *Oxford Review of Economic Policy*, 1996, Vol 12, No 3.

Chapter 12: Oxford University Press, India for an extract from *Trade and Industrialization* by Deepak Nayyar © Deepak Nayyar, 1997.

Chapter 13: Oxford University Press for an extract from *Governments, Globalization and International Business* by John H. Dunning © John H. Dunning, 1997.

Chapter 14: UNCTAD/DITE, *World Investment Report 1999* for 'Foreign Direct Investment and the Challenge of Development' in *Transnational Corporations,* Vol 8, No 3 © UNCTAD/DITE, *World Investment Report* 1999.

Chapter 15: The Random House Group Ltd for an extract from *On the Edge* by W. Hutton and A. Giddens, published by Jonathan Cape © M. Castells, 2000.

Chapter 16: Oxford University Press for C. Lawson, 'Towards a Competence Theory of the Region', *Cambridge Journal of Economics*, 1999, Vol 23, No 2.

Chapter 17: Oxford University Press for F. Belussi, 'Policies for the Development of Knowledge-Intensive Local Production Systems', *Cambridge Journal of Economics*, 1999, Vol 23, No 6.

Chapter 18: The Open University (1995) D216 *Economics and Changing Economics* Book 4, Chapter 27, 'Sustainable Development', © The Open University.

Chapter 18, Table 18.1: Kogan Page for *Blueprint 3: Measuring Sustainable Development* by David Pearce, et al., published by Earthscan Publications, Ltd. © D. Moran, 1994. Table 18.2: Oxford University Press for *World Without End: Economics Environment, and Sustainable Development* by David W. Pearce and Jeremy J. Warford © 1993 The International Bank for Reconstruction and Development/The World Bank.

P*olicy Issues for Business: A Reader* aims to provide undergraduate and postgraduate students of business, economics and management, including those studying for the MBA, with a critical analysis and discussion of policy issues relating to business.

The key objectives that this book endeavours to achieve include the recognition of the vital importance of policy for businesses, individuals and nations and an appreciation of the rationale for policy. It offers a critical evaluation of the link between different theoretical perspectives and policy and an in-depth understanding of selected policy issues. The book places business within the context of its legal, technological, economic and socio-cultural environment.

What is the relevance of policy to business?

Why is it important to study policy as part of one's study of business? Policy sets the rules of the game by which businesses have to play. But why do we need rules anyway? Shouldn't the operation of the 'free' market obviate the need for any rules? Who sets these rules? Do these rules promote the interests of some more than of others? Can governments and policy makers improve the performance of economies beyond what may be generated by the free play of spontaneous market forces?

It is questions such as the above that a study of policy seeks to answer. No market economy can operate without the establishment and enforcement of certain minimal rules such as those relating to property rights. But often, for markets to work effectively, much more than these minimalist rules are required. This constitutes the domain of economic and business policy.

One can hardly overstate the importance of policy. As Stiglitz demonstrates in Chapter 1 of this book, if policy makers get it wrong, whole nations can be destroyed. Equally, if policy makers get it right, this can enormously facilitate business growth and socio-economic welfare.

A neglected subject?

Despite the critical importance of policy for business, the study of business and management these days seems to neglect a proper study of policy. This is perhaps because the focus of business and management studies tends to be on the operations of the individual business. But, as mentioned above, a business's purposes and actions can be considerably influenced by the industry, national and international policy regime in which it operates. Businesses also need not be, and indeed are often not, passive reactants to the policy framework; they play a vital role in shaping policy. It is hence important that any study of business and management should include a systematic study of the subject of policy. This book is designed for such a purpose. We hope to stimulate the study of policy as a regular and integral part of business and management studies. This book endeavours to provide resources for such a purpose by collating some key readings in policy. There is presently a dearth of such a compendium; we hope that this book will go some way in fulfilling this need.

Is policy akin to strategic management?

Strategic management is currently an important and popular element in business and management studies. Just as firms need to be managed strategically, so too in many ways do other economic units such as industries, regions, nations and the international economy. Traditionally, aspects of governance relating to these economic units have been referred to as 'policy'. But, if we wished, we could also refer to these as 'strategic' management. The objectives underlying the strategic management of firms and the strategic management (policy governance) of regions, industries or nations have considerable similarity. In both cases, the aim is consciously and purposefully to plan for the long term, to integrate and co-ordinate diverse elements, and to try to achieve a degree of control over the environment and the future. A simple reaction to spontaneous market forces does not constitute strategic management at the level of the firm; nor does it constitute policy governance at the level of the industry, region, nation or the world.

If policy can be thought of as strategic management at a supra-firm level, why is it that while the subject of strategic management is so popular in business and management studies, the subject of policy suffers from relative neglect? We have already discussed one possible reason for this: the focus of business and management studies currently tends to be on the individual organization. The other probable reason for this has perhaps to do with the current economic and political climate of *laissez-faire*. While strategic management at the level of the firm is the responsibility of private entrepreneurs, many of the policy tasks are the responsibility of local, regional, national or international governmental bodies. Many today seem to believe that governments are incapable of doing anything right. So, the argument goes, even though policy may in principle be capable of improving upon market-mediated outcomes, in practice governments are likely to fail to deliver. This, however, is perhaps too pessimistic a view of the role that policy can play. As this book demonstrates, policy makers can play a highly useful role in improving economic performance. It is also critical to remember that while policy failures can carry significant costs, these costs may be outweighed by the costs of market failures that would occur in the absence of policy intervention. Not all policy is formulated and implemented by governments anyway: employer associations, trade unions, charities, clubs, regional associations – all can play an important role in the policy arena.

Conflicting theories, conflicting policies

One must bear in mind the distinction between a descriptive and a theoretical treatment of any subject. It is one thing to describe a policy, it is quite another to understand its rationale. Policies can only be properly understood in the context of their underpinning theoretical perspectives. But often there is more than one theory that 'explains' any business phenomenon, and these theories may offer conflicting perspectives. Consequently, policy prescriptions are often quite sensitive to the nature of one's theoretical position about how 'the world works'. This implies that any serious study of policy must be accompanied by an investigation of the various theoretical perspectives that relate to the business phenomenon under study. This is the approach that this book follows, offering a diversity of theoretical perspectives on the policy issues under consideration.

Self-interest, prejudice, ideology

Policy making is rarely neutral in terms of its consequences for economic participants. It is hence unlikely that those affected will view the analysis that underpins policy making in a dispassionate, even-handed or fair fashion. People's preferences for one theoretical standpoint over the other may be coloured, consciously or unconsciously, by the nature of economic, political and ideological consequences that follow for themselves or for their communities. Are academics likely to be truly neutral, however, untouched by motives of personal gain or by prejudice? Concern has been voiced, for example, that the close links that exist in some countries between the faculty of business schools and senior management in organizations pose the danger that academic discourse may be influenced such that it takes greater cognisance of the concerns of senior management than of the other stakeholders in the firm. Following a similar logic, it is possible to argue that academics working in the developed world may come to very different policy analysis and conclusions than academics working in developing nations. This points to the need for the exercise of the utmost vigilance when evaluating policy, and the need to consider critically a variety of perspectives.

Do values and culture matter?

Analysis of business policy issues is based to a very considerable degree on economic theory and analysis. It is therefore important that we pay special attention to the assumptions that, overtly or covertly, underlie theorizing in the discipline of economics. Casson (Chapter 4) points out that many theories in economics are based, explicitly or implicitly, on the assumptions that economic agents are exclusively selfish and exclusively materialistic. Human beings are assumed neither to care about the welfare of others, nor to care about non-material sources of satisfaction (such as emotional or spiritual satisfaction). Neo-classical economics argues that the working of the competitive market ensures that when such selfish and money-minded individuals try to maximize their rewards, the competitive process generally generates an outcome that is in everybody's collective interest. As Adam Smith pointed out, our dinner comes not from the butcher's generosity but from his self-interest. Being exclusively selfish, and being exclusively materialistic, is consequently no bad thing. Casson points out that such ideas are based on an incomplete understanding of how a market economy works. For many markets to work efficiently, a considerable degree of integrity and trust is required. An economic system that is able to invoke and make use of a high level of trust, integrity and character is likely to perform far more efficiently and effectively compared to a system that lacks these cultural attributes. But if trust and social norms are important for the functioning of a market economy, then this, in addition to leading us to question the assumptions of economic theory, also poses important issues for policy. How are trust and honesty in a society to be created and maintained, for example? And what role can policy play in this regard? This book argues that policy should no longer be seen to be limited to the manipulation of economic variables. Given the vital importance of cultural factors to the economy and society at large, culture must be given its due consideration by policy makers.

Is policy democratic?

How democratic is the formulation and choice of policy? There seem to be presently a number of impediments to having genuine democracy in the policy arena. On the one hand, many policy decisions are currently made by policy 'experts', bureaucrats or politicians without sufficient democratic scrutiny. Stiglitz (Chapter 1), for example, draws attention to the lack of transparency and accountability that surrounds decision making by the International Monetary Fund, even though the policies that emanate from this organization have major consequences for millions of people world-wide. Genuine democracy is also often hindered by the electorate's lack of sufficient knowledge of policy. If the fundamentals of policy were more widely known, this would probably generate a higher quality of debate on many policy issues. Governments would then have less of a pretext to refer important policy issues to the 'experts', and the expert advice would be subject to closer and wider scrutiny. The media also need to rethink their vital responsibilities in this regard.

Structure of the book

The book begins by outlining the significance and rationale for policy in a market economy (Section 1: 'Policy: Significance and Rationale'). Since it is unfeasible to explore in detail all the various aspects of business-related policy in a single book, we have had to be selective in our choice of policy topics. Consequently, the remainder of the book explores some of the key dimensions of business policy making. In Section 2, 'Competition Policy', we analyse policies that aim to maintain the 'right' degree and kind of competition in a market economy. The acceleration in national and cross-border mergers and acquisitions since the 1990s has made a consideration of such competition issues very pertinent and urgent. In Section 3, 'Science, Technology and Innovation Policy', we broaden our concern from the regulatory role of policy to the facilitative and supportive functions of policy. Why do we need to have a policy on science, technology and innovation? Shouldn't the free market take care of these matters? Is it more important to have such science and technology policies in developing countries than in developed ones? In Section 4, 'International Trade and Investment Policy', we investigate why policy is required at the supra-national level with respect to the international dimension of economic activity. The increased pace of globalization since the 1980s raises a number of questions about both the pace and the character of globalization that we are currently witnessing, and how (if at all) we should be trying to regulate or influence this process. While the importance of international policy is increasing, policy issues at the sub-national level, such as at the regional level, are becoming more important too. This is the subject of inquiry in Section 5, 'Regional Policy'. The increased integration of the global economy seems to be, in many ways, accentuating rather than diminishing the distinctiveness of geographic regions. The final section, Section 6, 'Environmental Policy', explores another important dimension of policy: that relating to the natural environment. With ever-increasing environmental degradation, the need for urgent action in this policy area is becoming increasingly obvious to all, but reaching agreement here has proved to be highly difficult so far. If some experts on climate change are to be believed, then time may be running out. But, as we shall see, environmental policy cannot be meaningfully considered without looking at many of the other policy areas, such as international trade and investment policy and policy on science, technology and innovation. This means that the whole subject of policy is assuming critical importance and urgency – indeed the very survival of our planet may depend on the wisdom with which we exercise our policy options.

A final remark

The purpose of this book is as much to raise questions as to seek to provide answers. We hope to provoke you into thinking and questioning. We hope you shall come up with some answers of your own and raise some new questions as well!

We hope you enjoy this book. *Bon voyage*!

Policy: Significance and Rationale

How important is policy? What is its rationale? What are the assumptions on which it is based? These are the fundamental questions that this section addresses.

We begin by looking at two pieces by Stiglitz and Dornbusch respectively that present starkly contrasting views on the role played by the International Monetary Fund in handling the East Asian financial crisis. During the time of the Asian crisis, Stiglitz was chief economist and vice-president of the World Bank. By virtue of his position, he was able to have an 'insider's' view of how the IMF went about handling the crisis. Stiglitz is highly critical of the theoretical and ideological analysis that underpins policy making by the IMF. He also questions the fund's motives. Dornbusch (Chapter 2) offers a vehement rebuttal to Stiglitz. It is indeed revealing how two reputed economists and policy makers can hold such vastly different views on policy and with such strength of feeling. These two chapters demonstrate the enormous impact policy can have on the affairs of businesses, individuals and nations. It is hence imperative that all of us seek to understand what policy is all about.

Chapter 3, by Heilbroner and Thurow, introduces us to why business-related policy is necessary in a market economy. Heilbroner and Thurow sketch out the economic rationale for policy making. This includes the existence of multiple kinds of market failure, such as externalities, public goods, information asymmetries, coordination failures and problems arising from imperfect competition. Market economies may also generate unacceptable inequities in income and wealth distribution. The existence of market failures does not automatically justify policy intervention: the benefits from intervention must exceed the costs of intervention.

Chapter 4, by Casson, is about the role of values, norms and culture in economic life. Casson demonstrates how narrow and unreal are the cultural assumptions of economic theory. The narrow cultural assumptions were introduced in economic theory as simplifying assumptions to make the economist's task easier. Although this abstraction has indeed made life simpler for the mathematical modeller in economics, and led to the creation of a vast super-structure of 'sophisticated' economic theory, the foundations on which this edifice has been created are not quite sound. Policy makers must take note of our capacity for non-material kinds of satisfaction, for caring about the welfare of others, and for self-restraint. Policy must also try to explore how integrity and character can be created and maintained in society. Religion, the family, the arts, the media, political institutions, cultural institutions – all may have an important role to play in this regard. So may business leaders – creating appropriate corporate cultures and standards of conduct. Policy makers may need to explore how they can encourage and support these various institutions in their cultural role.

C HAPTER 1

The Insider: What I Learned at the World Economic Crisis

JOSEPH STIGLITZ*

Next week's meeting of the International Monetary Fund will bring to Washington, D.C., many of the same demonstrators who trashed the World Trade Organization in Seattle. They'll say the International Monetary Fund (IMF) is arrogant. They'll say the IMF doesn't really listen to the developing countries it is supposed to help. They'll say the IMF is secretive and insulated from democratic accountability. They'll say the IMF's economic 'remedies' often make things worse – turning slowdowns into recessions and recessions into depressions.

And they'll have a point. I was chief economist at the World Bank from 1996 until last November [2000], during the gravest global economic crisis in a half-century. I saw how the IMF, in tandem with the U.S. Treasury Department, responded. And I was appalled.

The global economic crisis began in Thailand, on July 2, 1997. The countries of East Asia were coming off a miraculous three decades: incomes had soared, health had improved, poverty had fallen dramatically. Not only was literacy now universal, but, on international science and math tests, many of these countries outperformed the United States. Some had not suffered a single year of recession in 30 years.

But the seeds of calamity had already been planted. In the early '90s, East Asian countries had liberalized their financial and capital markets – not because they needed to attract more funds (savings rates were already 30 per cent or more) but because of international pressure, including some from the U.S. Treasury Department. These changes provoked a flood of short-term capital – that is, the kind of capital that looks for the highest return in the next day, week, or month, as opposed to long-term investment in things like factories. In Thailand, this short-term capital helped fuel an unsustainable real estate boom.

* *The New Republic* for 'The Insider' by J. Stiglitz © J. Stiglitz, 17 April, 2000.

And, as people around the world (including Americans) have painfully learned, every real estate bubble eventually bursts, often with disastrous consequences. Just as suddenly as capital flowed in, it flowed out. And, when everybody tries to pull their money out at the same time, it causes an economic problem. A big economic problem.

The last set of financial crises had occurred in Latin America in the 1980s, when bloated public deficits and loose monetary policies led to runaway inflation. There, the IMF had correctly imposed fiscal austerity (balanced budgets) and tighter monetary policies, demanding that governments pursue those policies as a precondition for receiving aid. So, in 1997 the IMF imposed the same demands on Thailand. Austerity, the fund's leaders said, would restore confidence in the Thai economy. As the crisis spread to other East Asian nations – and even as evidence of the policy's failure mounted – the IMF barely blinked, delivering the same medicine to each ailing nation that showed up on its doorstep.

I thought this was a mistake. For one thing, unlike the Latin American nations, the East Asian countries were *already* running budget surpluses. In Thailand, the government was running such large surpluses that it was actually starving the economy of much-needed investments in education and infrastructure, both essential to economic growth. And the East Asian nations already had tight monetary policies, as well: inflation was low and falling. (In South Korea, for example, inflation stood at a very respectable 4 per cent.) The problem was not imprudent government, as in Latin America; the problem was an imprudent private sector – all those bankers and borrowers, for instance, who'd gambled on the real estate bubble.

Under such circumstances, I feared, austerity measures would not revive the economies of East Asia – it would plunge them into recession or even depression. High interest rates might devastate highly indebted East Asian firms, causing more bankruptcies and defaults. Reduced government expenditures would only shrink the economy further.

So I began lobbying to change the policy. I talked to Stanley Fischer, a distinguished former Massachusetts Institute of Technology economics professor and former chief economist of the World Bank, who had become the IMF's first deputy managing director. I met with fellow economists at the World Bank who might have contacts or influence within the IMF, encouraging them to do everything they could to move the IMF bureaucracy.

Convincing people at the World Bank of my analysis proved easy; changing minds at the IMF was virtually impossible. When I talked to senior officials at the IMF – explaining, for instance, how high interest rates might increase bankruptcies, thus making it even harder to restore confidence in East Asian economies – they would at first resist. Then, after failing to come up with an effective counterargument, they would retreat to another response: if only I understood the pressure coming from the IMF board of executive directors – the body, appointed by finance ministers from the advanced industrial countries, that approves all the IMF's loans. Their meaning was clear. The board's inclination was to be even more severe;

these people were actually a moderating influence. My friends who were executive directors said they were the ones getting pressured. It was maddening, not just because the IMF's inertia was so hard to stop but because, with everything going on behind closed doors, it was impossible to know who was the real obstacle to change. Was the staff pushing the executive directors, or were the executive directors pushing the staff? I still do not know for certain.

Of course, everybody at the IMF assured me they would be flexible: if their policies really turned out to be overly contractionary, forcing the East Asian economies into deeper recession than necessary, then they would reverse them. This sent shudders down my spine. One of the first lessons economists teach their graduate students is the importance of lags: it takes 12 to 18 months before a change in monetary policy (raising or lowering interest rates) shows its full effects. When I worked in the White House as chairman of the Council of Economic Advisers, we focused all our energy on forecasting where the economy would be in the future, so we could know what policies to recommend today. To play catch-up was the height of folly. And that was precisely what the IMF officials were proposing to do.

I shouldn't have been surprised. The IMF likes to go about its business without outsiders asking too many questions. In theory, the fund supports democratic institutions in the nations it assists. In practice, it undermines the democratic process by imposing policies. Officially, of course, the IMF doesn't 'impose' anything. It 'negotiates' the conditions for receiving aid. But all the power in the negotiations is on one side – the IMF's – and the fund rarely allows sufficient time for broad consensus-building or even widespread consultations with either parliaments or civil society. Sometimes the IMF dispenses with the pretense of openness altogether and negotiates secret covenants.

When the IMF decides to assist a country, it dispatches a 'mission' of economists. These economists frequently lack extensive experience in the country; they are more likely to have firsthand knowledge of its five-star hotels than of the villages that dot its countryside. They work hard, poring over numbers deep into the night. But their task is impossible. In a period of days or, at most, weeks, they are charged with developing a coherent program sensitive to the needs of the country. Needless to say, a little number-crunching rarely provides adequate insights into the development strategy for an entire nation. Even worse, the number-crunching isn't always that good. The mathematical models the IMF uses are frequently flawed or out-of-date. Critics accuse the institution of taking a cookie-cutter approach to economics, and they're right. Country teams have been known to compose draft reports before visiting. I heard stories of one unfortunate incident when team members copied large parts of the text for one country's report and transferred them wholesale to another. They might have gotten away with it, except the 'search and replace' function on the word processor didn't work properly, leaving the original country's name in a few places. Oops.

It's not fair to say that IMF economists don't care about the citizens of developing nations. But the older men who staff the fund – and they are overwhelmingly older men – act as if they are shouldering Rudyard Kipling's white man's burden. IMF experts believe they are brighter, more educated, and less politically motivated than the economists in the countries they visit. In fact, the economic leaders from those countries are pretty good – in many cases brighter or better-educated than the IMF staff, which frequently consists of third-rank students from first-rate universities. (Trust me: I've taught at Oxford University, MIT, Stanford University, Yale University, and Princeton University, and the IMF almost never succeeded in recruiting any of the best students.) Last summer, I gave a seminar in China on competition policy in telecommunications. At least three Chinese economists in the audience asked questions as sophisticated as the best minds in the West would have asked.

As time passed, my frustration mounted. (One might have thought that since the World Bank was contributing literally billions of dollars to the rescue packages, its voice would be heard. But it was ignored almost as resolutely as the people in the affected countries.) The IMF claimed that all it was asking of the East Asian countries was that they balance their budgets at a time of recession. *All*? Hadn't the Clinton administration just fought a major battle with Congress to stave off a balanced-budget amendment in this country? And wasn't the administration's key argument that, in the face of recession, a little deficit spending might be necessary? This is what I and most other economists had been teaching our graduate students for 60 years. Quite frankly, a student who turned in the IMF's answer to the test question 'What should be the fiscal stance of Thailand, facing an economic down-turn?' would have gotten an F.

As the crisis spread to Indonesia, I became even more concerned. New research at the World Bank showed that recession in such an ethnically divided country could spark all kinds of social and political turmoil. So in late 1997, at a meeting of finance ministers and central-bank governors in Kuala Lumpur, I issued a carefully prepared statement vetted by the World Bank: I suggested that the excessively contractionary monetary and fiscal program could lead to political and social turmoil in Indonesia. Again, the IMF stood its ground. The fund's managing director, Michel Camdessus, said there what he'd said in public: that East Asia simply had to grit it out, as Mexico had. He went on to note that, for all of the short-term pain, Mexico emerged from the experience stronger.

But this was an absurd analogy. Mexico hadn't recovered because the IMF forced it to strengthen its weak financial system, which remained weak years after the crisis. It recovered because of a surge of exports to the United States, which took off thanks to the U.S. economic boom, and because of the North American Free Trade Association (NAFTA). By contrast, Indonesia's main trading partner was Japan – which was then, and still remains, mired in the doldrums. Furthermore, Indonesia was far more politically and socially explosive than Mexico, with a much deeper history of ethnic strife. And renewed strife would produce massive capital flight (made easy by relaxed currency-flow restrictions encouraged by the IMF). But none of these arguments mattered. The IMF pressed ahead, demanding reductions in government spending. And so subsidies for basic necessities like food and fuel were eliminated at the very time when contractionary policies made those subsidies more desperately needed than ever.

By January 1998, things had gotten so bad that the World Bank's vice president for East Asia, Jean Michel Severino, invoked the dreaded r-word ('recession') and d-word ('depression') in describing the economic calamity in Asia. Lawrence Summers, then deputy treasury secretary, railed against Severino for making things seem worse than they were, but what other way was there to describe what was happening? Output in some of the affected countries fell 16 per cent or more. Half the businesses in Indonesia were in virtual bankruptcy or close to it, and, as a result, the country could not even take advantage of the export opportunities the lower exchange rates provided. Unemployment soared, increasing as much as tenfold, and real wages plummeted – in countries with basically no safety nets. Not only was the IMF not restoring economic confidence in East Asia, it was undermining the region's social fabric. And then, in the spring and summer of 1998, the crisis spread beyond East Asia to the most explosive country of all – Russia.

The calamity in Russia shared key characteristics with the calamity in East Asia – not least among them the role that IMF and U.S. Treasury policies played in abetting it. But, in Russia, the abetting began much earlier. Following the fall of the Berlin Wall, two schools of thought had emerged concerning Russia's transition to a market economy. One of these, to which I belonged, consisted of a melange of experts on the region, Nobel Prize winners like Kenneth Arrow and others. This group emphasized the importance of the institutional infrastructure of a market economy – from legal structures that enforce contracts to regulatory structures that make a financial system work. Arrow and I had both been part of a National Academy of Sciences group that had, a decade earlier, discussed with the Chinese their transition strategy. We emphasized the importance of fostering competition – rather than just privatizing state-owned industries – and favored a more gradual transition to a market economy (although we agreed that occasional strong measures might be needed to combat hyperinflation).

The second group consisted largely of macroeconomists, whose faith in the market was unmatched by an appreciation of the subtleties of its underpinnings – that is, of the conditions required for it to work effectively. These economists typically had little knowledge of the history or details of the Russian economy and didn't believe they needed any. The great strength, and the ultimate weakness, of the economic doctrines upon which they relied is that the doctrines are – or are supposed to be – universal. Institutions, history, or even the distribution of income simply do not matter. Good economists know the universal truths and can look beyond the array of facts and details that obscure these truths. And the universal truth is that shock therapy works for countries in transition to a market economy: the stronger the medicine (and the more painful the reaction), the quicker the recovery. Or so the argument goes.

Unfortunately for Russia, the latter school won the debate in the Treasury Department and in the IMF. Or, to be more accurate, the Treasury Department and the IMF made sure there was no open debate and then proceeded blindly along the second route. Those who opposed this course were either not consulted or not consulted for long. On the Council of Economic Advisers, for example, there was a brilliant economist, Peter Orszag, who had served as a close adviser to the Russian government and had worked with many of the young economists who eventually assumed positions of influence there. He was just the sort of person whose expertise Treasury and the IMF needed. Yet, perhaps because he knew too much, they almost never consulted him.

We all know what happened next. In the December 1993 elections, Russian voters dealt the reformers a huge setback, a setback from which they have yet really to recover. Strobe Talbott, then in charge of the noneconomic aspects of Russia policy, admitted that Russia had experienced 'too much shock and too little therapy.' And all that shock hadn't moved Russia toward a real market economy at all. The rapid privatization urged upon Moscow by the IMF and the Treasury Department had allowed a small group of oligarchs to gain control of state assets. The IMF and Treasury had rejiggered Russia's economic incentives, all right – but the wrong way. By paying insufficient attention to the institutional infrastructure that would allow a market economy to flourish – and by easing the flow of capital in and out of Russia – the IMF and Treasury had laid the groundwork for the oligarchs' plundering. While the government lacked the money to pay pensioners, the oligarchs were sending money obtained by stripping assets and selling the country's precious national resources into Cypriot and Swiss bank accounts.

The United States was implicated in these awful developments. In mid-1998, Summers, soon to be named Robert Rubin's successor as secretary of the treasury, actually made a public display of appearing with Anatoly Chubais, the chief architect of Russia's privatization. In so doing, the United States seemed to be aligning itself with the very forces impoverishing the Russian people. No wonder antiAmericanism spread like wildfire.

At first, Talbott's admission notwithstanding, the true believers at Treasury and the IMF continued to insist that the problem was not too much therapy but too little shock. But, through the mid-'90s, the Russian economy continued to implode. Output plummeted by half. While only 2 per cent of the population had lived in poverty even at the end of the dismal Soviet period, 'reform' saw poverty rates soar to almost 50 per cent, with more than half of Russia's children living below the poverty line. Only recently have the IMF and Treasury conceded that therapy was undervalued – though they now insist they said so all along.

Today, Russia remains in desperate shape. High oil prices and the long-resisted ruble devaluation have helped it regain some footing. But standards of living remain far below where they were at the start of the transition. The nation is beset by enormous inequality, and most Russians, embittered by experience, have lost confidence in the free market. A significant fall in oil prices would almost certainly reverse what modest progress has been made.

East Asia is better off, though it still struggles, too. Close to 40 per cent of Thailand's loans are still not performing; Indonesia remains deeply mired in recession. Unemployment rates remain far higher than they were before the crisis, even in East Asia's best-performing country, Korea. IMF boosters suggest that the recession's end is a testament to the effectiveness of the agency's policies. Nonsense. Every recession eventually ends. All the IMF did was make East Asia's recessions deeper, longer, and harder. Indeed, Thailand, which followed the IMF's prescriptions the most closely, has performed worse than Malaysia and South Korea, which followed more independent courses.

I was often asked how smart – even brilliant – people could have created such bad policies. One reason is that these smart people were not using smart economics. Time and again, I was dismayed at how out-of-date – and how out-of-tune with reality – the models Washington economists employed were. For example, microeconomic phenomena such as bankruptcy and the fear of default were at the center of the East Asian crisis. But the macroeconomic models used to analyze these crises were not typically rooted in microfoundations, so they took no account of bankruptcy.

But bad economics was only a symptom of the real problem: secrecy. Smart people are more likely to do stupid things when they close themselves off from outside criticism and advice. If there's one thing I've learned in government, it's that openness is most essential in those realms where expertise seems to matter most. If the IMF and Treasury had invited greater scrutiny, their folly might have become much clearer, much earlier. Critics from the right, such as Martin Feldstein, chairman of Reagan's Council of Economic Advisers, and George Shultz, Reagan's secretary of state, joined Jeff Sachs, Paul Krugman, and me in condemning the policies. But, with the IMF insisting its policies were beyond reproach – and with no institutional structure to make it pay attention – our criticisms were of little use. More frightening, even internal critics, particularly those with direct democratic accountability, were kept in the dark. The Treasury Department is so arrogant about its economic analyses and prescriptions that it often keeps tight – much too tight – control over what even the president sees.

Open discussion would have raised profound questions that still receive very little attention in the American press: To what extent did the IMF and the Treasury Department push policies that actually contributed to the increased global economic volatility? (Treasury pushed liberalization in Korea in 1993 over the opposition of the Council of Economic Advisers. Treasury won the internal White House battle, but Korea, and the world, paid a high price.) Were some of the IMF's harsh criticisms of East Asia intended to detract attention from the agency's own culpability? Most importantly, did America – and the IMF – push policies because we, or they, believed the policies would help East Asia or because we believed they would benefit financial interests in the United States and the advanced industrial world? And, if we believed our policies were helping East Asia, where was the evidence? As a participant in these debates, I got to see the evidence. There was none.

Since the end of the cold war, tremendous power has flowed to the people entrusted to bring the gospel of the market to the far corners of the globe. These economists, bureaucrats, and officials act in the name of the United States and the other advanced industrial countries, and yet they speak a language that few average citizens understand and that few policymakers bother to translate. Economic policy is today perhaps the most important part of America's interaction with the rest of the world. And yet the culture of international economic policy in the world's most powerful democracy is not democratic.

This is what the demonstrators shouting outside the IMF next week will try to say. Of course, the streets are not the best place to discuss these highly complex issues. Some of the protesters are no more interested in open debate than the officials at the IMF are. And not everything the protesters say will be right. But, if the people we entrust to manage the global economy — in the IMF and in the Treasury Department — don't begin a dialogue and take their criticisms to heart, things will continue to go very, very wrong. I've seen it happen.

C HAPTER 2

Stiglitz vs. the IMF: Another View

RUDI DORNBUSCH*

Asia is showing miracle growth rates once again. Korea, one of the hardest-hit countries in the 1997–98 crisis, has today a GDP level already 12 percent above the pre-crisis level. What is the lesson? IMF policies work, the notion of IMF malpractice and crackpot medicine argued by Joe Stiglitz [see Chapter 1] is out-and-out frivolous and, of course, mostly self-serving.

Most offensive and untrue is surely the suggestion that the IMF staff consists of 'third-rank students from first-rate universities'. (The same for his former colleagues at the World Bank?) At Harvard and MIT, and everywhere else, fresh Ph.D.s who can't get jobs at the top five universities in the world will pick the World Bank or the IMF. And that is all for the better. Anyone likely to be picked as top draft choice by the top schools may be a trifle too theoretical for the cruder work of policy making. Stiglitz himself with his predilection for the intriguing exceptions rather than the general rule is a great case in point. Neither the IMF nor the World Bank needs theorists; they need well-trained country doctors. As Princeton's great Edwin Kemmerer – the Jeff Sachs of the 1920s – said: on the periphery, the pickaxe is the rule.

Stiglitz's contention that ignorant and arrogant IMF staff used drastically wrong medicine – tight budgets and high interest rates – turning a difficult situation into an all-out disaster is as contrarian as it is wrong. What is he saying? In the face of the government taking a 50 percent of GDP (or more) hit in public finance from bank failure and pervasive bankruptcy, fiscal largesse should be the rule? And in the face of a collapse of currencies under the pressure of capital flight, interest rates should be cut to make it cheaper to take money out and crash the exchange rate? Strange, indeed. For the past 100 years, the rule has been without fail: stabilization starts with the exchange rate and public finance. Investors will take confidence and bring back money when they see fiscal conservatism and really high interest rates. Do that for a few months and you are on the right track. That was League of Nations policy in the '20s, with great success; that has been IMF policy forever. And

* The New Republic for 'Stiglitz vs. The IMF: Another View' by R. Dornbusch © R. Dornbusch, April 2000.

it still works: Korea is booming and so is all of Asia. Interest rates fell within month as capital reflows stabilized and pushed up currencies; public finance could start to ease once investors figured out that all this was not the end of the world. In the countries where IMF guidance was followed promptly and without fail, recovery was faster. But in places like Indonesia, where policy makers wavered, the crisis is still not overcome.

When countries arrive at the IMF, on a stretcher, this is not the time for cute ideas. Drastic policies are necessary to avoid hemorrhage, currency collapse and irreparable meltdown. Stabilization is neither a popularity contest nor a research seminar. Today no finance minister will opt for the Stiglitz Clinic of Alternative Medicine; they have the ambulance rush them to the IMF. And when they do, markets start taking confidence very soon and from there it is a short step to normalization.

Stiglitz complains that nobody listened to him, except Dr. Mahatir, the other quack. No surprise! True, Stiglitz is a distinguished economist, on the short-list for a Nobel Prize for his theoretical contributions on how markets fail. But nobody ever thought of him as a policy economist and even less as someone who has the remotest clue of macroeconomics and stabilization. After all, this is the World Bank chief economist who in the midst of the Asian crisis publicly urged China to devalue with the likely consequence of a massive extra round of collapse throughout Asia. And a good thing too that nobody listened; Asia is doing well. The chief lesson for the IMF is that next time they should apply exactly the same remedies and enjoy as spectacular success. Congratulations to that bright staff at the IMF.

C HAPTER 3

Why Do We Need Policy?

ROBERT HEILBRONER AND LESTER THUROW*

Where markets fail

L et us begin by looking at some situations where markets don't work. One of these has to do with instances where marketers lack information and have no way of making intelligent decisions and where, therefore, the results of the market will reflect ignorance, luck, or accident rather than informed behavior. A second case involves what are known as 'pure public goods' – goods whose intrinsic characteristics mean that they cannot be allocated efficiently by private markets. Closely related is a third category of goods whose purchase, or failure to purchase, affects third parties' welfares and not just those of buyers or sellers. Market economies also need some social investments with longer payback periods than private markets are prepared to endure. There are also some goods, health care being an example, which the public simply wants to see more equally distributed than goods and services in general. Finally, there is the issue of imperfect competition. We'll take these up, one at a time.

The prevalence of ignorance

The whole market system is built on the assumption that individuals are *rational* as well as acquisitive – that marketers will have at least roughly accurate information about the market. A good example of the importance of information is the situation faced by the tourist in a bazaar of a country where he or she doesn't know a word of the language. Such a buyer has no way of knowing what the price of an article ought to be. That's why tourists so often return triumphantly with their bazaar trophies – only to discover that the same items were for sale in their hotel at half the price.

Without correct or adequate information marketers obviously cannot make correct decisions. But typically many marketers do *not* have adequate information.

Consumers guide themselves by hearsay, by casual information picked up by random sampling, or by their susceptibility to advertising. Who has time to investigate which brand of toothpaste is really best or even tastes best? Even professional buyers, such as industrial purchasing agents, cannot know every price of every product, including all substitutes.

The lack of information can be remedied, at least up to a point, but the remedy costs money or its equivalent – time. Few of us have the resources or patience to do a complete research job on every item we buy, nor would it even be necessarily rational to do so. Thus a certain amount of ignorance always remains in all markets, causing prices and quantities to differ from what they would be if we had complete information. These differences can be very great, as anyone knows who has ever discovered, with sinking heart, that he or she paid 'much too much' for a given article or sold it for 'much too little'.

Another important cause of market failure lies in the destabilizing effect of 'perverse' expectations. Suppose that a rise in prices sets off rumors that prices will rise still more. This is common experience in inflationary times, when the mounting prices of goods leads us to expect that prices will be still higher tomorrow. In this case, we do not act as ordinary demanders, curtailing our purchases as prices go up. Instead, we all rush in, with the result that prices go higher still. Meanwhile, sellers, seeing prices go up, may decide not to take advantage of good times by increasing their offerings, but to hold back, waiting for tomorrow's even higher prices. Thus demand goes up and supply goes down – a recipe for skyrocketing market prices.

Such perverse price movements can lead to very dangerous consequences. They play a major role in the cumulative, self-sustaining processes of inflation or collapse. They can cause commodity prices to shoot to dizzying heights or plummet to the depths. At its worst, perverse behavior threatens to make an entire economy go out of control, as in the case of hyperinflations or panics. At best, it disrupts smooth orderly markets and brings shocks and dislocations to the economy.

Can these market failures be remedied? Some can; some cannot. Ignorance can certainly be reduced by better economic reporting or by truth-in-advertising laws. Perverse behavior can be lessened by persuasive pronouncements from important public figures.

But we must recognize that there is a residue of arbitrariness even in the best-intentioned remedies. Take the matter of consumer information. We 'inform' the consumer, through labels on cigarette packages, that smoking is dangerous, but we do not prohibit the advertising of cigarettes. We spread market information by having the incomprehensible contents of medications printed on their containers, but we allow the consumer to be misinformed through advertising that claim superiority of one kind of aspirin over another.

Why? There is no clear rationale in these cases. Essentially we are trying to repair omissions in the market system – injecting information so that consumers can make better choices – without becoming paternalistic. Perhaps we think more mistakes would be made by a government trying to prevent individuals from making mistakes than individuals would themselves make. Or perhaps we just don't want the large governments that would be necessary to prevent individual mistakes.

That is perhaps as it should be. But the consequence is that the market will continue to produce less than wholly satisfactory or efficient results because a residue of ignorance or misinformation is allowed to remain – or remains despite our best efforts.

Pure public goods

Now we must turn to the range of problems that derive from the fact that certain kinds of output in our system do not have the characteristics of the ordinary goods or services that allow them to be sold in private markets. We call such outputs *pure public goods*. Since pure public goods are not easy to define, let us start by illustrating the properties of goods such as defense, the national weather service, or lighthouses. Such goods have three peculiar characteristics:

First, the consumption of a public good by any one individual does not interfere with its consumption by another. A lighthouse is as effective for ten boats as for one. A weather service is as useful for one hundred million TV viewers as for one hundred. By way of contrast, private goods – the food, clothing, or doctors' services that we use – cannot also be consumed by you.

Second, no one can be excluded from the use of a public good. We can deny you the use of your cars. But there is no way of denying you the use of our national defense system.

Last, with normal goods our private consumption depends on our individual decisions to spend or not spend our incomes. But there is no way that we can, by ourselves, buy defense, weather services, or a lighthouse service.[1] We must agree how much to buy!

As a result of these three characteristics there is no way to set up a market where citizens will be willing to pay voluntarily for national defense even though everyone values it. [...]

Externalities

Our third source of market failure is closely connected with the attributes of public goods. It is the problem of allowing for what economists call the *externalities* of production; that is, for the effects of the output of private goods and services on persons other than those who are directly buying or selling or using the goods in question.

The standard example of an externality is the smoke from the local factory. The smoke imposes medical bills and cleaning bills on households that may not use any of the factory's output. Or take the noise near a jetport. That damages the eardrums – and lowers the real estate values – of individuals who may never benefit from the propinquity of the airport, indeed who may never fly.

Externalities bring us to one of the most vexing and sometimes dangerous problems in our economic system – controlling pollution.

What is pollution, from an economic point of view? It is the production of wastes, dirt, noise, congestion, and other things we do not want. Although we don't think of smoke, smog, traffic din, and traffic jams as part of society's production, these facts of economic life are certainly the consequences of producing things we do want. Smoke is a part of the output process that also gives us steel or cement. Smog arises from the production of industrial energy and heat, among other things. Traffic is a by-product of transportation. In current jargon, economists call these unwanted by-products 'bads,' to stress their relation to things we call 'goods.'

The basic reason that externalities exist is technological: we do not know how to produce many goods cleanly, i.e., without wastes and noxious by-products. But there is also an economic aspect to the problem. Even when we do know how to produce cleanly, externalities can exist because it is cheaper to pour wastes into a river than to alter the manufacturing process to eliminate waste. That is, it is cheaper for the individual or the firm, but it may not be cheaper for the community. A firm may dump its wastes in a river 'for free,' but people living downstream will suffer the costs of having to cope with polluted water. Yet the people buying paper, not living in the communities affected by paper production, are only interested in buying cheap paper. They will not voluntarily buy clean (expensive) paper.

Finally, we should note that some externalities are not 'bads,' but 'goods.' A new office building may increase the property value of a neighborhood. Here is *positive* externality. The benefit gained by others results from the new building but is not paid to the owners of that building. Such externalities give some private goods the partial attributes of public goods.

Faced with the ugly view of smoke belching from a factory chimney, sludge pouring from a mill into a lake, automobiles choking a city, or persons being injured by contaminants, most ecologically concerned persons cry for regulation: 'Pass a law to forbid smoky chimneys or sulfurous coal. Pass a law to make mills dispose of their wastes elsewhere or purify them. Pass a law against automobiles in the central city.'

What are the economic effects of regulation? Essentially, the idea behind passing laws is to internalize a previous externality. That is, a regulation seeks to impose a cost on an activity that was previously free for the individual or firm — although not free, as we have seen, for society. This means that individuals or firms must stop the polluting activity entirely or bear the cost of whatever penalty is imposed by law, or else find ways of carrying out their activities without giving rise to pollution.

Is regulation a good way to reduce pollution? Let us take the case of a firm that pollutes the environment in the course of producing goods or services. Suppose a regulation is passed, enjoining that firm to install antipollution devices — smoke scrubbers or waste treatment facilities. Who bears this cost?

The answer seems obvious at first look: The firm must bear it. But if the firm passes its higher costs along in higher selling prices, we arrive at a different answer. Now a little economic analysis will show us that the cost is in fact borne by three groups, not just the firm. First, the firm will bear some of the cost because at the higher price, it will sell less output. How much less depends on the price sensitivity of demand for its product. But unless demand is totally insensitive, its sales and income must contract.

Two other groups also bear part of the cost. One group is the factors of production – labor and the owners of physical resources. Fewer factors will be employed because output has fallen. Their loss of income is therefore also a part of the economic cost of antipollution regulation. Last, of course, is the consumer. Prices will rise so that the consumer must also bear some share of the cost of regulation.

Offsetting all these costs is the fact that each of these three groups and the general public now have a better environment. There is no reason, however, why each of these three groups, singly or collectively, should think that its benefit outweighs its cost. Most of the benefit is likely to go to the general public, rather than to the individuals actually involved in the production or consumption of the polluting good or service.

Thus a regulation forcing car manufacturers to make cleaner engines will cost the manufacturers some lost sales, will cost the consumer added expense for a car, and will reduce the income going to land, labor, and capital no longer employed making engines. As part of the public, all three groups will benefit from cleaner air, but each is likely to feel its specific loss more keenly than its general gain.

Is regulation useful? Case by case, it's often hard to say. That is why economists tend to apply a general rule: Regulations are good or bad, *mainly depending on their ease of enforcement*. Compare the effectiveness of speed limits, which attempt to lessen the externality of accidents, and of regulation against littering. It is difficult enough to enforce antilittering laws. On the other hand, regulation of the disposal of radioactive wastes is simpler to enforce because the polluters are few and easily supervised.

This in turn is largely a matter of cost. If we were prepared to have traffic policemen posted on every mile of highway or every city block, regulation could be just as effective for speed violations or littering as for radioactive waste disposal. Obviously the cost would be horrendous, and so would most people's reactions to being overpoliced.

A second way to cope with pollution is to tax it. When a government decides to tax pollution (often called effluent charges), it is essentially creating a price system for disposal processes. If an individual company found that it could clean up its own pollutants more cheaply than paying the tax, it would do so, thereby avoiding the tax. If the company could not clean up its own pollutants more cheaply than the tax cost, which is often the case, it would pay the necessary tax and look to the state to clean up the environment.

The effluent charge looks like, but is not, a license to pollute. It is a license that allows you to produce some pollutants for a price. Prices could be set to make all pollution prohibitively expensive but are usually set to allow some pollution since the environment has some 'free' self-cleaning capacity.

As a result of effluent charges, an activity that was formerly costless is no longer so. Thus, in terms of their economic impacts, these charges are just like government regulations. In fact, they are a type of government regulation. The difference is that each producer can decide whether it pays to install clean-up equipment and not pay the tax, or to pollute and pay whatever tax costs are imposed.

Which is better, regulation or taxation? Practical considerations are likely to decide. For example, taxation on effluents discharged into streams is likely to be more practical than taxation on smoke coming from chimneys. The state can install a sewage treatment plant, but it cannot clean up air that is contaminated by producers who find it cheaper to pay a pollution tax than to install smoke-suppressing equipment. Moreover, to be effective, a pollution tax should vary with the amount of pollution; a paper mill or a utility plant would pay more taxes if it increased its output of waste or smoke. One of the problems with taxation is that of installing monitoring equipment. It is difficult to make accurate measurements of pollution or to allow for differences in environmental harm caused by the same amount of smoke or noxious gases or just plain heat coming from two factories located in different areas.

The third way of dealing with pollution is to subsidize polluters to stop polluting. In this case the government actually pays the offending parties to clean up the damage they have caused or to stop causing it. For example, a township might lessen the taxes on a firm that agreed to install filters on its stacks. This is, of course, paying the firm to stop polluting.

There are cases when subsidies may be the easiest way to avoid pollution. For example, it might be more effective to pay homeowners to turn in old cans and bottles than to try to regulate their garbage-disposal habits or to tax them for each bottle or can thrown away. Subsidies may therefore sometimes be expedient means of achieving a desired end, even if they may not be the most desirable means from other points of view.

Lengthening time horizons

Now consider another instance of market failure far removed from those we have mentioned. It has to do with the time horizon that can be rationally applied to market processes – if by 'rational' we mean profitable. In a word, will markets provide a setting in which very long-term, very risky, but potentially invaluable research and development take place?

Consider what are probably the two hottest private industries in America today – biotechnology firms and the new telecommunications Internet firms. How did these two industries come into existence?

In the early 1960s the federal National Institutes of Health started spending several billion dollars per year on research and development in what was then called biophysics. Seminal breakthroughs followed – the double helix, DNA, recombinant DNA, etc. Twenty-five to thirty years later a big important profitable private industry with tens of billions of dollars in sales came into existence. But no private firm using normal private decision-making rules would ever have made these original investments. Risks were too high and the time lags until profits could be made were too long. Using discounted net present values (the normal market mechanism for evaluating the value of future returns) today's market value of a dollar that will not be received until ten years from now is approximately zero.

The Internet started twenty-five years ago as a nuclear-bomb-proof communications system; thereafter as a National Science Foundation project; and only recently as a field where firms can make a lot of money. That last would not have happened without social investments made with time horizons far beyond those of private firms.

Or consider education. No hard-nosed capitalistic mother or father would ever invest in sixteen years of education for their children. Sixteen years of money in with no money out – the payoffs are too uncertain and too far into the future. No society has ever become literate solely based upon private education. Yet nothing pays off economically for a society more than having an educated work force.

As a result, investments in education, infrastructure, and research and development have to be at least partly financed by governments. Markets underprovide them.

The trouble is that markets distribute goods and services in accordance with the distribution of income and wealth. Those with money get; those without money do not get. For many products, distributions based upon market incomes yield acceptable social outcomes. But there are some products, such as health care, where we, as a society, have far more egalitarian preferences. We aren't willing to see ourselves, or others, go without health care simply because we do not have enough money to pay for health care – the market result. As a result governments interfere with the market, helping to pay for health care for the elderly or fully paying for it with the poor. Subsidized private health insurance helps those in-between with special tax breaks. [...]

The costs of imperfect competition

Let's now talk about monopoly and oligopoly. These are bad words to most people, just as competition is a good word, although not everyone can specify exactly what is good or bad about them.[2] Often we get the impression that the aims of the monopolist are evil and grasping, while those of the competitor are wholesome and pure. Therefore the difference between a world of pure competition and one of monopoly seems to be one of motive and intent – the well-meaning competitor versus the ill-intentioned monopolist.

The truth is that exactly the same motives drive both the monopolist and the competitive firm. Both seek to maximize profits. Indeed, the competitive firm, faced with the need to watch costs closely in order to survive, may be more penny-pinching and profit-oriented than the monopolist, who can afford to take a less hungry attitude because he is not so close to the edge. In a word, bad motives have nothing to do with the problem of less-than-perfect competition.

Then what is so good about competition? In theory the answer is clear: In a purely competitive market, the consumer is king. Indeed the rationale for such a market is often described as *consumer sovereignty*.

The term means two things. First, in a pure competitive market the consumer determines the allocation of resources by virtue of his or her demand – the public calls the tune to which the businessman dances. Second, the consumer enjoys goods that are produced as abundantly and sold as cheaply as possible. In such a market, each firm is producing the goods the consumer wants, in the largest quantity and at the lowest cost possible.

In a monopolistic or oligopolistic market the consumer loses much of this sovereignty. Firms have *strategies*, including that of increasing consumer demand for their particular products by describing them as different from, and better than, those of their competitors. If its advertising is successful, a firm will be able to sell its product at a price higher than the purely competitive one – a price that contains an element of monopoly because, however small the additional profit, it represents a return over and above that of a truly competitive setting. [...]

No one contests these general conclusions. Prices in an 'imperfectly competitive' market, where advertising seeks to make each product seem unique, will be higher than in a market where all products are obviously the same. Because they cost more, the volume of goods sold in such an imperfectly competitive market will be less than that sold in a perfectly competitive one.

But how important are these imperfections in actuality? Here the problem becomes muddier. Take the question of consumer demand. In 1867 we [in the USA] spent an estimated $50 million to persuade consumers to buy 'name brand' products of all kinds. By 1900, advertising expenditures were $500 million. Today they are roughly $130 billion, about a third as much as we spend on all primary and secondary education. Indeed, advertising expenditures can be considered a kind of campaign to educate individuals to be good consumers, buying a different set of goods than they would have if the advertising did not exist.

To what extent does this infringe on consumer sovereignty? The question is perplexing. Once we go beyond a subsistence economy it is no longer possible to think of consumers as having 'natural' tastes. For that reason, at least some advertising serves a genuinely educational purpose. Back in the 1910s people had to be educated into thinking that an ordinary family like themselves could actually own a car. Not so long ago, our parents had to be educated to think that flying was not only fast, but comfortable and safe.

Moreover, not all advertising works. In the 1950s, the Ford Motor Company spent a quarter of a billion dollars to persuade people that a new car called the Edsel was exactly what everyone had been looking for. Despite the barrage of ads, people looked the other way. Every year brings advertising fiascos of one kind or another.

Yet it is obvious that not all advertising serves a useful purpose. It is impossible to watch the raptures of 'housewives' extolling different brands of soap, laxatives, or canned goods without thinking that perhaps the single most persuasive message of these minidramas is that grown-ups will say things they obviously don't really believe because they are paid money to do so. Is that perhaps the residual effect of advertising on our culture, including, not least, on our children?

So we find ourselves in a quandary. Few consumers would like to have the absolutely standardized outputs that would do away with the need for advertising, and most consumers accept the make-believe of advertising as a mildly irritating, occasionally useful, interruption of their TV watching. From the advertisers' standpoint, advertising is one big expense, but one that must be undertaken if a firm selling brand-name goods is to survive in a 'competitive' world, however 'imperfect' economists may call that kind of market.

What is the answer to this dilemma? Here is where the economists' claim to expertise ceases. The question is properly referred to experts on culture or morality, or to the collective wisdom of consumers themselves when they put on their political caps and vote for more or less government regulation of markets. As economists we are bound to raise these questions, but we would be overstepping our bounds if we presume to answer them.

What about the second main attribute of consumer sovereignty – the ability to buy goods as cheaply as possible? To what extent does oligopoly introduce inefficiency into the system?

Once again the evidence in fact is murkier than in theory. For one thing, we tend to leap to the conclusion that a competitive firm is also an efficient one. Is this really so? Suppose that the competitive firm cannot afford the equipment that might lead to economies of large-scale production. Suppose it cannot afford large expenditures on research and development. Suppose its workers suffer from low morale and therefore do not produce as much as they might.

These are not wild suppositions. There is good evidence that many large firms are more efficient, in terms of productivity per man-hour, than small firms, although of course some large, monopolistic firms tolerate highly inefficient practices simply because of the lack of competition. Big businesses generate higher rates of technical progress than small, competitive firms, and may well justify their short-run monopoly profits by long-run technical progress.

Once again, however, we must consider the other side. Profits in oligopolistic industries as a whole are 50 to 100 percent higher than those in competitive industries. In certain fields, such as over-the-counter medicines, there is evidence that consumers are sometimes badly exploited. Brand-name aspirins sell for up to three times the cost on non-brand versions, but few buyers know that they are paying more for an *identical* product. Certain medicines, such as antibiotics and the like, have enjoyed enormous profits – which is to say, have forced consumers to pay far more than they would have had to pay were the rate of profit a competitive one – but here the issue becomes more complicated. Patents, and hence monopoly profits, are given to firms deliberately to encourage them to invent new drugs. We make a trade-off – more expensive drugs today for more drugs tomorrow.

To turn the coin over once more, a further complication is introduced by virtue of the fact that oligopolies often have provided more agreeable working conditions, more handsome offices, and safer plants than have small competitive firms. Thus some of the loss of consumers' well-being is regained in the form of workers' well-being. Needless to say, this is not solely the result of a kindlier attitude on the part of big producers, but reflects their sheltered position against the harsh pressures of competition. Nonetheless, the gains in work conditions and morale are real and must be counted in the balance.

Notes

1   Not even if we were immensely rich or absolute monarchs? In that case we would not have a market system, but a command economy catering to one person. Then indeed there would be no distinction between public and private goods.

2   Pure monopoly is a rarity. Most 'monopolistic' corporations operate in a market structure of oligopoly (a *few* sellers) rather than monopoly (only *one* seller). In an oligopolistic market a few sellers divide up the bulk of the business, and a long tail of smaller firms share the leftovers. For example, in the soap industry, the four biggest producers supply about 60 percent of all [USA] demand, and some six hundred-plus producers share the rest. Similarly, over one hundred companies make auto tires and tubes, but the top four do two-thirds of total business.

Culture, Social Norms and Economics: Some Implications for Policy

MARK CASSON*

1. The scope and purpose of this chapter

Economists are often accused of failing to take proper account of culture and social norms in their explanation of human behaviour. The stereotype economist is the practitioner of a 'dismal science' in which the law of competition regulates the behaviour of selfish individuals. Compared to other social scientists, the economist is committed to a very narrow view of human nature which is pessimistic about the prospects for improving social welfare. Other social sciences suggest that cultural change, and in particular the raising of social norms, will lead to higher standards of behaviour. The evolution of higher norms thus offers a direct route to the improvement of social welfare – a route which for the stereotype economist remains permanently blocked. Not all economists conform to this stereotype, however. [...]

This chapter is organized into two main parts. The first (Sections 1–5) is mainly concerned with the issue 'Where are we coming from?' It considers how the present narrow concept of 'economic man' came into being, and what needs to be done to escape from its mental straitjacket. The second part (Sections 6–12) addresses the question 'Where are we now?' It summarizes the modern literature and takes stock of recent developments.

2. The economic approach to culture

There is already a vast literature on culture generated by sociologists, anthropologists and social historians. As indicated above, this chapter focuses mainly on

* Edward Elgar Publishing Limited for an extract from *Culture, Social Norms and Economics* by Mark Casson © Mark Casson, 1997.

economic research. The defining characteristic of the economic approach is the use of the rational action model of human behaviour (see Blaug, 1980). According to this model, individuals have preferences which rank all the alternatives that they perceive in a consistent way. They collect information to assess the feasibility of these alternatives, and then select the best of the feasible ones. The rational action model is introspectively plausible insofar as it stresses the intentionality of actions, and the existence at the time of action of a definite expectation of what the outcome will be. It is less plausible in the sense that it suggests that a large amount of computation is associated with each decision. Economists usually respond to this criticism by arguing that *on average* people behave *as if* they were carrying out such computations, even though no single individual is conscious of having done so. A more sophisticated response is to argue that individuals respond to the costliness of information by economizing on the amount of information that they use. The amount of computation is tailored to the importance of the decision, which is why trivial decisions are taken with relatively little thought. This approach, based on the economics of information, is particularly useful in explaining the behaviour of people within organizations (Casson, 1997a).

While rational action is sufficient to explain the behaviour of a single isolated individual ('Robinson Crusoe' in standard economics texts), it needs to be supplemented by some other principle where a group of people is concerned. This is because the actions planned by different individuals may be incompatible with each other. There needs to be some mechanism which allows each individual to adjust their perception of what is feasible to allow for the impact upon them of the decisions that other individuals are about to make. This is a complex information-processing problem. To reduce the problem to manageable proportions economists normally invoke the principle of equilibrium. This principle asserts that the expectations that individuals form before they act are consistent with the actions of other people, even though they do not necessarily know what those actions are. This ensures that the actions of different people harmonize with each other so that, in retrospect, no one wishes to change the decision they have made.

In forming their expectations people do not normally need to know about every aspect of other people's plans. It is usually sufficient for them simply to know their aggregate effect. This means, though, that there must be some mechanism to aggregate the effects of individuals' provisional plans, and to communicate the results back to individuals so that they can modify their plans if necessary (Hayek, 1937). In some situations, such as that of bilateral monopoly, there is no obvious equilibrating mechanism. In other situations, such as competitive markets, publicly quoted prices play the equilibrating role. A set of competitive equilibrium prices summarizes all the aspects of other people's plans that individuals need to know about in order to optimize their own behaviour. Social situations in which people exchange gossip or reciprocate gifts typically occupy an intermediate position. There is no explicit price, in the sense that nothing is formally bought and sold, but there may, nevertheless, be an 'implicit price' which supports an equilibrium. The price is implicit in the sense that every one is agreed how much sacrifice, on average, is entailed in gaining some favour. The implicit price represents a consensus view of the situation. It is an equilibrium price insofar as it reconciles each individual's plans with those of other people.

3. From selfishness to altruism

The narrowness of vision associated with the dismal science is a consequence not of adopting the principles of rational action and equilibrium but of assuming that rational action is directed towards purely selfish and materialistic ends. Rationality itself is perfectly compatible with an optimistic view of human nature – indeed, in the early nineteenth century European intellectuals regarded rationality (which they defined as freedom from superstition as well as the ability to calculate) as the key to social progress. From the more formal standpoint of modern economic theory, the principle of rational action applies just as much to individuals whose aims are altruistic, or even purely spiritual, as it does to those whose aims are selfish and materialistic. Of course, theory must link these ultimate altruistic and spiritual ends to more proximate ends in order to explain people's everyday behaviour. This is done by specifying an appropriate transmission mechanism. In the case of the altruist, the purchase of goods for the purpose of making gifts, and their subsequent transfer, links his purchases to their intended effect on other people's welfare. In the case of a person pursuing spiritual goals, the symbolic significance of goods – especially in the context of social and religious ritual – links their purchase to the individual's strategy for acquiring peace of mind (Douglas, 1970).

But if selfishness is not essential to the theory then why have economists chosen to focus so narrowly on selfish and material ends? There are four main reasons. The first is that selfish preferences are easier to model than altruistic preferences because only one individual is involved. To model altruism it is necessary to evaluate the different ways in which empathy for other people can manifest itself. It is necessary to address the difficult question of how far an altruist can reasonably claim to know the preferences of his intended beneficiaries. One way out of this difficulty is to assume that altruists wish to benefit other people in general, so that each altruist is effectively concerned with only two people – himself, and a composite person who represents the rest of society (Margolis, 1982). Each individual formulates his own view of how this representative person feels. Although this specification of preferences is still more complex than a purely selfish one, the additional complexity is of manageable proportions.

The problem of specifying altruistic preferences leads in turn to the question of whether altruists really do feel empathy for other people, or whether they simply derive a hypocritical sense of satisfaction from manipulating the behaviour of other people through the gifts that they provide. Is altruism just a distorted form of self-interest, in other words? From a purely formal point of view it does not really matter whether it is or not. Nevertheless, the philosophical problems raised by question of this nature explain why many economists maintain that altruism is a complicating factor that a parsimonious model of human nature should really do without.

A third reason is that selfish preferences tend to focus on material consumption, and material consumption is easier to measure than other forms of consumption. It naturally lends itself to quantification, and the tangibility of the goods consumed makes these quantities relatively easy to observe. This in turn makes propositions about material preferences easy to test. By contrast, altruistic preferences are often concerned with the provision of intangible services, such as the emotional security that a parent attempts to provide for his child. Since, however, these intangible services feed through to generate tangible effects elsewhere (for example, in the behaviour of the child), it is still possible to formulate preferences in a testable way. In any case, the advantages of quantification are easily overstated, since many qualitative variables can be expressed using categorization instead. To some extent, the emphasis on material consumption in conventional economics is simply a legacy of the scientific materialism of the late nineteenth century, which was in fashion at the time that the mathematical utility theory used by modern economists was being refined. In this respect, a change in the professional attitude towards the specification of the utility function is long overdue.

Finally, the assumption of selfishness seems particularly appropriate in the context of competitive markets. Competition works by each person playing other people off against each other in order to secure more favourable terms for themselves. Each buyer plays off different sellers against each other, whilst at the same time each seller plays off the different buyers against each other. The simplest motivation for such behaviour is a selfish concern to obtain the best possible deal, even though this is against the interests of other people. The traditional preoccupation of economists with explaining how markets work has therefore led them to assume that selfishness is pervasive because this is the simplest basis on which to construct a model of competitive market behaviour. From this perspective, the typical economist is not really interested in people at all, but only in a particular type of institution – the market – which is characterized by an unusually impersonal and competitive form of social relation. This means, though, that when it comes to explaining other social structures, where co-operation is stronger and competition is less intense, it is helpful to relax the assumption of selfishness on which the competitive market model is based.

4. Beyond the market

Economists' preoccupation with markets has been unfortunate in other ways as well. It has led some economists to believe that the concept of equilibrium is somehow logically prior to, or at least on an equal footing with, the principle of rational action whereas, if anything, the opposite is actually the case. Rational action is a principle that applies almost universally within the social sciences. In whatever social context human motivation is discussed, rational action modelling has a contribution to make. The concept of equilibrium, however, is of more restricted scope. Few social systems have equilibrium tendencies as strong as those of a competitive market. Even where social equilibria exist, they may not be unique. Emphasizing equilibrium rather than rational action therefore understates the scope of economic reasoning by highlighting some of its major limitations. It thereby discourages people from applying rational action modelling to social situations where it is useful simply because they recognize that the equilibrium tendencies are weak.

Emphasis on markets has also led some economists to believe that the market is the only form of co-ordinating mechanism that merits serious study. Although economists have always grudgingly recognized that governments and firms have co-ordinating capabilities as well, they have been reluctant to scrutinize their internal mechanisms as closely as they scrutinize the role of competition in the market. Yet governments, firms and markets are all just alternative forms of co-ordinating mechanism (Coase, 1937). To understand why some activities are co-ordinated by governments, some by firms, and others by markets, it is necessary to understand the internal workings of each type of institution. Only then can a proper comparison of their effectiveness be made.

5. The social basis of the market process

Focusing on government and firms highlights the importance of social interaction in the co-ordination process. It is by sharing information with each other, in both formal committees and informal gatherings, that managers and bureaucrats are able to take complex decisions. Reflecting further on this role of social interaction shows that there are many other institutions – such as clubs, societies, and local communities – which participate in the co-ordination process. These other institutions typically operate – like government – on a non-profit basis. But – unlike government – they operate on a voluntary basis too, relying on the goodwill of their members to get most of the work done.

Finally, consideration of the social dimension of co-ordination reveals that, in important respects, markets are social institutions too. Many markets for consumer goods are established by innovating firms. Because consumers interact socially, knowledge of a new product spreads by word of mouth. This stimulates the growth of market demand – especially when consumption of the product becomes a sign of social status. The diffusion of information through social networks is important on the supply side of the market too. As information about the innovator's profits spreads throughout the business community, so imitators begin to appear. Competition between the innovator and the imitators drives down prices and eventually restores profits in the industry to a normal level.

Although firms in the same industry compete, they may also co-operate – for example, in lobbying for 'infant industry' protection, or pressing for the abolition of restrictions that inhibit further growth in demand for the good. Many organized commodity markets, in fact, originate not with individual innovation, but with collective innovation – they begin as clubs formed by dealers, whose members agree to meet at a certain place and to trade under certain rules. Only later do these clubs acquire formal legal recognition as self-regulating institutions. By focusing on markets that are already well established, economists have failed to recognize the importance of social processes in bringing these markets into being in the first place. If economists paid more attention to the origins of contemporary institutions such as markets, they would not only acquire a better understanding of the social dynamics of institutional innovation, but they would also achieve a better under-standing of how markets work today.

6. The political economy tradition

To understand the origins of institutions properly it is important to have an adequate theory of human motivation. [...] Creating a broader view of human motivation within economics does not involve beginning from scratch. A broad perspective on human motivation can be found in the early literature of political economy. Casson (1997b) explains the insights into human motivation, the holistic view of social science, and the progressive view of society that inspired the economic writers of the Scottish Enlightenment. Aspects of this vision continued to inspire leading British scholars such as John Stuart Mill, John Elliott Cairnes and Henry Sidgwick, right down to the time of Alfred Marshall. While these scholars valued the technical contributions made by David Ricardo (and subsequently by William Stanley Jevons), they never fell completely under the influence of radical utilitarians like Jeremy Bentham, despite the growing influence of Bentham's legacy on this technical work. They did not believe, as Bentham did, that the enormous complexities of social organization amongst selfish people could be successfully tackled by simple incen-tive mechanisms embodied in formal legal rules. This affirmation of the broader view is particularly clear in the case of Mill, who successfully freed himself from the Benthamite utilitarianism imparted by his father to reassert the broader view in his later work.

In contrast to many leading economists of today, these political economists saw no need to distinguish sharply between 'rigorous' economic theory and 'non-rigorous' social theory, nor were they so pessimistic about the possibilities for social reform as modern economists have become. Contemporary attitudes amongst economists can, to some extent, be justified as a reaction against the excesses of twentieth-century sociological theory, which has been preoccupied more with ideo-logical debate than with fixing an agenda for sustained empirical research. On the other hand, it must be recognized that both sociology and political science 'spun off' from political economy partly out of frustration with the increasingly narrow intel-lectual concerns of the economics profession. Furthermore, part of the political radicalism of the sociologists was due to the fact that, by the turn of the twentieth century, many professional economists had aligned themselves ideologically with the principle of *laissez faire*. The modern economics profession is thus essentially what remains of this rump of *laissez faire* economists three or four generations after those who were seriously interested in the human dimension of economic problem quit to go elsewhere.

7. Modelling individual preferences

This section addresses various aspects of modelling individual preferences when the assumption of selfishness is dropped. It discusses altruism and envy, in the form of positive or negative feelings about the consumption patterns of other people. The basic aim of these models is to capture the pain and pleasure to be earned by vicarious participation in the consumption activities of other people.

An important focus of envy relates to the social status enjoyed by other people. Status encourages people to think in terms of relative rather than absolute levels of consumption, and in particular about where they stand in the overall ranking of consumption levels within society. Thus when they obtain an increase in income, people are even happier if others do not share their good fortune. Status is one of the few effects discussed by political economists that has experienced a significant revival in recent years. Status effects were widely discussed amongst policy-makers in the 1970s – in the context of 'relative deprivation' amongst the poor, the bargaining tactics of trade union negotiators in raising their members' pay relative to that of other groups, and so on. Unfortunately, however, interest in status appears to have subsided during the 1980s and 1990s, partly because of prevailing political ideology in the US and UK.

Advocates of a free market economy often attack status as a source of rigidity, failing to recognize that in certain circumstances status mechanisms can in fact augment conventional market forces in a useful way. Because of the limitations of the legal system, conventional markets are often costly to use and invariably incomplete in their scope. There is thus an opportunity for other mechanisms, such as status, to help to 'complete the market'. Whether status effects can do so depends upon how status is ascribed. If it is ascribed by birth, or some other characteristic that the individual cannot control, then status effects are certainly of limited use. But when status is ascribed on the basis of performing socially useful tasks which are difficult to reward through conventional market mechanisms, then stimulating the desire to earn status can stimulate the supply of effort too. Thus the provision of public goods, such as useful inventions, whose value is difficult to appropriate through contractual means, may be stimulated by rewarding inventors with status instead.

There is, however, a negative side to status. An improvement in one person's status usually implies a reduction in someone else's status, so that the search for status tends to be a zero-sum game. If everyone agreed that no one would seek status then everyone might well be better off. But given that such agreements are difficult to enforce, it is probably easier to harness it for motivating public service, in the manner described above, than to try to suppress it altogether.

Many economists, though, continue to believe that status is too much of a complicating factor to warrant taking seriously, despite abundant evidence that it influences demand for fashion goods, affects the occupational choices of school-leavers, and continues to be a major factor in conflicts over pay. [...]

If modelling status is complicated, then modelling the economics of self-control is potentially more complicated still. Once again, the stereotype economist will ask what is to be gained from an exercise of this kind. The main advantage of a theory of self-control is that it can 'rationalize' apparently quite irrational behaviour. For a start, it can explain why individual behaviour may be apparently inconsistent over time. People say one thing, quite sincerely, and then do exactly the opposite, or they follow one action with another that seems to defeat the purpose of the first. Such behaviour can be explained in terms of lapses of self-control. If self-control depends upon a scarce resource, then lapses may be unavoidable when supplies of this resource run out. In the short run, all a rational economic agent can do is to allocate the scarce resource so that the lapses that do occur cause as little damage as possible. In the long run, the individual may be able to invest in 'personal development' in order to acquire greater reserves of self-control.

Perhaps the most significant application of a theory of self-control, however, is to explain why people deliberately 'tie their own hands'. For example, they may ask a friend to control their own behaviour (such as their intake of alcoholic drinks at a party) because they are afraid that they may be unable to exercise sufficient control themselves. People may support campaigns for censorship on the grounds that they do not wish to be corrupted at some future time when their self-control is relatively weak. The theory explains why people may desire not to maximize their range of choice, but rather to restrict it; a self-imposed restriction may be rational for a person who believes that, while their self-control is currently strong, they need to insure themselves against the consequences of it becoming weak.

8. Co-operation

How do cultural values affect the incentive to co-operate? It is often suggested that co-operation can be explained purely in terms of enlightened self-interest. The prospect of being punished by your victim in some future repetition of your encounter with them may well be sufficient to encourage good behaviour at the outset (Kreps and Wilson, 1982). In particular, if you believe that other people behave according to the principle of 'tit-for-tat', then it often pays to adopt the strategy of 'tit-for-tat' yourself. Tit-for-tat therefore becomes an equilibrium strategy for the group.

But what happens if a repeated encounter is unlikely? Tit-for-tat becomes inoperative in this case, because the opportunity to punish disappears. As a result, cheating may well pay instead. Indeed, if everyone else is going to cheat then it is doubly important that when you encounter them you cheat yourself. If you do not wish to cheat then you simply avoid contact with other people. In this way all economic activities based on a division of labour – which means all activities involving employment or trade – come to a stop.

To restart activity under these circumstances people need to have credible grounds for believing that others will be honest even if they have a material incentive to cheat. One reason that others may be honest is that they will feel guily if they cheat. If everyone knows that everyone else feels this way then everyone can afford to be honest because everyone else will be honest too. In this way a 'high-trust' equilibrium can be sustained by self-fulfilling beliefs in the integrity of other people.

Some economists appear to be mystified by arguments of this kind because they are used to premising their analysis on the existence of a system of law. It is true that if every form of cheating was covered by a perfect system of law then cheating could in principle be eliminated at a stroke. But, in reality, the law is a social institution which itself needs trust in order to sustain it. A legal system cannot work efficiently when the police or the judiciary is corrupt. The law is essentially an intermediating institution, allowing people who cannot trust each other to trust the law instead. The law conserves a scarce resource like integrity by concentrating honest people on the resolution of disputes between people less honest than themselves. But the arrangement still requires a core of honest people to make it work.

The law can be a very expensive intermediating mechanism. The law makes intensive use of information, and consequently information costs are a major constraint on the legal process. It is not just a matter of the cost of collecting evidence, but also the cost of testing its veracity given the strong incentive for those who have cheated to lie about what they have done. Indeed, the fairer the law attempts to be, the more expensive it becomes. Accurate judgments delivered by formal court proceedings are much more costly to arrive at than the 'rough justice' of the 'kangaroo court'. This suggests that for cost-effective co-operation, alternatives to the law must be explored.

9. Social alternatives to the law

Alternatives to the law include intermediation by society, in the form of peer regard, and intermediation by a leader to whom others naturally defer. The first mechanism tends to rely heavily on custom and conformity; it works best in small groups with a stable membership and regular face-to-face communication. Because it depends on custom, however, it is not very good at adapting to new sets of circumstances that arise. Although custom is more than just the 'dead hand of the past', its legitimacy certainly derives to some extent from the fact that no one can remember when things were done a different way. Thus while custom can adapt, there are definite limits to the speed at which this can take place.

The second mechanism – leadership – is much more flexible. A leader can act in an entrepreneurial way. He has the authority to exercise discretion in dealing with an unprecedented situation. The disadvantage of leadership is that it may confer excessive power upon a single individual. In this respect, consultative leadership is normally superior to autocratic leadership, in the sense that a consultative leader pools opinions in order to synthesize information from different sources, whereas an autocratic leader does not. The autocrat relies only on those sources of information which he can directly consult himself. A consultative leader is also more likely to be altruistic because, through the process of consulting other people, he is likely to develop a sympathetic understanding of the effects of his actions upon people other than himself. Nevertheless, there may be certain crisis situations in which autocracy is preferable; when it is crucial to act quickly, but opinions are divided, whatever the autocrat decides to do may work better than a consultative decision.

10. Religion

Let us now address two specific aspects of culture – religious belief and entrepreneurship. There is plenty of evidence to suggest that people care about the kind of society in which they live, in the sense that they are willing to pay, through higher house prices and a higher cost of living, to move to countries, or to local communities, which offer a higher 'quality of life'. Concerns may well extend beyond the community, to embrace the global environment, and the future of humanity as a whole. Concern for the well-being of future generations is also reflected in parental concerns about the kind of society in which children will grow up to live. The widest concerns of all are religious concerns with the ultimate 'meaning of life', and with the prospects for an after-life. Such concerns are so strong that in polite society it may be unacceptable to raise them in casual conversation for fear of provoking an argument.

It would be strange indeed if people's passionate feelings about these issues were not reflected in their ordinary behaviour in some way. One indication of such feelings is the magnitude of the voluntary contributions that people make to support churches, charities, and other 'good causes' of their choice. It is difficult to rationalize such giving – especially anonymous donations, which cannot be used to 'buy' status – without invoking some purely emotional reward that the donor receives. The existence of an altruistic impulse is not sufficient to explain why some societies sustain far higher levels of giving than others. It must be recognized that organized religion plays an important part in directing emotions not only into support for established beliefs about the after-life, but also into support for established ways of doing good. The standardization of belief through organized religion helps to realize economies of scale both in the provision of religious buildings and in the organization of charitable work.

Organized religion does not provide reassurance as a 'free good', however. The believer has to pay a price, and the voluntary donation to the church is only a part of that price. It is incorrect to suggest that churches merely 'sell' a form of supernatural reassurance in return for the gifts of the 'faithful'. For in most religions, deeds as well as gifts are required to buy reassurance, and the most important aspect of these deeds is they involve behaving honestly towards other people. Organized religion therefore provides powerful emotional incentives to live by functionally useful moral principles (see below), and thereby generates a potentially large economic surplus.

The survival of religious belief at a time when many progressive thinkers have expected such belief to wane is easily explained on these grounds. Religious belief confers economic value on communities in which it is strong. These communities prosper, and attract people from outside who assimilate the religion in order to participate fully in the economic gains. Conversely, societies in which religion decays need to replace it with other more expensive intermediating mechanisms. They need to strengthen their law, and promote 'communitarian' welfare policies, in order to combat the threat of rising crime – especially 'economic crimes' such as theft of property and cheating on trades. These costly mechanisms require either higher taxes, which undermine incentives to innovate and to work hard, or the displacement of public expenditure from services and infrastructure such as hospitals, schools and roads. These societies therefore become less attractive places in which to live, and those who can afford to, choose to leave. In this way societies that discard religion without putting another cost-effective institution in its place eventually decline. Amongst the societies that survive and prosper, religious observance is a prominent feature of the way of life.

11. Entrepreneurship

Some scholars disagree strongly with arguments of this kind. They tend to place religion in the same category as custom, regarding it as an obstacle to change and innovation. They argue that, while it may be successful in binding people together, it binds them together inflexibly and makes them collectively resistant to change. In the very long run – over several centuries, for example – the societies that survive are those that are the most dynamic, it is claimed, rather than the ones that simply afford the highest quality of life. New York and Chicago may both be violent cities, it is said, but they are full of highly entrepreneurial people as well. The violence and the crime is a natural by-product of aggressive enterprise – and on balance, the crime is an acceptable price to pay. If the price of crime were not acceptable then the entrepreneurs would move elsewhere. This implies that the only characteristic of a culture that matters in the long run is whether it is entrepreneurial or not.

Such a one-dimensional view of culture cannot be sustained, however. Entrepreneurship can be highly competitive and individualistic, it is true, but it can also be co-operative and familistic as well. There is a limit to what a single entrepreneur can achieve without the support of other entrepreneurs in related lines of business undertaking investments that complement his own. An entrepreneur who cannot trust other people in related lines of business will be reluctant to share his plans with people he regards as his potential rivals, and as a result these people will be reluctant to expand their businesses in line with his because they are unsure about whether he would play them off against competitors if they did. On the other hand, an entrepreneur who trusts people in related lines of business can share his vision with them; provided that they know him, and are convinced that his judgement is sound, they will expand their businesses in line with his own. This second approach is, on average, likely to be more successful than the first. It is particularly easy to implement when trust is underpinned by family links, common schooling and, of course, shared religious commitments of the kind described above. This shows that custom and religion, far from inhibiting entrepreneurship, can be used to promote it by strengthening co-operation within the business community.

12. Culture and economic performance

This result ties in quite nicely with the trend of recent political debate, in which the key ideological issue is no longer one of capitalism versus socialism. Instead, it is about what kind of capitalism works best. The erroneous idea that there is just one kind of capitalism, which is entrepreneurial but low-trust, has finally given way to the idea that there are at least two main forms of capitalism. One may be low-trust, but the other is based on high-trust relations instead. In some cases these high-trust relations may be confined to a business elite – dominated, for example, by a small number of politically-networked family dynasties. In other cases, effective national leadership and a strong religious tradition may extend the network of trust to other social classes – notably professionals, skilled workers and the self-employed.

The larger the country, however, and the more diverse its industrial and commercial base, the more difficult it is for extended networks to operate effectively. As countries expand their borders, and population is increased through conquest, migration, high fertility, or longer life, social networks become less effective. They may still be effective at the regional level, but at the national level more impersonal and legalistic mechanisms have to be used instead. Thus during the nineteenth century the US evolved a low-trust competitive and legalistic culture in response to multicultural immigration and rapid urban growth – a culture significantly different from the high-trust culture of the early communities of New England.

There may still be networks that operate at the national level in a large country, but if its society has become multicultural then they will be increasingly organized along ethnic lines.

If antagonisms develop between the different networks then the economic viability of the nation may be undermined. The antagonisms may be regional, religious or racial; or they may be just class antagonisms – for example, between landowners and capitalists, or between capitalists and workers. A trend towards lower trust generated by class antagonisms can be observed at the end of the Victorian era in Britain, when the increasingly cosmopolitan nature of City financial trading, and the gradual stagnation of manufacturing industry exacerbated class divisions between bankers and industrialists, and – more prominently – between industrialists and workers.

The legacy of these changes is that in many countries the region and the ethnic group appear to many people to be more viable economic units than the traditional nation state. This suggests that if nations are to survive without becoming increasingly repressive (through continual recourse to law) then political leaders need to do their very best to promote an inclusive high-trust culture. Merely preaching tolerance will not suffice; respect for cultural diversity needs to be combined with a focus on standardized core values – values such as honesty, loyalty and hard work. These core values will not only reinforce the cultures of the existing local networks but – most significantly – help to sustain co-operation between these networks too.

There is already growing recognition in many countries of the need for greater trust in supporting national business networks, but unfortunately many of the social mechanisms for engineering trust at the national level have been so neglected that they are in a poor state of repair. In the UK, for example, many of the key institutions – the monarchy, parliament, the established church – are currently held in low esteem. The same goes, unfortunately, for key professional groups such as teachers, doctors and civil servants too. More than mere incantation of the need for greater trust is required in order to rebuild the national networks on which they depend. There is still a long way to go in reviving or replacing these institutions in order to sustain a better kind of capitalism.

[...]

References

Blaug, M. (1980) *The Methodology of Economics: How Economists Explain*, Cambridge: Cambridge University Press.

Casson, M.C. (1997a) *Information and Organization*, Oxford: Clarendon Press.

Casson, M.C. (ed.) (1997b) *Culture, Social Norms and Economics*, Aldershot: Edward Elgar.

Coase, R.H. (1937) 'The Nature of the Firm', *Economica* (New series), **4**, 386–405.

Douglas, M. (1970) *Natural Symbols*, London: Barrie and Rockliff.

Hayek, F.A. von (1937) 'Economics and Knowledge', *Economica* (New series), **4**, 33–54.

Kreps, D. and Wilson, R. (1982) 'Sequential Equlibria', *Econometrica*, **50**, 863–894.

Margolis, H. (1982) *Selfishness, Altruism and Rationality: A Theory of Social Choice*, Cambridge: Cambridge University Press.

Competition Policy

Having examined the overall rationale for policy intervention in market economies, we now turn to exploring some specific policy areas in greater depth. We begin by investigating competition policy.

Competition policy is concerned with maintaining desirable kinds and levels of competition in an economy. But what do we mean by desirable? We seem to have been conditioned to think of competition as being universally good, so does 'desirable' mean 'maximum'? Should the aim of policy makers be to convert all monopolistic and oligopolistic markets into perfectly competitive ones?

Chapter 5, by Young and Metcalfe, seeks to answer questions pertaining to the theory and practice of competition policy. The chapter emphasises the vital link between theoretical perspectives and competition policy and demonstrates how different theories of competition, such as the neo-classical, Austrian and Marxian, lead to divergent policy prescriptions. Young and Metcalfe demonstrate how a study of the theory of competition leads us to take a more qualified view of competition: more competition may not always be preferable to less; temporary monopolies may sometimes be beneficial to the economy. Their analysis also makes us sensitive to the importance of context: competition authorities need to take account of the *specific* industry, product and process characteristics relating to the case under consideration. This is why many competition authorities handle competition matters on a case-by-case basis. This process involves the deployment of considerable administrative resources but is considered worthwhile in view of the importance of maintaining desirable levels and kinds of competition. As you read this chapter, remember that while policy frameworks are constantly evolving, the basic approaches remain valid, even as legislative detail changes.

Competition policies were traditionally devised in the context of national economies. With the development of (supra-national) trading blocks and the rapid growth of cross-border trading and investment links, the need for supra-national competition policy has increased very considerably. Young and Metcalfe explore the development of the competition policy of the European Union. One of the key challenges that the European Commission has faced in the development of European competition policy is the reconciliation of the diverse traditions of competition policy in the member nation states. Chapter 6, by Sykes, extends the discussion of competition policy to the wider international arena. He points out that national governments are likely to permit monopolistic practices of nationally owned firms that sell most of their output in foreign markets. If all nations condone monopolistic practices of this sort, then all nations may end up suffering. Developing countries may be especially vulnerable to such monopolistic practices because they often lack strong indigenous firms that can compete on equal terms with multinationals from the developed world. Consequently, there is a need for co-ordinating national competition policies or devising an international competition policy. Sykes makes some suggestions as to how such a competition policy may be devised and implemented at the international level.

Competition Policy

DAVID YOUNG AND STAN METCALFE*

The rationale for competition policy

Competition policy is concerned with maintaining competition between firms in all sections of the economy in an attempt to promote the efficient working of the market. The fundamental rationale for such policy is that the market does not, by itself, function perfectly or that there are certain necessary conditions for the proper functioning of markets which the state can attempt to create. Competitive markets are normally viewed as having a number of inherent advantages, such as the efficient allocation of resources, the maintenance of consumer choice, the promotion of technological innovation, and the autonomy of industrial enterprises, which it is believed is important for long-run economic progress. Mainstream economics has long emphasized the possible imperfections which may arise and that monopoly power, public goods, externalities, and such like provide grounds for a degree of state intervention on public policy in order to attempt to alleviate such problems. [...] There are, however, a variety of opinions as to the exact nature of competition and the extent to which state intervention is required. Moreover, it is also the case that any view as to the desirability of any type of competition policy is founded on a particular view of the nature of the competition process and the workings of a market economy.

The nature of the competitive process

In order to develop effective competition policy it is necessary to have a clear view of the meaning of competition. Competition policy is often seen as being necessary or helpful in aiding the competitive process and to correct any inadequacies or distortions existing in product (or less often factor) markets. But this view is based on a specific notion of the competitive process. Although there is a dominant theory

* Oxford University Press for an extract from *The Economics of the European Union, 2nd Edition* by M.J. Artis and Normal Lee © D. Young and S. Metcalfe, 1997.

of competition in economics, there are, in fact, a number of different theories or views of the nature of competition, and the dominant view sometimes draws on ideas from these alternative approaches. Before we can discuss and evaluate competition policy, we must explore the meaning of competition itself.

The mainstream view of competition is founded on the neoclassical notion of perfect competition. Although there are many dissenters from the application of such a strict condition, perfect competition still forms the theoretical basis of modern mainstream analysis of competition and hence competition policy. Perfect competition provides a bench-mark against which all and any actual form of competition may be judged. It defines a position of equilibrium which represents an optimal allocation of resources. This specifies a situation involving zero super-normal profits and free entry and exit. A deviation from this state is definitionally sub-optimal (although there may be dynamic gains which offset such static inefficiencies). Firms which possess a degree of market power, that are able to influence the market price, are regarded as distorting the allocation of resources from the socially optimal position. The conception of monopoly/market power as a distortion or imperfection is particularly important and is associated with the view that the market process is basically competitive but that at any point in time there may be a number of reasons why this is not so. The role of competition policy, therefore, is to correct these distortions and restore the market process to its correct competitive path.

However, some economists have been dissatisfied with such an abstract and static notion of the welfare bench-mark and in response have tried to develop a more suitable description of a baseline from which actual competition may be judged. In particular, the idea of 'workable' competition has been proposed. This does not involve any fundamentally different conception of what competition is, but rather is concerned with defining a state which relates more clearly to 'real-world' competitive conditions. It involves a neoclassical view of competition but eschews perfect competition as a realistic objective. Unfortunately, there are a number of different views and definitions of what workable competition actually is (see, for example, Devine et al. 1985). All, however, may be regarded as an attempt to describe a market which has an 'acceptable' set of competitive conditions from a policy perspective. Indeed, it is from a policy, rather than a theoretical, perspective that workable competition has been mainly thought to be a useful notion. Early attempts to define the term have focused on conditions where there are large numbers of sellers of similar products who do not collude, and where entry is not seriously restricted.

More radically different views of the nature of competition are offered by alternative schools of economic thought, such as the Austrian school, which emphasizes the 'process' character of competition. This view has enjoyed something of a revival in recent years (see, for example, Reid 1987) and has arguably been influential in determining changes in government policy on monopolies (since the early 1980s). The essence of the Austrian view is that competition is an ongoing *process* and that the neoclassical conception of competition, being essentially static, does not provide an appropriate basis for assessing actual markets. Competition, according to this view, is a continual process of entrepreneurial rivalry. Entrepreneurs are alert to profit opportunities and it is their purposeful pursuit of profit which is the driving force of the economy. This Austrian view, therefore, regards profit as necessary for motivating agents and also forms the basis of coordination and market order in the economy. Given that it is argued that perfect competition is not an appropriate baseline, this argument applies to profits generally and may include profits which neoclassical analysis would regard as super-normal. Therefore the argument that super-normal profits necessarily result from firms' monopoly power and that this should be a concern of state competition policy is denied. Rather, in the Austrian view, profits reflect superior firm-specific competence. Another significant dimension of the Austrian approach is the emphasis it places on innovation. This is particularly so in Schumpeterian theories, which develop the idea that the efficiency gains from innovations over time may out-weigh any short-term inefficiencies resulting from market imperfections. For example, a degree of monopoly power may result in an inefficient use of resources at a particular point in time, but if the profits generated by such market power generate greater innovation then there will be offsetting advantages in the longer term.

Another important alternative view of competition is propounded by radical or Marxian theorists. Though these views have had less impact on mainstream economics in general and competition policy in particular, some of the policy implications to which these approaches give rise represent important alternative perspectives on policy options. There are, in fact, two lines of thought (at least) in radical views on competition. One is based on the notion that market structure has an important influence on market performance, which is clearly similar in certain respects to the neoclassical view; the other is based on a radically different conception of competition as involving competing 'blocks' of capital. According to this latter view, the process of accumulation which drives the economic system involves each block of capital attempting to expand into, and therefore to invade, the domain of other blocks of capital; and it is this process of different capitals expanding and competing with each other which describes the nature of the competitive process. The alternative view accepts the concept of market structure proposed by neoclassical theory, but argues that the market system has a natural tendency towards monopoly. The process of competition involves the gradual monopolization of product markets by large corporations. Oligopoly and market power are seen as the norm. This contrasts with the standard neoclassical view of market power as an imperfection or deviation from a competitive state. Rather, competition is fundamentally about market power and more generally the exercise of economic and political power.

The theoretical basis of competition policy: impediments to competition

Having outlined the different views of competition, we are now able to consider the principal sources of departure from a competitive state which might provide the basis for the main issues of concern in competition policy. It should be emphasized at the outset that posing the problem in terms of a departure from an optimal state does in itself form the question in a neoclassical/mainstream way. But, given that it is the most familiar and influential approach, this seems acceptable in the present contest.

The most obvious obstacle to competitive behaviour in a market is the presence of monopoly. The standard theoretical approach to monopoly defines it as a situation in which there is a single seller of a given product, where there are no close substitutes for this product, and where entry into the market is blocked. [...]

There have been numerous attempts to estimate the social costs of monopoly power. Obviously some idea of the magnitude of welfare losses is of great importance, in as much as this can provide some basis for assessing the need for a competition policy. (It might also be noted that it may also be important in assessing the competing claims regarding the inherent tendency of the system towards competition or monopoly.) Early estimates, produced for the USA (such as Harberger 1954), tended to suggest that welfare losses were very low, leading to a 'conventional' view that the social costs of monopoly are in fact rather trivial. However, in the last twenty years there have been a number of studies which have produced quite different estimates, suggesting that the cost of monopoly, associated with the reduction in gross output, is quite significant. For example, Cowling and Mueller (1978) and Sawyer (1980) have published estimates for the UK which suggest that welfare losses might be as high as 9 per cent of gross output. Similarly, significant 'high' estimates have been produced for France by Jenny and Weber (1983). There are a variety of reasons for the differences between these estimates, but the principal factors which have led to the higher estimates include attempts to include the costs of attempting to acquire and maintain monopoly positions (by including advertising expenditures in some form) and different assumptions regarding demand elasticities.

Other assessments of the magnitude of social costs arising from monopoly power have produced an even more diverse set of estimates. Littlechild (1981), in criticizing the Cowling and Mueller (1978) estimates, adopted an Austrian position, arguing that welfare losses were considerably smaller than Cowling and Mueller suggested. This was due, in his view, to the positive role of profits as the reward for risk-taking and the necessity of profits for encouraging innovation, as well as a number of other factors, such as alleged aggregation bias and price discrimination. At the other end of the spectrum, Baran and Sweezy (1966) report estimates of surplus value for the US economy which suggest that more than 50 per cent of total US national product may take the form of surplus value produced by the monopolistic character of modern capitalism.

Although basic monopoly theory does provide some basis for identifying the social costs of non-competitive outcomes, it would be helpful if this theory provided an analysis of the consequences of monopoly power and not only of monopoly pricing. However, at present, a full theoretical explanation of monopoly power does not exist. Attempts to remedy this situation may arise out of developments in oligopoly theory, which is now firmly based on game-theoretic models. Although it is not possible or appropriate to discuss these developments here, it is important to consider the principal dimensions of oligopoly as they relate to the state of industrial competitiveness and therefore the formation of competition policy.

A particularly important factor is the notion of dominance. This is of specific concern from a policy perspective, because much legislative action has been concerned with dominant positions. The theoretical basis for this begins with the idea that a particular firm, or group of firms, may, by virtue of its relatively high share of industry/market output, be in a position to exert a degree of dominance over that market. The basic theoretical model which attempts to represent such a situation is referred to as the dominant firm or dominant firm-price leadership model (see, for example, Hay and Morris 1991). Such a model embodies the assumption that the dominant firm or dominant group acts as the price leader by setting the price for the market in accordance with maximizing its own profits subject to a demand constraint. This demand constraint (i.e. the dominant firm's demand curve) is obtained by deducting the total supply of all other producers in the industry from total industry demand, which is exogenously given. The other producers in the industry are assumed to be a competitive 'fringe', each firm being a price-taker. All of these firms take the dominant firm's (group's) price as given and produce the output which maximizes their profit given this price. This model has been criticized for a number of reasons, including its essentially static nature and its assumption that the dominant firm knows the supply of the 'fringe'; the conception of dominance involved is also rather narrow. In particular, the fact that the 'fringe' treats prices as given, but is important in determining the residual demand curve facing the dominant firm, limits the nature of the leading firm's dominance.

A broader view of dominance often involves the idea that a firm can restrict other firms' choices via strategic behaviour. (See, for example, Geroski's and Jacquemin's [1984] discussion of the persistence of dominant firms.) There are potentially many aspects to such behaviour, such as a firm's attempt to secure market share through advertising and attempts to establish a 'reputation' with regard to pricing or output strategies. Another crucial dimension of the interaction between firms which is particularly important is the degree of collusion. Overt collusion is normally the direct concern of competition policy and in many countries is effectively outlawed. There are various forms which collusion may take, but the main examples may be categorized as either some form of price-setting or some type of explicit agreement concerning outputs. (This is often analysed in terms of cartel behaviour. A cartel is the most formal and explicit form of collusion and normally involves a common price structure and some agreement over the output of the firms within the cartel.)

Although there is a wide variety of issues which must be evaluated when considering a firm's dominance, it should be noted that its relative size in terms of market share is still seen as a singularly important indicator of its potential dominance. This is clearly reflected, for example, in a number of previous European competition policy decisions. The well-known *Continental Can* case in the early

1970s invoked the company's substantial market share in establishing its abuse of a dominant position. (For a discussion of this and other cases, see Jacquemin and de Jong 1977 and Utton 1995). Further, examples of the importance of market share are provided by various competition policies within the European Union (EU), which we shall discuss later.

Another source of restriction on competition is merger activity. Mergers are normally categorized under three main types: horizontal, vertical, and conglomerate. Each, at least potentially, has welfare implications arising from a variety of effects on the degree of competition. Perhaps the simplest case is that of horizontal merger, which at certain times in the past, such as the famous merger boom of the late 1960s, has been the dominant type of merger. Definitionally horizontal mergers involve the merging of firms at the same stage of the production process. This can result in direct changes in the level of concentration in a given industry and this may result in increased market power and higher price–cost margins. For example, two firms merging within a particular industry will clearly reduce the number of firms and increase size inequalities between firms, hence leading to an increase in concentration (as measured by, for instance, the Herfindahl index). The newly formed firm (resulting from the merger) will have a higher market share and greater market power than either of the previous firms. This market power might be used to increase profit margins.

Cases involving vertical mergers – i.e. mergers between firms at different stages of the production process – also have welfare implications. Usually, the principal concern here is the restrictions placed on the suppliers of the vertical outlets for the particular products concerned. For example, if a firm at an intermediate stage of the production process merges with a firm at a later stage (retail), then there might be some welfare concern with regard to the restriction of supplies to other retail outlets supplied by the old intermediate firm, now part of the 'new' merged firm.

Conglomerate mergers have in recent years become the most important type of merger and their welfare implications are potentially very significant. These involve firms merging across different markets (i.e. mergers in which there are no vertical or horizontal relations). The analysis of the effects of mergers of this type, however, is the most complex, as by their very nature they involve activities in a number of different markets, and therefore it is impossible easily to assess their effects in terms of changes in concentration or vertical constraints. However, the overall effect on the economy may be indicated by changes in aggregate concentration, and specific pricing and/or output effects may be identified. The case of conglomerate merger also raises broader aspects concerning firms' 'power', and this may be of great importance from a policy perspective. For example, Jacquemin and de Jong (1977) have stated that the eventual goals of competition policy should include 'the diffusion of economic power' and the protection of the 'economic freedom of market participants'. However, these are much more difficult aspects of economic life to regulate, partly because there are quite different interpretations of what constitutes 'economic freedom' and 'economic power'. An important point to note, however, is that such consideration of such policy issues broadens our conception of competition to include the Austrian and radical viewpoints outlined previously. For example, Austrians might argue that maintaining the freedom of economic agents is of primary importance, whilst a radical approach might suggest that competition policy should take greater steps to contain the economic (and political) power attained by large corporations.

Having outlined some of the main theoretical issues, we may now turn to actual policy. Before doing so, however, it is worth emphasizing that, although the insights of economic theory are important in determining the nature of competition policy, there are many other influences. The perception of the problems arising from monopoly power, for example, are much influenced by political ideas and are not necessarily closely related to particular elements of economic theory. This said, the economic theories of the day are a critical ingredient in determining actual competition policies.

Competition policy in different EU countries

In order to illustrate how the principles of competition policy are applied in practice and to describe the different interpretations and methods of application which exist, it is useful to consider some examples of competition policy in some of the member states of the EU. In particular, we shall consider the basic legislation and policy measures which have been developed in the UK, Germany, and France, before proceeding to discuss policy at the EU level. [...]

There are a number of critical problems which arise when considering competitive policies in an international context. For example, there may be difficulties in deciding on the relevant jurisdiction of a particular policy or piece of legislation. Similarly, problems arising from price discrimination across different national markets ('dumping') have also raised difficult economic and legal questions. However, it is first necessary to consider individual national policies.

The United Kingdom

The main piece of legislation underpinning much of modern competition policy in the UK is the 1973 Fair Trading Act. This extended previous legislation concerning monopolies and mergers and established the Office of Fair Trading (OFT), which has the task of monitoring competition. The OFT is under the headship of the Director-General of Fair Trading, who has the legal power to refer any cases of anti-competitive behaviour to the Monopolies and Mergers Commission (MMC). Such anti-competitive behaviour concerns cases which involve the exploitation of a 'monopoly situation' which exists in relation to the acquisition or supply of goods within the UK. The definition of monopoly was amended in the 1973 Act to apply to a firm holding a 25 per cent market share or more (the previous definition specified a one-third market share); a 'complex monopoly', where two or more firms account for at least a 25 per cent share of the market and are deemed to act in such a way as to restrict competition, may also be referred. The definition of the relevant market is, of course, crucial in making such definitions meaningful. This is decided on the basis of a specific range of products and is determined by the Secretary of State for Trade and Industry on the advice of the Director-General.

Once a reference has been made, it is then incumbent upon the MMC to decide whether a monopoly situation exists (in accordance with the Act) and whether or not it operates against the 'public interest'. What is or is not against the public interest involves a balancing of the possible efficiency gains (such as scale economies) against the restriction of competition (as caused by the abuse of market power), and this has normally been considered on a case-by-case basis. The criteria used to decide this include the maintenance of effective competition for supply within the UK; promoting competition through cost reduction by the use of new techniques and products, and facilitating entry into existing markets; maintaining/promoting a balanced distribution of industry and employment throughout the UK; and the maintenance of competitive activities outside the UK by UK suppliers and producers. If a firm (or firms) is found to be acting against the public interest, then it will normally be required by law to agree to refrain from the activities identified by the MMC as anti-competitive and harmful to the public interest. The decision on this rests with the Secretary of State.

Two other pieces of legislation of significance for contemporary policy are the Resale Prices Act 1976 and the Restrictive Trade Practices Act 1976. These build on previous Acts in 1964 and 1956 respectively. The 1976 Restrictive Trade Practices Act broadened the information which firms are required to register, which was established in the 1956 Act and requires the Director-General to act against agreements which significantly restrict competition. This usually attempts to prohibit collusion and price-fixing agreements.

Much of the legislative basis of competition policy was altered in the Competition Act of 1980, which widened the investigating power of the Director-General. It also provided for the recommendation that a firm's activities were against the public interest on the grounds of only one outstanding effect (such as higher future prices) rather than having to weigh all possible pros and cons. Associated with this principle was the introduction of the concept of an 'anti-competitive practice', which has been interpreted to include refusal to supply 'tie-ins' and discounts, predatory pricing, and forcing retailers to stock a whole range of products ('full-line forcing').

The 1980 Act also provided for the investigation, by the MMC, of public enterprise 'monopolies', which was strongly associated with the government's drive towards privatization and was perhaps inspired in part by the Austrian notion that most (if not all) impediments to competition have their origins in state intervention. The subsequent privatization of many utilities has, of course, greatly reduced the number of references made on these grounds.

The continued development of the EU internal market has created new pressures for further revision of the UK legislative framework. A series of White and Green papers, from 1989 onwards, culminated in a government statement of policy in April 1993. In brief, reform will involve the replacement of the 1976 Restrictive Practices Act with a prohibition of cartels, anti-competitive arguments, and concerted practices, and a strengthening of the powers of the Director-General of Fair Trading in relation to investigation, the importance of interim measures, and abuses of market power. The model for this policy framework is Article 85 of the Treaty on European Union (TEU). It certainly makes sense to bring regulatory consistency and certainty to the appraisal of the activities of those UK-located companies which involve cross-border trade, while, at the same time, not losing sight of subsidiarity considerations in relation to competitive issues which are purely national in character. The central features of the new framework will include the *prohibition* of anti-competitive practices, the definition of *exemptions and exclusions*, and provisions for *penalties* and an *institutional framework* including rights of appeal. It is also the intention to extend competition law to the exercise of certain property rights – e.g. access to land – where there is the potential to damage competition.

Germany

German competition policy is based on the 1957 Act against Restraints on Competition. This Act prohibits actions/agreements to restrain competition, production, or market conditions with regard to trade in goods and commercial services. This includes any form of cartel arrangement, price-fixing, resale price maintenance, exclusive deals, and 'buying' arrangements. The distinguishing feature of German competition policy embodied in this Act is the emphasis on market dominance by large corporations. The Act has been amended several times since its inception, specifically in 1965, 1973, 1976, 1980, and 1989. The 1973 amendments established merger controls and notification requirements for proposed mergers, expanded the legal definition of market dominance, and extended the exemptions of small firms, which was the main amendment introduced by the previous alteration in 1965. The 1980 amendments were particularly significant in clarifying the definitions of abuse of dominant positions by illustrating the principal characteristics of dominant firms, and in specifying the criteria for control of vertical and conglomerate mergers.

The amendment in 1989 extended the dominance issue to 'powerful' buyers (in addition to sellers) and to situations involving smaller trading partners rather than the hitherto exclusive concern with large firms. This introduced a new dimension to German anti-trust policy, which has, generally speaking, always been primarily concerned with the abuse of dominant market positions, typically by large single suppliers. The system of law supporting this, which is in contradistinction to US legislation, has been adopted by a number of other anti-trust systems, including those in Japan and the EU itself, which we shall discuss later. The actual size of firm is crucial, in that the law is formulated to protect the interest of small firms against the exercise of market power/dominant positions by large firms. Activities of small firms are allowed which would be illegal if they were carried out by large firms, which are regarded as having a natural market advantage. This allows small firms, for example, to attempt to exploit economies of scale without fear of contravening competition policy. This exemption clause is important in simplifying the enforcement of anti-trust law, which, in comparison with the UK (and also the USA), is generally simpler, as it does not require the balancing of anti-competitive behaviour with efficiency. Under German law, conduct which is found severely to restrict competition is generally illegal. Efficiency is treated under grounds for exception rather than by the case-by-case evaluation typified by the UK, as discussed in the previous section.

France

Modern competition policy in France also has its legislative roots in the early post-Second World War years. Anti-trust policies of some type, however, are significantly older and represent one of the oldest systems of anti-monopoly legislation in the world. Most current legislation and policy is based on the post-war system, which was substantially revised in 1977. This included a much tougher policy on mergers, which in the 1950s and 1960s had been broadly encouraged in an attempt to strengthen domestic companies in order to make them better able to compete with foreign/international rivals. (This was also an important view prevailing in the UK during this time, and was, in part, responsible for the merger 'boom' of the late 1960s.) The new policy on mergers required post-merger notice, and provided for the prohibition of mergers, including firms with large (domestic) market shares. This Act also established the Commission de la Concurrence, which is empowered to investigate anti-trust violations and to recommend corrective measures. These changes, though altering the underlying laws very little, significantly expanded the means of enforcing anti-trust legislation.

Further changes in 1985 and 1986 strengthened merger policy by subjecting more mergers to the controls established in 1977, and the applicability of competition and anti-trust norms was broadened. This seems to have resulted in a significant increase in enforcement activity in France. The 1986 amendment also replaced the Commission by the Conseil de la Concurrence, which, unlike the Commission, is independent from the Ministry of Economics. Most significantly, this coincided with the separation of the administration from the interpretation and enforcement of anti-trust law. The interpretation of the law became the responsibility of the judiciary. This was an important change, which essentially shifted the onus of anti-trust enforcement from political discretion to judicial assessment. This is in contradistinction to the UK, where control of implementation rests with the Secretary of State, as noted previously. Merger control, on the other hand, has remained the subject of political review, and in this area recommendations by the Conseil require the authorization of the Minister of Economics.

Finally, it should be noted that these amendments (particularly the 1986 amendment) have drawn heavily on Articles 85 and 86 of the Treaty of Rome in formulating a view on competition. This illustrates, as do other national policies, the increasing influence and importance of EU competition policy, to which we now turn.

EU competition policy

The development of competition policy

An essential element in the concept of a common market is the unfettered mobility of goods, services, and factors of production so as to ensure the greatest efficiency in resource allocation. This was an essential theme throughout the development of the European Community, culminating in the establishment of the Single European Market (SEM) in 1992. Naturally, the first concern of the founders of the EC was the free mobility of goods, and, since it would have been pointless to eliminate national tariff barriers to trade if private firms could construct their own countervailing barriers, the whole question of competition policy was central to its progress. As with so many areas of EC activity, competition policy evolved steadily from the founding guidelines established in the Treaty of Rome. The advent of the single market is bound to result in further developments, as the experience of trading in different markets identifies new areas of anti-competitive practice previously sheltering in national backwaters. The production of services is one likely focus of attention, as is the enduring question of subsidiarity and the respective domains of national and EU competition authorities. Among the factors shaping the evolution of policy, in addition to the guidance provided by economic theory, are the diverse traditions of different countries, the extension of the EU to include other nations, and the changing role of public monopoly in the member states. Of some relevance here are the differing Anglo-Saxon and continental approaches to competition. The Anglo-Saxon viewpoint is best exemplified by the US anti-trust practice, of which the UK legislation is a loose imitation based on a case-by-case approach. In the USA, firms are subject to stringent scrutiny and fierce compliance regulations, including provision for triple damages to be awarded to injured third parties. In contrast, the continental view has always been more relaxed, accepting social dimensions to competition, close links between suppliers and customers, and the establishment of group interests to the detriment of outsiders. Agreements not to compete have traditionally been part of a European business mentality. It is not surprising, therefore, that, from the outset, the Commission has faced difficulties in imposing a competition policy on the Member States. At one extreme were Germany, and subsequently the UK, with well-developed frameworks for dealing with monopoly and restrictive practices, and, at the other, states such as Italy and Belgium, where a competition policy tradition scarcely existed. Out of this diversity a clear European dimension has emerged, and our purpose now is to sketch its main features in the light of the previous discussion of economic principle.

Some history

The central feature of EU policy is the belief in the static and dynamic benefits of competition, and the origins of this view can be traced back to the Treaty of Paris in 1951 and the subsequent establishment of the European Coal and Steel Community (ECSC) in May 1953. Given its concern with these strategic commodities, it is not surprising that the Treaty identified certain business practices and state aids as being incompatible with the foundation of an integrated market in coal and steel. Thus the High Authority of the ECSC was empowered to identify and rule on cases of anti-competitive behaviour. From this foundation, the next step was the Messina conference of May 1955 and the subsequent Spaak Report, which laid the foundations for the Treaty of Rome. By then it was well recognized, within the Commission and more generally, that static considerations relating to the abuse of market power had to be weighed in the balance against the more dynamic considerations relating to technological and organizational innovation. The Treaty of Rome established the Commission as the authority in all matters of competition policy, with DG IV being established as the appropriate branch of the Commission. To this branch fell the complex task of turning the guidelines of the treaty into a workable policy. The relevant Articles of the Treaty are 85, which deals with anti-competitive practices, and 86, which deals with dominant market practices and their abuse. In addition we should note that Articles 37 and 90 cover the conduct of public enterprises and Article 91 covers dumping of goods across national boundaries. However, our prime concern here is with Articles 85 and 86. The former has certainly been the more actively used of the two. Between 1964 and 1990 a total of 284 formal Commission decisions were made with respect to Article 85 and only twenty-one with respect to Article 86. Indeed, the first referral under the latter did not occur until 1971, an index of the jealousy with which national governments viewed this matter.

Article 85

This article sets out the practices deemed to be incompatible with a common market: all agreements between undertakings which may affect trade between Member States and have as their object or effect the prevention, reduction, or distortion of competition within the common market. It covers horizontal and vertical distortions of all kinds, price-fixing, price discrimination, agreements to predetermine market shares, and any controls on production, investment, or technical development. All such practices are declared void and unenforceable. However, it is also recognized that such agreements may, in clearly specified circumstances, be in the public interest and on these grounds exempt from the provisions of this article. The general rule here permits agreements if they promote efficiency in production and distribution, promote technical progress, and provide consumers with a fair share of the benefits. Provided an agreement is essential to the provision of these beneficial effects, it could be approved. The immediate consequence of these negative (85/1) and positive sides (85/3) to Article 85 is that each situation has to be treated on its own merits, and so DG IV's principal task has been to build the appropriate body of case law. To assist in this process, regulations have had to be drafted which translate the general principles of Article 85 into clear-cut practice.

We should first note that the Commission has very substantial powers of investigation, supported by the relevant national authorities (in the UK case, the OFT) and bolstered by a system of fines for failure to cooperate with an investigation. Investigations can be prompted by the Commission or by the complaints of third parties. These matters are codified in Regulation 17/62, which was the practical response to the experience of the early years gained in DG IV. This regulation empowered the Commission to enforce the rules of competition on a uniform basis throughout the Community and to exempt small firms with less than a 5 per cent market share from the provisions of Article 85, and instituted a system of fines for breaches of the competition rules. In principle, the fine could amount to up to 10 per cent of a company's world-wide turnover. Pressure of work on the Commission soon led to further regulations defining a category of group exemptions to Article 85 – that is, a class of practices which by their generic nature are considered not to have anti-competition effects. Thus Regulation 19/65 proposed exemption for resale agreements within the EC and restriction on the acquisition and use of industrial property rights. Group exemptions of this nature are typically granted for a period of ten to fifteen years. Not only do they limit the Commission's workload; they also save firms legal and other costs incurred in seeking an individual exemption. In the light of the Schumpeterian conflict between the static and dynamic aspects of innovation-based competition, it is particularly interesting to note the group exemptions which have been developed to accommodate firms' arrangements jointly to develop new technology. Thus, Council Regulation 2821/71 established that Article 85(1) does not apply to agreements between undertakings which have, as their objective, the application of standards or the joint undertaking of an R&D programme up to the stage of industrial exploitation, provided the results are shared between the partners in relation to their contributions. The increasing importance of high-technology competition to the perceived success of the EC *vis-à-vis* the rest of the world led, in the 1980s, to further refinements. Commission Regulation 418/85 extended the group exemptions to cover the joint exploitation of a joint R&D programme. In this context, joint exploitation covers production and marketing, the assignment of licences and other intellectual property, and the commercial know-how required for manufacture. One could hardly find a better example of the continually evolving nature of the Commission's competition policy.

Once a case has been dealt with by the Commission, a number of outcomes are possible. At one extreme is a negative clearance: that is, a declaration that the practice does not violate the conditions of Article 85(1). At the other extreme, a violation is found and fines may be imposed. The policy on fines has grown bolder with the acquisition of experience. The first case occurred in 1969, when a quinine cartel involving Dutch, German, and French firms was decreed in violation of

85(1), and was duly fined by the Commission. Relatively small beer one might think, but large firms in major sectors have not been exempt. Then a market-sharing agreement between ICI and Solvay for the production of soda ash was considered a violation in 1990 and fines of Ecu 17 million and Ecu 30 million were imposed on the respective companies. Nor were non-EC companies exempt: in 1991, Toshiba was fined Ecu 2 million for illegal arrangements with its European distribution companies. In between these extremes are the many cases where the partners involved voluntarily abandon their restrictive agreement or agree to modify it in a way in which the Commission considers is compatible with Article 85(3).

It would be a mistake to imagine that all the cases dealt with by the Commission relate to industrial markets. An interesting illustration of this is provided by the case of the Official Association of Industrial Property Agents (COAPRI), the Spanish trade association, which fixed scales of charges in relation to services provided for the acquisition of patent rights and trade marks in Spain and externally. Reporting in January 1995, the Commission found that, in determining categories of activity and setting the related charges, the Articles of COAPRI restricted the freedom of competitive action of agents and constituted an entry barrier to aspiring agents. Such collective action was deemed to be a serious restriction on competition that could not be justified on the grounds that the ensuing market stability resulted in a higher quality of service. COAPRI was obliged to cease these practices.

Some examples of the grounds on which the Commission has granted negative clearance may prove helpful at this stage. An early example was provided in 1965 concerning a German manufacturer of mechanical cultivators (Hummel) and its Belgian distribution company (Isbecque). The exclusive nature of the agreement was considered to bring it within the scope of Article 85(1), but, none the less, negative clearance was granted on the grounds that the arrangement led to superior customer services without any adverse pricing effects. Two more recent examples indicate the complexities of a case-by-case approach. In 1988 an arrangement between AEI and Reyroll Parsons to set up a joint manufacturing company (Vacuum Interrupters Limited) was granted exemption in spite of being the sole European supplier, entirely on the grounds that the associated product innovations would benefit consumers. A further example of the Commission's attitude to the dynamics of the competitive process is provided by the decision in 1990 to exempt a joint venture to develop and produce electronic components for satellites (Alcatel Esaci/ANT Nachrichten Technik). Notwithstanding the fact that this agreement was judged to affect competition adversely within the Community, it was allowed on the grounds that it strengthened European industry relative to the foreign competition.

A final, and very interesting, example is provided by the clearance in December 1992 of the joint venture agreement between Ford and Volkswagen to develop, engineer, and manufacture a multi-purpose vehicle (MPV). The proposal was to build one plant (in Portugal) and produce two products, one for each partner, distinguished by their engines and body-design details. In reaching its decision to clear this venture, the Commission noted that the venture related to a new market segment (MPVs) and that the venture would influence competition in a number of dimensions, including cross-border trade and the sharing of technical know-how. However, the agreement did not raise any issues of market dominance and fulfilled all the criteria for exemption noted above. It is worth noting that clearance was granted subject to a number of important conditions, including a request to ring-fence commercially sensitive information from the parent companies and to seek the approval of the Commission should either partner seek not to market its model in a Member State.

Article 86

Article 86 prohibits the abuse by one or more undertakings of a dominant position within the single market or a substantial part of it, but only in so far as the abuse may affect trade between Member States. It would cover, for example, restrictions on supply or technical development and unfair pricing. Unlike Article 85, there is no provision for granting an exemption, but like that Article the system of fines is used to penalize abuses of dominance. One example is the heavy fine imposed on Tetra Pak (a Swiss company): this was fined Ecu 75 million in 1991 on a turnover of Ecu 3.6 billion for engaging in discriminatory pricing and other practices, including unfair charges for early termination of contracts by its customers. Tetra Pak held 90 per cent of the EC market in one market segment and 50 per cent in the other relevant segment, and not only set limits on cross-border competition as a basis for discrimination but also set some limitations on the use of the machinery it supplied to certain manufacturers. One interesting aspect of this case was that, although the abuses were EC-wide, the complaint came from a competitor in the Italian market, who claimed that Tetra Pak was selling at predatory prices and excluding it from certain advertising media. Although the complaint was in a national context, the Commission judgment applied to abuse of market power in all the EC markets. As with decisions reached under Article 85, the European Court of Justice stands as the court of appeal in all cases.

We have already pointed to the relatively infrequent use of Article 86, in part due to the hostility of national authorities. More telling though is the failure of this Article to provide clear guidance on the treatment of mergers and acquisitions within the EU. At best it gives grounds for a decision *ex post* once a merger has been carried out and is judged to lead to adverse dominant behaviour. What it does not do is to provide guidance *ex ante* as to whether a merger is permissible. Equally, it becomes clear that mergers created a loophole in Article 85 in that two independent parties to an anti-competitive arrangement could merge and thereby avoid scrutiny – the Commission having no jurisdiction over the internal practices of companies.

The merger boom of the 1980s created very real concerns that a policy on mergers consistent with the principles of the Treaty of Rome was conspicuously absent. The outcome of this debate was the European Commission Merger Regulation, introduced in 1990.

The European Commission Merger Regulation

To understand the current position some history is again useful. In 1971 the Commission deployed Article 86 to judge a takeover by the Continental Can Company of New York of a West German and a Dutch company. It found against Continental Can on the grounds that its acquisitions had created a monopoly position for metal cans and bottle tops within the Community. The case went to appeal and the Court of Justice overturned the Commission's judgment. However, in its judgment it ruled that Articles 85 and 86, while they did not mention mergers, possessed a unity of purpose to protect competition and that, on these grounds, Article 86 applied on principle to merger situations. The period of drafting and consultation which followed led finally to Regulation 4064/89, the merger regulation which came into force in September 1990. This outlines the procedure for assessing whether cross-member State mergers create a dominant position which may have abusive effects, and it may also be applied to mergers between EU and non-EU companies. Authority to judge is again vested in DG IV, which has established a Merger Task Force to handle these cases. The essence of the EU position is that a merger falls within the regulation's scope if it leads to concentration and passes three tests. First, the aggregate world-wide turnover of all the undertakings involved (including parent companies of merging subsidiaries) must exceed Ecu 5 million. Secondly, the aggregate EU turnover of each of at least two of the firms involved must exceed Ecu 250 million. Finally, the regulation does not apply if each of the firms involved has two-thirds of its EU-wide turnover within one Member State. In these calculations, turnover is to be calculated net of all sales taxes. It is apparent that the identification of turnover will be a crucial and contentious aspect of the application of this regulation, although it is not obviously the most relevant measure of market dominance. It remains the responsibility of the merging parties to notify the Commission of their intention to merge, and the relevant national authorities lose jurisdiction whenever a merger has the identified EU dimension. We should also note that the merger provisions also apply to cooperative agreements between firms if that agreement is judged to be concentrative rather than cooperative – that is, creates a lasting economic unit to produce a product or develop a technology. The latter remains subject to the provisions of Articles 85 and 86.

As to its procedures, the Merger Task Force has one month from notification to decide whether to proceed with a case, and a further four months to reach a final decision. Having defined the appropriate market, the emphasis of the investigation is on the maintenance of competitive conditions. Perhaps the most pressing issues concerning the merger regulation relate to the relationship between the Commission and national authorities. National authorities are kept informed of the progress of an investigation, and they can, under Article 9 of the Regulation, request the referral of the merger back to themselves – a procedure which had happened only once, in response to a UK request. Also important here is the requirement further to limit the operation of the Regulation in 1993 with a view to reducing the turnover criteria which provide the tests for potential dominance. The Commission has proposed a reduction of the aggregate turnover threshold to Ecu 2 billion, and this is certain to meet with opposition from those members with well-established merger policies (the UK, Germany, and France). Not surprisingly, this has become entangled with post-Maastricht Treaty sensitivities about subsidiarity and the relative roles of national and European-level authorities. Finally, we note that some commentators are in favour of a European Central Office as the focus for merger policy at EU level.

Overview

It will be apparent from the above that competition policy at the European level has evolved considerably since 1958 and must continue to evolve as the EU grows in membership and the internal market develops. Central to this development will be its relationship with competition policies at national level within the EU and increasingly outside the EU as global competition plays an increasing role in EU thinking.

The extent to which national governments will be willing to forgo the adjudication of monopoly, merger, and anti-competitive practices remains the great practical conundrum for the future of EU policy. But deeper issues are also at work, reflecting the contrasting perspectives on competition outlined in the opening section of this chapter. Broadly speaking, these views may be typified in terms of competition as a state of equilibrium versus competition as a process of change. According to the first view, a firm is more competitive to the extent that it has less power to charge a price in excess of marginal costs (itself a vague concept depending on whether a short-run or long-run view is taken) and to control entry into its specific markets. According to the second view, a firm is more competitive to the extent that it has cost and product advantages relative to its rivals and can turn these advantages into gains in market share. Thus competition implies change in the relative market position of the different rivals, a situation of stable market shares indicating a neutral balance of competitive forces. Whichever view one takes of these contrasting positions, the openness of markets to entry by new firms, new products, and new methods of production is a central feature of a competitive environment. Thus policy to limit entry barriers, deregulate markets, and stimulate innovation through technology policy is immediately recognizable as a pro-competitive policy. Whenever entry entails the outlay of irrevocably sunk costs, it is clear that competition cannot be too fierce: as Downie (1956) pointed out, the effective operation of competition requires a modicum of grit in the market mechanism. The obvious example here is when entry is premised on product or process innovations, which require a firm to sink outlays in research, design, and development programmes. If imitation is too easy or the market too competitive, the incentive to undertake those innovation expenditures can be undermined to the detriment of the dynamics of competition. Within the EU, an obvious case is provided by the regulation of the pharmaceutical industry, which will be one important test-bed for competitive policy. Pressure to cut health-service costs and open markets to generic producers will have to be weighed carefully against the need for sufficient profitability to fund the science and technology base of the major drug companies. An important policy issue here relates to the question of the optimum length of life of a patent under European law, and the associated regulatory limitations placed on drug developers. In short, firms have to be given sufficient monopoly power to induce the development of beneficial pharmaceutical products, the dynamic gains from product improvement taking precedence over any static losses from granting these companies an element of patent-protected market power.

While open-entry conditions are common to all views of competition, the interpretation of market power and the profits so generated are not. In all practical cases, it is very difficult to decide the extent to which reported profits are the result of market power or the result of the superior competence of the firm in generating lower costs or better service to consumers. The great danger always lies in penalizing the successful for their very success and thus constraining the long-run development of the economic system. None of this, of course, is a recipe for turning a blind eye to anti-competitive practices intended to rig markets and offset the dynamic effects of customers' choice on the relative position of competing firms. Rather, it is a case for careful treatment of each situation on its merits, and an awareness that the competitive process generates losers as well as winners. As with so much in economic theory, the powerful general insights which it provides must always be qualified by the details of the specific circumstances of the individual case. Since these circumstances transcend national boundaries, it is clear that much will be learned (and need to be learned) by the practitioners of competition policy at both EU and national level.

Further reading

Much of the theoretical background concerning the various impediments to competition can be found in Devine et al. (1985) or, at a more advanced level, in Hay and Morris (1991) and Reid (1987). The latter includes some material relating to Austrian views. For a 'radical' perspective, Cowling and Mueller (1982) is an important source. In addition, Downie (1956) is a classic reference on the control of monopoly. On EU competition policy *per se*, Jacquemin and de Jong (1977) contains a useful introductory chapter. For recent analysis and discussion, Sapir et al. (1992) is valuable, as is mush of Comanor et al. (1990).

References

Baran, P., and Sweezy, P. (1966), *Monopoly Capital* (New York: Monthly Review Press).

Comanor, W.S., George, K., and Jacquemin, A. (1990), *Competition Policy in Europe and North America: Issues and Institutions* (Chur: Harwood Academic).

Cowling, K., and Mueller, D. (1978), 'The Social Costs of Monopoly Power', *Economic Journal*, 88/4: 727–48.

Cowling, K., and Mueller, D. (1982), *Monopoly Capitalism* (London: Macmillan).

Devine, P.J., Lee, N., Jones, R.M., and Tyson, W.J. (1985), *An Introduction to Industrial Economics*, 4th edn (London: Unwin Hyman).

Downie, J. (1956), 'How should We Control Monopoly?', *Economic Journal*, 66/2: 573–7.

Geroski, P., and Jacquemin, A. (1984), 'Dominant Firms and their Alleged Decline', *International Journal of Industrial Organization*, 2/1: 1–27.

Harberger, A. (1954), 'Monopoly and Resource Allocation', *American Economic Review Proceedings*, 44/2: 77–87.

Hay, D., and Morris, D. (1991), *Industrial Economics and Organization: Theory and Evidence* (Oxford: Oxford University Press).

Hay, D., and Vickers, J. (1988), 'The Reform of UK Competition Policy', *National Institute Economic Review* (Aug.): 56–67.

Jacquemin, A., and de Jong, H. (1977), *European Industrial Organisation* (London: Macmillan).

Jacquemin, A., and Sapir, A. (eds) (1989), *The European Internal Market: Trade and Competition* (Oxford: Oxford University Press).

Jenny, F., and Weber, A.P. (1983), 'Aggregate Welfare Loss Due to Monopoly Power in the French Economy', *Journal of Industrial Economics*, 32/2: 113–30.

Littlechild, S. (1981), 'Misleading Calculations of the Social Costs of Monopoly Power', *Economic Journal*, 91/2: 348–63.

Reid, G. (1987), *Theories of Industrial Organisation* (Oxford: Blackwell).

Sapir, A., Buigues, P., and Jacquemin, A. (1992), 'European Competitive Policy in Manufacturing and Services: A Two-Speed Approach', *Oxford Review of Economic Policy*, 9: 113–32.

Sawyer, M. (1980), 'Monopoly Welfare Losses in the U.K.', *Manchester School*, 48/4: 331–54.

Schumpeter, J. (1944), *Capitalism, Socialism and Democracy* (London: Allen & Unwin).

Utton, M. (1995), *Market Dominance and Antitrust Policy* (Aldershot: Edward Elgar).

International Competition Policy

ALAN O. SYKES*

[…] The theorietical case for international cooperation is a powerful one and rests on the existence of substantial external effects from national antitrust policies in an open economy – an economy with international trade. It is difficult to imagine a mechanism short of international cooperation that could adequately address these important externalities, but it is also clear that international consensus on 'optimal' antitrust policy is lacking in many particulars. Accordingly, I argue for a modest initial agreement aimed at encouraging all nations to formulate policy with reference to global rather than national welfare concerns where the two conflict. The legal principles most pertinent to that task would include non-discrimination, transparency, and due process requirements.

National antitrust policy with international trade

Every basic microeconomics course teaches the evils of monopoly […] For the most part, however, the discussion considers only antitrust policy in a closed economy, by which I mean an economy in which all consumers and producers are domestic citizens. […] But let us instead consider an open economy, in which goods and services may be traded internationally and producers and consumers may be of different nationalities. Does the argument against monopoly still hold? The answer is, 'it depends,' and it will turn on whose welfare 'counts' in the formulation of policy. If 'global welfare' is the proper criterion for implementing policy, then the analysis does not change at all. But if nations look to the welfare of their own citizens primarily or exclusively – the 'national welfare' criterion – their view of monopoly may change dramatically.

* *Harvard Journal of Law and Public Policy* for 'Externalities in Open Economy Antitrust and their Implications for International Competition Policy' by A. Sykes, Vol 23, Issue 1 © *Harvard Journal of Law and Public Policy*, 1999.

[...] From the national perspective, monopoly is far more harmful when the monopolist is a foreigner (as the United States discovered during the heyday of OPEC). Alternatively, suppose that the monopolist is domestic and the consumers are foreign. Then, from the national perspective, the increase in profit to the monopolist is a national gain, and the harm to consumers is of no concern.[1]

I will skirt the question of whose welfare 'ought' to count in the formulation of national policy and simply observe that it is exceptionally unlikely that the welfare of foreign citizens will be weighted equally with the welfare of domestic citizens in the domestic political process. Foreign citizens do not vote in domestic elections, they cannot be taxed, they generally do not donate money to foreign politicians, and so on. Consequently, it will certainly be the rare case in which their interests are taken into account by domestic policymakers to the same degree as the interests of domestic constituents. This claim is not mere theoretical speculation, as we see innumerable manifestations of it in practice. Indeed, examples can be found in the antitrust statutes themselves. For instance, the Webb–Pomerene Act creates an exemption from the Sherman Act for cartels that operate exclusively in export markerts.[2]

The implications of these observations are clear: not only will national antitrust policies have significant external effects in an open economy, but there is little reason to believe that national policymakers, acting on their own, will give much systematic weight to those external consequences in deciding how to behave. Accordingly, national governments acting on their own may tend to make decisions that promote the national interest – or at least the interests of their well-organized domestic constituents – at the expense of the global interest.

I have already offered the Webb–Pomerene Act's exemption for export cartels as an illustration of this problem, but it is important to recognize that it may surface in a variety of other, and typically less transparent, policy decisions. For example, a horizontal merger between two domestic companies that export extensively might reduce global welfare because of its tendency to produce higher prices, yet it may appear attractive to the government because the injured consumers are largely foreign. Similarly, if the same horizontal merger were efficient from a global perspective of economies made possible by the merger, foreign jurisdictions might nonetheless object to it because their consumers bear any rise in prices and do not realize any of the profits from cost savings in the merged company. One can develop numerous other illustrations.[3]

The potential benefits of international cooperation in the face of this problem are obvious, and indeed one can conceptualize the situation as a classic Prisoner's Dilemma. Nations acting on their own will tend to pursue the national interest at the expense of the global interest, but if they could cooperate and credibly promise not to behave in that fashion, all nations would benefit on average. Thus, we can make out a case, at least in theory, for an international agreement committing its signatories in some fashion to pursue global welfare rather than national welfare.

What legal obligations are appropriate?

The task of structuring a useful international competition policy agreement is not a trivial one. I do not imagine for an instant that a treaty of the form 'we promise to use global welfare as a touchstone for policy' would accomplish much or would be politically attractive to national officials. Rather, the task is to fashion an agreement that would promote that general objective, yet stand on much more precise and concrete obligations.

I cannot in this short piece hope to elaborate all the details and options for such an agreement,[4] but I will suggest a few particulars. A central principle should be the 'national treatment principle,' which is simply a rule of nondiscrimination. Here, it would require that nations not discriminate in their competition policy rules or enforcement actions according to the nationality of producers or consumers affected by them.

This principle has a number of immediate corollaries. For example, the Webb–Pomerene exemption for export cartels expressly discriminates in favor of cartels that burden foreign consumers only and could not survive under the national treatment principle. Likewise, a merger review policy that was more lenient towards mergers of firms that export a great deal would violate the national treatment obligation. A national treatment obligation would also require nations to grant private rights of action to foreign nationals injured by anticompetitive conduct within the jurisdiction just as it does to domestic nationals. A substantive commitment to national treatment is worthless unless deviations from that commitment can be detected. Accordingly, a useful agreement must embody certain 'transparency' requirements, such as a requirement for the publication of decisions accompanied by a statement of reasons and a requirement that decisions be based on information in a public record. Such requirements make it harder for nations to violate their obligations without somehow signaling their wrongdoing. Related 'due process' requirements, such as a requirement that all interested parties be given notice of proceedings and an opportunity to be heard, are useful to ensure that competition policy authorities and courts take account of the effects of their decisions on foreign nationals.

Finally, a dispute resolution system is required to afford some avenue for nations to enforce their rights under the agreement. One can readily imagine such a system modeled on that of the World Trade Organisation (WTO), where international bodies of experts can review national decisions for compliance with WTO obligations.

Indeed, the WTO is probably the logical umbrella entity for the agreement, in part because of a fairly well-functioning dispute resolution system that is already in place. Further, by locating the agreement within the WTO, an opportunity for side payments arises that may sway nations otherwise reluctant to sign the agreement. Some nations may be hesitant to make commitments on competition policy because they may benefit on balance from opportunities to pursue national interests at the expense of global interests. Such nations can be 'bribed' within the WTO by giving them concessions on market access issues involving trade in goods and services.

The framework outlined here, to be sure, will not resolve all issues, and some must no doubt remain unresolved for the time being. For example, there is no global consensus on the proper antitrust treatment of vertical restraints or on tight criteria for the treatment of horizontal mergers. Substantive differences in policy on these and other subjects will persist, and are, of course, permitted under an agreement that merely requires non-discrimination, transparency, and due process. Is an agreement along the lines sketched here realistic as a political matter? I do not know the answer to this question. I suggest only that significant gains from cooperation on antitrust policy are possible in principle and that simple commitments on non-discrimination, transparency, and due process could realize some of them. Formal competition policy negotiations under WTO auspices would permit the trading community to determine whether such commitments are attainable in the near term.

Notes

1   To be sure, the world may be more subtle – shareholders in the monopolist may be of many nationalities, for example, so the physical location of the monopolist's production facilities is not determinative of whose citizens earn the monopoly profit. Moreover, the monopolist may sell to consumers both domestically and abroad. Such observations, however, merely complicate matters without changing the basic point that, from the national welfare perspective, the welfare effects of monopoly may differ dramatically between the closed economy case and the open economy case.
2   See 15 U.S.C. Subsection 61–65 (1994).
3   See, e.g., Ordover and Sykes (1988). I wish to be clear that I am not claiming that national antitrust policy decisions are in fact made systematically on the basis of careful national welfare calculations. Many antitrust policies rest on no discernible welfare criterion, and indeed Janusz Ordover and I have argued that the U.S. Antitrust Guidelines for International Operations in particular cannot be understood with reference to either a global or a national welfare criterion. See ibid. Likewise, the tendency of the Antitrust Division of the U.S. Department of Justice to initiate cases against major exporters like IBM and Microsoft suggests that leniency toward national champions with the capacity to earn monopoly profits abroad is by no means systematic. Yet, there are enough examples of self-interested national policies and decisions (such as the Webb–Pomerene Act, Federal Trade Commission approval of the Boeing/McDonnell–Douglas merger, and the European Community challenge to it) to suggest that national policymakers do give more weight to domestic interests than to foreign interests, and indeed it would be surprising were it otherwise.
4   There is a large amount of literature on these issues. See, e.g., Fox (1999).

References

Fox, E.M. (1999) 'Competition Policy and the Millennium Round', *Journal of International Economic Law*, 2: 665–79.

Ordover, J.A., and Sykes, A.O. (1988) 'The Antitrust Guidelines for International Operations: An Economic Critique', Fordham Corp. L. Inst. 4–1.

Science, Technology and Innovation Policy

Science, technology and innovation are distinct from each other but interrelated and interdependent. This section explores the role that policy can play in facilitating progress in these three areas. This can be a crucial factor in generating and sustaining economic advancement.

Chapter 7, by Metcalfe, begins by exploring the similarities and differences between science and technology. Metcalfe thinks that it is misleading to think of technology as applied science. While technological progress may sometimes significantly draw upon science, it may also cause scientific advance, and science and technology are distinctive bodies of knowledge. However, in the modern age, technological and scientific developments are often closely interrelated, posing policy issues with respect to facilitating co-ordination between these two fields. This co-ordination is necessary because while most science, being of a public good nature, is financed through taxation, most of the technological effort is carried out in firms that are compensated through the market. Metcalfe contrasts the policy implications that follow from the traditional market failure arguments on technology with the arguments that draw upon the more recent work on the evolutionary theories of the firm, capability, technology and innovation.

Chapter 8, by Freeman, widens the discussion from science and technology to the broader notion of innovation. Freeman emphasises that a firm cannot innovate in isolation, and that technological innovations depend upon a host of social innovations. Many of the social factors may be strongly influenced by national characteristics. Consequently it is important to look at the national system aspects of the innovation process. Freeman illustrates his arguments by demonstrating how distinctive national systems of innovation emerged in some nations such as Germany, Japan and the former USSR.

Chapter 9, by Porter, further develops the discussion of national influences on innovation. For Porter, it is the 'diamond of national competitive advantage' that is key for determining the character and pace of innovation in an economy. The diamond is constituted by four sets of interrelated attributes of the national economy: factor conditions; demand conditions; related and supporting industries and firm strategy, structure and rivalry. Both Porter and Freeman regard the role of national factors to be more critical in determining innovation performance relative to international factors. This view may, however, be questioned. We revisit this issue in Section 4, where we consider the role that international trade and multinational firms may play in the innovation process.

In Chapter 10, Lall examines whether developing countries require policies on science, technology and innovation to a greater degree and of a different kind relative to developed nations. He shows us how the theories of neo-classical economics distort our understanding of the process of technology and capability acquisition and lead to inappropriate *laissez-faire* policy prescriptions. The more realistic evolutionary theories on capability and innovation demonstrate why firms in developing nations may need to be supported by a host of policy measures that may encompass trade and investment policies. Governments may be fallible, but markets too may be imperfect and incapable of inducing desirable scientific, technological and innovative effort and capability building.

C HAPTER 7

Science Policy and Technology Policy

J.S. METCALFE*

Introduction

In the past four decades, the relationship between science, technology and economic performance has rarely been off the agenda for public discussion and debate. [...] Over this time quite fundamental changes have occurred in the funding of science and technology and many of these changes have proved controversial with industry and academia alike but, of course, for different reasons. However, there is, I shall argue, a logical strand which runs through the evolution of policy in recent years, a strand which recognizes that if science and technology are funded as national investments the crucial issue becomes one of ensuring that those investments yield an adequate return, a return ultimately reflected in enhanced competitiveness, wealth-creating potential, and the quality of life. This thread has characterized technology policy in the USA and Europe as well as in the UK. A small country such as the UK will *never* be able to match the scale of expenditure on science and technology achieved in the USA and other larger economies. However, it can legitimately expect to ensure that institutional and other arrangements are in place to make more effective use of its investment in science and technology. Indeed, to the extent that a more effective return is obtained from science and technology, this of itself provides the most powerful of arguments for increased expenditure on research and development of all kinds. Moreover, it can include in these arrangements ways of importing knowledge generated overseas.

In a nutshell, my argument will be that this requires recognition that science and technology are distinctive but interdependent branches of knowledge, jointly required as inputs into wealth creation, and that their effective alignment requires the creation of appropriate technology support systems. The chief distinguishing characteristic of such systems is the collaborative involvement of industry (my shorthand for the major user of science and technology) and academia in the

* MCB University Press for 'Science Policy and Technology Policy in a Competitive Economy' by J.S. Metcalfe © *International Journal of Social Economics*, Vol 24, No 7/8/9.

execution of technology development programmes so that all the relevant and vastly different advances in understanding required to develop innovation are tackled simultaneously: for the crucial point about the modern innovation process is its multidisciplinarity and multiple institutional sources of relevant knowledge. No firm can expect to innovate in isolation and the question of how it is embedded within the wider matrix of knowledge-generating institutions becomes an issue of the first importance for technology policy. One natural consequence of all this for the science base, is, as Weinberg (1967) put it, a matching of external criteria with the traditional internal criteria for allocating funds to scientific development. The principal aim of technology and science policy is thus to ensure the creation of effective technology support systems which bridge between industry and the science base. It must recognize that firms, universities and public research bodies are distinctively different kinds of institution each adapted to a specific purpose. It would be as foolhardy to make academic institutions commercial as it would be to make private firms non-commercial. The division of labour between them is not accidental and the central problem of policy is how to connect these different institutions together in a more productive fashion. In short, science and technology policy should be concerned with proper process and not directly with specific innovation events which are inherently unpredictable. It is perhaps aptly expressed as policy for a non-linear world.

Precautionary remarks

Technology involves much more than science and innovation involves much more than technology: this is a recurrent background theme of this paper in which I want to draw out the implications for recent developments in policy. That technology policy is important should not be in doubt given the connection between technological advance, wealth creation and the quality of life. Everybody will accept that new technology is central to the innovation process. However, before we plunge into this theme three cautionary observations are in order. Particularly important is the fact that not all significant innovations involve the application of technology in the generally understood interpretation of the word. Many important innovations are primarily organizational and one can think here of just-in-time methods of stock control or the retailing revolution and the creation of supermarket chains. Certainly these innovations influenced important processes of transformation, the temporal and spatial availability of goods, but neither of them is primarily technological, even if they do draw extensively on information technology for their realization. Second, technology of itself is of no significance unless it is translated into innovations which are subsequently diffused into the economy, with the social and economic consequences being dependent on the degree of diffusion. Now innovation and diffusion are primarily economic and social processes which involve many other actors and behaviours besides those directly involved in the creation of technology itself.

Behind innovation is not only technology but marketing knowledge and production capability, let alone an entrepreneurial perception of the unification of these important considerations. Effective innovation always requires responses from users as well as suppliers and the former may have to be as creative as the latter. Consequently, technology policy, and science policy for that matter, are best presented as aspects of a broader innovation policy, not as policies standing free from other considerations. As we shall see, this viewpoint is of considerable relevance when interpreting the results of the recent UK technology foresight programme, to which I will turn subsequently. Thus in focusing this paper on technology policy, I must inevitably tread on science policy issues and sadly ignore many other concerns of innovation policy.[1] Third, let us not forget that these are immensely complex matters to do with the exercise of creativity by individuals and teams in highly decentralized market economies. There are no easy answers and the questions are not always obvious either.

With these cautionary remarks in mind I turn to the main themes. I wish to explore four issues to help us define better the nature and contribution of science and technology policy. These are, in order of treatment:

- the distinctive differences between science and technology as bodies of knowledge;

- the economic arguments for different kinds of technology policy;

- the importance of institutional coupling between firms and universities in the generation of scientific and technological knowledge; and

- the UK foresight in science exercise as an example of a technology policy, the fundamental purpose of which is to create a set of appropriate technology support systems.

The distinctiveness of technology

It is not fanciful to begin by observing that public debate rarely makes adequate distinctions between science and technology or of the activities which lead to their development. Let us begin then by noting two possible justifications for the public support of science. The first sees scientific output as a cultural consumer good which enlightens and entertains the public at large. This is, of course, a perfectly valid viewpoint: the discovery of a new star or a hitherto unknown species of plant are, in these terms, no less meritworthy than the performance of a new symphony. They enrich and enliven the understanding of our universe. Sadly, but understandably, this is not a style of argument which is usually appealed to when justifying public support of science. Instead, a second view is taken, promoted and accepted by government and the science establishment, that science is an investment which generates a more than compensatory return in terms of wealth creation or improved living standards via medical advances or better control of the environment. This modern, science-based investment argument was a theme first made public by the Vannevar Bush report *Science — The Endless Frontier* published in 1945 (although the 'golden egg' view of science goes back at least to Francis Bacon in 1635) in which the strong claim was made that

> New products, new industries and more jobs require continuous additions to knowledge of the *laws of nature* ... essential new knowledge can be obtained *only* through basic scientific research. (emphasis added)

As Wise (1985) has suggested, this is the original statement of the modern, linear or production line model of the innovation process.[2] Also in the UK as late as 1968, the Central Advisory Council for Science and Technology was able to claim that basic science is the origin of 'all new knowledge without which opportunities for further technical progress *must rapidly become* exhausted' (emphasis added). This, by now discredited, view was nonetheless extremely influential for about two decades, as were its twin corollaries that technology stood below science in a hierarchy of importance, that technology was merely applied science, and that the flow of new scientific knowledge would increase in proportion to the funds allocated to basic research (Keller, 1984; Wise, 1985). I need not detail the wealth of empirical material on the inadequacy of this view (Langrish et al., 1972; Layton, 1974) or the acceptance of more interactive models of the innovation process. Instead let me outline its clear conceptual deficiencies.

The first and crucial point is that at best it covers only a small fraction of the activities involved in the innovation process. The return in terms of innovation and wealth creation depends on a wide range of other non-scientific and technological activities and expenditures of a quite different kind. Unless these activities are carried out effectively to transfer science into exploitation the economic return to extra scientific expenditure is likely to reduce very rapidly. Indeed, as Charles Carter and Bruce Williams (1964) once suggested, if all scientific research ceased there would still be handsome returns from better exploitation of the existing stock of knowledge at least in the short and medium term. Rather more sharply the inverse correlation between GNP growth rates and Nobel Laureates per head of population makes the same point (Rosenberg, 1995). The point is simply that the economic returns from science will depend on the scale and effectiveness of two classes of complementary expenditures: the one to develop the technologies behind new products and processes and the other to diffuse those technologies in the relevant applications.

This brings us to the second flaw in the production line model concerning the relevant status of science and technology. A wealth of recent research has established quite clearly that science and technology are largely independent but mutually beneficial bodies of knowledge, created by different processes of accumulation within distinctly different communities located in different institutional contexts (Falkner, 1994; Keller, 1984; Layton, 1987; Vincenti, 1990). Both solve problems, are creative, imaginative, but the problems are quite distinctly different and the communities respond to different incentive mechanisms.[3] In broad terms science is naturally academic; its legitimate output is additions to the existing stock of knowledge for their own sake. Science is open; the outputs are widely diffused in an international publication culture and the primary incentives are in terms of priority in publication. Pure physics is the model many would recognize as exemplifying these attributes. Conversely, technology is naturally practical; its legitimate outputs are artefacts and the means by which they are designed, constructed and operated and its intrinsic worth is to be judged not by the truthfulness of the knowledge but by its practical utility. Does it work more beneficially than current practice, that is the only deciding question for technology. As science is open so technology is closed with quite different publication practices and a natural concern for secrecy or patent protection when private property rights are involved. Moreover, while it is essential to the replicability of scientific results that they be codifiable, much of technological practice rests in a tacit realm only easily communicated through observation and trial, not publication.

An immediate consequence of this is to deny that technology is merely science applied. Rather technology is a distinctive body of knowledge with its own operating principles and norms for design activity. While scientific knowledge constrains what technologists design, it does so at a level which is often very general. Concepts such as voltage, current and resistance and the relationships between them are necessarily obeyed in any electrical design, but this does not mean that only one design for an electrical system is possible (Vincenti, 1995). In many cases of important everyday technologies the current state of scientific understanding simply lacks the precision to determine technological development. In short, while modern technology may apply science, it is not applied science. Indeed the term 'applied science' (frequently a pejorative term) is something of a misnomer for what is involved is not application *per se* but the elucidation of the natural law basis underpinning man-made phenomena. Better still is the term 'transfer sciences' (OECD, 1992) to indicate a bridging position between pure science and technology proper. Pharmacology, agronomy, computer science and materials science are clear examples of activity with this intermediate position: knowledge is being pursued for its own sake but that knowledge is linked closely to technological practices. Indeed de Solla Price (1980) has argued that at best a third of scientific expenditure is what is normally understood as pure or basic research. If technology is distinctively different from science it is nonetheless the case that in adding to the stock of product knowledge, technologists draw on the accumulated stock of scientific understanding in a number of ways. They use methods of analysis, concepts and theoretical relationships about natural phenomena, instrumentation developed in the laboratory enables precise measurement and, perhaps most significant of all, well-trained scientific minds are in a position to make excellent contributions to technological advance.

There is another way of looking at the science–technology relationship which is illuminating. It is not difficult to see that if the choice of technological problems were decided randomly then there would not be much technological progress. Rather technological advance is cumulative; within a set of given design principles it proceeds along paths which, at least *ex post*, seem to involve their own inner logic. Technical advance involves guided variation in which a knowledge of where to search in the set of possible options is absolutely crucial to rapid advance. Here lies a key contribution of science: providing knowledge of where to look, and crucially where not to look, in advancing technology (Pavitt, 1991; Vincenti, 1995). Better scientific understanding is thus a contributor to more effective technological search (Gibbons and Johnson, 1974; Nelson, 1982) and so reduces the cost of technological advance.

But as has been hinted at above, the relationship runs two ways. Technologists have designed and operated artefacts well in advance of any scientific understanding and their labours have directly stimulated the search for an understanding of the natural laws which underpin the operation of the artefacts. The steam engine and the development of thermodynamics are the most oft-cited cases but there are many other industry examples (Rosenberg, 1990). It is thus not helpful to claim that science leads and technology follows, or vice versa. They are distinctive mutually supporting bodies of knowledge created for different purposes. That they illuminate one another is scarcely surprising, and the interesting question is how this process of mutual enlightenment works and is institutionalized along the spectrum from the most pure to the most applied. There is, however, one crucial unique aspect which follows from the practical directedness of technological knowledge, and this involves the close interaction between economic and social stimuli. What technologists design and construct has to pass the test of economic viability and social acceptability. Design is ultimately normative: what is the best, read most profitable, combination of materials is turned into components and linked into systems of varying scales of grandeur which reduce costs to a minimum or raise product value to a maximum. Such an approach, dependent on the specific economic and social context, has no meaning when one is seeking for the unique truth about a natural phenomenon. Equally important is the fact that many technological advances arising within a given set of design principles flow from experience gained in using and producing specific artefacts. Learning phenomena are rightly seen as central to technical advance in terms of a sequence of incremental improvements, the occurrence of which rarely depends on a formal R&D programme (Dosi, 1988; Malerba, 1992). This dependence of technological advance on practical experience gained in the diffusion and integration of artefacts into the economy is a quite distinctive factor of technological change which science does not share. Markets and technologies co-evolve and the way in which technology develops is strongly shaped by the rate and direction of market application. This is, of course, one of the key implications of the product/technology life-cycle literature (Utterback, 1995) and the modern analysis of diffusion.

The economics of technology policy

Central to an understanding of science and technology policy is the need to recognize that technology can be defined in a number of complementary ways – as knowledge, as skills and as artefacts – and that the focus of policy can involve any combination of these elements, for example as a programme of engineering research, or a programme of training, or a programme to construct a specific device. In each case the traditional rationale for policy intervention is market failure: relative to the (Pareto) efficient yardstick of a perfectly competitive economy the actual performance of the economy will be suboptimal and potentially improvable through policy intervention. The sources of market failure are well known (Australian Industry Commission, 1995; Branscomb, 1993; Metcalfe, 1995a) and may be outlined briefly as follows. Consider first the arguments about market inefficiency in the production and dissemination of new knowledge.

Here a major source of difficulty lies in the public good aspect of technological knowledge; it is used, not consumed, and once discovered is in principle useable by any individual on any number of occasions. In the terminology of economics there is non-rivalry and non-excludability. Hence, runs the argument, the incentives for any one individual to reveal how much they value an item of knowledge are deficient. Notice, however, that the public good dimension does not imply that the communication of knowledge is costless: in many cases it is communication between 'like minds', only open to those who have acquired comparable abilities to understand the significance of new technological information. Knowledge is a public good in the sense of non-rivalry in use but it is not necessarily a free good, and this is particularly true of complex technological knowledge. Hence the oft-remarked point that to benefit from the information generated by others one must make one's own substantial investment in technological capability. Or as it has been expressed, if one is to be an effective member of a network of information exchange or a collaborative programme one can only do so by having items of one's own information to contribute. A crucial issue, then, is the non-codifiable nature of some important aspects of technology, which makes it difficult to calculate and to transfer; it can only be shared between individuals or firms which have similar levels of understanding.

Divergences between private and social cost and benefit add a second source of difficulty. Once a technology has been created, the public good argument suggests that the knowledge should be made widely available at no more than the marginal cost of dissemination to maximize the social benefits from exploitation. However, to do so would undermine the ability of the creators of that technology to cover their costs of creation. More generally, spillovers of knowledge, as such externalities are termed, mean that many beneficiaries of that knowledge do not contribute to its cost of production and many exploit it to the disadvantage of the creator of that knowledge. Hence the argument for patent rights in which a temporary monopoly is permitted to enable the creators of technology to at least partially protect this property. In the case of breakthroughs of wide significance, generic knowledge, this divergence between private and social consequences is of particular importance: no individual firm, for example, is likely to have the capability to exploit such a breakthrough across all its potential applications.

The third source of market inefficiency in technology creation lies in uncertainty proper and the difficulties of estimating the technical or commercial returns to an innovation. Certainly the idea that innovation-related risks can be accurately computed and used in actuarial calculations of expected costs and benefits is fanciful in the extreme. Innovations are unique events for which the probability calculus is an inappropriate method of analysis. Much decision making about technology creation is at root an act of faith, with necessarily unpredictable time delays between knowledge creation and application. One immediate consequence of this is asymmetric information between firms and potential suppliers of capital and between the R&D managers and the firm's board of directors. Potential lenders cannot judge accurately the credibility of claims made by a firm nor can boards of directors always evaluate accurately the claims of technical personnel. [...] Firms then find it difficult to get others to accept the risks of technology development: in short it is difficult to insure technology projects. Again this puts large firms at an advantage in that they can pool the risks from a portfolio of projects, and it helps us understand the pressures towards more collaborative work in R&D and towards mergers and acquisitions between technology-based companies.

Taken together, the consequence of these various market failures is the absence of markets to promote the efficient creation and exchange of technological knowledge. This is particularly transparent when we consider more radical innovations where not only a new technology but a new market has to be created to exploit the innovation. In normal competitive markets the object of trade is sufficiently homogeneous to make the identity of buyers and sellers irrelevant to the outcome of the transaction. Not so with technological knowledge, where the identities of the buyer and seller greatly influence the valuation process. Bilateral exchanges are the norm, exchanges which are frequently facilitated by the presence of the parties in an existing network of relationships. The Arrow paradox (1962) adds to the problem when one recognizes that if full information of a discovery must be communicated prior to the transaction this obviates the subsequent need to purchase that information: sellers of technology have an incentive not to reveal all they know to purchasers. The consequence of all this is that transactions are mediated by non-market methods, primarily through networks and other forms of arrangement between organizations. [...]

I have spent some time outlining the arguments for market failure because of their considerable influence on policy debate among economists interested in technology and innovation. These ideas underpin a belief that market mechanisms will not allocate the right amount of support to innovative activity not least because of the peculiarities of knowledge as an economic commodity. In short there is a divergence between private incentives and social incentives which governments in principle can correct.

Leaving aside the well-recognized imperfections to which governments can be subject when they intervene, it is also clear that market failure as a technology policy framework leaves much to be desired (Metcalfe, 1995b).

The logical underpinning it provides tells us nothing about the design of policy instruments nor their appropriate method of implementation nor the areas which are most appropriately in need of support in their attempts to innovate. Is the focus to be on new knowledge, new skills or new artefacts? Is it to be concerned with design, with construction or with operation? Is it to focus on the creation of innovation or on the diffusion of innovation? The answers to these questions generate very different policy initiatives, in part because the incidence of market failure varies considerably across the wide spectrum of science and technology.

A second difficulty is the fact that the vision of a (Pareto) efficient [perfectly competitive] economy is a distorting mirror in which to reflect the operation of an economy in which innovation is at the heart of the competitive process. This is one reason why the policy implications for innovation are very sensitive to the way in which market competition is modelled. Private firms can be argued to do too much innovation or too little, to do it too quickly or too slowly or to be too risk-averse or not risk-averse enough in the breadth of their innovation activities. More fundamentally, to define degrees of competition in terms of equilibrium market structures fails to grasp the fact that competition is a process of change and that innovation is the major countervailing factor in offsetting the natural competitive tendency for markets to concentrate. Competition depends on a will to compete, which need bear no close relation to any traditional concept of market structure. It is essential to recognize that competition requires active not passive behaviour and that a framework based on price competition between identical firms can scarcely come to grips with competition which is based on the ability to innovate differently. The imperfections identified in the market failure approach therefore can be viewed in a different perspective, as integral and necessary aspects of the production and dissemination of knowledge in a market economy. In this perspective it is surely perverse to call them imperfections. This is, of course, not a new point: for those who have studied Schumpeter they are the natural features of an economic process driven by creative destruction.

It is worth, therefore, coming at the matter from a different direction, one in fact which is being actively developed by scholars working on evolutionary themes of technological and institutional change.

An evolutionary perspective

While recognizing the significance of the public good dimension of knowledge, the imperfections of intellectual property rights, indivisibilities and uncertainty, the thrust of the above section is that their significance is to be judged not by a world of equilibrium competition but by a world of change in which competition is a process. This is the view taken in the evolutionary approach to economic change, with its strong connections with a process view of competition.

In this perspective, competition depends on the possibility of firms behaving differently, and no source of difference is more significant in the longer term than the articulation of different product and process combinations to serve the needs of the consumer differentially. Another way of putting this is to say that without assymetries of knowledge the competitive process has nothing with which to work. Thus competition is at root a process of diffusing diverse discoveries. Competition depends on variety in behaviour, and those firms with superior product–process combinations are able over time to win customers from rivals and increase their share of the market. In this process, technological and organizational innovation is at the heart of the matter. Innovation drives competition and competition drives innovation as those who have fallen behind seek to protect and improve their market position. Thus the social benefits of competition are transmitted into increasingly more efficient allocations of resources as superior combinations supply a greater proportion of the market and as inferior combinations are continually improved (Downie, 1958; Metcalfe, 1995c; Nelson and Winter, 1984). Hence in a market situation in which all firms are behaving identically, whatever they are doing they are not competing for there is no basis for rivalry. Now because the possibility of effective competition is predicted on diversity in behaviour one major consequence of this process is to erode over time the economic significance of the differences in behaviour. Two eroding mechanisms are of predominant importance: imitation of the behaviour of other firms; and competition proper as firms with superior products and processes gain market share at the expense of less efficient rivals. Left to themselves such processes destroy economic diversity and concentrate economic behaviour on a narrow range of alternatives. Thus they destroy the diversity and the choice between alternatives on which the long-term maintenance of competition depends. Indeed the major long-run cost of monopoly is the elimination of plurality in the innovation process. If competition is to be preserved, mechanisms must be in place to re-create diversity, and it is the innovation mechanism primarily on which this burden falls and, by various stages of reason, on technology policy in particular.

In truly competitive situations all positions are open to challenge, and it is this link between innovation and competition which has proved to be the mainspring of economic growth. Hence technology policy becomes an essential component of competition policy, the objective being to maintain open economic conditions. Within this perspective a programme of technology support which privileges a small number of established and often large firms is clearly open to question. General support is more appropriate than specific support: policy makers do not have to beg the question of which firms are more likely to succeed in making significant technical developments and they can concentrate on questions of which technological opportunities are most promising.

In many aspects this captures the drift of policy in the UK since the 1970s. Specific innovation grants and technology development projects have been phased out by a shift from the support of close-to-market artefacts to the support of far-from-market knowledge generation carried out in collaborative contexts. In an unpredictable, rapidly changing world it is essential to keep options open and ensure a broad understanding of the whole spectrum of opportunities to innovate.

Innovation opportunities and firm capabilities

If technology policy is intended to change the innovation behaviour of firms it must take into account the perceived relationships firms seek to exploit relating their expenditure on technology creation and the subsequent outputs, new or improved products and production processes. We may term these relationships the 'innovation opportunities frontier' of the firm, recognizing that this concept must be used cautiously, particularly given the difficulties in deciding how to measure the inputs and outputs in the innovation process. Nonetheless, without some such relationship there really is nothing useful to say on the technology policy front. Our current state of understanding about these frontiers may be summarized as follows.

Innovation opportunities vary greatly between technologies, and within technologies there are considerable differences in the innovation opportunity frontiers identified by individual firms. Within a given area opportunities grow in a cumulative fashion although there is very considerable uncertainty concerning the relationship between inputs and outputs. The quality of the individual minds involved is obviously crucial, as is the way in which research and development teams are organized. Uncertainty also implies the failure of many attempts to develop technology. It is a trial-and-error process, governed by methods of blind variation; that is, the outcomes to any given programme are not knowable, they are necessarily conjectures. Given the current state of knowledge the allocation of additional resources to the development of technology is subject to diminishing returns in the 'short run' but the discoveries from that development process become part of the next period's knowledge base so that there can be phases of increasing returns in the development of a technology. This is what is involved in the idea of cumulative technological development and, for example, in Machlup's (1962) concept of agenda-increasing breakthroughs in the knowledge base of a technology. This balance of short-run and long-run patterns of returns defines a trajectory of advance for any given technology, a trajectory defined by accumulating knowledge and a sequence of related innovations. The trajectory is ultimately determined by the sets of design principles which define the technological opportunity, the way in which their principles interact and the systemic properties of the resulting artefacts. The latter define interface problems between components and subsystems and determine a pattern of constraints or imbalances which shape development. Consequently, paths of technological development are not random, they represent patterns of guided variation: a simple reflection of the fact that to make progress one must limit progress. Innovation opportunities are also characterized by plurality in the kinds of knowledge which contribute to technological, cross-disciplinarity, and plurality in the range of institutions in which relevant knowledge is generated. The firm may be the final determinant of innovation opportunities but it is a firm embedded in a wider network of knowledge-generating and -disseminating institutions. It is this perspective which is central to the idea of technology support systems and more generally to the idea of national systems of innovation. Finally there are also wide differences between firms in their ability to perceive the relevant innovation opportunities and in their ability to manage the process of technology creation, and it is these differences between firms which pose difficult problems for policy.

The consequence of all this is the great diversity in the patterns and timing of innovation across technologies and firms. Medicine is different from aeronautical engineering, agronomy is different from computing, large firms innovate in ways quite different from small firms, and if technology policy is to be effective it must be sensitive to these differences.

A policy dichotomy

In the light of our understanding of innovation opportunities we can divide technology policies into two clear categories (Metcalfe, 1995a, 1995b). One is primarily concerned with resources and incentives, taking the technological possibilities and capabilities of firms as given. In short, there are policies intended to encourage firms to locate at a different place in their given opportunities by changing the scale and focus of their effort. These policies work by changing net marginal returns to developing technology. Tax allowances for R&D, specific innovative subsidies, public purchasing of innovative products, the terms and duration of patent protection, and regulatory policies on such factors as the health and safety of medicines are the most familiar examples of this kind of policy, which are ultimately intended to correct any discrepancy between private and public incentives to innovate.

The second category of policy is quite different, for its purpose is to change and enhance the innovation possibilities that firms face by improving their access to knowledge and by improving managerial capabilities. The central feature of these policies is their relation to the support system for a particular technology, that set of institutions and relationships which support firms in their technology development activities. These are policies which have been implemented with increasing frequency in the past 15 years and they are all concerned to improve the connectivity between firms and their appropriate technology support systems. In their detailed investigation of the Swedish factory automation industry, Carlsson and colleagues distinguish these aspects of a technology support system: academic infrastructure, bridging institutions and user–supplier linkages (Carlsson, 1995). Programmes of collaboration in R&D are typical examples, between firms alone or between firms and the academic community, in which the complementarity between different knowledge bases is exploited to the mutual benefit of the participants. In many cases their collaborations are a reflection of the links between a firms and its customers and suppliers, which can be a fruitful way of enhancing innovation opportunities (Carlsson, 1995). A second way of treating collaboration has been to create new bridging institutions at the interface between industry and the science base to ensure the effective transfer of knowledge and to shape research agendas.

Technology foresight

There is no more appropriate indication of the switch in policy from matters of resources and incentives to matters of opportunities and capabilities than the Technology Foresight Programme initiated by the UK Government. Foresight activities have been defined as

> a systematic means of assessing those scientific and technological developments which could have a strong impact on industrial competitiveness, wealth creation and the quality of life. (Georghiou, 1995)

And they appear to have been applied on a most consistent, long-term basis within the Japanese science and technology system (Freeman, 1987). The process involved in conducting a large-scale foresight programme is precisely a matter of bridging and connectivity within a nation's science and technology base. Before commenting on recent UK experience it is worth noting that the case for a UK foresight programme was extensively discussed in an ACARD report, *Exploitable Areas of Science*, published in May 1986. The report made a strong connection between the investment view of science and what the report termed 'exploitable areas of science': an area of science

> in which the body of scientific understanding supports a generic (or enabling) area of *technology knowledge*: a body of knowledge out of which many specific products and processes may emerge in the future. (ACARD, 1986, para. 2.3.1, emphasis added)

A policy of identifying and supporting such areas of knowledge was carefully distinguished from a policy of picking commercial winners, potentially 'winning artefacts'; rather the intention was to support the creation of opportunities and capabilities via a reservoir of knowledge from which as yet undeveloped products and processes will emerge. Naturally this is a long-term process and the report worked explicitly with a ten- to twenty-year time horizon. Recognizing that the identification of such areas involves difficult matters of judgement, it was argued that a framework was needed to draw together the various knowledge inputs, establish communication between science and industry and mobilize resources according to the development of strategic objectives. Thus effective interaction between the scientific community and industry was considered of vital importance if the idea of science as investment was to be more than rhetorical. Given the appropriate framework, the principal elements in identifying exploitable science could be summarized at three levels:

- identifying the link between areas of technology and the underpinning scientific knowledge base;

- identifying the product classes which would be significantly affected by technological developments over a twenty-year horizon; and

- identifying the relevant markets and the related pressures for change in so far as they influence commercial incentives.

Of course, the provisional, tentative nature of any such analysis was well understood and from this followed the need to update the analysis continually, recognizing that

> A policy for exploitable science is a process, in which decisions are made in the light of the best available information and reviewed as and when new information becomes available. (ACARD, 1986, para. 2.10.3)

From this followed the principal recommendation of the ACARD group, namely that

> a process should be established for identifying exploitable areas of science, which has some degree of certainty of continuity, for the long-term economic health of the country. (p. 12)

Almost a decade after the ACARD group began its work (October 1993) their principles and objectives were included in the UK's own Technology Foresight Programme. This was announced in the 1993 White Paper 'Realizing our Potential' and produced its first outputs in 1995: the result of the bringing together of scientists, engineers, industry and government in a major exercise to identify opportunities in markets and technology likely to emerge in the next ten to twenty years, and to identify the actions needed to exploit them. In the process it did not attempt to pick winners but, as ACARD had suggested, to involve the main parties in the development of shared visions of the way in which the future may unfold. Behind all this lay the view that the competitive future of the UK is with high value-added sectors of economic activity. The principal issues involved the identification of market, social and economic trends, the identification of the matching knowledge bases in science, engineering and technology and the implications for public funding of research, skill formation and education.

The process involved the creation of fifteen sectoral panels of 'experts' which consulted on a wide basis with the relevant communities in industry, academia and government through regional workshops, a major delphi survey and numerous other activities. Each panel has produced a report indicating the main forces for change and the policy issues which flow from the analysis as well as identifying the likely constraints on change. It is without question the most extensive consultation of industrial and scientific opinion which has ever occurred in the UK. It is a fact, alluded to above, that the development of modern technology is so heterogeneous with respect to its discipline base and institutional context that it makes the sounding of opinion in the broadest possible fashion so important.

It is too early yet to come to clear conclusions concerning implementation: indeed it is central to the exercise that the consequences may not be fully realized until a quarter century from now: it really is about the long-term health of the economy, recognizing that the lead time for technology development can be substantial.

It may be that one outcome of Foresight will be a reallocation of resources within publicly funded science and technology in the UK. Be that as it may, the lasting benefit of the exercise is in the process and what the process does to the formation of commercial and academic strategies to promote innovation; to the creation of lasting networks between industry, government and the science and technology community; and to the emergence of coherent visions within their communities on complementary developments in science and technology. By 'coherent vision' it is definitely not meant a consensus view about specific technologies or routes to innovation but rather an understanding of the breadth of opportunities open to a particular sector. Government would be foolish to predict which of the options might succeed; this is very much a matter for the market process. If all these developments ever come to pass not only will the key priorities become clearer but the case for enhanced public and private funding of knowledge creation will be difficult to resist. In short, enhanced opportunities and capabilities provide their own incentives and make their own case for additional resources.

In summary, the Foresight Programme reflects an increasing concern with matters of co-ordination, creating and supporting the technology support systems of particular groups of firms, those formal and informal institutions which interact in a specific technological area for the purpose of generating, diffusing and utilizing technology (Carlsson, 1995; Carlsson and Stankiewicz, 1991). To create effective networks the policy maker must know the relevant communities of scientists and practitioners, understand the rival design configurations and ensure that incentives between the various parties are aligned appropriately. The sequence of innovations which emerge and the firms which are successful are the outcomes of the process and are not a specific concern of the policy maker. Winners emerge, they are not pre-chosen. All this is entirely consistent with the evolutionary perspective. Government can predict neither which are the likely innovations nor which are the promising markets. Rather its proper role is to build an infrastructure in support of firms and let the innovations follow from the market process.

Conclusion

In this chapter I have reviewed recent developments in technology policy and attempted to view them through the lens of evolutionary economics. Here the fundamental insight is the experimental nature of a market economy. As Schumpeter aptly observed, capitalism works by means of creative destruction, a process which is now played out on a global scale. Patterns of international competition are ever-changing and an advanced country must be ever aware of new opportunities if its standard of living is to be sustained. Central to this must be the rate of innovative, new technology-based experimentation, and I have suggested that a consistent thread to policy has emerged in the past twenty years of which the Foresight Programme in the UK is a leading example. The central focus of this change has been the emphasis on enhancing the innovation opportunities and innovative capabilities of firms. The ultimate test of this shift will be the technological creativeness of UK industry over the next two to three decades. From a political point of view this will be a lot to ask. Experimental economies have many failures as well as successes; blind variation means that a great deal of effort comes to nought and that patience is the sure companion to long-term success.

Notes

1   Freeman (1995) provides an admirable summary of the modern state of academic thinking on innovation.
2   Branscomb (1993) also refers to this as the pipeline model of the science–technology relationship.
3   Falkner (1994) provides a perceptive and thorough review of the more important aspects of the science–technology relationship, and the links with innovative activity.

References

ACARD (1986), *Exploitable Areas of Science*, HMSO, London.

Arrow, K. (1962), 'Economic welfare and the allocation of resources to invention', in R. Nelson (ed.), *The Rate and Direction of Inventive Activity: Economic and Social Factors*, Princeton University Press for the National Bureau of Economic Research, Princeton.

Australian Industry Commission (1995), *Research and Development*, Australian Government Publishing Service, Canberra.

Branscomb, L.M. (1993), *Empowering Technology*, MIT Press, Boston.

Carlsson, B. (ed.) (1995), *Technological Systems and Economic Performance: The Case of Factory Automation*, Kluwer-Academic, Dordrecht.

Carlsson, B., and Stankiewicz, R. (1991), 'On the nature, function and composition of technological systems', *Journal of Evolutionary Economics*, Vol. 1, pp. 93–118.

Carter, C., and Williams, B. (1964), 'Government science policy and the growth of the British economy', *Manchester School*, Vol. 32, pp. 117–214.

de Solla, J. Price (1980), 'A theoretical basis for input:output assessment of R&D policies', in D. Sahal (ed.), *Research, Development and Technological Innovation*, Lexington Books, Lexington, MA.

Dosi, G. (1988), 'Sources, procedures and microeconomic effects of innovation', *Journal of Economic Literature*, Vol. 36, pp. 1126–71.

Downie, J. (1958), *The Competitive Process*, Duckworth, London.

Falkner, W. (1994), 'Conceptualizing knowledge used in innovation: a second look at the science–technology distinction and industrial innovation', *Science, Technology and Human Values*, Vol. 19, pp. 425–58.

Freeman, C. (1987), *Technology Policy and Economic Performance*, Pinter, London.

Freeman, C. (1995), 'The economics of technical change', *Cambridge Journal of Economics*, Vol. 18, pp. 463–514.

Georghiou, L. (1995), 'The United Kingdom technology foresight programme', mimeo, PREST, University of Manchester.

Gibbons, M., and Johnson, R. (1974), 'The role of science in technological innovation', *Research Policy*, Vol. 3, No. 3, pp. 220–42.

Keller, A. (1984), 'Has science created technology?', *Minerva,* Vol. 22, pp.161–82.

Langrish, J., Jevons, F., Evans, W., and Gibbons, M. (1972), *Wealth from Knowledge*, Macmillan, London.

Layton, E.T. (1974), 'Conditions of technological development', in T. Spiegel-Rosing and D. de Solla Price (eds), *Science, Technology and Society*, Sage, London.

Layton, E.T. (1987), 'Through the looking glass, or news from lake mirror image', *Technology and Culture*, Vol. 15, pp. 594–601.

Machlup, F. (1962), 'The supply of inventors and innovations', in R. Nelson (ed.), *The Rate and Direction of Inventive Activity: Economic and Social Factors*, Princeton University for the National Bureau of Economic Research, Princeton.

Malerba, F. (1992), 'Learning by firms and incremental change', *Economic Journal*, Vol. 102, pp. 845–59.

Metcalfe, J.S. (1995a), 'The economic foundations of technological policy: equilibrium and evolutionary perspectives', in P. Stoneman (ed.), *Handbook of the Economics of Innovation and Technological Change*, Blackwell, Oxford.

Metcalfe, J.S. (1995b), 'Technology systems and technology policy in an evolutionary framework', *Cambridge Journal of Economics*, Vol. 19, pp. 25–46.

Metcalfe, J.S. (1995c), 'The design of order: notes on evolutionary principles and the dynamics of innovation', *Revue Economique*, Vol. 46, No. 6, pp. 1561–83.

Nelson, R. (1982), 'The role of knowledge in R&D efficiency', *Quarterly Journal of Economics*, Vol. 97, pp. 453–70.

Nelson, R., and Winter, S. (1984), *An Evolutionary Theory of Economic Change*, Belknap, Cambridge, MA.

OECD (1992), *Technology and the Economy*, Paris.

Pavitt, K. (1991), 'What makes basic research economically useful', *Research Policy*, Vol. 20, pp. 109–19.

Rosenberg, N. (1990), 'Why do firms do basic research (with their own money)?', *Research Policy*, Vol. 19, pp. 165–74.

Rosenberg, N. (1995), 'Science–technology–economy interactions', in O. Grandstand (ed.), *Economics of Technology*, North Holland, Amsterdam.

Utterback, J.M. (1995), *Mastering the Dynamics of Innovation: How Companies Can Seize Opportunities in the Face of Technological Change*, Harvard University Press, Cambridge, MA.

Vincenti, W.G. (1990), *What Engineers Know and How They Know It,* Johns Hopkins University Press, Baltimore, MD.

Vincenti, W.G. (1995), 'The technical shaping of technology: real world constraints and technical logic in Edison's electrical lighting system', *Social Studies of Science*, Vol. 25, pp. 553–74.

Weinberg, A. (1967), *Reflections on Big Science*, Pergamon, London.

Wise, G. (1985), 'Science and technology', *Osiris*, Vol. 1, pp. 229–48.

National Systems of Innovation

CHRIS FREEMAN*

1. Introduction: The national system of Friedrich List

According to this author's recollections, the first person to use the expression 'National System of Innovation' was Bengt-Åke Lundvall, and he is also the editor of a highly original and thought-provoking book (1992) on this subject. However, as he and his colleagues would be the first to agree (and as Lundvall himself points out), the idea actually goes back at least to Friedrich List's conception of 'The National System of Political Economy' (1841), which might just as well have been called 'The National System of Innovation'.

The main concern of List was with the problem of Germany overtaking England, and, for underdeveloped countries (as Germany then was in relation to England), he advocated not only protection of infant industries but also a broad range of policies designed to accelerate, or to make possible, industrialisation and economic growth. Most of these policies were concerned with learning about new technology and applying it. [...] List clearly anticipated many contemporary theories.

After reviewing the changing ideas of economists about development in the years since the Second World War, the World Bank (1991) concludes that it is intangible investment in knowledge accumulation which is decisive rather than physical capital investment, as was at one time believed (pp. 33–35). The Report cites the 'New Growth Theory' (Grossman and Helpman, 1991; Romer, 1986) in support of this view but the so-called 'New Growth Theory has in fact only belatedly incorporated into neoclassical models the realistic assumptions which had become commonplace among economic historians and neo-Schumpeterian economists. Indeed, it could just as well have cited Friedrich List (1841), who, in criticising a passage from Adam Smith, said:

* Oxford University Press for C. Freeman, 'The National System of Innovation in Historical Perspective', *Cambridge Journal of Economics*, 1995, Vol 19, No 1.

> in opposition to this reasoning, Adam Smith has merely taken the word *capital* in that sense in which it is necessarily taken by rentiers or merchants in their book-keeping and their balance sheets. ... He has forgotten that he himself includes (in his definition of capital) the intellectual and bodily abilities of the producers under this term. He wrongly maintains that the revenues of the nation are dependent only on the sum of its material capital. (p. 183)

And further:

> The present state of the nations is the result of the accumulation of all discoveries, inventions, improvements, perfections and exertions of all generations which have lived before us: they form the intellectual[1] capital of the present human race, and every separate nation is productive only in the proportion in which it has known how to appropriate those attainments of former generations and to increase them by its own acquirements. (p. 113)

List's clear recognition of the interdependence of tangible and intangible investment has a decidedly modern ring. He saw too that industry should be linked to the formal institutions of science and of education:

> There scarcely exists a manufacturing business which has no relation to physics, mechanics, chemistry, mathematics or to the art of design, etc. No progress, no new discoveries and inventions can be made in these sciences by which a hundred industries and processes could not be improved or altered. In the manufacturing State, therefore, sciences and arts must necessarily become popular. (p. 162)

It was thanks to the advocacy of List and like-minded economists, as well as to the long-established Prussian system, that Germany developed one of the best technical education and training systems in the world. This system was not only, according to many historians (e.g. Barnett, 1988; Hobsbawm, 1968; Landes, 1970), one of the main factors in Germany overtaking Britain in the latter half of the nineteenth century, but to this day is the foundation for the superior skills and higher productivity of the German labour force (Prais, 1981) in many industries. Many British policies for education and training for over a century can be realistically viewed as spasmodic, belated and never wholly successful attempts to catch up with German technological education and training systems.

Not only did List anticipate these essential features of current work on national systems of innovation, he also recognised the interdependence of the import of foreign technology and domestic technical development. Nations should not only acquire the achievements of other more advanced nations, they should increase them by their own efforts. Again, there was already a good model for this approach to technological learning in Prussia: the acquisition of machine tool technology. It was British engineers (especially Maudslay) and mechanics who were responsible for the key innovations in machine tool technology in the first quarter of the nineteenth century. This technology was described by Paulinyi (1982) as the 'Alpha and Omega of modern machine-building' because it enabled the design and construction of metal-working precision machinery for all other industries. Those involved attempted to maintain a considerable degree of secrecy, but its importance was recognised by the Prussian government, who took decisive steps to acquire the technology, despite the fact that the British government was attempting to ban the export of machine tools (with the imposition of heavy fines for contravention).

The Prussian government, which had set up Technical Training Institutes (Gewerbe-Institut), made sure that they received imported British machine tools for reverse engineering and for training German craftsmen, who then disseminated the technology in German industry (Paulinyi, 1982). British craftsmen were also attracted to Prussia, as much of the technology depended on tacit knowledge. (Three out of four of the leading machine tool entrepreneurs in Britain at that time had themselves spent years with Maudslay in his workshop.) The transfer of technology promoted and coordinated by the Prussian state was highly successful: the German machine tool industry and machine-building proved capable of designing and manufacturing the machinery necessary to make steam locomotives in the 1840s and 1850s. This set Prussia (later Imperial Germany) well on the road to overtaking Britain. Thus, although he did not cite this particular example, List was talking not in a purely abstract way about industrialisation and technology transfer but about a process which was unfolding before his eyes. It was summed up by Landes (1970):

> Only the government could afford to send officials on costly tours of inspection as far away as the United States; provide the necessary buildings and equipment; feed, clothe, house, and in some cases pay students for a period of years. Moreover, these pedagogical institutions were only part – though the most important part – of a larger educational system designed to introduce the new techniques and diffuse them through the economy; there were also non-teaching academies, museums, and most important perhaps, expositions.
>
> Finally, the government provided technical advice and assistance, awarded subventions to inventors and immigrant entrepreneurs, bestowed gifts of machinery, allowed rebates and exemption of duties on imports of industrial equipment. Some of this was simply a continuation of the past – a heritage of the strong tradition of direct state interest in economic development. Much of it, in Germany particularly, was symptomatic of a passionate desire to organize and hasten the process of catching up.
>
> In so far as this promotional effort stressed the establishment of rational standards of research and industrial performance, it was of the greatest significance for the future. (p. 151)

Not only did List analyse many features of the national system of innovation which are at the heart of contemporary studies (education and training institutions, science, technical institutes, user–producer interactive learning, knowledge accumulation, adapting imported technology, promotion of strategic industries, etc.), he also put great emphasis on the role of the state in coordinating and carrying through long-term policies for industry and the economy. Here, as often, he took issue with Jean-Baptiste Say, the favourite target in his polemics with the classical school, who had argued that governments did not make much difference, except in a negative way.

The United States was of course even more successful than Germany in overtaking Britain in the second half of the nineteenth century and List had learnt a great deal from his residence in the United States and especially from Hamilton's (1791) *Report on Manufactures*. The widespread promotion of education (though not of industrial training) was even more remarkable in the United States than in Germany. However, the abundance of cheap, accessible materials, energy and land together with successive waves of immigration imparted to the United States' national system some specific characteristics without parallel in Europe. The pro-active role of the state was greater in Germany whilst foreign investment played a greater role in the United States.

Although List anticipated many features of the contemporary debate about national systems of innovation (even though his terminology was different), it would of course be absurd to imagine that he could have foreseen all the changes in the world economy and national economies over the next century and a half. In particular, he did not foresee the rise of in-house professionalised research and development (R&D) in industry, still less the rise of multinational (or transnational) corporations (MNCs/TNCs), operating production establishments in many different countries and increasingly also setting up R&D outside their original base. These are major new developments which deeply affect the whole concept of national systems. This chapter will discuss the rise of R&D in Section 2, and types of comparison of national systems which this has led to in Section 3. It will discuss the role of TNCs and the ways in which they may affect the performance of national economies in different continents in Section 4.

2. The rise of specialised research and development

Bjørn Johnson (1992) in an excellent chapter in the Lundvall book on 'National Systems of Innovation' emphasises the important point that institutions are often thought of simply as a source of 'institutional drag' (i.e. of inertia in the system), whereas of course institutional innovations may also give new impetus to technical and economic change.

Appropriately enough it was in Germany that the major institutional innovation of the in-house industrial R&D department was introduced in 1870. Product and process innovation by firms took place of course for more than a century before that, but it was the German dyestuffs industry (Beer, 1959) which first realised that it could be profitable to put the business of research for new products and development of new chemical processes on a regular, systematic and professional basis. Hoechst, Bayer and BASF have continued and strengthened this tradition down to the present day, when their R&D labs now employ many thousands of scientists and engineers. Undoubtedly such discoveries and innovations as synthetic indigo, many other synthetic dyestuffs and pharmaceuticals and the Haber–Bosch process for fertilisers were the main factors in establishing the German chemical industry's leading position before and after the First World War. When the three companies merged in 1926 to form the giant IG Farben Trust they further reinforced their R&D (Freeman, 1974) and made many of the key innovations in synthetic materials, fibres and rubbers (PVC, polystyrene, urea-formaldehyde, Buna, etc.).

The enormous success of the German chemical industry led to imitation of the social innovation of the R&D Department in the chemical firms of other countries (e.g. CIBA in Switzerland). The in-house R&D lab also emerged in other industries which had the same need to access the results of basic research from universities and other research institutions and to develop their own new products. In the United States and German electrical industries, in-house R&D labs appeared in the 1880s, but contract labs, such as Edison's Institute, played a bigger part in the US system (Hughes, 1989).

From their origins in the chemical and electrical industries gradually during the latter part of the nineteenth century and the first half of the twentieth, specialised R&D labs became characteristic features of most large firms in manufacturing industry (although not of the vast majority of small firms or of service industries) (Hounshell, 1992; Hughes, 1989; Mowery, 1980, 1983). This change in industrial behaviour and the growth of government laboratories, of independent contract research institutes and university research impressed many observers and led to the comment by a leading physicist that the greatest invention of the nineteenth century was the method of invention itself. A great many inventions had of course been made for centuries or indeed for millennia before 1870, but the new professional R&D labs seemed like a giant step forward. This perception was powerfully reinforced in the Second World War. Science was already important in the First World War – more important than most people realised at the time – but it was the Manhattan Project and its outcome at Hiroshima which impressed on people throughout the world the power of science and especially, as it seemed, Big Science. Many other developments on both sides, such as radar, computers, rockets and explosives, resulted from large R&D projects, mobilising both government, industrial and academic engineers and scientists.

It was, therefore, hardly surprising that in the climate which existed after the Second World War, the prestige of organised, professional R&D was very high. The proposals made by a visionary physicist (Bernal, 1939) to increase British R&D by an order of magnitude seemed absurdly Utopian at the time but this was in fact achieved in the new political climate after the Second World War. A similar rapid expansion occurred in all industrial countries in the 1950s and 1960s (Table 8.1), and even in developing countries there was a trend to establish research councils, national R&D labs and other scientific institutions to do nuclear physics and in some cases to try to make nuclear weapons (e.g Argentina, India, Brazil, Israel, Yugoslavia). It was hardly surprising either that a simplistic linear model of science and technology 'push' was often dominant in the new science councils that advised governments. It seemed so obvious that the atom bomb (and it was hoped nuclear power for electricity) was the outcome of a chain reaction: basic physics → large-scale

Table 8.1   *Estimated gross expenditure on research and development as a fraction of GNP (GERD/GNP ratio) 1934–1983*

	1934	1967	1983	1983 civil R&D only
USA	0.6	3.1	2.7	2.0
EC*	0.2	1.2	2.1	1.8
Japan	0.1	1.0	2.7	2.7
USSR	0.3	3.2	3.6	1.0

* Estimated weighted average of 12 EC countries.
Source: Author's estimates based on Bernal (1939) adapted to 'Frascati' definitions (OECD, 1963a), OECD statistics, and adjustments to Soviet statistics based on Freeman and Young (1965)

development in big labs → applications and innovations (whether military or civil). The 'Linear Model' was specifically endorsed in the influential Report of Vannevar Bush, 'Science, the Endless Frontier' (see Stokes, 1993).

This meant that the R&D system was seen as *the* source of innovation – an impression that was reinforced by the system of measurement which was adopted, first by the National Science Foundation in the United States and later during the 1950s and 1960s by all the other OECD countries. This was standardised by the so-called 'Frascati Manual' (OECD, 1963a) and, despite the fact that the authors pointed out that technical change did not depend just on R&D but on many other related activities, such as education, training, production engineering, design, quality control, etc., etc., nevertheless R&D measures were very frequently used as a surrogate for all these activities which helped to promote new and improved products and processes. Furthermore, the importance of all the feedback loops from the market and from production into the R&D system was often overlooked or forgotten. The simple fact that the R&D measures were the only ones that were available reinforced these tendencies.

Their effect could be seen in many national Reports as well as in the 'Science Policy Reviews' conducted by the OECD in its member countries in the 1960s and 1970s. The admirable aim of these reviews, like the reviews of member countries' economic policies, which still continue and on which they were modelled, was to produce a friendly but independent and critical assessment of each country's performance by an international comparative yardstick. In practice they concentrated mainly on the formal R&D system and technical education. This was of course still quite a useful thing to do but it meant that the 'national system' was usually defined in rather narrow terms. Academic research on invention and innovation had amply demonstrated that many factors were important for innovative success other than R&D. However, the practical difficulties of incorporating these factors in international comparisons were very great. 'League table' comparisons of R&D were much easier and more influential.

Gradually, during the 1950s and 1960s, the evidence accumulated that the rate of technical change and of economic growth depended more on efficient diffusion than on being first in the world with radical innovations and as much on social innovations as on technical innovations. This was reflected in the change of emphasis in various OECD Reports (OECD, 1963b, 1971, 1980, 1988, 1991, 1992) and in the introduction of Country Reports on 'Innovation'. Basic science was of course still recognised as being very important but much more was said about technology and diffusion than hitherto.

Although various OECD Reports are a convenient record of changing ideas and policies for science and technology, they rarely originated these changes. The OECD documents summed up and reflected recent experience and changes in the member countries and disseminated what were thought to be the lessons of this experience. The OECD was also, however, more ready than most international organisations to involve independent researchers, so that their reports also embody some input from academic research on technical change as well as from industrial R&D management sources. The next section will very briefly summarise the relevant results of some of this work (more fully surveyed in Freeman, 1994) and especially the results of international comparisons. Comparisons with Japan were especially influential after Japan joined the OECD in the 1970s.

3. Some contrasting features of national systems of innovation in the 1970s and 1980s

As empirical evidence and analysis began to accumulate about industrial R&D and about innovation, both in Japan and in the United States and Europe, it became increasingly evident that the success of innovations, their rate of diffusion and the associated productivity gains depended on a wide variety of other influences as well as formal R&D. In particular, *incremental* innovations came from production engineers, from technicians and from the shop floor. They were strongly related to different forms of work organisation (see especially Hollander, 1965). Furthermore, many improvements to *products* and to services came from interaction with the market and with related firms, such as sub-contractors, suppliers of materials and services (see especially Lundvall, 1988, 1992; Sako, 1992; von Hippel, 1976, 1988). Formal R&D was usually decisive in its contribution to *radical* innovations but it was no longer possible to ignore the many other contributions to, and influences upon, the process of technical change at the level of firms and industries (Carter and Williams, 1957; Jewkes et al., 1958; Mansfield, 1968, 1971; Nelson, 1962).

Not only were inter-firm relationships shown to be of critical importance, but the external *linkages* within the narrower professional science–technology system were also shown to be decisive for innovative success with radical innovations (Gibbons and Johnson, 1974; NSF, 1973). Finally, research on diffusion revealed more and more that the *systemic* aspects of innovation were increasingly influential in determining both the rate of diffusion and the productivity gains associated with any particular diffusion process (see especially Carlsson and Jacobsson, 1993). The success of any specific technical innovation, such as robots or CNC, depended on other related changes in *systems* of production. As three major new 'generic' technologies (information technology, bio-technology and new materials technology) diffused through the world economy in the 1970s and 1980s, systemic aspects of innovation assumed greater and greater importance.

At the *international* level two contrasting experiences made a very powerful impression in the 1980s both on policy-makers and on researchers: on the one hand extraordinary success of first Japan and then South Korea in technological and economic catch-up; and on the other hand the collapse of the Socialist economies of Eastern Europe.

At first, in the 1950s and 1960s, the Japanese success was often simply attributed to copying, imitating and importing foreign technology, and the statistics of the so-called 'technological balance of payments' were often cited to support this view. They showed a huge deficit in Japanese transactions for licensing and know-how imports and exports and a correspondingly large surplus for the United States. It soon became evident, however, as Japanese products and processes began to out-perform American and European products and processes in more and more industries, that this explanation was no longer adequate even though the import of technology continued to be important. Japanese industrial R&D expenditures as a proportion of civil industrial net output surpassed those of the United States in the 1970s and total civil R&D as a fraction of GNP surpassed USA in the 1980s (Table 1). The Japanese performance could now be explained more in terms of R&D intensity, especially as Japanese R&D was highly concentrated in the fastest growing civil industries, such as electronics. Patent statistics showed that the leading Japanese electronic firms outstripped American and European firms in these industries, not just in domestic patenting but also in patents taken out in the United States (Freeman, 1987; Patel and Pavitt, 1991, 1992).

However, although these rough measures of research and inventive activity certainly did indicate the huge increase in Japanese scientific and technical activities, they did not in themselves explain how these activities led to higher quality of new products and processes (Grupp and Hofmeyer, 1986; Womack et al., 1990), to shorter lead times (Graves, 1991; Mansfield, 1988) and to more rapid diffusion of such technologies as robotics (Fleck and White, 1987; Mansfield, 1989). Moreover, the contrasting example of the (then) Soviet Union and other East European countries showed that simply to commit greater resources to R&D did not in itself guarantee successful innovation, diffusion and productivity gains. It was obvious that *qualitative* factors affecting the national systems had to be taken into account as well as the purely *quantitative* indicators.

Some major differences between the two national systems of Japan and the Soviet Union as they were functioning in the 1970s are summarised in Table 2. The most striking contrast of course was the huge commitment of Soviet R&D to military and space applications with little direct or indirect spin-off to the civil economy. It has now been shown that the desire to keep pace with the USA in the super-power

Table 8.2 *Contrasting national systems of innovation: 1970s*

Japan	USSR
High GERD/GNP Ratio (2.5%)	Very high GERD/GNP Ratio (*c.* 4%)
Very low proportion of military space R&D (< 2% of R&D)	Extremely high proportion of military/space R&D (> 70% of R&D)
High proportion of total R&D at enterprise level and company-financed (approx. 67%)	Low proportion of total R&D at enterprise level and company-financed (< 10%)
Strong integration of R&D, production and import of technology at enterprise level	Separation of R&D, production and import of technology and weak institutional linkages
Strong user–producer and subcontractor network linkages	Weak or non-existent linkages between marketing, production and procurement
Strong incentives to innovate at enterprise level involving both management and workforce	Some incentives to innovate made increasingly strong in 1960s and 1970s but offset by other negative disincentives affecting both management and workforce
Intensive experience of competition in international markets	Relatively weak exposure to international competition except in arms race

arms race led to about three-quarters of the massive Soviet R&D resources going into defence and space research. This amounted to nearly 3% of GNP, so that only about 1% remained for civil R&D. This *civil* R&D GNP ratio was less than half of most West European countries and much smaller than the Japanese ratio (Table 8.1).

Nevertheless, it could have been far more productive if the social, technical and economic linkages in the system and the incentives to efficient performance had been stronger. The Soviet system grew up on the basis of separate Research Institutes within the Academy system (for fundamental research), for each industry sector (for applied research and development) and for the design of plant and import of technology (the Project Design organisations) (Amann et al., 1979; Barker and Davies, 1965). The links between all these different institutions and enterprise-level R&D remained rather weak despite successive attempts to reform and improve the system in the 1960s and 1970s.

Moreover, there were quite strong negative incentives in the Soviet system retarding innovation at enterprise level (Gomulka, 1990), such as the need to meet quantitative planned production targets. Thus, whereas the integration of R&D, production and technology imports at firm level was the strongest feature of the Japanese system (Baba, 1985; Freeman, 1987; Takeuchi and Nonaka, 1986), it was very weak in the Soviet Union except in the aircraft industry and other defence sectors. Finally, the user–producer linkages which were so important in most other industrial countries were very weak or almost non-existent in some areas in the Soviet Union.

There were some features of their national systems in which both countries resembled each other, and both did of course enjoy high economic growth rates in the 1950s and 1960s. Both had (and still have) good education systems with a high proportion of young people participating in tertiary education and a strong

Table 8.3   *Divergence in national systems of innovation in the 1980s*

East Asia	Latin America
Expanding universal education system with high participation in tertiary education and with high proportion of engineering graduates	Deteriorating education system with proportionately lower output of engineers
Import of technology typically combined with local initiatives in technical change and at later stages rapidly rising levels of R&D	Much transfer of technology, especially from the United states, but weak enterprise-level R&D and little integration with technology transfer
Industrial R&D rises typically to >50% of all R&D	Industrial R&D typically remains at < 25% of total
Development of strong science–technology infrastructure and at later stages good linkages with industrial R&D	Weakening of science–technology infrastructure and poor linkages with industry
High levels of investment and major inflow of Japanese investment and technology with strong yen in 1980s. Strong influence of Japanese models of management and networking organisation	Decline in (mainly US) foreign investment and generally lower levels of investment. Low level of international networking in technology
Heavy investment in advanced telecommunications infrastructure	Slow development of modern telecommunications
Strong and fast-growing electronic industries with high exports and extensive user feedback from international markets	Weak electronic industries with low exports and little learning by international marketing

emphasis on science and technology. Both also had methods of generating long-term goals and perspectives for the science–technology system, but whereas in the Japanese case the long-term 'visions' are generated by an interactive process involving not only MITI and other government organisations but also industry and universities (Irvine and Martin, 1984), in the USSR the process was more restricted and dominated to a greater extent by military/space requirements.

A similar sharp contrast can be made between the national systems of innovation typically present in Latin American countries in the 1980s and those in the '4 Dragons' of East Asia (Table 8.3) and especially between two 'newly industrialising countries' (NICs) in the 1980s: Brazil and South Korea (Table 8.4). The Asian countries started from a *lower* level of industrialisation in the 1950s but, whereas in the 1960s and 1970s the Latin American and East Asian countries were often grouped together as very fast-growing NICs, in the 1980s a sharp contrast began to emerge: the East Asian countries' GNP grew at an average annual rate of about 8%, but in most Latin American countries, including Brazil, this fell to less than 2%, which meant in many cases a falling per capita income. There are of course many explanations for this stark contrast. Some of the Asian countries introduced more radical social changes, such as land reform and universal education, than did most Latin American countries, and clearly a structural and technical transformation of this

Table 8.4   *National systems of innovation: 1980s, some quantitative indicators*

Various indicators of technical capability and national institutions	Brazil	South Korea
Percent age group in third-level (higher) education	11 (1985)	32 (1985)
Engineering students as a percentage of population	0.13 (1985)	0.54 (1985)
R&D as percentage of GNP	0.7 (1987)	2.1 (1989)
Industry R&D as a percentage of total	30 (1988)	65 (1987)
Robots per million in employment	52 (1987)	1060 (1987)
CAD per million in employment	422	1437 (1986)
NCMT per million in employment	2298 (1987)	5176 (1985)
Growth rate electronics	8% (1983–1987)	21% (1985–1990)
Telephone lines per 100 (1989)	6	25
Per capita sales of telecommunication equipment (1989)	$10	$77
Patents (US) (1989)	36	159

magnitude in this time was facilitated by these social changes. In the case of Brazil and South Korea it is possible to give some more detailed quantitative indicators of some of these contrasting features. As Table 8.4 shows, the contrast in educational systems was very marked as well as enterprise-level R&D, telecommunication infrastructure and the diffusion of new technologies (see Nelson, 1993, for more detailed comparisons and Villaschi, 1993, for a detailed study of the Brazilian national system).

4. 'Globalisation' and national systems

It has been argued in Section 3 that a variety of *national* institutions have powerfully affected the relative rates of technical change and hence of economic growth in various countries. The variations in national systems which have been described are of course extreme contrasting cases. Nevertheless, they have certainly been important features of world development in the second half of the twentieth century and they point to *uneven* development of the world economy and *divergence* in growth rates. Moreover, differences in national systems are also very important between Japan, the United States and the EC and between European countries themselves, as the major comparative study between more than a dozen national systems of innovation illustrates (Nelson, 1993). The comparative study of Ireland with other small countries by Mjøset (1992) also demonstrates this point, and the comparison of Denmark and Sweden by Edqvist and Lundvall (1993) shows that big differences exist between neighbouring countries which superficially appear very similar in many ways. Moreover, Archibugi and Pinta (1992) have demonstrated the growing pattern of specialisation in technology and trade and Fagerberg (1992) has shown the continuing importance of the home market for comparative technological advantage.

However, the whole concept of *national* differences in innovative capabilities determining national performance has been recently challenged on the grounds that transnational corporations (TNCs) are changing the face of the world economy in the direction of globalisation. For example, Ohmae (1990) in his book *The Borderless World* argues that national frontiers are 'melting away' in what he calls the 'ILE' (inter-linked economy) – the triad of the USA, the EC and Japan, now being joined by NICs. This 'ILE' is becoming 'so powerful that it has swallowed most consumers and corporations, made traditional national borders almost disappear, and pushed bureaucrats, politicians and the military towards the status of declining industries' (p. xii).

As against this, Michael Porter (1990) has argued that:

> Competitive advantage is created and sustained through a highly localized process. Differences in national economic structures, values, cultures, institutions and histories contribute profoundly to competitive success. The role of the home nation seems to be as strong or stronger than ever. While globalization of competition might appear to make the nation less important, instead it seems to make it more so. With fewer impediments to trade to shelter uncompetitive domestic firms and industries, the home nation takes on growing significance because it is the source of the skills and technology that underpin competitive advantage. (p. 19 [see also Chapter 9 below])

In addition to Porter's argument, Lundvall (1993) points out that if uncertainty, localised learning and bounded rationality are introduced as basic and more realistic assumptions about microeconomic behaviour, rather than the traditional assumptions of perfect information and hyperrationality, then it must follow that local and national variations in circumstances may often lead to different paths of development and to increasing diversity rather than to standardisation and convergence.

At first sight, the activities of multinational corporations might appear to offer a powerful countervailing force to this local variety and diversity. The largest corporations in the world, whether their original domestic base was in Europe, the United States, Japan or elsewhere, have often been investing in many different new locations. This investment, even though initially it may have been distribution and service networks, or in production facilities, has more recently also included R&D. Whilst the greater part of the 1980s' investment was within the OECD area itself and in oil-producing countries and could be more accurately described therefore as 'triadisation' rather than 'globalisation', it has also flowed, even though very unevenly, to other countries of the Third World and there is now a small trickle to the former socialist group of countries.

As Harry Johnson (1975) long ago pointed out, in this sense the multi-nationals do indeed unite the human race. Since the basic laws of physics, chemistry, biology and other sciences apply everywhere, there is an underlying unified tech-nology which can in principle be applied anywhere with identical or very similar results. Insofar as large 'global' TNCs are able to sell their products and services world-wide and to produce them in many different locations, they can and do act as a very powerful agency tending towards the world-wide standardisation of techno-logy and output. As the model developed by Callon (1993) indicates, the diffusion process can tend to enhance similarities between adopters.

Even in the case of consumer goods where it might be reasonable to suppose that there would continue to be wide variations in consumer tastes, we are all sufficiently familiar with such products as 'Coca-Cola' and such services as those provided by McDonald's to recognise the reality of such global production and distribution networks, offering standardised products and services and services world-wide. Is it not realistic to suppose that an ever-larger proportion of world production and trade will take this form? Supporting such a view are not only the obvious examples of hotel chains, soft drinks, canned beer, tourist agencies and credit cards but theoretical economic arguments based on static and dynamic economies of scale in production, advertising, marketing, design and finance, as well as the ability of large multinationals to take advantage of surviving differences between nations in costs of capital, labour, energy and other inputs.

However, it would be unwise to assume that these tendencies are the only or even necessarily the strongest tendencies within the world economy. Nor are they so unequivocally desirable that they should be promoted by both national and international economic policies. In fact, the arguments for preserving and even encouraging diversity may sometimes outweigh the shorter-term advantages of the scale economies derived from standardisation and their propagation through trans-national companies, free trade and free flows of investment. In fact both processes (global standardisation in some areas but increasing diversity in others) co-exist.

Whilst there are certainly some products and services, such as those already mentioned, where there is indeed a demand which is 'global' in nature and where local variations in taste, regulation, climate and other circumstances can be largely or wholly ignored, there are far more products and services where such variations certainly cannot be ignored without dire consequences. Innumerable examples leap to mind where climatic conditions affect the performance of machines, instru-ments, vehicles and materials and even more examples are obvious in relation to variations in national standards, specifications and regulations. Whilst it is true that international standardisation is a countervailing force through the activities of the International Standards Organisation (ISO) and many other bodies attempting to achieve harmonisation of technical standards, it is also true that the experience of the European Community over the past 20 years demonstrates the extreme diffi-culties attending this process in many areas (as well as its feasibility in others). And all this still does not take into account the cultural aspects of the problem which deeply affect such areas as food, clothing and personal services.

So far we have been discussing mainly the case of established products and pointing to some factors which limit global standardisation even in the simplest cases. Advocates of a strong globalisation hypothesis would of course accept most of these points, although they might argue that some will constantly tend to diminish as the media, travel, education and international organisations all exert their long-term influence. Rothwell (1992) has pointed to the 'electronification' of design as an important factor facilitating the internationalisation of design and R&D. It can be argued further that local variations can easily be dealt with inside the framework of the global strategies of the multinational corporations. Indeed, globalisation of R&D has already led to local adaptation and modification of products to meet national variations, as a normal and almost routine activity of TNCs. Companies such as Honda go one step further and claim to have a strategy of diversity in world-wide design which goes beyond the simple modification of a standard product to the idea of local variation at the design stage in several different parts of the world. However, the vast majority of Japanese-based TNCs remain essentially Japanese companies with international operations rather than truly international companies, and the same is true of US and most other MNCs in relation to their home environment (Hu, 1992). Most R&D activities of MNCs are still overwhelmingly conducted in the domestic base of the company and are heavily influenced by the local national system of innovation. Moreover, ownership and control still remain overwhelmingly based on the domestic platform.

The statistics are rather poor but analysis of all the available data and cross-checking with the patent statistics (Patel, 1993; Patel and Pavitt, 1991) suggests that the R&D activities of US companies outside the USA amount to less than 10% of the total, whilst those of Japanese companies are much lower – less than 2% – though rising. The picture in Europe is more complex both because of the development of the European Community and the Single European Market, and because of the existence of several technically advanced small countries where the domestic base is too small for the strong MNCs which are based there (Netherlands, Sweden, Belgium, Switzerland). A larger part of national R&D activities in these countries and most other parts of Europe is undertaken by foreign multinationals and their 'own' TNCs perform much more R&D abroad than is the case with the USA or Japan. Only a small part of total world R&D is conducted outside the leading industries countries and only a very small part of this is financed by TNCs.

Qualitative analysis of the transnational activities of corporations shows that most of it is *either* local design modification to meet national specifications and regulations *or* research to facilitate monitoring of local science and technology. The more original research, development and design work is still overwhelmingly concentrated in the domestic base, although there are important exceptions in the drug industry and electronics industry where specialised pools of scientific ability play an important role.

As long as we are dealing with a static array of products and discussing only minor variations to adjust to local consumer tastes and environments, then the standardisation arguments, the globalisation arguments and even some of the simplifying neoclassical assumptions about perfect information are at the borderlines of credibility and usefulness. But once we leave this world and enter the dynamic world of radical innovations, both technical and organisational, and of extremely uneven and unequal access to new developments in science and technology, then the whole picture is transformed. More realistic assumptions and a more realistic vision are essential if economic theory is to be of any help in policy-making.

Lundvall (1993) points out that, even in the case of continuous *incremental* innovation in open economies, the drive towards standardisation is limited. Geographical and cultural proximity to advanced users and a network of institutionalised (even if often informal) user–producer relationships are an important source of diversity and of comparative advantage, as is the local supply of managerial and technical skills and accumulated tacit knowledge. He gives several examples of such localised learning generating strong positions in the world market. Whilst he accepts that TNCs might locate in such 'national strongholds' in order to gain access to the fruits of this interactive learning process, he points out that it is not always simple to enter such markets because of the strength of the non-economic relationships involved. Competing standards for the global market may be important weapons in such situations as well as other forms of product differentiation and quality improvement.

When it comes to *radical* innovations the importance of institutional variety and localised learning is even greater. Posner's (1961) theory of technology gaps and imitation lags is of fundamental importance here. It may be many years before imitators are capable of assembling the mix of skills, the work organisation and other institutional changes necessary to launch into the production and marketing of entirely new products.

It is of course true that in the global diffusion of radical innovations, TNCs may have an extremely important role. They *are* in a position to transfer specialised equipment and skills to new locations if they so wish and to simulate and organise the necessary learning processes. They are also in a position to make technology exchange agreements with rivals and to organise joint ventures in any part of the world. It is for this reason that many governments in Europe as well as in the Third World and the ex-socialist countries have been anxious to offer incentives to attract a flow of inward investment and associated technology transfer from firms based in Japan and the USA.

However, such efforts will meet with only limited success unless accompanied by a variety of institutional changes designed to strengthen autonomous technological capability within the importing countries. This is especially true of those generic technologies which have been at the centre of the world-wide diffusion process over the past two decades. Here it is essential to emphasise the interdependencies between innovations and between technical innovations and organisational innovations. A theory of technical change which ignores these interdependencies is no more helpful than a theory of economics which ignores the interdependencies of prices and quantities in the world economy.

Perez (1983) has pointed out that the social and institutional framework which is hospitable to one set of technologies will not be so suitable for a radically new technology. Whereas incremental innovations can be easily accommodated, this may not be the case with radical innovations, which by definition involve an element of creative destruction. When we are talking about large clusters of radical innovations combined with rapid processes of incremental innovation, then the problems of structural and social adjustment can be very great. This is quite obvious when we consider such aspects as the change in management techniques and skill-mix which are called for, but it also applies to many other types of institutional change in standards, patents, new services, new infrastructure, government policies and public organisations.

It is in this context that the concept of 'national systems of innovation' assumes such great importance, and in the light of this approach it is not surprising that the recognition of the scope and depth of the computer revolution, which was accelerated by the microprocessor in the 1970s, has been followed by a growing recognition of the importance of organisational and managerial change ('multi-skilling', 'lean production systems', 'down-sizing', 'just-in-time' stock control, worker participation in technical change, quality circles, continuous learning, etc., etc.).

The diffusion of a new techno-economic paradigm is a trial-and-error process involving great institutional variety. There are evolutionary advantages in this variety and considerable dangers in being locked in too early to a standardised technology. A technological monoculture may be more dangerous than an ecological monoculture. Even when a technology matures and shows clear-cut advantages and scale economies it is important to retain flexibility and to nourish alternative sources of radically new technology and work organisation.

National and international policies thus confront the need for a sophisticated dual approach to a complex set of problems. Policies for diffusion of standard generic technologies are certainly important and these may sometimes entail the encouragement of inward investment and technology transfer by MNCs. But also important are policies to encourage local originality and diversity.

5. Conclusions

This chapter has attempted to show that historically there have been major differences among countries in the ways in which they have organised and sustained the development, introduction, improvement and diffusion of new products and processes within their national economies. These differences can perhaps be most easily demonstrated in the case of Britain in the late eighteenth and early nineteenth centuries when she achieved leadership in world technology and world trade and could temporarily claim to be 'the workshop of the world'.

Historians (Mathias, 1969; von Tunzelmann, 1994) are generally agreed that no single factor can explain this British success; it can be rather attributed to a unique combination of interacting social, economic and technical changes within the national economic space. It was certainly not just a succession of remarkable inventions in the textile and iron industries, important though these were. Among the more important changes were the transition from a domestic 'putting out' system to a factory system of production; new ways of managing and financing companies (partnership and later joint stock companies); interactive learning between new companies and industries using new materials and other inputs as well as new machinery; the removal of many older restrictions on trade and industry and the growth of new markets and systems of retail and wholesale trade; a new transport infrastructure; a hospitable cultural environment for new scientific theories and inventions; and, certainly not least important, the dissemination and widespread acceptance of economic theories and policies which facilitated all these changes. It was the British Prime Minister who said to Adam Smith: 'We are all your pupils now.' The benefits from foreign trade and in some cases piracy and plunder also played their part, especially in the process of capital accumulation, but it was the mode of investment of this capital within the national economy, rather than the simple acquisition of treasure or luxury expenditure, which was a decisive impulse to economic growth.

Of course, many of these changes also took place within other European countries, but there were distinct and measurable differences in the rate and direction of institutional and technical change, the rate of economic growth, of foreign trade and of standards of living, which were fairly obvious at the time as well as to historians since. This can be seen not only from the writings of economists but from novelists and travellers. It was therefore hardly surprising that Friedrich List and other economists on the Continent of Europe were concerned to develop theories and policies which would help them to understand the reasons for British commercial supremacy and enable Germany (and other countries) to catch up. Section 1 attempted to show that in this endeavour, List anticipated many contemporary ideas about 'national systems of innovation' including the crucial importance of technological accumulation through a combination of technology imports with local activities and pro-active interventionist policies to foster strategic 'infant' industries.

In the second half of the nineteenth century, new developments in the natural sciences and in electrical engineering led to progressive entrepreneurs and reformers realising that in the new and fastest-growing industries, learning by doing, using and interacting in the old British ways had to be accompanied or replaced by more professional and systematic processes of innovation and learning. The organisational innovation of the in-house R&D department put the introduction of new products and processes on a firmer foundation whilst new institutions and departments of higher education and secondary education provided the new, more highly qualified scientists, engineers and technicians. Section 2 of the chapter argued that it was in Germany and the United States that these institutional innovations began and made the greatest impact on national systems in the second half of the nineteenth century and early twentieth century.

The rapidly widening gap between a small group of industrialised countries and the rest of the 'under-developed' world (Dosi et al., 1992; Durlauf and Johnson, 1992), as well as the 'forging ahead', 'catching up' and 'falling behind' (Abramovitz, 1986) among the leaders, clearly called for some explanation of why growth rates differed so much. The brave simplifying assumptions of neoclassical economics might lead people to expect convergence rather than divergence in growth rates (perfect information and costless, instant transfer of technology). Nor did formal growth theory and models provide much help since most of the interesting phenomena were confined to a 'residual' which could not be satisfactorily disaggregated and because of the interdependencies involved (Nelson, 1973).

Many economic historians and proponents of what have now become known as 'national systems of innovation' would claim that the differences were due to varying types of institutional and technical change which may be the subject of quali-tative description, even though difficult to quantify. Sections 2 and 3 of the chapter argued that the over-simplification of quantitative R&D comparisons was an inade-quate method in itself. Section 3 attempted to show by the examples of Japan and the former Soviet Union, and of the East Asian and Latin American 'NICs', that institutional differences in the mode of importing, improving, developing and diffusing new technologies, products and processes played a major role in their sharply contrasting growth rates in the 1980s.

Finally, in Section 4 the chapter discussed the controversial issue of 'globali-sation' and its bearing on national systems of innovation. It is ironical that just as the importance of technology policies and industrial policies has been increasingly recognised alike in OECD and in developing countries, the limitations of *national* policies are increasingly emphasised and the relevance of *national* systems increasingly questioned (see, for example, Humbert, 1993). The global reach of transnational corporations, the drastic cost reductions and quality improvements in global telecommunications networking and other rapid and related changes in the world economy must certainly be taken into account in any satisfactory analysis of national systems (Chesnais, 1992).

It is tempting at first sight to follow Ohmae and to discard national economies and nation states as rapidly obsolescent categories. The speed of change and the difficulties of focusing analysis may be illustrated by the confusion in terminology. Ohmae maintains that nation states are losing their power and their influence both 'upwards' and 'downwards', on the one hand to supra-national institutions (the EC, NAFTA, UN organisations, etc., as well as transnational companies) and, on the other hand, to sub-national (or 'infra-national') provin-cial, urban or local authorities and organisations (the disintegration of federal and centralised states, the growing importance in some areas of local government agencies and even of various forms of Tariff-Free Zones, and of 'Silicon Valleys'). Unhappily, at least in the English language, the same word 'regions' has to be used to describe both processes – the very large 'regional' trading blocs such as NAFTA or the emerging East Asian 'region', and the much smaller sub-national 'regions'. Some terminological innovation is needed here, and for the purposes of this paper, the expressions 'upper regions' and 'nether regions' will be used. It is undoubtedly important to keep track of both and of their interaction with national systems.

The work of geographers as well as economists (e.g. Antonelli, 1994; Lundvall, 1992; Saxenian, 1991; Scott, 1991; Storper and Harrison, 1991) has convincingly demonstrated the importance of nether regions for network developments and new technology systems. They have argued that local infrastructure, externalities, especially in skills and local labour markets, specialised services and, not least, mutual trust and personal relationships have contributed greatly to flourishing nether regions. It should not be forgotten, however, that 'nether-regional systems of innovation' and 'economies of agglomeration' have always underpinned national systems from the beginnings of the industrial revolution (Arcangeli, 1993). Marshall (1890) already stressed the importance of what were then known as 'industrial districts' where 'the secrets of industry were in the air' (Foray, 1991). Piore and Sabel (1984) have especially underlined the importance of these nether regions in many parts of Europe both in the nineteenth century and again today.

Moreover, the vulnerability of national economies to external shocks is also by no means a new phenomenon of the last decade or two, even though the liberalisation of capital markets and international flows of trade and investment combined with computerisation and new telecommunications networks may have increased this vulnerability. Small and distant nations were already affected by shocks from the City of London under the Gold Standard and the Popular Front Government in France suffered just as severely from the 'flight of capital' in the 1930s as the Socialist government of France in the 1980s.

This chapter has argued that nation states, national economies and national systems of innovation are still essential domains of economic and political analysis, despite some shifts to upper and nether regions. Indeed, Michael Porter (1990) may well be right in his contention that the intensification of global competition has made the role of the home nation more important, not less. Particularly from the standpoint of developing countries, national policies for catching up in technology remain of fundamental importance. Nevertheless, the interaction of national systems both with 'nether-region systems of innovation' and with transnational corporations will be increasingly important, as will be the role of international cooperation in sustaining a global regime favourable to catching up and development.

Note

1   I have used the expression 'intellectual capital' rather than 'mental capital' used
    in the early English edition, [C.F.]

References

Amann, R., Berry, M. and Davies, R.W. 1979. *Industrial Innovation in the Soviet Union*, New Haven, Yale University Press.

Antonelli, C. 1994. Technological districts, localized spillovers and productivity growth, *International Review of Applied Economics*, Vol. 8, No. 1, pp. 18–30.

Arcangeli, F. 1993. Local and global features of the learning process, in M. Humbert (ed.), *The Impact of Globalisation on Europe's Firms and Industries*, London, Pinter.

Archibugi, D. and Pinta, M. 1992. 'The Technological Specialisation of Advanced Countries', Report to the EC on International Science and Technology Activities, Dordrecht, Kluwer.

Baba, Y. 1985. 'Japanese Colour TV Firms. Decision-making from the 1950s to the 1980s', DPhil. dissertation, Falmer, University of Sussex.

Barker, G.R. and Davies, R.W. 1965. The research and development effort of the Soviet Union, in C. Freeman and A. Young (eds), *The Research and Development Effort in Western Europe, North America and the Soviet Union*, Paris, OECD.

Barnett, C. 1988. *The Audit of War*, Cambridge, Cambridge University Press.

Beer, J.J. 1959. *The Emergence of the German Dye Industry*, Chicago, University of Illinois Press.

Bernal, J.D. 1939. *The Social Function of Science*, London, Routledge and Kegan Paul.

Callon, M. 1993. Variety and irreversibility in networks of technique conception and adoption, in D. Foray and C. Freeman (eds), *Technology and the Wealth of Nations*, London, Pinter.

Carlsson, B. and Jacobsson, S. 1993. Technological systems and economic performance: the diffusion of factory automation in Sweden, in D. Foray and C. Freeman (eds), *Technology and the Wealth of Nations*, London, Pinter.

Carter, C.F. and Williams, B.R. 1957. *Industry and Technical Progress*, Oxford, Oxford University Press.

Chesnais, F. 1992. National systems of innovation, foreign direct investment and the operations of multinational enterprises, in B.-Å. Lundvall (ed.), *National Systems of Innovation: Towards a Theory of Innovation and Interactive Learning*, London, Pinter.

Dosi, G., Freeman, C., Fabiani, S. and Aversi, R. 1992. 'The Diversity of Development Patterns: On the Processes of Catching Up, Forging Ahead and Falling Behind', International Economics Association, Varenna, Italy, October.

Durlauf, S. and Johnson, P.A. 1992. 'Local versus Global Convergence across National Economies', mimeo, Stanford University.

Edqvist, C. and Lundvall, B.-Å. 1993. Denmark and Sweden, in E.R. Nelson (ed.), *National Innovation Systems: A Comparative Analysis*, Oxford, Oxford University Press.

Fagerberg, J. 1992. The home market hypothesis re-examined: the impact of domestic-user–producer interacation in exports, in B.-Å. Lundvall (ed.), *National Systems of Innovation: Towards a Theory of Innovation and Interactive Learning*, London, Pinter.

Fleck, J. and White, B. 1987. National policies and patterns of robot diffusion: UK, Japan, Sweden and United States, *Robotics*, Vol. 3, No. 1.

Foray, D. 1991. The secrets of industry are in the air: industrial cooperation and the organisational dynamics of the innovative firm, *Research Policy*, Vol. 20, No. 5.

Freeman, C. 1974. *The Economics of Industrial Innovation*, 1st edn, Harmondsworth, Penguin; 2nd edn, 1982 London, Frances Pinter.

Freeman, C. 1987. *Technology Policy and Economic Performance: Lessons from Japan*, London, Pinter.

Freeman, C. 1994. The economics of technical change, *Cambridge Journal of Economics*, Vol. 18, No. 5, October.

Freeman, C. and Young, A. (eds) 1965. *The Research and Development Effort in Western Europe, North America and the Soviet Union*, Paris, OECD.

Gibbons, M. and Johnson, R.D. 1974. The role of science in technological innovation, *Research Policy*, Vol. 3, No. 3, 220–242.

Gomulka, S. 1990. *The Theory of Technological Change and Economic Growth*, London, Routledge.

Graves, A. 1991. 'International Competitiveness and Technological Development in the World Automobile Industry', DPhil. thesis, Falmer, University of Sussex.

Grossman, I. and Helpman, E. 1991. *Endogenous Growth Theory*, Cambridge, MA, MIT Press.

Grupp, H. and Hofmeyer, O. 1986. A technometric model for the assessment of technological standards and their application to selected technology comparisons, *Technological Forecasting and Social Change*, Vol. 30, 123–137.

Hamilton, A. 1791. 'Report on the Subject of Manufactures', reprinted by the US Government Printing Office, Washington, 1913.

Hobsbawm, E. 1968. *Industry and Empire*, London, Weidenfeld and Nicolson.

Hollander, S. 1965. *The Sources of Increased Efficiency: A Study of DuPont Rayon Plants*, Cambridge. MA, MIT Press.

Hounshell, D.A. 1992. Continuity and change in the management of industrial research: the DuPont Company 1902–1980, in G. Dosi, R. Giannetti and P.A. Toninelli (eds), *Technology and Enterprise in a Historical Perspective*, Oxford, Oxford University Press.

Hu, Y.S. 1992. Global or transnational corporations are national firms with international operations, *Californian Management Review.*

Hughes, T.P. 1989. *American Genesis*, New York, Viking.

Humbert, M. (ed.) 1993. *The Impact of Globalisation on Europe's Firms and Industries*, London, Pinter.

Irvine, J. and Martin, B.R. 1984. *Foresight in Science: Picking the Winners*, London, Pinter.

Jewkes, J., Sawers, D. and Stillerman, R. 1958. *The Sources of Invention*, London, Macmillan.

Johnson, B. 1992. Institutional learning, in B.-Å. Lundvall (ed.), *National Systems of Innovation: Towards a Theory of Innovation and Interactive Learning*, London, Pinter.

Johnson, H.G. 1975. *Technology and Economic Interdependence*, London, Macmillan.

Landes, M. 1970. *The Unbound Prometheus: Technological and Industrial Development in Western Europe from 1750 to the Present*, Cambridge, Cambridge University Press.

List, F. 1841. *The National System of Political Economy*, English edn 1904, London, Longman.

Lundvall, B.-Å. 1988. Innovation as an interactive process: from user–producer interaction to the national system of innovation, in G. Dosi et al. (eds), *Technical Change and Economic Theory*, London, Pinter.

Lundvall, B.-Å. (ed.) 1992. *National Systems of Innovation: Towards a Theory of Innovation and Interactive Learning*, London, Pinter.

Lundvall, B.-Å. 1993. User–producer relationships, national systems of innovation and internationalisation, in D. Foray and C. Freeman (eds), *Technology and the Wealth of Nations*, London, Pinter.

Mansfield, E. 1968. *The Economics of Technical Change*, New York, W.W. Norton.

Mansfield, E. 1971. *Research and Innovation in the Modern Corporation*, New York, W.W. Norton.

Mansfield, E. 1988. Industrial innovation in Japan and in the United States, *Science*, Vol. 241, 1760–1764.

Mansfield, E. 1989. The diffusion of industrial robots in Japan and in the United States, *Research Policy*, Vol. 18, 183–192.

Marshall, A. 1890. *Principles of Economics*, London, Macmillan.

Mathias, P. 1969. *The First Industrial Nation*, London, Methuen.

Mjøset, L. 1992. *The Irish Economy in a Comparative Institutional Perspective*, Dublin, National Economic and Social Council.

Mowery, D.C. 1980. 'The Emergence and Growth of Industrial Research in American Manufacturing 1899–1946', PhD dissertation, Stanford University.

Mowery, D.C. 1983. The relationship between intrafirm and contractual forms of industrial research in American manufacturing 1900–1940, *Explorations in Economic History*, Vol. 20, No. 4, October.

National Science Foundation 1973. *Interactions of Science and Technology in the Innovative Process*, NSF-667, Washington, DC.

Nelson, R.R. (ed.) 1962. *The Rate and Direction of Innovative Activity: Economic and Social Factors*, Princeton, Princeton University Press for the National Bureau of Economic Research.

Nelson, R.R. (ed.) 1993. *National Innovation Systems: A Comparative Analysis*, Oxford, Oxford University Press.

OECD 1963a. *The Measurement of Scientific and Technical Activities* (Frascati Manual), Paris, OECD.

OECD 1963b. *Science, Economic Growth and Government Policy*, Paris, OECD.

OECD 1971. *Science, Growth and Society*, (Brooks Report), Paris, OECD.

OECD 1980. *Technical Change and Economic Policy*, Paris, OECD.

OECD 1988. *New Technologies in the 1990s: A Socio-Economic Strategy* (Sundqvist Report), Paris, OECD.

OECD 1991. *Technology and Productivity: The Challenges for Economic Policy*, Paris, OECD.

OECD 1992. *Technology and the Economy: The Key Relationships*, Paris, OECD.

Ohmae, K. 1990. *The Borderless World*, New York, Harper.

Patel, P. 1993. 'Localised Production of Technology for Global Markets', mimeo, SPRU, University of Sussex.

Patel, P. and Pavitt, K. 1991. Large firms in the production of the world's technology: an important case of 'non-globalisation', *Journal of International Business Studies*, Vol. 22, No. 1.

Patel, P. and Pavitt, K. 1992. The innovative performance of the world's largest firms: some new evidence, *Economics of Innovation and New Technology*, Vol. 2, 91–102.

Paulinyi, A. 1982. Der technologietransfer für die Metallbearbeitung und die preussische Gewerbeförderung 1820–1850, in F. Blaich (ed.), *Die Rolle des Staates für die wirtschaftliche Entwicklung*, Berlin, Blaich.

Perez, C. 1983. Structural change and the assimilation of new technologies in the economic and social system, *Futures*, Vol. 15, No. 5.

Piore, M. and Sabel, C. 1984. *The Second Industrial Divide: Possibilities for Prosperity*, New York, Basic Books.

Porter, M.E. 1990. *The Competitive Advantage of Nations*, New York, Free Press, Macmillan.

Posner, M. 1961. International trade and technical change, *Oxford Economic Papers*, Vol. 13, 323–341.

Prais, S.J. 1981. Vocational qualifications of the labour force in Britain and Germany, *National Institute Economic Review*, Vol. 98, 47–59.

Romer, P. 1986. Increasing returns and long-run growth, *Journal of Political Economy*, Vol. 94, No. 5.

Rothwell, R. 1992. 'Successful Industrial Innovation: Critical Factors for the 1990s', SPRU 25th Anniversary, Brighton, University of Sussex, reprinted in *R&D Management*, Vol. 22, No. 3.

Sako, M. 1992. *Contracts, Prices and Trust: How the Japanese and British Manage Their Sub-contracting Relationships*, Oxford, Oxford University Press.

Saxenian, A. 1991. The origins and dynamics of production networks in Silicon Valley, *Research Policy*, Vol. 20, No. 5.

Scott, A.J. 1991. The aerospace–electronics industrial complex of Southern California: the formative years 1940–1960, *Research Policy*, Vol. 20, No. 5.

Stokes, D.E. 1993. 'Pasteur's Quadrant: A Study in Policy Science Ideas', mimeo, Princeton University.

Storper, M. and Harrison, B. 1991. Flexibility, hierarchy and regional development: the changing structure of industrial production systems and their forms of governance in the 1990s, *Research Policy*, Vol. 20, No. 5.

Takeuchi, H. and Nonaka, I. 1986. The new product development game, *Harvard Business Review*, January/February, 285–305.

Villaschi, A.F. 1993. 'The Brazilian National System of Innovation: Opportunities and Constraints for Transforming Technological Dependency' DPhil. thesis, University of London.

von Hippel, E. 1976. The dominant role of users in the scientific instrument innovation process, *Research Policy*, Vol. 5, 212–239.

von Hippel, E. 1988. *The Sources of Innovation*, Oxford, Oxford University Press.

von Tunzelmann, N. 1994. Technology in the early nineteenth century, in R.C. Floud and D.N. McCloskey (eds), *The Economic History of Great Britain*, Vol. 1, 2nd edn, Cambridge, Cambridge University Press.

Womack, J., Jones, D. and Roos, D. 1990. *The Machine that Changed the World*, New York, Rawson Associates (Macmillan).

World Bank 1991. *World Development Report*, New York, Oxford University Press.

C HAPTER 9

The Competitive Advantage of Nations

MICHAEL E. PORTER*

N ational prosperity is created, not inherited. It does not grow out of a country's natural endowments, its labor pool, its interest rates, or its currency's value, as classical economics insists.

A nation's competitiveness depends on the capacity of its industry to innovate and upgrade. Companies gain advantage against the world's best competitors because of pressure and challenge. They benefit from having strong domestic rivals, aggressive home-based suppliers, and demanding local customers.

In a world of increasingly global competition, nations have become more, not less, important. As the basis of competition has shifted more and more to the creation and assimilation of knowledge, the role of the nation has grown. Competitive advantage is created and sustained through a highly localized process. Differences in national values, culture, economic structures, institutions, and histories all contribute to competitive success. There are striking differences in the patterns of competitiveness in every country; no nation can or will be competitive in every or even most industries. Ultimately, nations succeed in particular industries because their home environment is the most forward-looking, dynamic, and challenging.

These conclusions, the product of a four-year study of the patterns of competitive success in ten leading trading nations, contradict the conventional wisdom that guides the thinking of many companies and national governments – and that is pervasive today in the United States. [...] According to prevailing thinking, labor costs, interest rates, exchange rates, and economies of scale are the most potent determinants of competitiveness. In companies, the words of the day are merger, alliances, strategic partnerships, collaboration, and supra-national globalization. Managers are pressing for more government support for particular industries. Among governments, there is a growing tendency to experiment with various policies intended to promote national competitiveness – from efforts to manage exchange rates to new measures to manage trade to policies to relax antitrust – which usually end up only undermining it. (See Appendix A: 'What is National Competitiveness?')

These approaches, now much in favor in both companies and governments, are flawed. They fundamentally misperceive the true sources of competitive advantage. Pursuing them, with all their short-term appeal, will virtually guarantee that the United States – or any other advanced nation – never achieves real and sustainable competitive advantage.

We need a new perspective and new tools – an approach to competitiveness that grows directly out of an analysis of internationally successful industries, without regard for traditional ideology or current intellectual fashion. We need to know, very simply, what works and why. Then we need to apply it.

How companies succeed in international markets

Around the world, companies that have achieved international leadership employ strategies that differ from each other in every respect. But while every successful company will employ its own particular strategy, the underlying mode of operation – the character and trajectory of all successful companies – is fundamentally the same.

Companies achieve competitive advantage through acts of innovation. They approach innovation in its broadest sense, including both new technologies and new ways of doing things. They perceive a new basis for competing or find better means for competing in old ways. Innovation can be manifested in a new product design, a new production process, a new marketing approach, or a new way of conducting training. Much innovation is mundane and incremental, depending more on a cumulation of small insights and advances than on a single, major technological breakthrough. It often involves ideas that are not even 'new' – ideas that have been around, but never vigorously pursued. It always involves investments in skill and knowledge, as well as in physical assets and brand reputations.

Some innovations create competitive advantage by perceiving an entirely new market opportunity or by serving a market segment that others have ignored. When competitors are slow to respond, such innovation yields competitive advantage. For instance, in industries such as autos and home electronics, Japanese companies gained their initial advantage by emphasizing smaller, more compact, lower capacity models that foreign competitors disdained as less profitable, less important, and less attractive.

In international markets, innovations that yield competitive advantage anticipate both domestic and foreign needs. For example, as international concern for product safety has grown, Swedish companies like Volvo, Atlas Copco, and AGA have succeeded by anticipating the market opportunity in this area. On the other hand, innovations that respond to concerns or circumstances that are peculiar to the home market can actually retard international competitive success. The lure of the huge U.S. defense market, for instance, has diverted the attention of U.S. materials and machine-tool companies from attractive, global commercial markets.

Information plays a large role in the process of innovation and improvement – information that either is not available to competitors or that they do not seek. Sometimes it comes from simple investment in research and development or market research; more often, it comes from effort and from openness and from looking in the right place unencumbered by blinding assumptions or conventional wisdom.

That is why innovators are often outsiders from a different industry or a different country. Innovation may come from a new company, whose founder has a nontraditional background or was simply not appreciated in an older, established company. Or the capacity for innovation may come into an existing company through senior managers who are new to the particular industry and thus more able to perceive opportunities and more likely to pursue them. Or innovation may occur as a company diversifies, bringing new resources, skills, or perspectives to another industry. Or innovations may come from another nation with different circumstances or different ways of competing.

With few exceptions, innovation is the result of unusual effort. The company that successfully implements a new or better way of competing pursues its approach with dogged determination, often in the face of harsh criticism and tough obstacles. In fact, to succeed, innovation usually requires pressure, necessity, and even adversity: the fear of loss often proves more powerful than the hope of gain.

Once a company achieves competitive advantage through an innovation, it can sustain it only through relentless improvement. Almost any advantage can be imitated. Korean companies have already matched the ability of their Japanese rivals to mass-produce standard color televisions and VCRs; Brazilian companies have assembled technology and designs comparable to Italian competitors in casual leather footwear.

Competitors will eventually and inevitably overtake any company that stops improving and innovating. Sometimes early-mover advantages such as customer relationships, scale economies in existing technologies, or the loyalty of distribution channels are enough to permit a stagnant company to retain its entrenched position for years or even decades. But sooner or later, more dynamic rivals will find a way to innovate around these advantages or create a better or cheaper way of doing things. Italian appliance producers, which competed successfully on the basis of cost in selling midsize and compact appliances through large retail chains, rested too long on this initial advantage. By developing more differentiated products and creating strong brand franchises, German competitors have begun to gain ground.

Ultimately, the only way to sustain a competitive advantage is to *upgrade it* – to move to more sophisticated types. This is precisely what Japanese automakers have done. They initially penetrated foreign markets with small, inexpensive compact cars of adequate quality and competed on the basis of lower labor costs. Even while their labor-cost advantage persisted, however, the Japanese companies were upgrading. They invested aggressively to build large modern plants to reap economies of scale. Then they became innovators in process technology, pioneering just-in-time production and a host of other quality and productivity practices. These process improvements led to better product quality, better repair records, and better customer-satisfaction ratings than foreign competitors had. Most recently, Japanese automakers have advanced to the vanguard of product technology and are introducing new, premium brand names to compete with the world's most prestigious passenger cars.

The example of the Japanese automakers also illustrates two additional prerequisites for sustaining competitive advantage. First, a company must adopt a global approach to strategy. It must sell its product worldwide, under its own brand name, through international marketing channels that it controls. A truly global approach may even require the company to locate production or R&D facilities in other nations to take advantage of lower wage rates, to gain or improve market access, or to take advantage of foreign technology. Second, creating more sustainable advantages often means that a company must make its existing advantage obsolete – even while it is still an advantage. Japanese auto companies recognized this; either they would make their advantage obsolete, or a competitor would do it for them.

As this example suggests, innovation and change are inextricably tied together. But change is an unnatural act, particularly in successful companies; powerful forces are at work to avoid and defeat it. Past approaches become institutionalized in standard operating procedures and management controls. Training emphasizes the one correct way to do anything; the construction of specialized, dedicated facilities solidifies past practice into expensive brick and mortar; the existing strategy takes on an aura of invincibility and becomes rooted in the company culture.

Successful companies tend to develop a bias for predictability and stability; they work on defending what they have. Change is tempered by the fear that there is much to lose. The organization at all levels filters out information that would suggest new approaches, modifications, or departures from the norm. The internal environment operates like an immune system to isolate or expel 'hostile' individuals who challenge current directions or established thinking. Innovation ceases; the company becomes stagnant; it is only a matter of time before aggressive competitors overtake it.

The diamond of national advantage

Why are certain companies based in certain nations capable of consistent innovation? Why do they ruthlessly pursue improvements, seeking an evermore sophisticated source of competitive advantage? Why are they able to overcome the substantial barriers to change and innovation that so often accompany success?

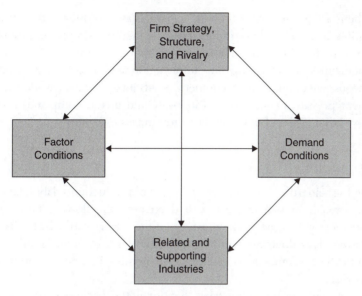

Figure 9.1 *Determinants of national competitive advantage*

The answer lies in four broad attributes of a nation, attributes that individually and as a system constitute the diamond of national advantage, the playing field that each nation establishes and operates for its industries. These attributes are as follows:

1. *Factor Conditions*. The nation's position in factors of production, such as skilled labor or infrastructure, necessary to compete in a given industry.

2. *Demand Conditions*. The nature of home-market demand for the industry's product or service.

3. *Related and Supporting Industries*. The presence or absence in the nation of supplier industries and other related industries that are internationally competitive.

4. *Firm Strategy, Structure, Rivalry.* The conditions in the nation governing how companies are created, organized, and managed, as well as the nature of domestic rivalry.

These determinants create the national environment in which companies are born and learn how to compete (see Figure 9.1). Each point on the diamond – and the diamond as a system – affects essential ingredients for achieving international competitive success: the availability of resources and skills necessary for competitive advantage in an industry; the information that shapes the opportunities that companies perceive and the directions in which they deploy their resources and skills; the goals of the owners, managers, and individuals in companies; and, most important, the pressures on companies to invest and innovate. (See Appendix B: 'How the Diamond Works: The Italian Ceramic Tile Industry.')

When a national environment permits and supports the most rapid accumulation of specialized assets and skills – sometimes simply because of greater effort and commitment – companies gain a competitive advantage. When a national environment affords better ongoing information and insight into product and process needs, companies gain a competitive advantage. Finally, when the national environment pressures companies to innovate and invest, companies both gain a competitive advantage and upgrade those advantages over time.

Factor conditions

According to standard economic theory, factors of production – labor, land, natural resources, capital, infrastructure – will determine the flow of trade. A nation will export those goods that make most use of the factors with which it is relatively well endowed. This doctrine, whose origins date back to Adam Smith and David Ricardo and which is embedded in classical economics, is at best incomplete and at worst incorrect.

In the sophisticated industries that form the backbone of any advanced economy, a nation does not inherit but instead creates the most important factors of production – such as skilled human resources or a scientific base. Moreover, the stock of factors that a nation enjoys at a particular time is less important than the rate and efficiency with which it creates, upgrades, and deploys them in particular industries.

The most important factors of production are those that involve sustained and heavy investment and are specialized. Basic factors, such as a pool of labor or a local raw-material source, do not constitute an advantage in knowledge-intensive industries. Companies can access them easily through a global strategy or circumvent them through technology. Contrary to conventional wisdom, simply having a general workforce that is high school- or even college-educated represents no competitive advantage in modern international competition. To support competitive advantage, a factor must be highly specialized to an industry's particular needs – a scientific institute specialized in optics, a pool of venture capital to fund software companies. These factors are more scarce, more difficult for foreign competitors to imitate – and they require sustained investment to create.

Nations succeed in industries where they are particularly good at factor creation. Competitive advantage results from the presence of world-class institutions that first create specialized factors and then continually work to upgrade them. Denmark has two hospitals that concentrate in studying and treating diabetes – and a world-leading export position in insulin. Holland has premier research institutes in the cultivation, packaging, and shipping of flowers, where it is the world's export leader.

What is not so obvious, however, is that selective disadvantages in the more basic factors can prod a company to innovate and upgrade – a disadvantage in a static model of competition can become an advantage in a dynamic one. When there is an ample supply of cheap raw materials or abundant labor, companies can simply rest on these advantages and often deploy them inefficiently. But when companies face a selective disadvantage, like high land costs, labor shortages, or the lack of local raw materials, they *must* innovate and upgrade to compete.

Implicit in the oft-repeated Japanese statement, 'We are an island nation with no natural resources,' is the understanding that these deficiencies have only served to spur Japan's competitive innovation. Just-in-time production, for example, economized on prohibitively expensive space. Italian steel producers in the Brescia area faced a similar set of disadvantages: high capital costs, high energy costs, and no local raw materials. Located in Northern Lombardy, these privately owned companies faced staggering logistics costs due to their distance from southern ports and the inefficiencies of the state-owned Italian transportation system. The result: they pioneered technologically advanced minimills that require only modest capital investment, use less energy, employ scrap metal as the feedstock, are efficient at small scale, and permit producers to locate close to sources of scrap and end-use customers. In other words, they converted factor disadvantages into competitive advantage.

Disadvantages can become advantages only under certain conditions. First, they must send companies proper signals about circumstances that will spread to other nations, thereby equipping them to innovate in advance of foreign rivals. Switzerland, the nation that experienced the first labor shortages after World War II, is a case in point. Swiss companies responded to the disadvantage by upgrading labor productivity and seeking higher value, more sustainable market segments. Companies in most other parts of the world, where there were still ample workers, focused their attention on other issues, which resulted in slower upgrading.

The second condition for transforming disadvantages into advantages is favorable circumstances elsewhere in the diamond – a consideration that applies to almost all determinants. To innovate, companies must have access to people with appropriate skills and have home-demand conditions that send the right signals. They must also have active domestic rivals who create pressure to innovate. Another precondition is company goals that lead to sustained commitment to the industry. Without such a commitment and the presence of active rivalry, a company may take an easy way around a disadvantage rather than using it as a spur to innovation.

For example, U.S. consumer-electronics companies, faced with high relative labor costs, chose to leave the product and production process largely unchanged and move labor-intensive activities to Taiwan and other Asian countries. Instead of upgrading their sources of advantage, they settled for labor-cost parity. On the other hand, Japanese rivals, confronted with intense domestic competition and a mature home market, chose to eliminate labor through automation. This led to lower assembly costs, to products with fewer components and to improved quality and reliability. Soon Japanese companies were building assembly plants in the United States – the place U.S. companies had fled.

Demand conditions

It might seem that the globalization of competition would diminish the importance of home demand. In practice, however, this is simply not the case. In fact, the composition and character of the home market usually has a disproportionate effect on how companies perceive, interpret, and respond to buyer needs. Nations gain competitive advantage in industries where the home demand gives their companies a clearer or earlier picture of emerging buyer needs, and where demanding buyers pressure companies to innovate faster and achieve more sophisticated competitive advantages than their foreign rivals. The size of home demand proves far less significant than the character of home demand.

Home-demand conditions help build competitive advantage when a particular industry segment is larger or more visible in the domestic market than in foreign markets. The larger market segments in a nation receive the most attention from the nation's companies; companies accord smaller or less desirable segments a lower priority. A good example is hydraulic excavators, which represent the most widely used type of construction equipment in the Japanese domestic market – but which comprise a far smaller proportion of the market in other advanced nations. This segment is one of the few where there are vigorous Japanese international competitors and where caterpillar does not hold a substantial share of the world market.

More important than the mix of segments per se is the nature of domestic buyers. A nation's companies gain competitive advantage if domestic buyers are the world's most sophisticated and demanding buyers for the product or service. Sophisticated, demanding buyers provide a window into advanced customer needs; they pressure companies to meet high standards; they prod them to improve, to innovate, and to upgrade into more advanced segments. As with factor conditions, demand conditions provide advantages by forcing companies to respond to tough challenges.

Especially stringent needs arise because of local values and circumstances. For example, Japanese consumers, who live in small, tightly packed homes, must contend with hot, humid summers and high-cost electrical energy – a daunting combination of circumstances. In response, Japanese companies have pioneered compact, quiet air-conditioning units powered by energy-saving rotary compressors. In industry after industry, the tightly constrained requirements of the Japanese market have forced companies to innovate, yielding products that are *kei-haku-tan-sho* – light, thin, short, small – and that are internationally accepted.

Local buyers can help a nation's companies gain advantage if their needs anticipate or even shape those of other nations – if their needs provide ongoing 'early-warning indicators' of global market trends. Sometimes anticipatory needs emerge because a nation's political values foreshadow needs that will grow elsewhere. Sweden's long-standing concern for handicapped people has spawned an increasingly competitive industry focused on special needs. Denmark's environmentalism has led to success for companies in water-pollution control equipment and windmills.

More generally, a nation's companies can anticipate global trends if the nation's values are spreading – that is, if the country is exporting its values and tastes as well as its products. The international success of U.S. companies in fast food and credit cards, for example, reflects not only the American desire for convenience but also the spread of these tastes to the rest of the world. Nations export their values and tastes through media, through training foreigners, through political influence, and through the foreign activities of their citizens and companies.

Related and supporting industries

The third broad determinant of national advantage is the presence in the nation of related and supporting industries that are internationally competitive. Internationally competitive home-based suppliers create advantages in downstream industries in several ways. First, they deliver the most cost-effective inputs in an efficient, early, rapid, and sometimes preferential way. Italian gold and silver jewelry companies lead the world in that industry in part because other Italian companies supply two-thirds of the world's jewelry-making and precious-metal recycling machinery.

Far more significant than mere access to components and machinery, however, is the advantage that home-based related and supporting industries provide in innovation and upgrading – an advantage based on close working relationships. Suppliers and end -users located near each other can take advantage of short lines of communication, quick and constant flow of information, and on ongoing exchange of ideas and innovations. Companies have the opportunity to influence their suppliers' technical efforts and can serve as test sites for R&D work, accelerating the pace of innovation.

The illustration of 'The Italian Footwear Cluster' (Figure 9.2) offers a graphic example of how a group of close-by, supporting industries creates competitive advantage in a range of interconnected industries that are all internationally competitive. Shoe producers, for instance, interact regularly with leather manufacturers on new styles and manufacturing techniques and learn about new textures and colors of leather when they are still on the drawing boards. Leather manufacturers gain early insights into fashion trends, helping them to plan new products. The interaction is mutually advantageous and self-reinforcing, but it does not happen automatically: it is helped by proximity, but occurs only because companies and suppliers work at it.

The nation's companies benefit most when the suppliers are, themselves, global competitors. It is ultimately self-defeating for a company or country to create 'captive' suppliers who are totally dependent on the domestic industry and prevented from serving foreign competitors. By the same token, a nation need not be competitive in all supplier industries for its companies to gain competitive advantage. Companies can readily source from abroad materials, components, or technologies without a major effect on innovation or performance of the industry's

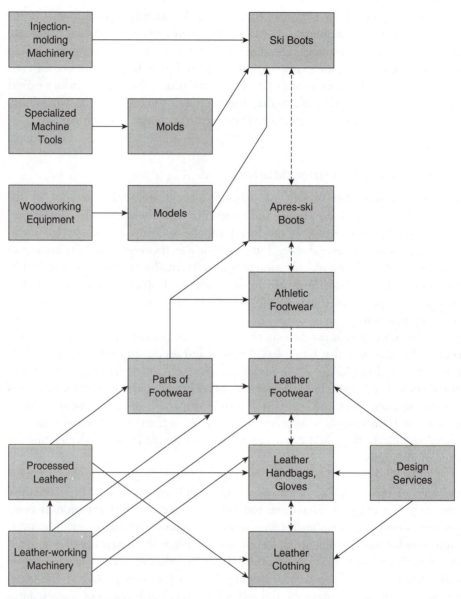

Figure 9.2 *The Italian footwear cluster*

products. The same is true of other generalized technologies – like electronics or software – where the industry represents a narrow application area.

Home-based competitiveness in related industries provides similar benefits: information flow and technical interchange speed the rate of innovation and upgrading. A home-based related industry also increases the likelihood that companies will embrace new skills, and it also provides a source of entrants who will bring a novel approach to competing. The Swiss success in pharmaceuticals emerged out of previous international success in the dye industry, for example; Japanese dominance in electronic musical keyboards grows out of success in acoustic instruments combined with a strong position in consumer electronics.

Firm strategy, structure, and rivalry

National circumstances and context create strong tendencies in how companies are created, organized, and managed, as well as what the nature of domestic rivalry will be. In Italy, for example, successful international competitors are often small or medium-sized companies that are privately owned and operated like extended families; in Germany, in contrast, companies tend to be strictly hierarchical in organization and management practices, and top managers usually have technical backgrounds.

No one managerial system is universally appropriate – notwithstanding the current fascination with Japanese management. Competitiveness in a specific industry results from convergence of the management practices and organizational modes favored in the country and the sources of competitive advantage in the industry. In industries where Italian companies are world leaders – such as lighting, furniture, footwear, woolen fabrics, and packaging machines – a company strategy that emphasizes focus, customized products, niche marketing, rapid change, and breathtaking flexibility fits both the dynamics of the industry and the character of the Italian management system. The German management system, in contrast, works well in technical or engineering-oriented industries – optics, chemicals, complicated machinery – where complex products demand precision manufacturing, a careful development process, after-sale service, and thus a highly disciplined management structure. German success is much rarer in consumer goods and services where image marketing and rapid new-feature and model turnover are important to competition.

Countries also differ markedly in the goals that companies and individuals seek to achieve. Company goals reflect the characteristics of national capital markets and the compensation practices for managers. For example, in Germany and Switzerland, where banks comprise a substantial part of the nation's shareholders, most shares are held for long-term appreciation and are rarely traded. Companies do well in mature industries, where ongoing investment in R&D and new facilities is essential but returns may be only moderate. The United States is at the opposite extreme, with a large pool of risk capital but widespread trading of public companies and a strong emphasis by investors on quarterly and annual share-price appreciation. Management compensation is heavily based on annual bonuses tied to individual results. America does well in relatively new industries, like software and biotechnology, or ones where equity funding of new companies feeds active domestic rivalry, like specialty electronics and services. Strong pressures leading to underinvestment, however, plague more mature industries.

Individual motivation to work and expand skills is also important to competitive advantage. Outstanding talent is a scarce resource in any nation. A nation's success largely depends on the types of education its talented people choose, where they choose to work, and their commitment and effort. The goals a nation's institutions and values set for individuals and companies, and the prestige it attaches to certain industries, guide the flow of capital and human resources – which, in turn, directly affects the competitive performance of certain industries. Nations tend to be competitive in activities that people admire or depend on – the activities from which the nation's heroes emerge. In Switzerland, it is banking and pharmaceuticals. In Israel, the highest callings have been agriculture and defense-related fields. Sometimes it is hard to distinguish between cause and effect. Attaining international success can make an industry prestigious, reinforcing its advantage.

The presence of strong local rivals is a final, and powerful, stimulus to the creation and persistence of competitive advantage. This is true of small countries, like Switzerland, where the rivalry among its pharmaceutical companies, Hoffmann-La Roche, Ciba-Geigy, and Sandoz, contributes to a leading worldwide position. It is true in the United States in the computer and software industries. Nowhere is the role of fierce rivalry more apparent than in Japan, where there are 112 companies competing in machine tools, 34 in semiconductors, 25 in audio equipment, 15 in cameras – in fact, there are usually double figures in the industries in which Japan boasts global dominance (see Table 9.1). Among all the points on the diamond, domestic rivalry is arguably the most important because of the powerfully stimulating effect it has on all the others.

Conventional wisdom argues that domestic competition is wasteful: it leads to duplication of effort and prevents companies from achieving economies of scale. The 'right solution' is to embrace one or two national champions, companies with the scale and strength to tackle foreign competitors, and to guarantee them the necessary resources, with the government's blessing. In fact, however, most national champions are uncompetitive, although heavily subsidized and protected by their government. In many of the prominent industries in which there is only one national rival, such as aerospace and telecommunications, government has played a large role in distorting competition.

Static efficiency is much less important than dynamic improvement, which domestic rivalry uniquely spurs. Domestic rivalry, like any rivalry, creates pressure on companies to innovate and improve. Local rivals push each other to lower costs, improve quality and service, and create new products and processes. But unlike rivalries with foreign competitors, which tend to be analytical and distant, local rivalries often go beyond pure economic or business competition and become intensely personal. Domestic rivals engage in active feuds; they compete not only for market share but also for people, for technical excellence, and perhaps most important, for 'bragging rights.' One domestic rival's success proves to others that advancement is possible and often attracts new rivals to the industry. Companies often attribute the success of foreign rivals to 'unfair' advantages. With domestic rivals, there are no excuses.

Geographic concentration magnifies the power of domestic rivalry. This pattern is strikingly common around the world: Italian jewelry companies are located around two towns, Arezzo and Valenza Po; cutlery companies in Solingen,

Table 9.1   *Estimated number of Japanese rivals in selected industries*

Air conditioners	13
Audio equipment	25
Automobiles	9
Cameras	15
Car audio	12
Carbon fibres	7
Construction equipment*	15
Copiers	14
Facsimile machines	10
Large-scale computers	6
Lift trucks	8
Machine tools	112
Microwave equipment	5
Motorcycles	4
Musical instruments	4
Personal computers	16
Semiconductors	34
Sewing machines	20
Shipbuilding†	33
Steel‡	5
Synthetic fibers	8
Television sets	15
Truck and bus tires	5
Trucks	11
Typewriters	14
Videocassette recorders	10

*The number of companies varied by product area. The smallest number, 10, produced bulldozers. Fifteen companies produced shovel trucks, truck cranes, and asphalt-paving equipment. There were 20 companies in hydraulic excavators, a product area where Japan was particularly strong
† Six companies had annual production exports in excess of 10,000 tons
‡ Integrated companies
Sources: Field interviews; *Nippon Kogyo Shinbun, Nippon Kogyo Nenkan,* 1987; Yano Research, *Market Share Jitan,* 1987; researchers' estimates

West Germany and Seki, Japan; pharmaceutical companies in Basel, Switzerland; motorcycles and musical instruments in Hamamatsu, Japan. The more localized the rivalry, the more intense. And the more intense, the better.

Another benefit of domestic rivalry is the pressure it creates for constant upgrading of the sources of competitive advantage. The presence of domestic competitors automatically cancels the types of advantage that come from simply being in a particular nation – factor costs, access to or preference in the home market, or costs to foreign competitors who import into the market. Companies are forced to move beyond them, and as a result, gain more sustainable advantages. Moreover, competing domestic rivals will keep each other honest in obtaining government support. Companies are less likely to get hooked on the narcotic of government contracts or creeping industry protectionism. Instead, the industry will seek – and benefit from – more constructive forms of government support, such as assistance in opening foreign markets, as well as investments in focused educational institutions or other specialized factors.

Ironically, it is also vigorous domestic competition that ultimately pressures domestic companies to look at global markets and toughens them to succeed in them. Particularly when there are economies of scale, local competitors force each other to look outward to foreign markets to capture greater efficiency and higher profitability. And having been tested by fierce domestic competition, the stronger companies are well equipped to win abroad. If Digital Equipment can hold its own against IBM, Data General, Prime, and Hewlett-Packard, going up against Siemens or Machines Bull does not seem so daunting a prospect.

The diamond as a system

Each of these four attributes defines a point on the diamond of national advantage; the effect of one point often depends on the state of others. Sophisticated buyers will not translate into advanced products, for example, unless the quality of human resources permits companies to meet buyer needs. Selective disadvantages in factors of production will not motivate innovation unless rivalry is vigorous and company goals support sustained investment. At the broadest level, weaknesses in any one determinant will constrain an industry's potential for advancement and upgrading.

But the points of the diamond are also self-reinforcing: they constitute a system. Two elements, domestic rivalry and geographic concentration, have especially great power to transform the diamond into a system – domestic rivalry because it promotes improvement in all the other determinants, and geographic concentration because it elevates and magnifies the interaction of the four separate influences.

The role of domestic rivalry illustrates how the diamond operates as a self-reinforcing system. Vigorous domestic rivalry stimulates the development of unique pools of specialized factors, particularly if the rivals are all located in one city or region: the University of California at Davis has become the world's leading center of wine-making research, working closely with the California wine industry. Active local rivals also upgrade domestic demand in an industry. In furniture and shoes, for example, Italian consumers have learned to expect more and better products because of the rapid pace of new product development that is driven by intense domestic rivalry among hundreds of Italian companies. Domestic rivalry also promotes the formation of related and supporting industries. Japan's world-leading group of semiconductor producers, for instance, has spawned world-leading Japanese semiconductor-equipment manufactures.

The effects can work in all directions: sometimes world-class suppliers become new entrants in the industry they have been supplying. Or highly sophisticated buyers may themselves enter a supplier industry, particularly when they have relevant skills and view the new industry as strategic. In the case of the

Japanese robotics industry, for example, Matsushita and Kawasaki originally designed robots for internal use before beginning to sell robots to others. Today they are strong competitors in the robotics industry. In Sweden, Sandvik moved from specialty steel into rock drills, and SKF moved from specialty steel into ball bearings.

Another effect of the diamond's systemic nature is that nations are rarely home to just one competitive industry; rather, the diamond creates an environment that promotes *clusters* of competitive industries. Competitive industries are not scattered helter-skelter throughout the economy but are usually linked together through vertical (buyer–seller) or horizontal (common customers, technology, channels) relationships. Nor are clusters usually scattered physically; they tend to be concentrated geographically. One competitive industry helps to create another in a mutually reinforcing process. Japan's strength in consumer electronics, for example, drove its success in semiconductors toward the memory chips and integrated circuits these products use. Japanese strength in laptop computers, which contrasts with limited success in other segments, reflects the base of strength in other compact, portable products and leading expertise in liquid-crystal display gained in the calculator and watch industries.

Once a cluster forms, the whole group of industries becomes mutually supporting. Benefits flow forward, backward, and horizontally. Aggressive rivalry in one industry spreads to others in the cluster, through spin-offs, through the exercise of bargaining power, and through diversification by established companies. Entry from other industries within the cluster spurs upgrading by stimulating diversity in R&D approaches and facilitating the introduction of new strategies and skills. Through the conduits of suppliers or customers who have contact with multiple competitors, information flows freely and innovations diffuse rapidly. Interconnections within the cluster, often unanticipated, lead to perceptions of new ways of competing and new opportunities. The cluster becomes a vehicle for maintaining diversity and overcoming the inward focus, inertia, inflexibility, and accommodation among rivals that slows or blocks competitive upgrading and new entry.

The role of government

In the continuing debate over the competitiveness of nations, no topic engenders more argument or creates less understanding than the role of the government. Many see government as an essential helper or supporter of industry, employing a host of policies to contribute directly to the competitive performance of strategic or target industries. Others accept the 'free market' view that the operation of the economy should be left to the workings of the invisible hand.

Both views are incorrect. Either, followed to its logical outcome, would lead to the permanent erosion of a country's competitive capabilities. On one hand, advocates of government help for industry frequently propose policies that would actually hurt companies in the long run and only create the demand for more helping. On the other hand, advocates of a diminished government presence ignore the legitimate role that government plays in shaping the context and institutional structure surrounding companies and in creating an environment that stimulates companies to gain competitive advantage.

Government's proper role is as a catalyst and challenger; it is to encourage – or even push – companies to raise their aspirations and move to higher levels of competitive performance, even though this process may be inherently unpleasant and difficult. Government cannot create competitive industries; only companies can do that. Government plays a role that is inherently partial, that succeeds only when working in tandem with favorable underlying conditions in the diamond. Still, government's role of transmitting and amplifying the forces of the diamond is a powerful one. Government policies that succeed are those that create an environment in which companies can gain competitive advantage rather than those that involve government directly in the process, except in nations early in the development process. It is an indirect, rather than a direct, role.

Japan's government, at its best, understands this role better than anyone – including the point that nations pass through stages of competitive development and that government's appropriate role shifts as the economy progresses. By stimulating early demand for advanced products, confronting industries with the need to pioneer frontier technology through symbolic cooperative projects, establishing prizes that reward quality, and pursuing other policies that magnify the forces of the diamond, the Japanese government accelerates the pace of innovation. But like government officials anywhere, at their worst Japanese bureaucrats can make the same mistakes: attempting to manage industry structure, protecting the market too long, and yielding to political pressure to insulate inefficient retailers, farmers, distributors, and industrial companies from competition.

It is not hard to understand why so many governments make the same mistakes so often in pursuit of national competitiveness: competitive time for companies and political time for governments are fundamentally at odds. It often takes more than a decade for an industry to create competitive advantage; the process entails the long upgrading of human skills, investing in products and processes, building clusters, and penetrating foreign markets. In the case of the Japanese auto industry, for instance, companies made their first faltering steps toward exporting in the 1950s – yet did not achieve strong international positions until the 1970s.

But in politics, a decade is an eternity. Consequently, most governments favor policies that offer easily perceived short-term benefits, such as subsidies, protection, and arranged mergers – the very policies that retard innovation. Most of the policies that would make a real difference either are too slow and require too much patience for politicians or, even worse, carry with them the sting of short-term pain. Deregulating a protected industry, for example, will lead to bankruptcies sooner and to stronger, more competitive companies only later.

Policies that convey static, short-term cost advantages but that unconsciously undermine innovation and dynamism represent the most common and most profound error in government industrial policy. In a desire to help, it is all too easy for governments to adopt policies such as joint projects to avoid 'wasteful' R&D that undermine dynamism and competition. Yet even a 10 per cent cost saving through economies of scale is easily nullified through rapid product and process improvement and the pursuit of volume in global markets – something that such policies undermine.

There are some simple, basic principles that governments should embrace to play the proper supportive role for national competitiveness: encourage change, promote domestic rivalry, stimulate innovation. Some of the specific policy approaches to guide nations seeking to gain competitive advantage include the following:

Focus on specialized factor creation

Government has critical responsibilities for fundamentals like the primary and secondary education systems, basic national infrastructure, and research in areas of broad national concern such as health care. Yet these kinds of generalized efforts at factor creation rarely produce competitive advantage. Rather, the factors that translate into competitive advantage are advanced, specialized, and tied to specific industries or industry groups. Mechanisms such as specialized apprenticeship programs, research efforts in universities connected with an industry, trade association activities, and, most important, the private investments of companies ultimately create the factors that will yield competitive advantage.

Avoid intervening in factor and currency markets

By intervening in factor and currency markets, governments hope to create lower factor costs or a favorable exchange rate that will help companies compete more effectively in international markets. Evidence from around the world indicates that these policies – such as the Reagan administration's dollar devaluation – are often counterproductive. They work against the upgrading of industry and the search for more sustainable competitive advantage.

The contrasting case of Japan is particularly instructive, although both Germany and Switzerland have had similar experiences. Over the past 20 years, the Japanese have been rocked by the sudden Nixon currency devaluation shock, two oil shocks, and most recently, the yen shock – all of which forced Japanese companies to upgrade their competitive advantages. The point is not that government should pursue policies that intentionally drive up factor costs or the exchange rate. Rather, when market forces create rising factor costs or a higher exchange rate, government should resist the temptation to push them back down.

Enforce strict product, safety, and environmental standards

Strict government regulations can promote competitive advantage by stimulating and upgrading domestic demand. Stringent standards for product performance, product safety, and environmental impact pressure companies to improve quality, upgrade technology, and provide features that respond to consumer and social demands. Easing standards, however tempting, is counterproductive.

When tough regulations anticipate standards that will spread internationally, they give a nation's companies a head start in developing products and services that will be valuable elsewhere. Sweden's strict standards for environmental protection have promoted competitive advantage in many industries. Atlas Copco, for example, produces quiet compressors that can be used in dense urban areas with minimal disruption to residents. Strict standards, however, must be combined with a rapid and streamlined regulatory process that does not absorb resources and cause delays.

Sharply limit direct cooperation among industry rivals

The most pervasive global policy fad in the competitiveness arena today is the call for more cooperative research and industry consortia. Operating on the belief that independent research by rivals is wasteful and duplicative, that collaborative efforts achieve economies of scale, and that individual companies are likely to underinvest in R&D because they cannot reap all the benefits, governments have embraced the idea of more direct cooperation. In the United States, antitrust laws have been modified to allow more cooperative R&D; in Europe, mega-projects such as ESPRIT, an information-technology project, bring together companies from several countries. Lurking behind much of this thinking is the fascination of Western governments with – and fundamental misunderstanding of – the countless cooperative research projects sponsored by the Ministry of International Trade and Industry (MITI), projects that appear to have contributed to Japan's competitive rise.

But a closer look at Japanese cooperative projects suggests a different story. Japanese companies participate in MITI projects to maintain good relations with MITI, to preserve their corporate images, and to hedge the risk that competitors will gain from the project – largely defensive reasons. Companies rarely contribute their best scientists and engineers to cooperative projects and usually spend much more on their own private research in the same field. Typically, the government makes only a modest financial contribution to the project.

The real value of Japanese cooperative research is to signal the importance of emerging technical areas and to stimulate proprietary company research. Cooperative projects prompt companies to explore new fields and boost internal R&D spending because companies know that their domestic rivals are investigating them.

Under certain limited conditions, cooperative research can prove beneficial. Projects should be in areas of basic product and process research, not in subjects closely connected to a company's proprietary sources of advantage. They should constitute only a modest portion of a company's overall research program in any given field. Cooperative research should be only indirect, channeled through independent organizations to which most industry participants have access. Organizational structures, like university labs and centers of excellence, reduce management problems and minimize the risk to rivalry. Finally, the most useful cooperative projects often involve fields that touch a number of industries and that require substantial R&D investments.

Promote goals that lead to sustained investment

Government has a vital role in shaping the goals of investors, managers, and employees through policies in various areas. The manner in which capital markets are regulated, for example, shapes the incentives of investors and, in turn, the behavior of companies. Government should aim to encourage sustained investment in human skills, in innovation, and in physical assets. Perhaps the single most powerful tool for raising the rate of sustained investment in industry is a tax incentive for long-term (five years or more) capital gains restricted to new investment in corporate equity. Long-term capital gains incentives should also be applied to pension funds and other currently untaxed investors, who now have few reasons not to engage in rapid trading.

Deregulate competition

Regulation of competition through such policies as maintaining a state monopoly, controlling entry into an industry, or fixing prices has two strong negative consequences: it stifles rivalry and innovation as companies become preoccupied with dealing with regulators and protecting what they already have; and it makes the industry a less dynamic and less desirable buyer or supplier. Deregulation and privatization on their own, however, will not succeed without vigorous domestic rivalry – and that requires, as a corollary, a strong and consistent antitrust policy.

Enforce strong domestic antitrust policies

A strong antitrust policy – especially for horizontal mergers, alliances, and collusive behavior – is fundamental to innovation. While it is fashionable today to call for mergers and alliances in the name of globalization and the creation of national champions, these often undermine the creation of competitive advantage. Real national competitiveness requires governments to disallow mergers, acquisitions, and alliances that involve industry leaders. Furthermore, the same standards for mergers and alliances should apply to both domestic and foreign companies. Finally, government policy should favor internal entry, both domestic and international, over acquisition. Companies should, however, be allowed to acquire small companies in related industries when the move promotes the transfer of skills that could ultimately create competitive advantage.

Reject managed trade

Managed trade represents a growing and dangerous tendency for dealing with the fallout of national competitiveness. Orderly marketing agreements, voluntary restraint agreements, or other devices that set quantitative targets to divide up markets are dangerous, ineffective, and often enormously costly to consumers. Rather than promoting innovation in a nation's industries, managed trade guarantees a market for inefficient companies.

Government trade policy should pursue open market access in every foreign nation. To be effective, trade policy should not be a passive instrument; it cannot respond only to complaints or work only for those industries that can muster enough political clout; it should not require a long history of injury or serve only distressed industries. Trade policy should seek to open markets wherever a nation has competitive advantage and should actively address emerging industries and incipient problems.

Where government finds a trade barrier in another nation, it should concentrate its remedies on dismantling barriers, not on regulating imports or exports. In the case of Japan, for example, pressure to accelerate the already rapid growth of manufactured imports is a more effective approach than a shift to managed trade. Compensatory tariffs that punish companies for unfair trade practices are better than market quotas. Other increasingly important tools to open markets are restrictions that prevent companies in offending nations from investing in acquisitions or production facilities in the host country – thereby blocking the unfair country's companies from using their advantage to establish a new beachhead that is immune from sanctions.

Any of these remedies, however, can backfire. It is virtually impossible to craft remedies to unfair trade practices that avoid both reducing incentives for domestic companies to innovate and export and harming domestic buyers. The aim of remedies should be adjustments that allow the remedy to disappear.

The company agenda

Ultimately, only companies themselves can achieve and sustain competitive advantage. To do so, they must act on the fundamentals described above. In particular, they must recognize the central role of innovation – and the uncomfortable truth that innovation grows out of pressure and challenge. It takes leadership to create a dynamic, challenging environment. And it takes leadership to recognize the all-too-easy escape routes that appear to offer a path to competitive advantage, but are actually short-cuts to failure. For example, it is tempting to rely on cooperative research and development projects to lower the cost and risk of research. But they can divert company attention and resources from proprietary research efforts and will all but eliminate the prospects for real innovation.

Competitive advantage arises from leadership that harnesses and amplifies the forces in the diamond to promote innovation and upgrading. Here are just a few of the kinds of company policies that will support that effort:

Create pressures for innovation

A company should seek out pressure and challenge, not avoid them. Part of strategy is to take advantage of the home nation to create the impetus for innovation. To do that, companies can sell to the most sophisticated and demanding buyers and channels; seek out those buyers with the most difficult needs; establish norms that exceed the toughest regulatory hurdles or product standards; source from the most advanced suppliers; treat employees as permanent in order to stimulate upgrading of skills and productivity.

Seek out the most capable competitors as motivators

To motivate organizational change, capable competitors and respected rivals can be a common enemy. The best managers always run a little scared; they respect and study competitors. To stay dynamic, companies must make meeting challenge a part of the organization's norms. For example, lobbying against strict product standards signals the organization that company leadership has diminished aspirations. Companies that value stability, obedient customers, dependent suppliers, and sleepy competitors are inviting inertia and, ultimately, failure.

Establish early-warning systems

Early-warning signals translate into early-mover advantages. Companies can take actions that help them see the signals of change and act on them, thereby getting a jump on the competition. For example, they can find and serve those buyers with the most anticipatory needs; investigate all emerging new buyers or channels; find places whose regulations foreshadow emerging regulations elsewhere; bring some outsiders into the management team; maintain ongoing relationships with research centers and sources of talented people.

Improve the national diamond

Companies have a vital stake in making their home environment a better platform for international success. Part of a company's responsibility is to play an active role in forming clusters and to work with its home-nation buyers, suppliers, and channels to help them upgrade and extend their own competitive advantages. To upgrade home demand, for example, Japanese musical instrument manufacturers, led by Yamaha, Kawai, and Suzuki, have established music schools. Similarly, companies can stimulate and support local suppliers of important specialized inputs – including encouraging them to compete globally. The health and strength of the national cluster will only enhance the company's own rate of innovation and upgrading.

In nearly every successful competitive industry, leading companies also take explicit steps to create specialized factors like human resources, scientific knowledge, or infrastructure. In industries like wool cloth, ceramic tiles, and lighting equipment, Italian industry associations invest in market information, process technology, and common infrastructure. Companies can also speed innovation by putting their headquarters and other key operations where there are concentrations of sophisticated buyers, important suppliers, or specialized factor-creating mechanisms, such as universities or laboratories.

Welcome domestic rivalry

To compete globally, a company needs capable domestic rivals and vigorous domestic rivalry. Especially in the United States and Europe today, managers are wont to complain about excessive competition and to argue for mergers and acquisitions that will produce hoped-for economies of scale and critical mass. The complaint is only natural – but the argument is plain wrong. Vigorous domestic rivalry creates sustainable competitive advantage. Moreover, it is better to grow internationally than to dominate the domestic market. If a company wants an acquisition, a foreign one that can speed globalization and supplement home-based advantages or offset home-based disadvantages is usually far better than merging with leading domestic competitors.

Globalize to tap selective advantages in other nations

In search of 'global' strategies, many companies today abandon their home diamond. To be sure, adopting a global perspective is important to creating competitive advantage. But relying on foreign activities that supplant domestic capabilities is always a second-best solution. Innovating to offset local factor disadvantages is better than outsourcing; developing domestic suppliers and buyers is better than relying solely on foreign ones. Unless the critical underpinnings of competitiveness are present at home, companies will not sustain competitive advantage in the long run. The aim should be to upgrade home-base capabilities so that foreign activities are selective and supplemental only to over-all competitive advantage.

The correct approach to globalization is to tap selectively into sources of advantage in other nations' diamonds. For example, identifying sophisticated buyers in other countries helps companies understand different needs and creates pressures that will stimulate a faster rate of innovation. No matter how favorable the home diamond, moreover, important research is going on in other nations. To take advantage of foreign research, companies must station high-quality people in overseas bases and mount a credible level of scientific effort. To get any thing back from foreign research ventures, companies must also allow access to their own ideas – recognizing that competitive advantage comes from continuous improvement, not from protecting today's secrets.

Use alliances only selectively

Alliances with foreign companies have become another managerial fad and cure-all: they represent a tempting solution to the problem of a company wanting the advantages of foreign enterprises or hedging against risk, without giving up independence. In reality, however, while alliances can achieve selective benefits, they always exact significant costs: they involve coordinating two separate operations, reconciling goals with an independent entity, creating a competitor, and giving up profits. These costs ultimately make most alliances short-term transitional devices, rather than stable, long-term relationships.

Most important, alliances as a broad-based strategy will only ensure a company's mediocrity, not its international leadership. No company can rely on another outside, independent company for skills and assets that are central to its competitive advantage. Alliances are best used as a selective tool, employed on a temporary basis or involving noncore activities.

Locate the home base to support competitive advantage

Among the most important decisions for multinational companies is the nation in which to locate the home base for each distinct business. A company can have different home bases for distinct businesses or segments. Ultimately, competitive advantage is created at home: it is where strategy is set, the core product and process technology is created, and a critical mass of production takes place. The circumstances in the home nation must support innovation; otherwise the company has no choice but to move its home base to a country that stimulates innovation and that provides the best environment for global competitiveness. There are no half-measures: the management team must move as well.

The role of leadership

Too many companies and top managers misperceive the nature of competition and the task before them by focusing on improving financial performance, soliciting government assistance, seeking stability, and reducing risk through alliances and mergers.

Today's competitive realities demand leadership. Leaders believe in change; they energize their organizations to innovate continuously, they recognize the importance of their home country as integral to their competitive success and work to upgrade it. Most important, leaders recognize the need for pressure and challenge. Because they are willing to encourage appropriate – and painful – government policies and regulations, they often earn the title 'statesmen,' although few see themselves that way. They are prepared to sacrifice the easy life for difficulty and, ultimately, sustained competitive advantage. That must be the goal, for both nations and companies: not just surviving, but achieving international competitiveness.

And not just once, but continuously.

Author's note

Michael J. Enright, who served as project coordinator for this study, has contributed valuable suggestions.

Appendix A:
What is national competitiveness?

National competitiveness has become one of the central preoccupations of government and industry in every nation. Yet for all the discussion, debate, and writing on the topic, there is still no persuasive theory to explain national competitiveness. What is more, there is not even an accepted definition of the term 'competitiveness' as applied to a nation. While the notion of a competitive company is clear, the notion of a competitive nation is not.

Some see national competitiveness as a macro-economic phenomenon, driven by variables such as exchange rates, interest rates, and government deficits. But Japan, Italy, and South Korea have all enjoyed rapidly rising living standards despite budget deficits; Germany and Switzerland despite appreciating currencies; and Italy and Korea despite high interest rates.

Others argue that competitiveness is a function of cheap and abundant labor. But Germany, Switzerland, and Sweden have all prospered even with high wages and labor shortages. Besides, shouldn't a nation seek higher wages for its workers as a goal of competitiveness?

Another view connects competitiveness with bountiful natural resources. But how, then, can one explain the success of Germany, Japan, Switzerland, Italy, and South Korea – countries with limited natural resources?

More recently, the argument has gained favor that competitiveness is driven by government policy: targeting, protection, import promotion, and subsidies have propelled Japanese and South Korean auto, steel, shipbuilding, and semiconductor industries into global preeminence. But a closer look reveals a spotty record. In Italy, government intervention has been ineffectual – but Italy has experienced a boom in world export share second only to Japan. In Germany, direct government intervention in exporting industries is rare. And even in Japan and South Korea, government's role in such important industries as facsimile machines, copiers, robotics, and advanced materials has been modest; some of the most frequently cited examples, such as sewing machines, steel, and shipbuilding, are now quite dated.

A final popular explanation for national competitiveness is differences in management practices, including management–labor relations. The problem here, however, is that different industries require different approaches to management. The successful management practices governing small, private, and loosely organized Italian family companies in footwear, textiles, and jewelry, for example, would produce a management disaster if applied to German chemical or auto companies, Swiss pharmaceutical makers, or American aircraft producers. Nor is it possible to generalize about management–labor relations. Despite the commonly held view that powerful unions undermine competitive advantage, unions are strong in Germany and Sweden – and both countries boast internationally preeminent companies.

Clearly, none of these explanations is fully satisfactory; none is sufficient by itself to rationalize the competitive position of industries within a national border. Each contains some truth; but a broader, more complex set of forces seems to be at work.

The lack of a clear explanation signals an even more fundamental question. What is a 'competitive' nation in the first place? Is a 'competitive' nation one where every company or industry is competitive? No nation meets this test. Even Japan has large sectors of its economy that fall far behind the world's best competitors.

Is a 'competitive' nation one whose exchange rate makes its goods price competitive in international markets? Both Germany and Japan have enjoyed remarkable gains in their standards of living – and experienced sustained periods of strong currency and rising prices. Is a 'competitive' nation one with a large positive balance of trade? Switzerland has roughly balanced trade; Italy has a chronic trade deficit – both nations enjoy strongly rising national income. Is a 'competitive' nation one with low labor costs? India and Mexico both have low wages and low labor costs – but neither seems an attractive industrial model.

The only meaningful concept of competitiveness at the national level is *productivity*. The principal goal of a nation is to produce a high and rising standard of living for its citizens. The ability to do so depends on the productivity with which a nation's labor and capital are employed. Productivity is the value of the output produced by a unit of labor or capital. Productivity depends on both the quality and features of products (which determine the prices that they can command) and the efficiency with which they are produced. Productivity is the prime determinant of a nation's long-run standard of living; it is the root cause of national per capita income. The productivity of human resources determines employee wages; the productivity with which capital is employed determines the return it earns for its holders.

A nation's standard of living depends on the capacity of its companies to achieve high levels of productivity – and to increase productivity over time. Sustained productivity growth requires that an economy continually *upgrade itself*.

A nation's companies must relentlessly improve productivity in existing industries by raising product quality, adding desirable features, improving product technology, or boosting production efficiency. They must develop the necessary capabilities to compete in more and more sophisticated industry segments, where productivity is generally high. They must finally develop the capability to compete in entirely new, sophisticated industries.

International trade and foreign investment can both improve a nation's productivity as well as threaten it. They support rising national productivity by allowing a nation to specialize in those industries and segments of industries where its companies are more productive and to import where its companies are less productive. No nation can be competitive in everything. The ideal is to deploy the nation's limited pool of human and other resources into the most productive uses. Even those nations with the highest standards of living have many industries in which local companies are uncompetitive.

Yet international trade and foreign investment also can threaten productivity growth. They expose a nation's industries to the test of international standards of productivity. An industry will lose out if its productivity is not sufficiently higher than foreign rivals' to offset any advantages in local wage rates. If a nation loses the ability to compete in a range of high-productivity/high-wage industries, its standard of living is threatened.

Defining national competitiveness as achieving a trade surplus or balanced trade per se is inappropriate. The expansion of exports because of low wages and a weak currency, at the same time that the nation imports sophisticated goods that its companies cannot produce competitively, may bring trade into balance or surplus but lowers the nation's standard of living. Competitiveness also does not mean jobs. It's the *type* of job, not just the ability to employ citizens at low wages, that is decisive for economic prosperity.

Seeking to explain 'competitiveness' at the national level, then, is to answer the wrong question. What we must understand instead is the determinants of productivity and the rate of productivity growth. To find answers, we must focus not on the economy as a whole but on *specific industries and industry segments*. We must understand how and why commercially viable skills and technology are created, which can only be fully understood at the level of particular industries. It is the outcome of the thousands of struggles for competitive advantage against foreign rivals in particular segments and industries, in which products and processes are created and improved, that underpins the process of upgrading national productivity.

When one looks closely at any national economy, there are striking differences among a nation's industries in competitive success. International advantage is often concentrated in particular industry segments. German exports of cars are heavily skewed toward high-performance cars, while Korean exports are all compacts and subcompacts. In many industries and segments of industries, the competitors with true international competitive advantage are *based in only a few nations*.

Our search, then, is for the decisive characteristic of a nation that allows its companies to create and sustain competitive advantage in particular fields – the search is for the competitive advantage of nations. We are particularly concerned with the determinants of international success in technology – and skill-intensive segments and industries, which underpin high and rising productivity.

Classical theory explains the success of nations in particular industries based on so-called factors of production such as land, labor, and natural resources. Nations gain factor-based comparative advantage in industries that make intensive use of the factors they possess in abundance. Classical theory, however, has been overshadowed in advanced industries and economies by the globalization of competition and the power of technology.

A new theory must recognize that in modern international competition, companies compete with global strategies involving not only trade but also foreign investment. What a new theory must explain is why a nation provides a favorable *home base* for companies that compete internationally. The home base is the nation in which the essential competitive advantages of the enterprise are created and sustained. It is where a company's strategy is set, where the core product and process technology is created and maintained, and where the most productive jobs and most advanced skills are located. The presence of the home base in a nation has the greatest positive influence on other linked domestic industries and leads to other benefits in the nation's economy. While the ownership of the company is often concentrated at the home base, the nationality of shareholders is secondary.

A new theory must move beyond comparative advantage to the competitive advantage of a nation. It must reflect a rich conception of competition that includes segmented markets, differentiated products, technology differences, and economies of scale. A new theory must go beyond cost and explain why companies from some nations are better than others at creating advantages based on quality, features, and new product innovation. A new theory must begin from the premise that competition is dynamic and evolving; it must answer the questions: Why do some companies based in some nations innovate more than others? Why do some nations provide an environment that enables companies to improve and innovate faster than foreign rivals?

Appendix B: How the diamond works: the Italian ceramic tile industry

In 1987, Italian companies were world leaders in the production and export of ceramic tiles, a $10 billion industry. Italian producers, concentrated in and around the small town of Sassuolo in the Emilia-Romagna region, accounted for about 30% of world production and almost 60% of world exports. The Italian trade surplus that year in ceramic tiles was about $1.4 billion.

The development of the Italian ceramic tile industry's competitive advantage illustrates how the diamond of national advantage works. Sassuolo's sustainable competitive advantage in ceramic tiles grew not from any static or historical advantage but from dynamism and change. Sophisticated and demanding local buyers, strong and unique distribution channels, and intense rivalry among local companies created constant pressure for innovation. Knowledge grew quickly from continuous experimentation and cumulative production experience. Private ownership of the companies and loyalty to the community spawned intense commitment to invest in the industry.

Tile producers benefited as well from a highly developed set of local machinery suppliers and other supporting industries, producing materials, services, and infrastructure. The presence of world-class, Italian-related industries also reinforced Italian strength in tiles. Finally, the geographic concentration of the entire cluster supercharged the whole process. Today foreign companies compete against an entire subculture. The organic nature of this system represents the most sustainable advantage of Sassuolo's ceramic tile companies.

The origins of the Italian industry

Tile production in Sassuolo grew out of the earthenware and crockery industry, whose history traces back to the thirteenth century. Immediately after World War II, there were only a handful of ceramic tile manufacturers in and around Sassuolo, all serving the local market exclusively.

Demand for ceramic tiles within Italy began to grow dramatically in the immediate postwar years, as the reconstruction of Italy triggered a boom in building materials of all kinds. Italian demand for ceramic tiles was particularly great due to the climate, local tastes, and building techniques.

Because Sassuolo was in a relatively prosperous part of Italy, there were many who could combine the modest amount of capital and necessary organizational skills to start a tile company. In 1955, there were 14 Sassuolo area tile companies; by 1962, there were 102.

The new tile companies benefited from a local pool of mechanically trained workers. The region around Sassuolo was home to Ferrari, Maserati, Lamborghini, and other technically sophisticated companies. As the tile industry began to grow and prosper, many engineers and skilled workers gravitated to the successful companies.

The emerging Italian tile cluster

Initially, Italian tile producers were dependent on foreign sources of raw materials and production technology. In the 1950s, the principal raw materials used to make tiles were kaolin (white) clays. Since there were red- but no white-clay deposits near Sassuolo. Italian producers had to import the clays from the United Kingdom. Tile-making equipment was also imported in the 1950s and 1960s: kilns from Germany, America, and France; presses for forming tiles from Germany. Sassuolo tile makers had to import even simple glazing machines.

Over time, the Italian tile producers learned how to modify imported equipment to fit local circumstances: red versus white clays, natural gas versus heavy oil. As process technicians from tile companies left to start their own equipment companies, a local machinery industry arose in Sassuolo. By 1970, Italian companies had emerged as world-class producers of kilns and presses; the earlier situation had exactly reversed: they were exporting their red-clay equipment for foreigners to use with white clays.

The relationship between Italian tile and equipment manufacturers was a mutually supporting one, made even more so by close proximity. In the mid-1980s, there were some 200 Italian equipment manufacturers; more than 60% were located in the Sassuolo area. The equipment manufacturers competed fiercely for local business, and tile manufacturers benefited from better prices and more advanced equipment than their foreign rivals.

As the emerging tile cluster grew and concentrated in the Sassuolo region, a pool of skilled workers and technicians developed, including engineers, production specialists, maintenance workers, service technicians, and design personnel. The industry's geographic concentration encouraged other supporting companies to form, offering molds, packaging materials, glazes, and transportation services. An array of small, specialized consulting companies emerged to give advice to tile producers on plant design, logistics, and commercial, advertising, and fiscal matters.

With its membership concentrated in the Sassuolo area, Assopiastrelle, the ceramic tile industry association, began offering services in areas of common interest: bulk purchasing, foreign-market research, and consulting on fiscal and legal matters. The growing tile cluster stimulated the formation of a new, specialized factor-creating institution: in 1976, a consortium of the University of Bologna, regional agencies, and the ceramic industry association founded the Centro Ceramico di Bologna, which conducted process research and product analysis.

Sophisticated home demand

By the mid-1960s, per-capita tile consumption in Italy was considerably higher than in the rest of the world. The Italian market was also the world's most sophisticated. Italian customers, who were generally the first to adopt new designs and features, and Italian producers, who constantly innovated to improve manufacturing methods and create new designs, progressed in a mutually reinforcing process.

The uniquely sophisticated character of domestic demand also extended to retail outlets. In the 1960s, specialized tile showrooms began opening in Italy. By 1985, there were roughly 7,600 specialized showrooms handling approximately 80% of domestic sales, far more than in other nations. In 1976, the Italian company Piemme introduced tiles by famous designers to gain distribution outlets and to build brand name awareness among consumers. This innovation drew on another related industry, design services, in which Italy was world leader, with over $10 billion in exports.

Sassuolo rivalry

The sheer number of tile companies in the Sassuolo area created intense rivalry. News of product and process innovations spread rapidly, and companies seeking technological, design, and distribution leadership had to improve constantly.

Proximity added a personal note to the intense rivalry. All of the producers were privately held, most were family-run. The owners all lived in the same area, knew each other, and were the leading citizens of the same towns.

Pressures to upgrade

In the early 1970s, faced with intense domestic rivalry, pressure from retail customers, and the shock of the 1973 energy crisis, Italian tile companies struggled to reduce gas and labor costs. These efforts led to a technological breakthrough, the rapid single-firing process, in which the hardening process, material transformation, and glaze-fixing all occurred in one pass through the kiln. A process that took 225 employees using the double-firing method needed only 90 employees using single-firing roller kilns. Cycle time dropped from 16 to 20 hours to only 50 to 55 minutes.

The new, smaller, and lighter equipment was also easier to export. By the early 1980s, exports from Italian equipment manufacturers exceeded domestic sales; in 1988, exports represented almost 80% of total sales.

Working together, tile manufacturers and equipment manufacturers made the next important breakthrough during the mid- and late 1970s: the development of materials-handling equipment that transformed tile manufacture from a batch process to a continuous process. The innovation reduced high labor costs – which had been a substantial selective factor disadvantage facing Italian tile manufacturers.

The common perception is that Italian labor costs were lower during this period than those in the United States and Germany. In those two countries, however, different jobs had widely different wages. In Italy, wages for different skill categories were compressed, and work rules constrained manufacturers from using overtime or multiple shifts. The restriction proved costly: once cool, kilns are expensive to reheat and are best run continuously. Because of this factor disadvantage, the Italian companies were the first to develop continuous, automated production.

Internationalization

By 1970, Italian domestic demand had matured. The stagnant Italian market led companies to step up their efforts to pursue foreign markets. The presence of related and supporting Italian industries helped in the export drive. Individual tile manufacturers began advertising in Italian and foreign home-design and architectural magazines, publications with wide global circulation among architects, designers, and consumers. This heightened awareness reinforced the quality image of Italian tiles. Tile makers were also able to capitalize on Italy's leading world export positions in related industries like marble, building stone, sinks, washbasins, furniture, lamps, and home appliances.

Assopiastrelle, the industry association, established trade-promotion offices in the United States in 1980, in Germany in 1984, and in France in 1987. It organized elaborate trade shows in cities ranging from Bologna to Miami and ran sophisticated advertising. Between 1980 and 1987, the association spent roughly $8 million to promote Italian tiles in the United States.

— *Michael J. Enright and Paolo Tenti*

C HAPTER 10

Imperfect Markets and Fallible Governments: The Role of the State in Industrial Development

SANJAYA LALL*

1. Introduction

This chapter considers the case of government intervention in promoting industrialization for 'industrial policy'. Industrial policy is not in favour with mainstream economists today, in developing as in formerly socialist and mature industrialized economies. Disillusionment with the ham-fisted and costly interventions associated with import substitution, planning and public-sector-led development, a growing faith in the efficiency of market forces, and a particular interpretation of the success of the Asian Newly Industrializing Economies (NIEs) have produced a powerful case for non-interventionist strategies. This now guides the processes of policy reform that are sweeping the developing world, generally (but by no means exclusively) in the form of structural adjustment programmes.

This approach has a strong foundation in neoclassical theory and in neo-liberal political economy. This chapter argues, however, that it is not justified on either theoretical or empirical grounds. The theoretical case rests on particular assumptions about how industrial efficiency and competitiveness are attained. If these assumptions are relaxed, standard theory can provide a sound case for selective government interventions. The argument that governments are incapable of intervening efficiently is also suspect – in any case the neo-liberal political economy that asserts that governments are inherently inefficient or corruptible is not something on which economics has much to say. The empirical evidence from East Asia shows the efficacy of interventions in the presence of widespread

* Oxford University Press, India for an extract from *Trade and Industrialization* by Deepak Nayyar © S. Lall, 1997.

market failures as well as the ability of governments to act in the national economic interest.

The case for industrial policy does not rest on the simple proposition that perfect competition does not hold: not every market failure calls for intervention. Moreover, mainstream economists accept a role for the government to remedy market failures in defence, law and order and the 'rules of the game'. Most would also accept the need for public provision of infrastructure, certain forms of education, basic science, and so on, where the public goods nature of the activity precludes exclusively private production. This does not constitute a case for industrial policy in the normal sense.

Market imperfections in the industrial sector, like certain forms of oligopolistic competition, uncertainty, some externalities, or proprietary owner-ship of technology, are inherent features of market economies in real life and may not detract from their efficient functioning. In particular, where imperfec-tions are associated with scale economies and Schumpeterian technological growth, the case for official intervention may be negligible: the costs of market failure may, in other words, be outweighed by its benefits. In certain circum-stances, moreover, markets can develop their own efficient institutional or cooperative solutions to perceived failures. Thus the mere existence of market failures is not necessarily a case for industrial policy. Only certain failures call for remedial interventions.

Interventions may only be justified *where market failures significantly retard industrial development, and where market-driven solutions fail, or take too long to emerge*. This case can indeed be made and justified empirically, based on a micro-level analysis of industrial efficiency and dynamism. Section 2 describes the neo-classical approach to this and contrasts it to the 'capability' approach that has evolved in recent years. Section 3 presents the case for interventions in trade and Section 4 for interventions in factor markets. Section 5 draws on the evidence of the East Asian NIEs and other industrializing countries like India to analyse the kinds of intervention that are desirable. Section 6 draws the main conclusions.

2. Approaches to industrial competence

The essence of successful industrial development lies in the ability of individual firms to be technically and managerially efficient. This obvious fact is often ignored in the analysis of industrial policy. The basic contention of this chapter is that dif-ferent approaches to industrial policy have been derived from different conceptuali-zations of the *enterprise-level process of gaining competence and efficiency*. This chapter focuses on the technological rather than the managerial and organizational aspects of efficiency, for which a very similar argument may also be made.

2.1 The neoclassical approach

Neoclassical economics has a clear and simple interpretation of how firms enter industry and grow. In textbook models of the neoclassical firm, an anonymous unit operates in perfectly competitive markets to optimize resource allocation and production.[1] It is assumed to operate with full knowledge of all possible technologies. Given the right (market-determined) prices for inputs and outputs, it picks the one that is appropriate to the factor endowments of the country. All firms in an industry facing the same prices choose the same technologies (otherwise they are allocatively inefficient). The international technology market is assumed to work efficiently, and all firms can buy the right technology 'off the shelf' without costs of search and negotiation. Given that developing countries have to import their industrial technology, they must be fully open to all channels of information inflow (foreign direct investment, licensing, capital goods imports, and so on).

Moreover, all firms can immediately use imported technologies with the same degree of efficiency (at best practice levels). There is no theoretical reason to expect the persistence of technical inefficiency. If such inefficiency exists, it is, *ex hypothesi*, due to managerial negligence or incompetence, and to government interventions that allow inefficient firms to continue in production. In essence, there is no process of *acquiring* technological capabilities (TCs).

Where extra costs of absorbing new technologies in developing countries are admitted, a simplified view of the learning process is taken. The learning curve is believed to be fairly short and predictable: largely confined to 'running in' a new plant until it reaches rated capacity and benefits of automatic learning-by-doing are realized. It is generally assumed that such costs are relatively trivial, predictable, and similar across industries. The learning process is relatively passive (rather than one that involves investment, risk and, in some activities, long maturation periods). Firms know what to do to reach best practice levels. There is consequently no need to devise measures to stimulate the capability to absorb new technologies, or to distinguish between industries in the financing of learning and start-up costs.

Firms are assumed to acquire and use technologies as individual units essentially in isolation. There are no linkages between them, and no externalities resulting from individual efforts to generate skills and information. The development of specialization among firms and industries thus relies on information exchanged in anonymous market transactions. There is no need to create or foster the information networks and institutions that have evolved in advanced industrial economies. Since there are no technological externalities, there is also no need to coordinate investment decisions across activities that may have intense linkages. Nor are some sets of activities more significant for industrial development than others because of externalities: no sector has the claim to be more 'strategic' than another.

It is assumed that firms have the foresight to finance their predictable and fully internalized 'running-in' costs in capital markets. If capital markets are not fully efficient, theory says that the market failure has to be addressed at source rather than by protection or subsidization of the industry. Since no technologies are more difficult, or involve more externalities, than others, there is no need for policy makers to be selective in their promotion of particular industries or technologies. There is also no need to devise different policies by the level of development of the countries in question, since markets are assumed to operate with equal degrees of efficiency. However, some analysts admit that the manufacturing sector as a whole may need some protection because of its externalities in skill creation and the lack of an industrial culture – such protection, if offered, should be uniform, low and limited in duration. This is as much industrial policy as neoclassical development, economists concede. There is no case for selective interventions to promote particular activities and to guide resource allocation.

In this essentially static framework, comparative advantage evolves according to the gradual accumulation of factor endowments, rather than by the deliberate efforts of industrial enterprises. As endowments grow, firms automatically move to the right factor combinations, costlessly absorbing the technologies concerned. If it is admitted that in developing countries some factor apart from markets may not operate efficiently (as with education or technology support), policy interventions may be recommended to support those markets. However, as with protection, this support has to be non-selective or 'market-friendly'.[2] The allocation of resources should not be influenced to encourage particular activities that governments consider desirable.

This approach logically leads to policy prescriptions for non-intervention and market-determined resource allocation in industry. Indeed, if the assumptions about technological learning, information, risk and externalities are accepted, any intervention is bound to be suboptimal. This is the theoretical underpinning of the liberal approach to industrial policy.

2.2 The capabilities approach

The assumption that technology is costlessly absorbed in efficient factor and product markets is an important, but often misleading, simplification. Empirical work in many different developing countries suggests that most industrial technologies are operated at low levels of technical proficiency, and that technical inefficiency is a much larger source of low productivity than allocative inefficiency. The process of selecting, mastering and adapting technology, and later improving upon it, requires the development of new knowledge, skills, organizational forms and interlinkages between enterprises. It is based, in other words, upon the acquisition of new TCs.[3]

Technological capabilities in industry are the information and skills – technical, organizational and institutional – that allow productive enterprises to utilize equipment and information efficiently. Such capabilities are *firm-specific*, a form of institutional knowledge that is made of the combined skills and experience of its members.[4] The development of TCs should not be thought of as the ability to undertake frontier innovation, though innovative capabilities are one form of TC. It comprises a much broader range of effort that every enterprise must itself undertake in order to absorb, adapt and build upon the knowledge that has to be utilized in production. The growth of capabilities may be defined as industrial technology development (ITD); this process is evolutionary, and depends on the conscious and purposive efforts undertaken by every enterprise.

The successful transfer of a new technology to a developing country has to include a major element of capability building: simply providing equipment and operating instructions, patents, designs or blueprints does not ensure that the technology will be properly used.[5] These 'embodied' elements of a technology have to be accompanied by a number of 'tacit' elements that have to be taught and learned. Only when such learning (entailing training, searching for new technical information, and in-house engineering and experimentation[6]) has taken place, and necessary adaptations made to local operating and market conditions, can the technology be considered to be 'mastered' in a static sense. Only then can it be used at or near the best-practice level of technical efficiency for which it was designed. The achievement of flexibility in a dynamic setting, with new technologies, changing market demands and the entry of new competitors, is a process far more complex and demanding.

Technological mastery, in a static or dynamic sense, cannot be an automatic or passive process. In order to successfully absorb and deploy new technical information, prior investments have to be made in human capital and organizational capabilities to 'decode' new technical information, and to incorporate it into manufacturing processes. Technological capability is not, however, simply the sum of the education and training of a firm's employees. It is based on the learning undergone with reference to particular technologies, and depends on the way in which the firm combines all the individual skills to function as an organization.

To some extent, any enterprise that tries to use a new technology acquires some TCs as an automatic result of the production process. Such *passive learning* goes some way towards developing the necessary capabilities. In simple industries, say the assembly of imported kits or garment manufacture for the domestic market, this may be enough for efficiency. Such passive learning is, however, generally insufficient to ensure efficiency as more complex technology is considered, or if more demanding markets are tackled. For more complex industries, to reach even static 'best-practice' levels as established in advanced countries involves an enterprise in a longer and more demanding process, sometimes taking years of production, engineering and research.[7]

Different firms can thus experience quite different rates of technological development and end up with different levels of efficiency in using the same technologies. There is *no predictable learning curve* along which all firms travel. Moreover, in most developing countries the learning process itself may have to be learned.[8] The systematic launching of the training, engineering, search and experimentation process that comprises capability development is generally not understood by the typical entrant to modern manufacturing in developing countries. And even if the need for capability development is recognized, enterprises may not know the best way to go about it: information of this sort cannot be assumed to be widely available in developing countries.

Manufacturing enterprises do not develop capabilities in isolation. They operate, in most industries, in a dense network of formal and informal relationships with suppliers, customers, competitors, consultants, and technology, research and educational institutions. These networks take the form of complex, long-lasting contractual and non-contractual relations. These linkages help individual firms to deal with each other, to gain access to expensive ('lumpy') information and facilities and to create information, skills and standards that all firms need but no individual firm will generate on its own ('public goods'). The case for factor market interventions is discussed below.

In addition, the existence of learning sequences in other firms in the vertical chain of production (suppliers and customers) means that there are strong *technological externalities*.[9] In industries with strong interlinkages (such as most engineering activities), one firm cannot therefore predict the learning process of its suppliers and subcontractors. It cannot, therefore, know its future cost structure or take rational investment decisions in isolation from other firms. Efficient resource allocation then requires an external agent to coordinate individual investments, the classic case for planning. These failures in the factor markets and information systems have important implications for policy.

Finally, while developing countries depend crucially on the *import of technology* and skills from advanced industrial countries, the best policy on technology transfer may not be the completely open and unselective one. There are well-known gaps in information and oligopolistic elements in international technology markets. More importantly, the same technology can be transferred with many different combinations of foreign and local technological effort. The choice of combination is not neutral with respect to effects on long-term technological development. Those that require more local effort, while perhaps more costly in the short term, are likely to improve the potential for future industrialization, because of the externalities and learning benefits that they generate, and the greater linkages with local suppliers of capital goods, engineering services and components they entail. Even the immediate costs of technology transfer are much lower where the recipient has developed absorptive capabilities. The longer-term gains for capability development, for further investments and greater local linkages, may be enormous.[10]

Moreover, given the need for technology import, the mode of technology import can have an effect on local TC development. 'Internalized' modes (like foreign direct investment, where the seller of technology retains ownership and control on the utilization of the technology) tend to centralize the innovation process in developed economies. They transfer, quite efficiently, the *results* of their research to affiliates. In 'externalized' modes (licensing, equipment purchase, arm's length contracts, etc.), the recipient may not get technology as rapidly, and has to do much more homework to absorb and build upon it. Again, this may lead to more technological learning and a better understanding of the technology being transferred. It is generally found that local firms tend to do more design and development activity than affiliates of foreign firms that have full access to their parent companies' network of services, information and skills.

This concludes the description of the process by which firms develop technological capabilities. It is evident that this description can lead to very different, and more complex and differentiated, policy conclusions on how industrialization may be promoted from the standard neoclassical approach. The basic unit of analysis emerges as the individual firm trying to develop capabilities and collect technical information in a world in which markets and factors of production are missing or highly imperfect. The crucial factor that distinguishes the developing country firm from its counterpart in advanced countries is that the former is struggling to learn something that has already been learned in more industrialized countries, and it has to manage with weaker market and institutional support. The costs, risks and processes involved are thus very different.

In this setting, just 'getting prices right' in developing countries may not be sufficient to promote industrial development – it may not even be desirable. Sole reliance on market forces, when market failures are endemic and widespread, may not ensure static efficiency or dynamic growth.

3. The case for interventions in trade

The above analysis allows us to look at the case for interventions in the product and factor markets within which technological learning takes place. There are a number of factors that affect the incentive to invest in TCs: the macroeconomic and political environments, domestic competition and market structures, technical progress, ownership, and so on. We shall not consider these here, since the real debate about the role of industrial policy has focused on interventions in trade. This section thus deals only with the *trade regime*.

It is now generally accepted that classic import-substitution industrialization strategies have been inefficient. The benefits of outward orientation to industrial development are well established and need not be analysed in detail here. The empirical evidence on the relative success of outward orientation over import substitution is overwhelming. We have no dispute with the superiority of Export-Orientation (EO) strategies; what needs analysis is *why* they succeeded, and whether these reasons support the neoclassical interpretation that they approximated free trade. The case is considered in two stages: first, whether there is a sound case for free trade (assuming that export orientation is equivalent to free trade) when some of its assumptions on technological learning are dropped; and, second, whether export-oriented economies actually practised free trade.

There is a clear and powerful case in neoclassical economics for the welfare benefits of free trade, arising from conformance to the comparative advantage that market-determined resource allocation provides. These benefits obtain under assumptions of perfect competition and efficient markets. Once they are relaxed, and a realistic portrayal of the technological learning process accepted, the welfare implications do not necessarily follow.[11] The prolonged, risky, costly and unpredictable nature of learning, with its externalities and information gaps, means that *free market prices cannot guide resource allocation correctly as far as investments in activities with 'difficult' technologies are concerned*. This gives rise to a case for infant industry protection, which may apply also to the temporary protection of existing activities that have to be restructured and upgraded.

The essential feature of industrial investment in developing countries is that they have to create new capabilities to utilize the technologies they import, even if these technologies are well known and used in other countries. This necessarily implies higher costs during the learning period relative to firms elsewhere that have already gone through the learning process. In a completely free market regime, therefore, firms in developing countries may underinvest in activities that have relatively costly learning periods (the relative costs depending on the nature of the technology, the existing level of skills, and the relevant cost advantages, such as cheaper unskilled labour or natural resources, that the developing country may have). Similarly, for existing activities with complex technologies that have not developed competitive capabilities in a protected environment, the 'relearning' of new capabilities takes time. If they are suddenly exposed to world competition, these activities may not be able to restructure and invest in the learning process, and may simply die out. Again, there is a case for protection to help overcome the learning costs.

The case for protection rests on the existence of a number of market failures in a free market that could distort resource allocation, between activities (with low and high learning costs) and within activities (between physical and capability investments). These may create a case for intervention to promote entry into complex activities and/or in capability building. The market failures are well known in the theoretical literature, but are worth mentioning:

- Firms may not be able to appropriate returns on technological investments because trained workers leave or knowledge leaks out (classic externalities of the type noted by Arrow, 1962).

- They may find that their own lack of experience and of supporting suppliers and institutions makes the learning process highly risky and unpredictable.

- They may not realize the need for capability investment to raise efficiency, or, if they do, they may not know how to set about raising capabilities (they have to 'learn to learn').

- They may be unable to anticipate learning in vertically linked suppliers (described above as 'technological' externalities).

- They may not be able to raise the finances to cover their losses during the learning period (capital market failures).

It has to be noted that failures in capital or information markets do not necessarily call for *trade* interventions. Such market failures should be treated at source (in financial or other markets), and offering protection or subsidies to producers can at most be a second-best solution. However, capital market failures are difficult to correct quickly, and in the interim their costs can be reduced by protection or subsidization.[12] Needless to say, simply prolonging this will do nothing to make the enterprise efficient unless measures are also undertaken on the supply side, especially in skill and information markets (see below).

The case for protection in industrial latecomers arising from technological learning has been cogently put by the most powerful advocate of free trade in the history of economic thought: John Stuart Mill. In his *Principles of Political Economy* of 1848, Mill, after a forceful and extended attack on protection, says:

> The only case in which, on mere principles of political economy, protecting duties can be defensible, is when they are imposed temporarily (especially in a young and rising nation) in the hopes of naturalising a foreign industry, in itself perfectly suitable to the circumstances of the country. The superiority of one country over another in a branch of production often arises only from having begun it sooner. There may be no inherent advantage on one part, or disadvantage in another, but only a present superiority of *acquired skill and experience*. A country which has this skill and experience yet to acquire, may in other respects be better adapted to the production than those which were earlier in the field; and besides … nothing has a greater tendency to promote improvements in any branch of production than its trial under a new set of conditions. But it *cannot be expected that individuals should, at their own risk, or rather to their certain loss, introduce a new manufacture, and bear the burden of carrying on until the producers have been educated to the level of those with whom the processes are traditional*. A protective duty, continued for a reasonable time, might sometimes be the least inconvenient mode in which the nation can tax itself for the support of such an experiment. But it is essential that the protection should be confined to cases in which there is good ground for assurance that the industry which it fosters will after a time be able to dispense with it; nor should the domestic producers ever be allowed to expect that it will be continued to them beyond the time necessary for a fair trial of what they are capable of accomplishing.[13]

Once the case for protection is accepted, there is no analytical basis for providing low, uniform rates of effective protection. The duration and extent of protection *cannot be uniform* when different technologies have different learning costs and periods. Complex, skill-intensive technologies necessarily require greater protection than those which have simple processes. The garment industry, for instance, may be able to reach competence in three months, while automobile manufacture may, depending on the level of local content, take ten to fifteen years.[14] Moreover, where there are strong complementarities and externalities between sets of activities resulting from their technical and production linkages, there is a valid case for treating them as a set (of what are often called 'strategic' sectors) and promoting them as a group.[15]

Any case for protection runs up against obvious *dangers*, and the manifest failures of highly protected import-substituting regimes in fostering efficient industries. Clearly, while protection allows industries the resources and grace period to invest in developing capabilities, it takes away the most important incentives to do so. Import-substitution is replete with infant industries that never grew up because there was no competitive pressure to invest in the costly and risky process of capability acquisition. As Mill notes, protection must be limited in duration. And it is possible to offset its disincentive effects by forcing protected industries to enter export markets at early stages (even while maintaining protection). This is the secret of the success of export orientation in East Asia. Entry into complex technologies could be promoted and the learning period subsidized while disciplining the firms and administrators concerned by the imperative to become export-competitive. Without such protection and offsetting measures, the story of East Asia would have been very different.

It has to be noted, moreover, that the learning process can be shorter and less costly for foreign investors who have the knowledge, experience, skills and financial resources to undertake capability development. While 'learning' costs always exist, complex technology may be more readily implemented by multinationals than by local firms. This accounts for the success of the second-tier NIEs in Asia, which have low indigenous capabilities but have attracted export-oriented multinationals from developed countries and the leading NIEs. Does this negate the case for trade interventions?

It does not. Even for countries that wish to depend on MNCs to drive their industrial development, there are many activities where the learning period may be too long and costly for multinationals to finance in free trade conditions.[16] Moreover, as economies move into more sophisticated activities, the need to develop local research capabilities grows simply to absorb new imported technologies. MNCs are generally reluctant to transfer their R&D activities to affiliates in developing countries, though they may do considerable adaptive work in larger countries. They are much better transferors of 'know-how' than of 'know-why'.[17] For countries that wish to develop know-why, therefore, there may be a case for intervening in foreign investment as well as in trade.

There are many countries, more importantly, that have technological ambitions – they do not wish to foster a passive dependence on foreign firms to transfer all the technologies they need or to conduct all sophisticated technological activity in their countries. As with Japan and South Korea, they wish to capture the externalities and dynamic benefits of indigenous innovative capability. In this case, trade strategy becomes necessary not only to allow difficult activities to be started but also, along with technology strategy, to encourage local firms to invest in developing 'know-why' capabilities.

The success of the NIEs has to be re-examined in the context of this analysis of costly learning in industrial development. Clearly, they developed considerable technological capabilities – what role did their governments play in promoting learning and overcoming the market failures that confront capability development? The NIEs intervened a great deal more than conventional wisdom allows, as will be shown in Section 5. Their success was due, not to conformance to efficient free markets, but to their *interventions to remedy imperfect markets by well-directed and selective interventions*. The benefits of export orientation arose not from static benefits to resource allocation, but from *the discipline and incentives it provided that enabled infant industries to be carefully selected and to invest in their capabilities*.[18] This is discussed in greater detail below.

4. Interventions in factor markets

Before this, however, let us deal with factor market interventions. The supply side of capability development essentially deals with the factor markets within which the firm operates. For present purposes, only three of these need be considered: skills, technical effort and finance. Each of these has its own set of private markets, and each may suffer from market failures. Each has, over time, evolved institutional intermediaries to remedy such failures, with the government usually playing a large role in launching the institutions.

4.1 Skills

The human capital needed for industrialization comprises the skills imparted by the formal education and training system, as well as those created by on-the-job training and experience. Less advanced or more specialized firms need a smaller range than those in large-scale and technologically complex industries. But even the simplest technology, if it is to be operated at world levels of efficiency, needs a range of worker, supervisory, maintenance, quality control and adaptive skills. At the lowest end of the technological spectrum, simple literacy and some vocational training, complemented by a few higher-level technical skills, may be sufficient to ensure adequate TCs. In more sophisticated technologies, the requirements are more diverse and the range of special skills wider.

While primary and secondary schooling provide the necessary base for building shop-floor capabilities in all activities, more advanced technical training becomes critical as the industrial structure develops. Since many forms of high-level skills are not fungible (a textile engineer cannot, for example, design electrical equipment), the range of specialization grows with industrial complexity. The education system has to match the skill needs of the industrial structure, not just in the quantity of the people it graduates in different disciplines, but also in the quality of the training and the relevance of the curriculum.

Formal pre-employment education is only one component of the skill creation process. The other is on-the-job training and experience, and also further formal training of employees sponsored by the enterprises. The latter is a rapidly increasing activity among developed-country firms. Most enterprises in developing countries, however, invest relatively little in upgrading the skills of their employees.

This may be due to several market failures. First, there may be an information failure: managers may not be fully aware of the skill needs of the technologies they are using. Or they may be rooted in traditional ways of manufacturing and training (such as the apprenticeship system in Africa) that are unsuited to the needs of modern technologies or to the upgrading of existing technologies.[19] Their own level of education may, in certain cases, make them averse to the further training of employees. Second, there may be missing or deficient markets for the provision of skills and training: managers may realize that employee skills are deficient, but may not be able to remedy this. They may not have access to trainers in-house. Overseas training may be out of the question. And there may be no local institutions, official or private, that can offer the right level and quality of training. Finally, there may be failures caused by the externalities inherent in training: employers may be unsure of recouping the full benefits of their investments. Trained employees may leave the firm, taking the benefits of training to competitors.

The risk of market failures in skill creation is generally accepted. Interventions to promote human capital formation are, however, assumed to be purely functional, i.e. they simply strengthen factor markets without attempting to support some activities over others.[20] This assumption is not always justified. Many forms of educational investments *are* non-selective, providing a general base of skills for all activities: particularly for schooling and non-technical higher education. However, by contrast, more specialized forms of tertiary education and vocational training are highly industry-specific, and policies to address these needs *have necessarily to be selective*. The selectivity of educational policies increases with the role that the government plays in determining the direction of industrial growth. If the government has an active industrial strategy, pushing the economy into selected complex areas of activity, it has to ensure that the necessary skills are created by the education system: selectivity in one sphere necessarily calls for selectivity in all related, supporting spheres. For purposes of industrial strategy, therefore, *interventions in skill markets have to be an integral part of interventions in trade and resource allocation*.

4.2 Technical effort

Most of the technological activity that firms undertake to cope with production problems, cost reduction, diversification, and so on, is an in-house affair. However, the undertaking of such effort may suffer from similar types of market failure as skill formation. Many firms in developing countries do not *know* that they have to undertake deliberate technological effort to resolve those problems. When they wish to undertake the effort, they may not have well-functioning information and technical support services to draw upon. The applied research that industrial firms conduct may need basic research and 'lumpy' testing and other facilities that may not exist in the country. Finally, the returns to investments in technology may be greatly reduced by the danger of losing the knowledge to other firms. Some of these market failures can also lead to underinvestment in technological effort in developed economies, as Arrow's (1962) classic article noted many years ago.

Government interventions in information and technology markets may be needed to remedy such failures. Let us start with technical information and support. Many forms of technical information are available free to firms: from journals, contacts with capital goods suppliers and buyers of export products, visits to fairs, plants and conferences, interactions with subcontractors and other suppliers, and so on. More complex or closely held information is available commercially from consultants, more advanced firms (on licence), or as part of a package of direct investment. There is little need for policy intervention here, except to guide firms to the right sources of information.

Apart from these, however, there are many information and support services that are not provided by the market in any country, especially by markets in developing countries. There are several essential technological functions that have 'public goods' features, whose rewards are difficult to appropriate by private firms and so suffer from market failure. These include the encouragement of technological activity in general (overcoming risk aversion and the 'learning to learn' barrier); the development of special research skills; the setting of industrial standards and the promotion of quality awareness; the provision of metrology (industrial measurement and calibration) services; the undertaking of contract research, testing or information search for firms that lack the facilities or skills; other extension services for small enterprises; and the undertaking and coordination of basic (pre-commercial) research activities. The provision of these services then has to be undertaken as an infrastructural service, or as a cooperative activity by the enterprises concerned.[21]

The public infrastructure for science and technology (S&T) may comprise a variety of institutions, from universities and research-financing bodies to standards institutes and R&D institutions. The efficacy of this infrastructure has been variable. In many developing countries S&T institutions have been inadequately staffed and poorly equipped and funded. In some a lot of money has been invested, but without a proper linkage between the technological needs of industry and the research or promotion work of the institutions. In the poorest and least developed countries, there is no industrial research conducted worth the name, and there is little effective extension work to support small enterprises. In the more advanced countries, the technical extension is somewhat better and some high-quality research is carried out, but most of the latter is divorced from industrial technology. There are exceptions, of course, but on the whole the infrastructure has not served the functions it was set up for.

From the viewpoint of industrial policy, again, interventions in technology markets have to be integrated with interventions in product markets. Industries being promoted *cannot* become efficient unless matching measures are undertaken to provide information and technical support. Yet most discussions of industrial policy fail to take this into account, as do measures to boost industry by liberalization and structural adjustment.

4.3 Finance

Since the development of TCs is an investment involving time and cost, the availability of finance at the appropriate time, in appropriate amounts and at the appropriate price is an important determinant of ITD. Capital market failures can constitute a barrier to capability development, in general terms by retarding the allocation of resources to, or within, manufacturing activity, and in particular by constricting resources for technology development.

Capital markets failures are widespread in developing countries.[22] Some such failures are policy-induced, while others are endemic to weak economic structures. Policies that lead to the arbitrary allocation of credit, repression of interest rates, suppression of competition among intermediaries, inadequate development of capital markets and segmentation among differing markets for finance are common causes of resource misallocation in developing countries. Apart from these policy-induced distortions, financial intermediaries may suffer from inadequate information, especially on small borrowers, and may be exceptionally risk-averse because of problems in collecting sufficient information and enforcing contracts. They may be particularly reluctant to finance technological development because of their lack of knowledge of what it involves (they know even less about it than the firms involved) and the risk inherent in all technological activity. Needless to say, capital market failures are likely to be worse for small and medium-sized enterprises than for large ones.

Industrial policy in many countries has involved the direct participation of governments in the allocation of investment resources, via directed credit, ownership of banks, ownership of industrial enterprises, or the promotion of large private firms that can internalize capital markets. Japan, Taiwan and Korea are the most striking examples of industrial success with such measures. There are also many failures, resulting from ill-chosen activities, lack of incentives to invest in capabilities or the lack of integration of the different elements of intervention (as in India).

This concludes the analysis of the various arguments for interventions in product and factor markets that affect industrial development. It is clear that a realistic analysis of the process of learning in developing country firms takes place in an environment in which many of the markets do not function optimally. The degree of failure depends on the initial conditions of the country and on the complexity of the technologies concerned, and there are innumerable possible strategies that could be adopted to remedy the failures. 'Getting prices right' in the current sense of following *laissez faire* economic policies may not get prices 'right' at all from the viewpoint of long-term resource allocation. It may remove gross distortions imposed by misguided interventions, but it may expose firms to market signals that are not conducive to industrial deepening and diversification.

5. Some country experiences

This section describes the industrial strategies pursued by some important developing countries, to illustrate the above arguments on the need for interventions and the effects of different patterns of intervention on industrial structure and competitiveness. We start with the four East Asian NIEs and go on to deal with a major import-substitution economy that I have some familiarity with: India.

5.1 The East Asian NIEs

There is a large and growing literature now on the role of government interventions in the industrialization of the East Asian NIEs.[23] Apart from the fact that they all adopted export orientation, the most interesting aspect of their experience is that there *is* no single East Asian 'model' of industrial development. There are four separate models for each of the NIEs, differing in significant respects from each other, and yielding different patterns of industry and technological capabilities. These differences are worth considering here because they have important implications for the kind of industrial flexibility that has emerged. These implications will be drawn out as the cases are discussed below.

It is useful to start with background data on some of the variables that are relevant to TC development. Table 10.1 shows the performance of the four NIEs and measures of their education levels, technical effort and reliance on foreign technology in different forms. The data are later compared with those from some least industrialized countries from sub-Saharan Africa to illustrate some of the basic needs for industrial development and flexibility.

At one end is Hong Kong, with a *laissez faire* trade policy that comes closest to the neoclassical paradigm of ideal industrial strategy. It has not intervened in product markets, either to support particular industries or to protect manufacturing in general. It has not guided investments in other ways, by interfering in the allocation of domestic credit or foreign investments. It has provided a stable administrative and macroeconomic regime. Its growth performance has been impressive, if not up to the level of the larger NIEs.

The Hong Kong government did intervene 'functionally' to provide education and training, subsidized land to manufacturers, export information and support services.[24] It set up the Hong Kong Productivity Centre to perform various technological services to help producers improve their technologies. It chose to support the clothing sector by setting up a large and well-funded textile and garments design and training centre. However, its interventions were predominantly non-selective, and there was no strong attempt to 'pick winners': at most, existing exporters were supported. Moreover, even its functional interventions in education, while impressive by Third World standards, were not as intense as those of the larger NIEs.[25] In particular, it lagged behind in the training of scientists and engineers, in vocational training, and in undertaking research and development locally

Table 10.1   *Background data on the East Asian NIEs*[a]

	Hong Kong	Singapore	South Korea	Taiwan
Mfg. growth				
1965–80	17.0	13.3	18.7	16.4
1980–90[b]	3.0	6.6	12.7	6.9
Mfd. Exports (1990)[c] (US $ billion)	27.8	38.4	60.3	62.3
Growth merch. exports				
1965–80	9.1	4.7	27.2	18.9
1980–90	6.2	8.6	12.8	10.3[d]
FDI as percentage of gross				
domestic investment (1957–87)	7	16.8	0.9	3.3
Educational enrolments				
Primary[e]	105	110	108	99
Secondary	73	69	87	94
Tertiary[f] (1989)	13	24	39	31
Teritary enrolment in				
S&T (as percentage of pop.)	0.67	0.89	1.39	1.06
Vocational training				
(per 100,000 pop.)	800	372	1970	2082
R&D (latest)				
Total (percentage GNP)	n.a.	0.9	2.3	1.8
By productive				
enterprises[g] (percentage GNP)	n.a.	0.3	1.9	1.0
Scientists & engineers				
in R&D (per million population)	n.a.	960	1283	1426
R&D (latest)				
Total (percentage GNP)	n.a.	0.9	2.3	1.8
By productive enterprises				
(percentage of GNP)	n.a.	0.3	1.9	1.0

Sources: [a] Lall (1992a); Lall and Kell (1991); Republic of China (Taiwan), *Statistical Yearbook*, 1990, 1992; UNDP, *Human Development Report 1992*; UNESCAP, *Statistical Yearbook for Asia and the Pacific*, 1991; UNIDO, *Industry and Development Global Report, 1992–93;* World Bank, *World Development Report (WDR) 1992.*
[b] Growth rates for Hong Kong and Taiwan calculated from UNIDO data, in constant 1985 US dollars. Rest from *WDR 1992.*
[c] *WDR* figures.
[d] Calculated from Taiwanese official data, in constant US dollars.
[e] Enrolment figures are with reference to populations in the relevant age groups: if enrolments are from other groups, a figure of over 100 per cent is obtained.
[f] Calculated for Hong Kong and Singapore from *UNESCAP Yearbook.* Taiwanese data from official statistics.
[g] R&D financed by productive enterprises.

(though precise data on R&D are not available, all the studies of Hong Kong manufacturing suggest that there is relatively little formal technology development).

Thus the level of intervention was fairly low, and trade was always free. Does this have lessons for other industrializing economies? It does, but not necessarily that *laissez faire* is everywhere the best way to promote competitive manufacturing. Two important features of the Hong Kong experience have to be noted in this context.

First, it started with several unique advantages for industrialization that other developing countries, even free trade centres, lacked. Its century and a half of entrepot trading experience gave it a range of capabilities and infrastructure for trading and finance. The presence of several British business and finance houses (the 'Hongs') provided a constant supply of foreign skills as well as training for local employees. Most important for manufacturing, its textile, garment and toy industries took off only after the communist takeover, when there was an influx of experienced Chinese entrepreneurs, engineers and technicians from Shanghai. Much of the 'learning' for these industries had already been undergone earlier and the technologies were sufficiently simple for subsequent training to be given to a workforce with good primary and secondary education. The free trade environment, combined with existing capabilities in trade and finance and a supply of cheap manpower, enabled these advantages to be fully exploited, mainly by Chinese entrepreneurs. There was considerable foreign investment, but in manufacturing the lead stayed firmly in local hands (in sharp contrast to Singapore, discussed later).

Second, the ensuing pattern of industrialization in Hong Kong reflected the non-selective policies of its government. The colony started and stayed with light labour-intensive manufacturing industry, though within this there was considerable upgrading of quality, a pattern of industrial development driven by the lack of selective interventions to promote more complex industries. Its success was based on the development of operational and marketing capabilities. Despite its dynamism in light industry, however, there was little industrial deepening and diversification. There was little natural progression up the ladder of industrial complexity, into more difficult and demanding technologies. As wage and land pressures mounted, the colony had to relocate its manufacturing to other countries, mainly mainland China, and suffered a significant loss of industrial activity at home (over 1986–92 it lost about 35 per cent of its manufacturing employment, and the process is continuing).[26]

Because of the size, location and history of the colony, this industrialization strategy is not one that may be open to other developing countries as well. Simple recourse to free trade is unlikely to lead to such dynamic industrial growth, and no other free trade centre, of which there are several in the developing world, has achieved much industrial success because even the relatively easy learning required of light industry has not been undergone. Even economies that can attract labour-intensive foreign investments are unlikely to be able to sustain their industrial deepening by 'natural' progression if they do not undertake interventions to promote the move into more complex activities. Reliance on foreign direct investments can reduce some of the learning requirements, but any development of local technological capabilities is bound to need supporting selective interventions.

The Hong Kong manufacturing sector thus has special characteristics that mark it off from the larger NIEs, and from the typical industrialization pattern of most other economies.[27] Its progress consists of moving upmarket in existing light industry and diversifying out of manufacturing altogether, not of taking on the more complex technologies that can enable it to retain a manufacturing base with rising wage costs. By contrast, Switzerland, with a population only 1 million larger than Hong Kong's, retains a growing and deep industrial sector (with chemicals, heavy machinery, food processing, and so on) with much higher wages than Hong Kong. The difference lies precisely in the fact that Switzerland has, with judicious periods of protection, promotion and disregard of intellectual property laws, over the past century built up a deep technological base. The industrial fate of Hong Kong is in essence to deindustrialize while exploiting its industrial capabilities to set up services and overseas facilities, a feature that depends crucially on its location and ability to act as a conduit for the mainland.

The relative lack of depth in its industrial structure has, nevertheless, led to considerable disquiet among Hong Kong's policy makers. As the *Financial Times* notes:

> The *laissez faire* prop against which the Hong Kong government has leaned since 1841 has prevented it from adopting the ambitious strategies that have spawned the computer components and telecommunications products of Singapore, South Korea and Taiwan. But as Hong Kong continues to evolve into a financial and services centre, the pressures of some of the highest land and labour costs in Asia appear to have given the government second thoughts about its stance. ... The government is taking serious measures to encourage the inflow of overseas technologies, so that Hong Kong can retain some kind of industrial base. ... The government has toned down its *laissez faire* inclinations to permit a new applied research and development scheme. This is a $HK 200m. fund, which will match the investment of any start-up company which fulfils certain criteria, in exchange for an equity stake. This represents the first step towards direct government funding for research and development, and by implication, the creation of a Government industrial policy.[28]

South Korea is at the other extreme. Its record of industrial development, in terms of growth, diversification and deepening, is perhaps the most impressive in modern economic history (even more so than Japan's in view of the shorter periods and more adverse initial conditions involved). Its government intervened extensively, both functionally and selectively, in all product and factor markets.[29] It offered high, variable and prolonged periods of protection to selected activities, while forcing those that approached competitiveness to export significant parts of their output. It directed domestic investible resources to infant industries, subsidized credit, and deliberately fostered the emergence of giant private conglomerates that could internalize various imperfect markets. It invested heavily in education, especially technical education,[30] and forced firms to launch employee training schemes; it also invested in R&D and technology infrastructure institutions, while inducing (through subsidies and other incentives) and cajoling local firms to develop their independent research capabilities.[31] All these factor market interventions had highly selective aspects, being integrated into the overall direction of industrial development as driven by trade and industrial policies. The selectivity was based on close interaction between the government, the bureaucracy and the *chaebol*, the giant conglomerates, which acted as interlocutors for industry at large. Industrial policy was based largely on emulating Japan (some twenty years or so later), though it was backed by intense and continuous monitoring of performance, flexibility in implementation and strict disciplining of non-performers.[32]

Perhaps the most interesting aspect of South Korea's industrial success for present purposes is that it was *largely based on indigenous enterprises* that imported and assimilated a range of complex technologies rather than on technology transfer via direct investment. The South Korean government was until very recently highly selective concerning foreign direct investments, and in some instances induced Japanese firms to sell out to the *chaebol* after some years in the country. In technological terms this strategy called for far more domestic skill and technology creation than one that set up the same range of industries but with a heavy reliance on direct foreign investment. South Korea's investments in education and R&D, and the fostering of the giant *chaebol*, were a necessary part of its nationalist strategy, driven by the objective of being efficient in world markets. A strategy of nationalism with inward orientation (like India) would have led to far less efficiency and would consequently have demanded less interventions in supporting factor markets. A strategy of outward orientation with reliance on foreign investors, like Singapore, may have led to less deepening or to lower domestic innovative capabilities.

The fact that South Korea has a research and manufacturing base that is able to copy, adapt and build upon state-of-the-art industrial technologies gives it a competitive capability that is probably unmatched, especially in advanced manufacturing activities. This capability is of a completely different order from that of Hong Kong – *it conduces to sustained industrial expansion rather than prolonged deindustrialization*. It is also different from that of liberalizing economies with diverse industrial economies which are heavily dependent on foreign direct investment (FDI) for technology, like Mexico. Such economies are unable to enter world-class production of new high-technology items of the type that Korea is launching, and their most important industrial exports (automobiles in the case of Mexico) are those that have matured behind long periods of import substitution and can now form part of the global sourcing strategies of multinational companies.

The implication of this is that indigenous research capability has many dynamic benefits for the industries that possess the capability. Apart from significantly lowering the cost of technology transfer, it allows independent diversification into more advanced areas than may be permitted by a foreign investor that fully controls the same technology.[33] The underlying market failure with FDI-driven technology transfer is that, in a Korean-type strategy, the local firm is forced to develop more advanced skills and technical knowledge than are needed simply to operate a technology imported in a fully 'packaged' form. The foreign investor who already has access to advanced design, research and development capabilities elsewhere will not find it in its interest to invest in them in a developing host country.

The development of local R&D capabilities can also have several externalities and linkages. It feeds into local capital goods and component production. It enables the accumulated technical knowledge to be applied by other industries or even by competitors. It leads to interaction between industry and the technology infrastructure (universities, research institutions, quality assurance centres, and so on). All this conduces to overall flexibility in the manner displayed by South Korea (and also, to a great extent, Taiwan).

In Singapore, by far the smallest of the NIEs, the government has been very interventionist, but the form of interventionism has been very different from South Korea.[34] The economy started with a base of trading, ship servicing and petroleum refining. After a brief period of import substitution, it moved into export-oriented industrialization based overwhelmingly on foreign investment and technology transfer by multinational companies. Unlike Hong Kong, there was a weak tradition of local entrepreneurship and there was no sudden influx of technical and entrepreneurial know-how from China. There was a decade or so of light industrial activity (garment and semiconductor assembly), after which the Singapore government acted firmly to upgrade the industrial structure by intervening in the entry of foreign investors to guide them to higher value-added activities, and in education to create specific high-level technical skills.

This latter set of interventions is not reflected fully in the figures in Table 10.1, though the figures for science and technology enrolments at the tertiary level are quite respectable (India, for instance, has 0.21 per cent of its population in these subjects, Mexico 0.7 per cent, and Brazil 0.4 per cent).[35] The main thrust of training in Singapore was via the setting up of institutes jointly with industry to give specialized instruction to employees rather than pre-employment education. This was subsidized by the state, and carefully targeted at the activities to be promoted.

Specific areas of both manufacturing and services (like banking, freighting and aircraft servicing) were selected for promotion, but the policy instruments used did not include trade protection. They comprised a range of incentives, pressure, subsidies and support, that guided the allocation of resources and lowered the cost of entry into difficult activities. Manufacturing activity was highly specialized in particular processes and products, with no attempt to increase local content or the degree of vertical integration. Such specialization, along with the heavy reliance on foreign investments for technology and skill transfer, greatly reduced the need for indigenous technological investments (as compared, say, to South Korea). Thus, while selective interventions led Singapore's industry into sophisticated producer and consumer electronics, precision instruments, optics, and so on, the technological depth of the enterprises located there was comparatively low. Some design and development activity did build up over time, again with considerable urging and support from the government,[36] but this is an area that is targeted for the island's future.

The lessons of Singapore, to the extent that an economy of 3 million can be considered relevant to most of the developing world, are twofold. First, FDI can take a small economy a long way if it is carefully selected and guided, supplied with superlative infrastructure and a disciplined and trained workforce, and given a competitive and stable investment environment. Second, it is not necessary to offer import protection to technologically complex activities if the main sources of operational and other technologies remain foreign, production is integrated with that in foreign countries (rather than with local suppliers) and is concentrated on some stages of production. This strategy requires both functional and selective interventions by the government: the contrasting experiences of Singapore and Hong Kong with respect to the deepening of industrial activity illustrate this clearly.

For larger countries that wish to develop *à la* South Korea (i.e. to deepen local supply capabilities, develop indigenous enterprise and foster innovative skills), however, this level of selectivity may not be enough. The significantly higher learning costs involved may only be met by local enterprises by higher levels of support (through protection or subsidies) and by the creation of large domestic firms that can partly internalize defective risk, capital and information markets.

Finally, we come to Taiwan. The Taiwanese economy, with a population about half the size of South Korea's, has been practically as dynamic as the latter. Some thirty years ago Taiwan was considerably more developed than South Korea, and was better endowed with human resources. Like Hong Kong, it had a large influx of capital, skills and entrepreneurship from mainland China after the revolution. Its development strategy had elements of Korean-style attempts to select and promote local industries, by protection, credit allocation and selectivity in letting in FDI, in areas of future comparative advantage. However, Taiwan's selectivity was far less detailed than South Korea's, and it did not attempt to create giant private conglomerates or to push so heavily into advanced technologies or capital-intensive activities. The government's less intense relationship with private industry in Taiwan meant that many of its more ambitious forays into heavy industry had to be led by the public sector and Taiwan has the largest public sector of the NIEs.

Taiwan's strength has lain in its small and medium enterprises that have tapped its large base of human capital and the infant industry promotion offered by the government to grow and diversify in skill-intensive activities. The resulting industrial structure is 'lighter' than South Korea's, with greater emphasis on meeting market niches rather than mass production, less in-house R&D, and less emphasis on creating international brand names.[37] The inherent disadvantages of small size for technical upgrading have been partly offset by the government's provision of a wide range of technology support services, including R&D, and its inherent flexibility in meeting changing demand conditions has till now enabled Taiwan to keep up nearly as high rates of export growth as South Korea.

Taiwanese industry is thus in some respects different from that of South Korea. A large proportion of small enterprises are specialized in labour-intensive manufacturing that faces the same problems as Hong Kong's industry, and may only survive by relocating overseas, perhaps moving upmarket in their domestic operations while winding down manufacturing.[38] Unlike Hong Kong, however, there are many firms with the ability to enter higher value-added activities and to tap a large technology infrastructure. There are also a growing proportion of larger firms that can invest in their own R&D and brand names. This gives it some of the flexibility arising from industrial depth, as in South Korea. It is a debatable point which of these two economies has the greater long-term dynamism, one dominated by giant *chaebol*, the other by smaller and more nimble, but technologically lighter, enterprises.

This concludes our brief survey of the successful industrializers. The evidence suggests that their success has different characteristics. Each started with a different set of endowments for industrial growth and adopted different approaches to improving those endowments and to pushing their enterprises into more productive activities. A variety of models emerged, depending on the strategy chosen to tackle market failures. Each was fairly good in addressing functional failures, especially in physical infrastructure and human capital. They differed in their approaches to capital markets: South Korea and Taiwan intervened heavily to direct domestic credit to chosen activities, while Singapore directed FDI inflows to its strategic ends. They also differed in their technology support activities, with South Korea and Taiwan investing most heavily in creating an S&T infrastructure. Their most important differences, however, lay in their trade and industrial policies. Interpreting these with the perspective of capability development yields very useful insights.

5.2 India

India started its industrial drive in the 1950s with a large, diverse, and long-established base of manufacturing. A number of heavy, complex industries like steel, paper, chemicals, cement and machinery (in addition to a broad array of consumer goods industries) had taken root some decades earlier. There was a thriving and accomplished indigenous entrepreneurial class, good physical infrastructure and a well-functioning legal and administrative system. The government invested in building up the human capital base and pursued sound macroeconomic policies. It also mounted a comprehensive strategy of industrial development, supplemented by a science and technology plan, one of the first such in the developing world. This section deals with the policy interventions that shaped the development of Indian industry until the late 1980s, until the recent wave of liberalization.

In the 1950s, the stage seems to have been set for the sustained and competitive development of Indian industry. This early promise was belied. The nature of the policies adopted by the government to promote industrial development produced a mixture of good and bad results.[39] The former included an extremely diverse and deep industrial structure capable of producing practically all industrial goods locally, a wide range of manufactured exports, a broad base of domestic capabilities to design and manufacture complex products, equipment and processes, and a high degree of local content. The bad results were more numerous.

Industrial growth rates were consistently below plan targets and substantially lower than in many other industrializing nations. Growth in manufacturing output, which averaged about 4 per cent per annum between 1974 and 1981, increased to only 5.7 per cent in the 1981–5 period. Rigid investment licensing and controls on output and technology acquisition led to a state of permanent product shortages that inhibited competitive behaviour. High import barriers effectively isolated many Indian enterprises from technological developments in the rest of the world. The rigidities created by the regulatory system not only constrained firms' ability to enter new markets and expand, but also limited their ability to restructure and close down. In many sectors, continued production by financially weak – 'sick' – firms, via subsidies, undermined the viability of the remaining more efficient units. Heavy indirect taxes on all stages of production had a cascading effect that raised domestic prices, further constraining firms' ability to expand markets and achieve economies of scale. As a result of these policies, Indian firms in many industrial sub-sectors are below international standards in terms of technology, scale and efficiency, and offer products at high prices and variable quality. This environment has also contributed to India's disappointing export performance and its weak record of total factor productivity growth.[40]

The *incentive structure* in India's industrial strategy was given by aspects of its trade regime and internal industrial and technology policies. As far as the *trade regime* is concerned, the prolonged and pervasive pursuit of self-reliance led to a system of import controls that virtually insulated domestic industry from foreign competition. Protection was non-selective, virtually permanent and unrelated to learning needs of industries. The powerful disincentives that this gave to exporting were only partially offset by a complex and cumbersome array of export incentives. Imports were controlled by quantitative restrictions and tariffs, the latter playing the predominant role until very recently. Even in their subsidiary role, tariffs were very high, among the highest in the world; they were also extremely complex, with many *ad hoc* exemptions. The licensing system, with several categories of banned, restricted and permissible products, was highly discretionary and subject to arbitrary, lengthy and often corrupt processes.

The *industrial policy* regime in India also exerted various disincentives to healthy development. Five features of the regulatory framework deserve special mention: industrial licensing, monopoly control, small-scale industry promotion, exit policies and price controls. Industrial licensing was the most important tool in the government's armoury directed at bending the progress of Indian industry to its will. The system covered the licensing of domestic industrial capacity as well as the licensing of technology imports and of foreign investment (under the purview of FERA, the Foreign Exchange Regulation Act). Licences were firm, product-, time- and location-specific, and were administered through a complex web of cumbersome controls that created enormous delays and rent seeking. The system was used as part of monopoly control and small-scale promotion, and was used essentially to guide resources into activities desired by the government, rather than into those with the highest economic returns or the potential for international competitiveness. The effect was to direct resource allocation into many non-economic uses, and to restrict competition in all sectors, including those which were accorded high priority by the policy-makers. Thus, productivity growth and competitiveness were held back, not only by static resource misallocation but also by the slow (or absent) upgrading of capabilities in existing activities.

On the technology front, licensing policy aimed at promoting self-reliance in both the production of capital goods and the generation of new technology by imposing a strict and cumbersome screening process for importing technology, entering into a foreign joint venture, employing foreign technicians and importing various categories of capital goods. The regime encouraged short-termism, weakened the bargaining position of Indian firms, narrowed their range of choice and hampered technology acquisition by smaller firms. While it succeeded in keeping down total expenditures on foreign technology by the country, it led to a lowering of the quality of technology imported and to a minimization of the commitment of the transferor to ensuring its full absorption and subsequent upgrading.[41] The restrictions were not, however, the primary cause of technological sloth in India – the most important reasons lay in the lack of competition and the barriers to entry and exit – but they fed into an environment where dynamism and competitiveness were low on the priorities of industrial enterprises.

Foreign direct investment has long been tightly restricted by the Indian government, with the most restricted period in the 1970s and some liberalization over the 1980s. Only some $367 million of FDI entered India in the entire period from 1970 to 1988.[42] This was far more restrictive than Korea, which was also very nationalistic in its approach to the acquisition of foreign skills, technology and capital via FDI. However, the dissimilarity in other aspects of industrial policies meant that the results were very different. The trade and industrial policy setting in India meant that local firms, as well as the foreign firms that were allowed to enter, had few incentives to be efficient, export-oriented and technologically dynamic. The competitive spur that foreign affiliates could have offered to domestic firms was blunted by the industrial policy regime, with restrictions on entry and exit exacerbated by additional controls on the growth of large (monopoly) firms and by reservations for the small-scale and public sectors.

In addition to the incentive effects of trade and industrial policies, the government's drive to place the 'commanding heights' of the economy in the *public sector* also had serious effects. Apart from the direct 'crowding out' of private enterprises from a variety of activities reserved for the public sector, the latter also had privileged access to factors of production like finance or infrastructure, and to the (largely public) science and technology system. Thus, the reduction of competition in product markets combined with dominance of some factor markets is likely to have reduced the incentives and capabilities for competitive industrial development, and guided it into suboptimal patterns.

There were also deficiencies in Indian strategies as far as the supply side is concerned. The *human capital base*, while large in absolute terms, was in fact rather weak in relation to the size of the economy. Thus, in comparison with South Korea, India had much lower investments in all categories of skill generation in the late 1980s. There was widespread illiteracy, which had been practically eliminated in South Korea. Indian secondary school enrolments were 43 per cent of the relevant age group (compared to 89 per cent) and tertiary enrolments about 10 per cent (38 per cent). Tertiary enrolments in science and engineering came to 0.06 per cent of the population (as compared to 0.54 per cent); scientists and engineers in R&D per million population were 150 in India and 1,283 in South Korea. The fact that even these low levels of skill formation were not fully exploited in India (with resulting graduate unemployment) was a reflection of the poor growth and technological performance of the industrial sector. It may also be a reflection of the poor quality of education in a large number of establishments in India.

Technological effort in India remained predominantly in the public sector, and within that in these R&D institutes largely divorced from direct involvement in productive activity. Although total R&D was creditable by developing country standards (around 1 per cent of GDP in 1990) – though still lagging well behind South Korea's 2.1 per cent – industry only accounted for some 21 to 25 per cent of the total (compared to 80 per cent for South Korea), with its share *declining* over time. As a proportion of GDP, in consequence, the share of 'productive sector' R&D in India was 0.2 per cent, and that financed by productive enterprises (including those in the public sector), the most realistic measure of applied technological effort in industry, only 0.1 per cent (compared to 1.5 per cent and 1.9 per cent respectively for South Korea). The R&D institutions remained largely peripheral to industrial technological effort.

To conclude on Indian industrial policy, the structure of incentives, capabilities and institutions set up was not conducive to the healthy development of industry. The problems lay predominantly, but not entirely, with the incentive structure, which reduced the need for sustained technological efforts by industry and distorted the nature of the efforts that did take place. The supply side of the technological equation also lagged. There were indications of incipient skill gaps: the S&T infrastructure was isolated and of variable utility; the financing of technological effort or technology imports was inadequate; technology imports themselves were constrained and there was minimal inflow of FDI. Of these, perhaps the most pressing gaps lay with the functioning of the technology institutions and their linkages with industry, and the financing of technological activity. [...]

6. Implications

The analysis of technological capabilities at the micro level is essential to an understanding of industrial development and the formulation of industrial policy. The usual simplifying assumptions that there are no learning costs in using industrial technologies, and that efficient production can be launched merely in response to 'right' prices, do not do justice to a complex reality. They often result in misleading policy recommendations. The discussion in this chapter suggests that the promotion of capability development is a vital part of the strategy of industrial development. It also suggests that, in the presence of market failures, active government involvement is required to ensure capability development. This involvement should comprise selective and functional interventions in both product and factor markets.

Today, the most pressing policy problem in most developing countries is less the setting up of new industries than of enhancing the competitiveness of existing inefficient and technologically stagnant industries. It must therefore address the *removal* of an accretion of many irrational and inefficient interventions that many governments have undertaken in the past four decades. The analytical approach proposed here is equally relevant: industrial reform policy must have the same basic elements as industrial development policy.

Industrial reform and restructuring have, in other words, to address various determinants of capability development: the incentive framework, the supply of human capital, the supporting technology infrastructure, finance for technological activity, and access to foreign technologies. However, they have to differ from conventional industrial policy because they have to take into account the 'relearning' costs and time required for existing industries to become efficient to shed the legacy of inherited attitudes, outdated skills and inappropriate technologies. Similarly, account has to be taken of the costs and time needed for the relevant factor markets to be upgraded to meet the needs of international competition.

If these factors are taken into account, the design of policy reforms would be very different from what the typical structural adjustment package contains. The ideal structural adjustment in the World Bank view consists of a rapid and sweeping liberalization, applied uniformly across all countries and industrial structures, and resulting in a 'minimalist' government. The reasoning here suggests that an appropriate reform package would be far more gradual and would retain a large role for the government to overcome market failures. It would be phased according to the needs of relearning and factor market upgrading. It would retain the instruments of intervention in trade and technology that are needed to set up new infant industries (and which are among the first casualties of structural adjustment programmes).

The pattern of interventions and their objectives would, however, be very different from those of classic import substitution regimes, where they were not geared to achieving international competitiveness and did not address the relevant market failures. They would be much more in the South Korean mould, which also underwent two structural adjustment programmes in the early 1980s but whose economy, despite considerable liberalization, still retains large elements of government control and direction.[43]

Let us reiterate the main considerations of rational industrial policy. In product markets, the best framework for efficient industrial development is one which provides constant competition to enterprises. Full exposure to world competition has, however, to be tempered by the fact that a new entrant has to incur the costs and risks of gaining technological mastery, when its competitors in more advanced countries have already gone through the learning process. Depending on the extent of the learning costs and the efficiency of the relevant factor markets and supporting institutions, there is a valid case for selective and variable infant industry protection, and for the gradual and phased exposure of existing activities to import competition.

Since protection reduces the incentive to invest in capability building, it has to be carefully designed, sparingly granted, strictly monitored and offset by measures to force firms to aim for world standards of efficiency. Protection has to be selectively granted to a few activities at a time, because only a few have the capacity to reach competitiveness and intervention resources on the supply side are limited. The most effective offset to the disincentives to capability development arising from protection seems to be strong pressures to enter export markets – a commitment to export disciplines not only from the firms but also from those who decide and administer the policies. The secret of the success of export orientation lies in this rather than in conforming to static comparative advantage.

Factor markets also need intervention. The markets for human capital, technical support, technology, information and finance in developing countries generally suffer from a number of deficiencies. A sound industrial promotion strategy must address each of these needs. Moreover, these interventions must be integrated with interventions in the incentive framework, so that activities being promoted are not penalized by the lack of production factors and information. Intervention resources are scarce, and their most effective use calls for selectivity and coherence. This seems so obvious as to sound banal – yet few governments have aimed at such coherence and selectivity. Current adjustment programmes ignore the supply side of capability building in their overwhelming urge to get prices right and reduce interventions.

There are many possible levels and patterns of industrial support. The greater the degree of selectivity exercised, the greater the potential benefits if the strategy works, but the larger also the risk of government failure (and of heavy ensuing economic costs). A few governments have managed to intervene selectively with great success, and have produced industrial growth rates perhaps unmatched in recent economic history. Most have not. This means that government intervention capabilities have to be assessed in drawing up technology development strategies. It also means that administrative capabilities and incentives themselves have to be developed to the extent possible. There is considerable debate about the capability of governments to undertake selective interventions at all, which takes us beyond the realm of economics into that of political economy. Some of the most important issues lie here; however, this chapter cannot explore them.[44] What is evident is that many governments have managed such interventions effectively, and that, given imperfect markets, the costs of non-intervention may be high.

Notes

1   This approach is succinctly analysed in Nelson (1981) and Nelson and Winter (1977).
2   The World Bank's *World Development Report 1991* is the best embodiment of this view.

3 Recent work on technological capabilities in developing countries includes Bell and Pavitt (1993), Bell et al. (1984), Dahlman et al. (1987), Enos (1992), Katz (1984, 1987), Lall (1987, 1990, 1992a, 1993b), Pack and Westphal (1986).

4 See Nelson and Winter (1982).

5 See Nelson (1987), Nelson and Winter (1977) and Pack and Westphal (1986).

6 For a detailed analysis for the constituent elements of the 'learning curve' see Adler and Clark (1991). Mody (1989) has a useful analysis of the need for engineering manpower in the absorption of complex technologies.

7 For an analysis of the long learning process in the Korean engineering industry, see Jacobsson (1993).

8 Stiglitz (1987) has an analysis of 'learning to learn'.

9 For a discussion, see Pack and Westphal (1986).

10 This is analysed for the case of Korea by Enos and Park (1987). Also see Amsden (1989).

11 This is quite distinct from the argument that neoclassical theory itself does not establish the causal links between optimal resource allocation in a static sense and higher rates of growth over time. As the proponents of 'new growth theories' note, even under ideal neoclassical assumptions trade liberalization can only provide a once-for-all improvement in resource allocation – by itself, it cannot lead to the higher rates of growth. A sustained increase in the growth rate can only come from investments in human capital and technology that raise the productivity of other factors of production. The growth benefits of outward-oriented strategies cannot therefore be traced to their resource allocation effects (Lucas, 1988; Young, 1991). Analysts of import liberalization note, in a similar vein, that the theoretical and empirical case for the link between import liberalization and improved efficiency is tenuous (Havrylyshyn, 1990; Rodrik, 1992).

12 Historically almost all governments trying to promote industrialization have used such second-best solutions. In addition to protection and subsidies, they have promoted the formation of large firms or cartels, directed credit, set up public enterprises, given tax incentives, favoured local procurement. Vernon (1989) describes the historical experience of the countries that are now highly industrialized.

13 Mill (1940), p. 922, emphasis added.

14 Jacobsson (1993).

15 The arguments for this are developed in Pack and Westphal (1986). 'New' growth theory (see Young, 1991) also provides a theoretical justification for promoting sets of activities with greater technological intensity that offer a higher learning potential than traditional activities. Thus, countries that can specialize in the former set can enjoy higher rates of sustained growth than others – analysts associate the former with the industrialized economies and the latter with developing ones.

16 The automobile industry in Mexico and Brazil, now fairly competitive in world markets, would never have been launched without a long period of protection to develop production capabilities and supplier networks.

17 See the editor's introduction to Lall (1993a).

18 See Moreira (1993) for an illuminating discussion and a comparison of South Korea and Brazil, with the former able to manage the process far better than the latter.

19 This is found in the study of Ghanaian enterprises by Lall et al. (1994).

20 The current jargon is that such interventions are 'market-friendly'; see the World Bank's *World Development Report 1991*.

21 For a good historical review of institutional support for technological activity in the industrialized countries, see Mowery and Rosenberg (1989).

22 See Stiglitz (1989).

23 See, among others, Amsden (1989, 1992), Lall and Kell (1991), Lall and associates (1992), Pack and Westphal (1986) and Wade (1990).

24 Chen (1989).

25 This remains true even if overseas enrolments are taken into account.

26 *Financial Times*, London, 4 May 1993, 'Survey of Hong Kong', p. 6.

27 The 'typical model' is given by the statistical work of Chenery et al. (1986).

28 *Financial Times*, see note 26.

29 The details are now well known, and are given in publications such as Amsden (1989, 1992), Lall and associates (1992), Pack and Westphal (1986).

30 Interestingly, industrialists participated in setting the curriculum for technical training.

31 For a case study of the electronics industry see Mody (1990).

32 Amsden (1989), Westphal (1990).

33 The capabilities may be mainly for absorption rather than for frontier innovation, but, as noted, even the absorption, adaptation and improvement of advanced technologies needs substantial local R&D effort.

34 See Hobday (1994).

35 See Lall (1990).

36 Hobday (1994).

37 See Mody (1990) on the electronics industry.

38 See Lall (1991).

39 Lall (1987).

40 India's productivity record is documented and analysed in Ahluwalia (1985, 1991).

41 For a detailed analysis of the technology regime see Desai (1988).

42 The inflow of FDI has greatly accelerated in the past two years after significant liberalization, but this chapter concentrates on the earlier period.

43 The World Bank holds up the Korean case as an example of successful adjustment. It is, but only because the pace and content of adjustment were tightly controlled by the government, see Westphal (1991). This deviates sharply from the typical adjustment programme that the Bank imposes on weaker economies, say in Africa, where the experience of rapid liberalization has been disastrous.

44 See, however, Streeten (1993) and Shapiro and Taylor (1990).

References

Adler, P.S. and Clark, K.B. (1991), 'Behind the Learning Curve: A Sketch of the Learning Process', *Management Science*, 37(3), 267–81.

Ahluwalia, I.J. (1985), *Industrial Growth in India: Stagnation Since the Mid-Sixties*, Delhi: Oxford University Press.

Ahluwalia, I.J. (1991), *Productivity and Growth in Indian Manufacturing*, Delhi: Oxford University Press.

Amsden, A.H. (1989), *Asia's New Giant: South Korea and Late Industrialization*, New York: Oxford University Press.

Amsden, A.H. (1992), 'A Theory of Government Intervention in Late Industrialization', in L. Putterman and D. Ruschmeyer (eds), *The State and the Market in Development*, Boulder, Colo.: Lynne Rienner Publishers, 53–84.

Arrow, K. (1962), 'Economic Welfare and the Allocation of Resources for Innovation', in R. Nelson (ed.), *The Rate and Direction of Innovative Activity: Economic and Social Factors*, Princeton: Princeton University Press for the National Bureau of Economic Research, 609–26.

Bell, M. and Pavitt, K. (1993), 'Accumulating Technological Capability in Developing Countries', *Proceedings of the World Bank Annual Conference on Development Economics 1992*, 257–81.

Bell, M., Ross-Larson, B. and Westphal, L.E. (1984), 'Assessing the Performance of Infant Industries', *Journal of Development Economics*, 16(1), 101–28.

Chen, E.K.Y. (1989), 'The Changing Role of the Asian NICs in the Asian-Pacific Region Toward the Year 2000', in M. Shinahora and F. Lo (eds), *Global Adjustment and the Future of the Asian-Pacific Economy*, Tokyo: Asian and Pacific Development Center, 207–31.

Chenery, H.B., Robinson, S. and Syrquin, M. (1986), *Industrialization and Growth: A Comparative Study*, New York: Oxford University Press.

Cohen, W.M. and Levinthal, D.A. (1989), 'Innovation and Learning: The Two Faces of R&D', *Economic Journal*, 99(4), 569–96.

Dahlman, C.J., Ross-Larson, B. and Westphal, L.E. (1987), 'Managing Technological Development: Lessons from the Newly Industrializing Countries', *World Development*, 15(6), 759–75.

Desai, A.V. (ed.) (1988), *Technology Absorption in Indian Industry*, New Delhi: Wiley Eastern.

Enos, J. (1992), *The Creation of Technological Capabilities in Developing Countries*, London: Pinter.

Enos, J. and Park, W.H. (1987), *The Adaptation and Diffusion of Imported Technologies in the Case of Korea*, London: Croom Helm.

Havrylyshyn, O. (1990), 'Trade and Productivity Gains in Developing Countries. A Survey of the Literature', *World Bank Research Observer*, 5(1), 1–24.

Hobday, M.G. (1994), 'Technological Learning in Singapore: A Test Case of Leapfrogging', *Journal of Development Studies* (forthcoming).

Jacobsson, S. (1993), 'The Length of the Learning Period: Evidence from the Korean Engineering Industry', *World Development*, 21(3), 407–20.

Katz, J. (1984), 'Domestic Technological Innovation and Dynamic Comparative Advantage: Further Reflections on a Comparative Case Study Program', *Journal of Development Economics*, 16(1), 13–38.

Katz, J.M. (ed.) (1987), *Technology Generation in Latin American Manufacturing Industries*, London: Macmillan.

Lall, S. (1987), *Learning to Industrialize*, London: Macmillan.

Lall, S. (1990), *Building Industrial Competitiveness in Developing Countries*, Paris: OECD Development Centre.

Lall, S. (1991), 'Direct Investment in S.E. Asia by the NIEs: Trends and Propects', *Banca Nazionale del Lavoro Quarterly Review*, 179, 463–80.

Lall, S. (1992a), 'Technological Capabilities and Industrialization', *World Development*, 20(2), 165–86.

Lall, S. (1992b), 'Structural Problems of African Industry', in F. Stewart, S. Lall and S. Wangwe (eds), *Alternative Development Strategies in Sub-Saharan Africa*, London: Macmillan.

Lall, S. (ed.) (1993a), *Transnational Corporations and Economic Development*, United Nations Library on Transnational Corporations, London: Routledge.

Lall, S. (1993b), 'Understanding Technology Development', *Development and Change*, 24(4).

Lall, S. (1993c), 'Trade Policies for Development: A Policy Prescription for Africa', *Development Policy Review*, 11(1), 47–65.

Lall, S. and Kell, G. (1991), 'Industrial Development in Developing Countries and the Role of Government Interventions', *Banca Nazionale del Lavoro Quarterly Review*, 178, 271–92.

Lall, S. and associates (1992), *World Bank Support for Industrialization in Korea, India and Indonesia*, Washington, DC: World Bank Operations Evaluation Department.

Lall, S., Navaretti, G.B., Teitei, S. and Wignaraja, G. (1994), *Technology and Enterprise Development: Ghana under Structural Adjustment*, Oxford: Draft prepared for the World Bank, Africa Technical Department's Regional Program on Enterprise Development.

Liang, N. (1992), 'Beyond Import Substitution and Export Promotion: A New Typology of Trade Strategies', *Journal of Development Strategies*, 28(3), 447–72.

Lucas, R.E. (1988), 'On the Mechanics of Economic Development', *Journal of Monetary Economics*, 22(1), 3–42.

Mill, J.S. (1940), *Principles of Political Economy* (first edition, 1848), with an introduction by W.J. Ashley, London: Longmans, Green and Company.

Mody, A. (1989), 'Firm Strategies for Costly Engineering Learning', *Management Science*, 33(4), 496–512.

Mody, A. (1990), 'Institutions and Dynamic Comparative Advantage: The Electronics Industry in South Korea and Taiwan', *Cambridge Journal of Economics*, 14(3), 291–314.

Moreira, M.M. (1993), 'Industrialization, Trade and Market Failures: The Role of Government Intervention in Brazil and the Republic of Korea', University College, London: PhD Thesis.

Mowery, D.C. and Rosenberg, N. (1989), *Technology and the Pursuit of Economic Growth*, Cambridge: Cambridge University Press.

Nelson, R.R. (1981), 'Research on Productivity Growth and Productivity Differences: Dead Ends or New Departures?', *Journal of Economic Literature*, 19(3), 1029–64.

Nelson, R.R. (1987), 'Innovation and Economic Development: Theoretical Retrospect and Prospect', in J.M. Katz (ed.), *Technology Generation in Latin American Manufacturing Industries*, London: Macmillan, 78–93.

Nelson, R.R. and Winter, S.J. (1977), 'In Search of Useful Theory of Innovation', *Research Policy*, 6(1), 36–76.

Nelson, R.R. and Winter, S.J. (1982), *An Evolutionary Theory of Economic Change*, Cambridge, Mass.: Harvard University Press.

Pack, H., (1992), 'Learning and Productivity Change in Developing Countries', in G.K. Helleiner (ed.), *Trade Policy, Industrialization and Development*, Oxford: Clarendon Press, 21–45.

Pack, H. and Westphal, L.E. (1986), 'Industrial Strategy and Technological Change: Theory versus Reality', *Journal of Development Economics*, 22(1), 87–128.

Republic of China (1990, 1992), *Taiwan Statistical Yearbook*, Taipei: Council for Economic Planning and Development.

Rodrik, D. (1992), 'Closing the Productivity Gap: Does Trade Liberalization Really Help?', in G.K. Helleiner (ed.), *Trade Policy, Industrialization and Development*, Oxford: Clarendon Press.

Shapiro, H. and Taylor, L. (1990), 'The State and Industrial Strategy', *World Development*, 18(6), 861–78.

Stiglitz, J.E. (1987), 'Learning to Learn, Localized Learning and Technological Progress', in P. Dasgupta and P. Stoneman (eds), *Economic Policy and Technological Development*, Cambridge: Cambridge University Press, 125–55.

Stiglitz, J. (1989), 'Markets, Market Failures and Development', *American Economic Review Papers and Proceedings*, 79(2), 197–202.

Streeten, P.P. (1993), 'Markets and States: Against Minimalism', *World Development*, 21(8), 1281–98.

UNDP (1992), *Human Development Report*, New York: United Nations Development Programme.

UNESCAP (1991), *Statistical Yearbook of Asia and the Pacific*, Bangkok: United Nations Economic Commission for Asia and the Pacific.

UNIDO (1993), *Industry and Development, Global Report 1992–93*, Vienna: United Nations Industrial Development Organization.

Vernon, R. (1989), 'Technological Development: The Historical Experience', Washington, DC: World Bank, Economic Development Institute, Seminar Paper No. 39.

Wade, R. (1990), *Governing the Market: Economic Theory and the Role of Government in East Asian Industrialization*, Princeton: Princeton University Press.

Westphal, L.E. (1990), 'Industrial Policy in an Export Propelled Economy: Lessons from South Korea's Experience', *Journal of Economic Perspectives*, 4(3), 41–59.

Westphal, L.E. (1991), 'Comments' on M. Dailami, 'Korea: Successful Adjustment', in V. Thomas et al. (eds), *Restructuring Economies in Distress*, New York: Oxford University Press for the World Bank.

World Bank (1991), *World Development Report 1991*, Washington, DC: World Bank.

World Bank (1992), *World Development Report 1992*, Washington, DC: World Bank.

Young, A. (1991), 'Learning by Doing and the Dynamic Effects of International Trade', *Quarterly Journal of Economics*, 106(2), 369–405.

International Trade and Investment Policy

Recent years have seen a sharp growth in cross-border trade, financial flows and the activity of multinational firms. Has this growth been desirable? Should policy makers seek to influence the degree and nature of international economic activity?

Chapter 11, by Krugman, contrasts some of the key theoretical perspectives on international trade. Krugman places trade theorists into four categories: the mercantilists, classicists, strategists and realists. He points out some of the simplistic and flawed assumptions that inform classical (and neo-classical) economic theorising on trade, such as the assumptions of perfect competition and exogenously given technology. He demonstrates how the more realistic assumptions of imperfect competition and the evolutionary, cumulative and endogenous nature of the process of knowledge and capability creation can provide the rationale for strategic interventions in trade. However, he rejects these arguments for trade intervention, fearing that such interventions may lead to a trade war.

Chapter 12, by Nayyar, explores the arguments on international trade in the context of the developing world. Nayyar agrees with Krugman in his criticism of classical and neo-classical trade theory, and in the argument that strategic interventions in trade may enhance national welfare. He then argues that while Krugman may be right in dismissing strategic trade intervention in the case of developed nations, this argument does not apply to the case of developing nations. Developing countries face an asymmetric position when they trade with developed nations: only the latter possess strategic industries. The trading relationship between developing and developed nations is thus likely to be unequal. Consequently, developing nations may need to institute trade policies that permit their infant industries to grow and mature.

Chapter 13, by Dunning, investigates the role of policy in the area of foreign direct investment activity of multinational forms. Multinationals now account for a quarter of global output and two-thirds of international trade. It is therefore important that a nation attracts the appropriate volume and appropriate kinds of multinational activity. Dunning draws upon Porter's work and 'internationalises' the latter's diamond of national competitiveness. He explores the role that policy may play in inducing multinational firms to upgrade Porter's diamond of national competitive advantage. He points out that multinationals are increasingly carrying out parts of their innovation activity in foreign locations, even though the bulk of research and early product development activity is still carried out in the home country. Developing countries, however, remain largely excluded from this growing internationalisation of innovation.

In Chapter 14, the authors of the UNCTAD 1999 World Investment Report explore how policy makers in developing countries may try to optimise the benefit from foreign direct investment. They emphasise that the objectives of multinational firms may substantially differ from the development priorities of developing nations. The policy challenge then is to institute measures that attract the appropriate volume and appropriate kinds of investment from multinational firms that help in enhancing indigenous capability development. Investment that is geared to the exploitation of a nation's cheap and unskilled labour is not likely to yield any dynamic sources of competitive advantage in the long run.

Chapter 15, by Castells, investigates policy issues with respect to the portfolio aspect of global finance. Castells explores how the deregulation of national capital markets and developments in information technology have led to an explosive growth in international financial markets. He questions the desirability of this development and the dilemmas that the globalised financial market poses for developed and developing economies.

C HAPTER 11

Making Sense of the Competitiveness Debate

PAUL R. KRUGMAN*

Introduction

Most of us, despite all the evidence, cling to a vision of public discourse in which great issues are decided by profound debates among deep thinkers. We like to imagine that the authors we read in intellectual magazines, the talking heads we see on television, are really engaged in such debates – that while they may have differences of opinion, they start from a shared base of knowledge and understanding.

When it comes to international economics, however, nothing could be further from the truth, Debates about international trade are a study in confusion and misconceptions, in which the 'experts' you see, hear, and read are usually misinformed about the most basic facts and concepts – and in which even those who are fairly sound on the economics do not understand the nature of the debate.

The discussion of competitiveness is a case in point. The idea that the economic success of a country depends on its international competitiveness took hold among business, political, and intellectual leaders in the late 1970s. The World Economic Forum, which hosts the famous Davos conferences, began issuing its annual World Competitiveness Report in 1980, and the rankings in that report soon became a major criterion by which national performance was judged. By the 1990s the concept of competitiveness was no longer even controversial among influential people. Of course competitiveness was the key; the only question was how to achieve it.

But what does national economic competitiveness mean? For the majority of those who use the term, it means exactly what it seems to mean: it is the view that nations compete for world markets in the same way that corporations do, that a nation which fails to match other nations in productivity or technology will face the

* Oxford University Press for P. Krugman, 'Making Sense of the Competitiveness Debate', *Oxford Review of Economic Policy*, 1996, Vol 12, No 3.

same kind of crisis as a company that cannot match the costs or products of its rivals. This is the view expressed, for example, in Lester Thurow's 1992 book, *Head to Head*, which repeatedly asserts that advanced nations are in a 'win–lose' competition for world markets. (Thurow's book not only was a massive best-seller but was approvingly cited by no less a figure than President Clinton.) It is also the view expressed in the European Commission's 1993 White Paper, 'Growth, Competitiveness, Employment', whose introduction argued that competition from newly industrializing economies was the most important reason for the upward trend in European unemployment rates.

While influential people have used the word 'competitiveness' to mean that countries compete just like companies, professional economists know very well that this is a poor metaphor. In fact, it is a view of the world so much in conflict with what even the most basic international trade theory tells us that economists have by and large simply failed to comprehend that this is what the seemingly sophisticated people who talk about competitiveness have in mind. To the extent that they even notice that most people who matter think that competitiveness is what economics is all about, economists imagine that the word must mean something other than what it seems to mean. Either they suppose that 'competitiveness' is a poetic way of saying productivity, and has nothing to do with any actual conflict between countries; or they suppose that people who talk about competitiveness must understand the basics and have in mind some sophisticated departure from standard economic models, involving imperfect competition, external economies, or both.

And the flip side of this misunderstanding is that those relatively few believers in the importance of competitiveness who do know that their view conflicts with simple trade theory are unintentionally given aid and comfort by economists who seem to be telling them that they have not failed to understand the simple economics, but rather have transcended it.

In this chapter I want to offer a sort of guide to the realities of this discussion – in particular, to the widely different levels of understanding among people who have managed to convince themselves and others that know something about international trade. Only if you understand that the people you hear or read are operating at very different intellectual levels – that there is no shared basis of mutually agreed facts and mutually understood concepts – can you make sense of what is otherwise a baffling discussion.

Four characters

To introduce the subject, let me describe four stock characters. All of them imagine themselves to be sophisticated about international economics, but in fact their grasp of the subject varies enormously. In order of increasing sophistication, they are:

- the Mercantilist;
- the Classicist;

- the Strategist;
- the Realist.

The Mercantilist

The Mercantilist is someone who has no problems at all with the term 'competitiveness'. To him, it seems obvious that countries compete with each other in the same way that corporations do. He has never heard of comparative advantage or, if he has, he thinks it means the same thing as 'competitive advantage'. He believes that the purpose of trade is to generate exports, which create jobs; if he has any sympathy for free trade, it is because we can make a deal to accept other countries' exports if they accept ours.

The important thing to understand about the subject of competitiveness is that the vast majority of people who use the term – politicians, business leaders, journalists, best-selling authors on economics – are Mercantilists. Anyone who writes about trade as a global struggle or war; anyone who compares countries to corporations; anyone who says that trade policy is about creating jobs; anyone who talks about 'high-value' sectors – all of these people reveal themselves to be Mercantilists. A few of them may try to put an intellectual gloss on their views by citing the works of Strategists, but a Mercantilist uses Strategic ideas as a drunk uses a lamppost – as a source of support, not of illumination.

Mercantilists need not be protectionists. Indeed, the relatively liberal trading system we actually have was achieved not via an understanding of the economist's case for free trade, but via the application of a doctrine of enlightened mercantilism, in which countries are willing to lower their trade barriers – to offer 'concessions' – only in return for access to other countries' markets. Both NAFTA and the Uruguay Round were sold politically not on the basis of economists' estimates of the gains from trade, but with the claim that the extra exports thereby generated would add hundreds of thousands of jobs. None the less, even the enlightened Mercantilist's attachment to free trade is very much conditional – he is for 'free and fair' trade, not free trade pure and simple.

The Classicist

Economists, of course, do not think about international trade in anything like that way. The classical model of trade is essentially that initially stated by Ricardo and formally nailed down by John Stuart Mill, and still remains the main subject of international economics as it is taught in universities. The difference in outlook between a Classicist and a Mercantilist is enormous – much greater than either the Classicist or the Mercantilist is likely to realize. Consider the following statement of the classical position:

> The purpose of trade is imports, not exports. Exports are a cost – something we must produce because our import suppliers are crass enough to demand payment.

Or to put it differently, an export is an indirect way to produce an import, which is worth doing because it is more efficient than producing our imports for ourselves.

This is standard economics – indeed, Mill put it almost exactly that way. Yet it is almost the opposite of what Mercantilists believe.

The Strategist

The Strategist's objection to the classical position can be summarized with two words: Silicon Valley. In the basic classical model, competition is perfect – that is, there are no monopolies or oligopolies; wages are equalized across industries; and national efficiency in any given industry is a datum, determined by factors outside the economist's brief. In reality, there are industries in which economies of scale imply that only a few, perhaps highly profitable firms dominate the market; there are industries that seem persistently to pay higher wages than others, even when the qualifications of the workers are taken into account; and there are industries in which technological prowess seems to be generated by the mutual spill-overs of knowledge from national producers, and in which exports, therefore, may create comparative advantage rather than the other way around.

These failures of the classical model were the dominant subject of theoretical and empirical research on international trade during the 1980s. The Strategist, however, is not a mere researcher: he or she is eager to go out and exploit the possibilities for activist government that these market imperfections may create. Strategists want the government to stand behind domestic firms wherever there seems to be a winner-takes-all competition for future monopoly profits; they want active promotion of industries that seem to pay exceptionally high wages, or that seem likely to generate strong spill-overs.

Although the Strategist draws on the work of the economic theorists who, during the 1980s, put together what came to be known as the 'new trade theory', surprisingly few of the new trade theorists themselves are Strategists. Instead, however excited they may have been about the intellectual contribution of the new trade theory, they have become increasingly sceptical about the extent to which this theory can justify government activism in practice. In short, most of the new trade theorists are Realists.

The Realist

The Realist is someone who understands both why the classical analysis of international trade refutes crude mercantilist views, and how the qualifications to classical trade theory create new, more subtle arguments for intervention. What distinguishes the Realist from the Strategist are two beliefs. First, the Realist has looked at the practical prospects for strategic trade policy, and found them unimpressive: while markets are indeed imperfect, the potential gains from trying to exploit those imperfections are, he believes, essentially small change. Second, the Realist is cynical about the likelihood that subtle arguments for intervention can be translated into productive policies in the real world. In particular, he suspects that Strategists who think that they can improve on the policy recommendations of Classicists will, in practice, simply provide a bit of intellectual cover for the crudely belligerent ideas of Mercantilists. As a result, the Realist ends up sounding quite a lot like the Classicist: he knows that the classical model is not the whole story, but it is a lot of the story, and he believes that most of those who criticize conventional views of trade do so not because they have transcended the classical model but because they have never understood it in the first place.

Obviously, I myself am a Realist – the paragraph above about why the major new trade theorists are not Strategists was a self-portrait. But rather than go straight into a defence of the Realist position, let me work my way there in stages.

My plan here is to illustrate the basis for these different positions by considering the transitions between them. That is, we will see how classical trade theory refutes mercantilism; how new trade theory offers the possibility of strategic trade policy; and, finally, why a realistic appreciation of both the economics and the politics of trade leads one back to something more like a classical than a strategic view of the issue.

From mercantilism to classicism

It cannot be emphasized too much that the vast majority of those who talk about national economic competitiveness – politicians, trade officials, editors of leading magazines, and professors of political science (and an occasional rogue economist) – are Mercantilists. Perhaps some of the readers of this chapter are Mercantilists, too. To test whether you are, consider the following rough reproduction of a discussion I had with an individual who routinely makes the lists of America's top ten intellectuals.

He said: 'Isn't the story of the automobile industry basically what is happening to the whole economy? Foreigners started to produce cars better and cheaper than ours, and as a result we lost hundreds of thousands of jobs.' I replied: 'You can't use that kind of story about what happens in an individual industry to make sense of what is happening to the economy as a whole. If foreigners become relatively more productive in a particular industry, then of course we will lose jobs in that industry. But that doesn't mean that we lose jobs in the economy as a whole, or that foreign productivity growth hurts us.' 'Why do you keep on talking about "a particular industry"? Isn't the economy just the sum of what happens in each industry? Haven't auto's gone the way of textiles, and won't computers be next?' 'No, of course not – that's the whole point of the idea of comparative advantage. You always have a comparative advantage in something.' 'Well, that's not what Lester Thurow says.'

If you side with the other speaker – if you can't follow or don't accept what I was trying to say – then you are a a Mercantilist. Conversely, if you think that everyone who talks knowingly about international trade must, at the very least, understand the basic idea of comparative advantage, you are naïvely mistaken. In fact, almost nobody does.

When someone who does understand comparative advantage spends any length of time discussing and debating international trade with the great majority of would-be sophisticates who do not, one of two things happen: either he goes native, and forgets what he used to know; or he develops a new, almost awed respect for the sophistication of the simplest trade models. In particular, the basic two-good, one-factor model of international trade that Ricardo sketched out and John Stuart Mill filled in begins to seem stunningly insightful. If you read the reports of the innumerable commissions and conferences on competitiveness, the articles published on the subject in learned magazines and upscale newspapers, you will again and again see propositions such as the following:

- The growth of new economies in Asia necessarily comes at the expense of the West.
- If our foreign rivals become more productive than we are across the board, we will have nothing that we can produce competitively, and our standard of living will collapse.
- As modern technology diffuses globally, the real incomes of advanced nations will be driven down towards Third World levels.
- Intensified competition between nations will lead to a simultaneous decline in everyone's incomes.

I have often wondered why it is so hard to explain that propositions like these are silly. The answer, I now believe, is that international trade is a quintessentially 'general equilibrium' subject. By this I do not mean that trade must be addressed in terms of an analysis that assumes that markets are perfectly competitive, or even that they are in equilibrium. I refer rather to what somebody once described as the essential insight of general equilibrium analysis: 'Everything in the economy affects everything else in at least two ways.' Well, not quite; but it is utterly crucial when discussing international trade to keep track of the interdependencies among the variables of interest, and not to hold constant things that will not stay constant. For example, the amateur pundit on international trade typically thinks of wages as a given, and so imagines that productivity growth in low-wage countries must always come at the expense of jobs elsewhere; or he thinks implicitly in terms of a world market of fixed size, in which one country's increased output can only come by crowding out production and jobs in other countries. But if one understands even the simplest textbook model of comparative advantage, one already has a picture of a world in which wages, prices, the pattern of specialization and production, and the size of the world market are all simultaneously and mutually determined; in which productivity growth will feed back to wages, in which output growth will feed back to demand.

How can such a simple model offer a world-view that is much more subtle and complex than that held by the vast majority of even highly intelligent commentators, no matter how many facts they know? The answer, I suspect, is that general equilibrium is a very difficult thing to understand unless you are willing and able to think about it mathematically. We are not talking about the kind of maths that physicists use – the Ricardo–Mill model requires no more than high school algebra, and can even be explained with numerical examples. But seven generations of economists, some of them very good writers and teachers, can attest that the insights one gets from Ricardo and Mill cannot be explained unless the listener is willing to accept the idea that a simplified mathematical model can shed light on the way the world economy works, and to spend a little while understanding the mechanics of that model.

Otherwise, even in a two-good, two-country, one-factor model there is too much going on to keep everything straight.

The prevalence of Mercantilists is thus easy to understand. Most people dislike maths in general and particularly hate the idea of doing anything that seems like going back to school.

One may therefore argue that the success of the doctrine of competitiveness owes much to the excuse it gives would-be experts on world trade for *not* going back to school. The rhetoric of competitiveness has, in effect, made the Mercantilist position seem not only respectable but sophisticated. Like the famed intellectual I was talking to, if an instinctive Mercantilist should be confronted with some puzzling economist's remark about something called 'comparative advantage', some suggestion that the economy is more than the sum of its parts, he need only reply, 'Well, that's not what Lester Thurow says.'

From classical to strategic trade

Once one has tried to talk seriously about trade with people who do not understand comparative advantage, one appreciates anew the astonishing beauty and sophistication of classical trade theory. None the less, there is more to life and even to international trade than comparative advantage; and since about 1980 much of the empirical and analytical effort of international economists has been devoted to departures from the classical approach.

The new trade theory has been the subject of many manifestos and surveys. Rather than try to restate what it was all about, let me simply quote myself, from the introduction to my own 1990 book, *Rethinking International Trade*:

> If one had to provide a concrete example of what the new trade theory is about, it might be this: conventional trade theory views world trade as taking place entirely in goods like wheat; new trade theory sees it as being largely in goods like aircraft. Since a good part of world trade is in goods like wheat, and since even trade in aircraft is subject to some of the same influences that bear on trade in wheat, traditional theory has by no means been disposed of completely. Yet the new theory introduces a whole set of new possibilities and concerns.
>
> Begin with the most basic question: Why is there international trade? The traditional theory answers: Because countries are different. Canada exports wheat to Japan because Canada has so much more arable land *per capita*, and as a result in the absence of trade wheat would be much cheaper in Canada. The differences between

countries that drive trade may lie in resources, technology, or even in tastes, but in any case, traditional theory takes it as axiomatic that countries trade in order to take advantage of their differences.

The new theory acknowledges that differences between countries are one reason for trade, but it adds another: Countries may trade because there are inherent advantages to specialization. The economies of scale in aircraft manufacture are so large that the world market can accommodate at best only a few efficient-scale producers and thus only a few centres of production. Even if Japan and the United States were identical, it is likely that only one country would be producing (say) wide-bodied jet aircraft, and as a result there must be trade in order to allow the centres of production to serve the world market. Of course, the United States and Japan are not identical, but the new theory says that much trade, especially between similar countries, represents specialization to take advantage of increasing returns rather than to capitalize on inherent differences between the countries.

What determines the international pattern of specialization? In traditional theory the answer emerges from the explanation of trade itself: Countries produce goods that would have been relatively cheap in the absence of trade. Comparative advantage may arise from a variety of sources, but in any case the attributes of a country determine what it produces.

In the new theory an important element of arbitrariness is added to this story. Why are aircraft manufactured in Seattle? It is hard to argue that there is some unique attribute of the city's location that fully explains this. The point is, instead, that the logic of increasing returns mandates that aircraft production be concentrated somewhere, and Seattle just happens to be where the roulette wheel came to a stop. In many of the new models of trade, the actual location of production is to some degree indeterminate. Yet what the example of Seattle suggests, and what is explicit in some of the models, is a crucial role for history: Because Seattle (or Detroit or Silicon Valley) was where an industry initially got established, increasing returns keep the industry there.

What are the effects of protection? In traditional trade models a tariff or import quota raises the price of a good for both domestic producers and domestic consumers, reduces imports, and generally, except in some well-understood cases, is a bad thing. In new trade theory the result could be either much worse or much better. Let all countries protect domestic aircraft industries, and the result will be a fragmented world market in which losses arise not only from failure to specialize in accord with comparative advantage but also from inefficient scale production. On the other hand, an individual country that protects its aircraft industry might conceivably increase the scale of that industry sufficiently to reap a net benefit, possibly even lower prices to domestic consumers.

Finally, what is the optimal trade policy? Traditional theory is the usual basis for advocating free trade, one of the most strongly held positions in the economics profession (although actually even in traditional theory a second-best case can be made for protection as a corrective for domestic market failures). The new trade theory suggests a more complex view. The potential gains from trade are even larger in a world of increasing returns, and thus, in a way, the case for free trade is all the stronger. On the other hand, the aircraft example clearly suggests that an individual country acting alone may have reasons not to adopt free trade. New trade models show that it is possible (not certain) that such tools as export subsidies, temporary tariffs, and so on, may shift world specialization in a way favourable to the protecting nation. (Krugman, 1990, pp. 1–3)

This certainly sounds as if the new trade theory not only represents a major change from classical views, but offers considerable scope for government intervention. And many people, ranging from Clyde Prestowitz (1992) to Laura D'Andrea Tyson (1992), have in fact taken this theory as a green light to advocate more or less aggressive, neo-mercantilist policies. So why are none of the people who created the new trade theory Strategists? What is the objection?

From strategic trade policy to cynical realism

A Realist appreciates the sophistication of classical trade theory, but also acknowledges its incompleteness; he is willing to take seriously the ideas of the new trade theorists (especially if he is one of them himself), and to examine the possibilities for productive departures from free trade. None the less, he does not share the interventionist propensities of the Strategist, because he regards acting on the theoretical possibilities for activism to be virtually certain to do more harm than good.

This judgement is essentially empirical rather than theoretical. It rests on three main observations.

First, while it may seem easy in theoretical models to state the conditions for a strategic trade policy, it is extremely hard to translate those conditions into practical advice for real industries. The reason is that while all perfectly competitive industries are pretty much alike, each imperfectly competitive industry is imperfect in its own way. It may not be hard to sound sophisticated about an industry such as aircraft; but if you are asked, say, to provide a quantitative assessment of the likely effects of an export subsidy, you quickly realize that there is a big difference between knowing a lot of facts and really knowing how a market works. And worse yet, if you should happen really to figure out aircraft, you will find that very little of that knowledge generalizes to computers, which are in turn utterly different from telecommunications, which do not at all resemble software…

The difficulty of converting the theoretical possibility of strategic trade policy into practical policy recommendations is well illustrated by the slightly comical story of punditry on the semiconductor industry.

During the 1980s the manufacture of chips took on a sort of iconic status, both as the supposedly canonical example of high-technology industry (although it is very different from other high-tech sectors) and as a supposed demonstration of the superiority of Japanese industrial policy over American *laissez-faire*. Indeed, even in the early 1990s James Fallows (1994) used the example of silicon chips to argue for the bankruptcy of conventional economic analysis. And semiconductors is definitely an industry that departs in important ways from the classical assumptions:

there are strong economies of scale, both at the level of the individual producer and, if real estate prices in Silicon Valley are any indication, at the level of the industry.

But to formulate a useful policy, one must have more than a general sense of the existence of market imperfections: one must be much more specific. Circa 1989, the conventional wisdom on semiconductors was based on two propositions: (i) the key to the industry – its 'technology driver' – was the manufacture of DRAMs (dynamic random access memories), a standardized product with much larger sales volume than more differentiated chips; and (ii) the market for DRAMs was a steadily narrowing circle – only some of those who had produced 16K DRAMs made it into the market for 64Ks, only some of those into the market for 256Ks, and so on.

The conclusion, then, was that Japan's apparent domination of the market for DRAMs would eventually give a few Japanese firms both a monopoly position in that market and technological dominance of the industry as a whole.

But it has not turned out that way at all. America's semiconductor companies have retained and even increased their technological edge in sophisticated special-purpose chips, despite losing the mass-produced memory market to Japan – so it turns out that the presumed spill-over between DRAMs and other chips was illusory, or anyway much weaker than imagined. And DRAMs themselves have turned out not to be the narrowing circle everyone had expected: the Japanese producers have faced new competition, mainly from developing Asian nations but also from re-entering US producers. In short, the conventional wisdom on the nature of the market imperfections in semiconductors appears, at this point, to have been almost completely wrong. And the semiconductor industry is, as modellers of industrial policy can attest, a comparatively easy market to study: its technology and product are relatively well-defined, as compared with such amorphous and complex industries as telecommunications.

The example of semiconductors shows, then, that it is extremely hard to gain enough understanding of an imperfectly competitive industry to formulate an effective strategic policy. But modellers of such industries have also learned something else: even if you think you do understand an industry well enough to devise an activist policy, or are willing for the sake of argument to assume that your model is really good enough, estimates of the gains from strategic trade policies almost always turn out to be very small.

This is not an easy point to explain without going through the details of the extensive modelling efforts in this area; interested readers might want to look at Krugman and Smith (1994) for a sampling of articles. However, the main point may be conveyed by considering a hypothetical scenario. US officials have argued that a true opening of the Japanese market might lead to $20 billion annually in additional US exports, many of them high-technology products; and they have argued that such exports are desirable because these are high-wage sectors. Well, all of this can be quantified. Value-added per worker in high-technology industries is about $80,000; thus $20 billion would mean 250,000 such jobs. The wage premium in high-tech has been estimated by Tyson (1992) at 15 per cent, or about $6,000 per worker. So under favourable assumptions the net gains in wages to the USA if Japan were to give it everything it wanted would be $6,000 times 250,000 or $1.5 billion. That may sound like a lot – but it is only one-fortieth of 1 per cent of America's GDP. And this is a wildly optimistic scenario; no real strategic trade policy is likely to be anywhere close to this effective. The fact is that nobody who has studied strategic trade policy quantitatively has been able to make it appear to be more than a very marginal issue for overall economic success.

Given this economic background – it is very difficult to formulate strategic trade policies, and the evidence we have suggests that, even if you could, it would not be worth much to the economy – one then arrives at the final reason why new trade theorists are generally Realists rather than Strategists: policy-makers are very unlikely to understand any of this. Again, it cannot be emphasized too much that almost everyone who matters is a Mercantilist. I have myself tried to make the numerical argument above to business leaders and pundits who regard themselves as well-informed about international trade. They invariably object to the idea that only the wage premium represents a net gain, wanting to count all of the people employed in producing goods for the Japanese market as a net addition to employment, and indeed wanting to invoke multiplier effects as well. In short, they do not understand even the most basic adding-up constraints.

What this means is that the Strategist who goes to politicians with clever ideas for strategic trade policies is kidding himself. He may imagine that they value the content of his ideas. In fact, they value him because what he says seems to confirm to them their Mercantilist views, and absolves them from the need to understand even classical, let alone 'new', trade theory. Or, to put it more broadly, Mercantilists value Strategists not because they want to be sophisticated, but because they want to feel sophisticated, without actually having to give up their crude but satisfying views. The Realist understands this, and thus ends up sounding very much like a Classicist in denouncing Mercantilists.

The idea of competitiveness

Economists, in general, do not use the word 'competitiveness'. Not one of the textbooks in international economics I have on my shelves contains the word in its index. So why are there so many councils on competitiveness, White Papers on competitiveness, and so on? Why have most people who think about international trade come to use 'competitiveness' as perhaps the central concept of their world-view? [...]

As I said at the beginning of this piece, most of us would like to believe that great public debates are driven by serious intellectual concerns. We would therefore like to believe that if famed intellectuals and powerful politicians talk about 'competitiveness', they must have something meaningful in mind. It seems far too cynical to suggest that the debate over competitiveness is simply a matter of time-honoured fallacies about international trade being dressed up in new and pretentious rhetoric.

But it is.

References

Commission of the European Communities (1993), 'Growth, Competitiveness, Employment: The Challenges and Ways Forward into the 21st Century', *Bulletin of the European Communities,* June.

Fallows, J. (1994), *Looking at the Sun: The Rise of the New East Asian Economic and Political System*, New York, Pantheon.

Krugman, P.R. (1990), *Rethinking International Trade*, Cambridge, MA, MIT Press.

Krugman, P.R. and Smith, M.A.M. (eds) (1994), *Empirical Studies of Strategic Trade Policy*, Chicago, University of Chicago Press.

Prestowitz, C. (1992), 'Beyond Laissez Faire', *Foreign Policy*, 87, 67–87.

Thurow, L. (1992), *Head to Head: The Coming Economic Battle among Japan, Europe, and America*, New York, Morrow.

Tyson, L. D'A. (1992), *Who's Bashing Whom? Trade Conflict in High-technology Industries*, Washington, DC, Institute for International Economics.

HAPTER 12

Themes in Trade and Industrialization

DEEPAK NAYYAR*

1. Introduction

In the post-colonial era, which began soon after the end of the second world war, most underdeveloped countries adopted strategies of development that provided a sharp contrast with their past during the first half of the twentieth century. For one, there was a conscious attempt to limit the degree of openness and of integration with the world economy, in pursuit of a more autonomous, if not self-reliant, development. For another, the State was assigned a strategic role in development because the market, by itself, was not perceived as sufficient to meet the aspirations of late-comers to industrialization. Both represented points of departure from the colonial era, which was characterized by open economies and unregulated markets. But this approach also represented a consensus in thinking about the most appropriate strategy for industrialization. It was, in fact, the development consensus at the time.

It is almost fifty years since then. And it would seem that, in terms of perceptions about development, we have arrived at the polar opposite. Most countries in the developing world, as also in the erstwhile socialist bloc, are reshaping their domestic economic policies so as to integrate much more with the world economy and to enlarge the role of the market *vis-à-vis* the State. This is partly a consequence of internal crisis situations in economy, polity or society. It is also significantly influenced by the profound transformation in the world economic and political situation. The widespread acceptance of this approach represents a new consensus in thinking about development. It has come to be known as the Washington Consensus.

This dramatic change in thinking is significant enough to be characterized as a shift of paradigm. The change, however, is not confined to the domain of thinking. It extends to reality. For the process of globalization is changing the character

* Oxford University Press, India for an extract from *Trade and Industrialization* by Deepak Nayyar © Deepak Nayyar, 1997.

of the world economy. Yet, the theme of trade and industrialization has remained central to the debate throughout this period. It was then. It is now.

[…] This essay seeks to explore themes in trade and industrialization which have not received sufficient attention in mainstream literature […]. Section 2 begins with the underlying economic theory. It sets out the logic of the free trade argument and explains the rationale of exceptions to this rule. Section 3 examines the evolution of thinking about the degree of openness (in the sphere of trade) and the degree of intervention (by the State in the market) in the process of industrialization, to provide a critical assessment of the consensus: old and new. […] Section 4 sketches the broad contours of globalization in the contemporary world economy, which has changed the international context, to discuss what it means for trade and industriali- zation in the developing world. […]

2. Economic theory and the free trade doctrine

It is necessary, as also appropriate, to begin by outlining the logic of the free trade doctrine, which has received so much emphasis in economic theory, and by explaining the rationale of departures for free trade, which have been central to the debate on trade and industrialization over the past two centuries.[1]

The analytical foundations of the orthodox theory of international trade, as it now exists, were laid in the era of classical political economy by Adam Smith, David Ricardo and John Stuart Mill. Smith (1776) enunciated the principle of absolute advantage to demonstrate that there were gains from trade, by extending his concept of the division of labour between men to a division of labour between countries. Ricardo (1812) formulated the theory of comparative advantage to develop an explicit argument against protection and an implicit argument for free trade. At the same time, Smith and Ricardo endeavoured to provide a rationale, as also to analyse the conditions, for a transition from the prevalent feudalism to a prospective capitalism. Thus, for Adam Smith, free trade was simply one dimension of the case for *laissez faire* which confirmed his belief in the magic of the invisible hand. Similarly, for David Ricardo, the formulation of comparative advantage was not simply about the pattern of trade or the gains from trade, as contemporary textbooks would have us believe. It was as much, if not more, about the impact of international trade on income distribution, capital accumulation and economic growth. The repeal of the Corn Laws and the adoption of free trade was advocated by Ricardo in the belief that it would redistribute incomes away from the reactionary landed gentry, who would at worst not save and at best invest in agriculture which promised diminishing returns, in favour of a progressive industrial capitalist class, who would earn more profits (given a lower corn wage) through cheap imports of wheat, and invest in manufacturing which promised increasing returns. The moral of the story was that, consequent upon the removal of restrictions on trade, an increase in profits would lead to an increase in the rate of accumulation, which in turn would lead to growth in employment, income and wealth.

Subsequent economic theorizing about international trade, beginning in the late nineteenth century, became much narrower in perspective.[2] The neoclassical paradigm, as it emerged, emphasized the gains from trade. The economic logic underlying the proposition was indeed simple. In the most elementary sense, there are gains to be derived from trade if it is cheaper for an economy to import a good than to produce it at home, in terms of domestic resources used, and pay for it by exporting another. The gains are attributable in part to international exchange when cost or price differ among countries before trade is introduced, and in part to international specialization in production after trade commences. In a world where countries enter into international trade on a voluntary basis, each partner must derive some benefit to be in the game. The very existence of trade, then, becomes proof of its mutual benefit, irrespective of how the gains from trade are distributed between countries. Orthodox theory combined the economic logic of the gains from trade proposition with the assumption of perfect competition to establish that free trade will enable an economy to operate with technical efficiency in production, in terms of resource allocation, and to optimize consumption through trade, in terms of utility maximization. The neat conclusion derived from this theorizing is that free trade ensures efficiency for a country and for the world as a whole.

The belief in free trade is almost a sacred tenet in the world of orthodox economics. Yet, from time to time, the profession of economics has recognized that there are reasons – orthodox and unorthodox – which may justify departures from free trade.[3] Economic theory has analysed these exceptions to the rule, mostly in response to developments in the real world which have questioned the free trade doctrine.

In the era of classical political economy, even before the doctrine gained widespread acceptance, it was recognized that there are two critical assumptions underlying the strong prescription of free trade: first, that market prices reflect social costs; and, second, that a country's trade in a good is not large enough to influence world prices. If these assumptions do not hold, free trade cannot ensure an efficient outcome. Market failure provides the basis of the infant industry argument, recognizing that free trade may prevent an economy from realizing its comparative advantage in manufacturing activities. Monopoly power provides the basis of the optimum tariff arguments recognizing that restricting the volume of trade may enable an economy to increase its real income at the expense of the rest of the world. These arguments were accepted as valid exceptions to the rule by Mill (1848), thus providing the analytical foundation for legitimate departures from free trade. It must be recognized that this thinking was prompted largely by the concerns of late industrializers such as the United States and Germany who wished to follow in the footsteps of England and France.[4] It was also motivated by the pursuit of economic interests rather than economic efficiency on the part of nation states.

More than a century later, at the beginning of the post-colonial era, the aspirations of underdeveloped countries were similar for they were latecomers to industrialization and wanted to accelerate the catching-up process. In the realm of politics, of course, the strong sentiment against free trade stemmed from the perceived association between openness and underdevelopment during the colonial era. In the sphere of economics, however, the argument against free trade was based on market failure. It had two dimensions. First, it was argued that there were significant positive externalities in any process of industrialization which were difficult to identify, let alone capture. Second, it was argued that imperfections in factor markets, both labour and capital, would pre-empt the realization of potential comparative advantages in manufacturing. The infant industry argument was, thus, generalized into the infant-manufacturing sector argument.[5] The industrial sector was protected from foreign competition and the pursuit of industrialization in most developing countries came to be based on the strategy of import substitution.

The response of modern neoclassical economics was twofold. At one level, it accepted the infant industry argument, or the optimum tariff argument, as the basis of justifiable departures from free trade, but reduced the validity of such arguments to a very demanding set of conditions.[6] At another level, it argued that if market prices did not measure social costs, whether on account of a divergence arising out of market failure or on account of a distortion arising out of government intervention, the optimum policy intervention is one which is applied at the point at which the divergence or the distortion arises; the simple solution which followed from this complex discussion was that, as a rule, intervention in the form of trade policies would be sub-optimal.[7] In sum, such theoretical analysis sought to strengthen the case for free trade by accepting that there is market failure and by arguing that protection is not the best corrective.

Recent developments in the theory of international trade which have relaxed the assumptions of constant returns to scale and perfect competition to model scale economies and market structures have, once again, questioned the free trade argument.[8] This literature on strategic trade policy, which surfaced in the industrialized countries during the 1980s, developed a theoretical case for government intervention in trade on the basis of assumptions which are different from those in orthodox theory but conform more to observed reality.[9] In terms of positive economics, the new theories suggest that trade flows are driven by increasing returns rather than comparative advantage in international markets which are characterized by imperfect competition. This has led to the formulation of two arguments against free trade in the sphere of normative economics.[10] The first is the strategic trade policy argument, which states that appropriate forms of government intervention can deter entry by foreign firms into lucrative markets and thus manipulate the terms of oligopolistic competition to ensure that excess returns are captured by domestic firms. The idea is that, in a market which has a small number of competitors, strategic support for domestic firms in international competition can raise national welfare at the expense of other countries. The second is an old argument in a new incarnation which states that governments should encourage activities that yield positive externalities. In a world of increasing returns and imperfect competition, such externalities are easier to identify in industries where R&D expenditures are large and firms cannot entirely appropriate the benefits from investment in technology and learning.

It should come as no surprise that the new trade theories received an asymmetrical response from economists: ready acceptance of the positive aspects and strong criticism of the normative aspects. Orthodox economics set out three criticisms: (a) it is difficult to model imperfect markets and thus impossible to formulate appropriate policies for intervention; (b) potential gains from intervention would be dissipated by the entry of rent-seeking firms; and (c) in a general equilibrium world, the benefits from explicit promotion of one sector may be less than the cost of implicit discrimination against other sectors. These criticisms may weaken the arguments against free trade, but they cannot eliminate them. Yet, the new theorizing has withdrawn in the face of criticism on the basis of what is described as wider considerations of political economy. The explanation runs as follows. For one, it is possible that successful intervention would have a beggar-thy-neighbour impact, which could lead to retaliation by trading partners, making everybody worse off. For another, governments are not Plato's guardians, who act in the national interest, and intervention may simply be manipulated by vested interests who can influence the State to appropriate economic gains. This strategic withdrawal leads Paul Krugman (1987, p. 143) to a revealing conclusion:

> The economic cautions about the difficulty of formulating useful interventions and the political economy concerns that interventionism may go astray combine into a new case for free trade. This is not the old argument that free trade is optimal because markets are efficient. Instead, it is a sadder but wiser argument for free trade as a rule of thumb in a world whose politics is as imperfect as its markets. ... It is possible, then, both to believe that comparative advantage is an incomplete model of trade and to believe that free trade is nevertheless the right policy. In fact, this is the position taken by most of new trade theorists themselves. So free trade is not passé – but it is not what it once was.

The preceding discussion suggests that economic theory has, from time to time, thrown up serious questions about free trade. The response of orthodoxy has been predictable. It has endeavoured to reduce the validity of the widely accepted arguments for protection to a set of stringent conditions. It has attempted to dilute the arguments against free trade, in the context of industrialization and development, by arguing that domestic economic policies provide the first-best corrective. It has coaxed the new trade theorists into an acceptance of free trade as the best policy by invoking the real world of politics. The exceptions, it would seem, have been explored to establish the rule.

Yet, these exceptions have provided the rationale for departures from free trade in the real world of policy choices. The infant industry argument, sometimes generalized into the infant manufacturing sector argument, has shaped the strategies of most countries that were, or are, latecomers to industrialization, at least in the earlier stages of their development. It has, therefore, been the focus of an extensive literature and an intensive debate on trade and industrialization, particularly with reference to the experience of the developing world during the second half of the twentieth century. In recent years, the new trade theories have revived the same issues and similar concerns by exploring the linkages between trade, industrialization and growth in a dynamic context. For one, these theories have emphasized, once again, the importance of externalities, scale or learning, and recognized, for the first time, the significance of market structures. For another, these theories have pointed to the inequalizing effects of trade (Krugman, 1981), given the importance of initial conditions, so that even if trade is good, more trade is not always better. Thus, unmindful of the conclusions reached by orthodoxy, economic theory has lent new dimensions to the discussion on openness and industrialization.

3. Openness, intervention and industrialization

The theme of trade and industrialization, situated in the wider context of development, has aroused considerable interest and stimulated much debate among economists over the past fifty years. It is striking that, throughout this period, the degree of openness *vis-à-vis* the world economy and the degree of intervention by the State in the market have remained the critical issues, despite the shift in paradigm from the development consensus of the early 1950s to the Washington Consensus of the early 1990s.

At the beginning of the post-colonial era, there was a clear consensus in thinking about development. It was widely accepted that underdeveloped countries must industrialize and that their industrialization must be based on import substitution in the manufacturing sector combined with a leading role for the State in the process of economic development. This consensus was dominant until the early 1970s.

It was the actual industrialization experience of economies in Asia, Africa and Latin America, during the quarter century which followed the second world war that led to questions. Research on the subject which attempted to describe, analyse and evaluate this experience suggested that industrialization in developing countries was characterized by success-stories in a few, muddling-through in some and near-failure in others. Such uneven development, over time and across space, should not have come as a surprise. For those who questioned conventional wisdom, however, the post-mortem of failures led to a diagnosis while the analysis of successes led to prescriptions. These lessons drawn from the experience of particular countries were sought to be generalized and transplanted elsewhere. Such an approach tended to ignore not only the complexities of the growth process but also the characteristics of economies which are specific in time and space.

Yet, this approach came to exercise a profound influence on thinking about development. Its origins can be traced to the work of Little et al. (1970), which attempted a systematic evaluation of the industrialization experience in selected developing countries to question the development consensus. Among the country-studies, India's industrialization experience was examined by Bhagwati and Desai (1970). This set of studies was followed by those of Bhagwati (1978) and Krueger (1978) some years later, in which Bhagwati and Srinivasan (1975) studied the Indian experience. These studies were among the first to provide an elaborate critique of the industrialization experience until then, from a neoclassical perspective, suggesting that the policy framework led to economic inefficiency and resource misallocation while the cumulative effect of these policies became an obstacle to growth. The basic object of these studies was an evaluation of import-substitution strategies and the economic efficiency of industrialization. The main conclusion was that industrialization policies, which protected domestic industries from foreign competition and led to excessive or inappropriate State intervention in the market, were responsible for the high cost and the low growth in these economies. Inward-looking policies, particularly in the sphere of trade, were seen as the prime culprit. The prescription followed from the critique. More openness and less intervention would impart both efficiency and dynamism to the growth process. And outward-looking policies, particularly in the sphere of trade, were seen as the prime saviour. Thus, trade policies were perceived as critical in the process of industrialization and development.

It needs to be said that this approach to trade and industrialization was narrow in its focus. For it was not recognized that there is more to trade policies than the distinction between import substitution and export promotion or inward and outward orientation, just as there is much more to industrialization than simply trade policies.[11] Even more important, perhaps, this approach was selective in its use of theory and history. For one, there was a striking asymmetry between the unqualified enthusiasm of policy prescriptions advocating free(r) trade, unmindful of the distinction between statics and dynamics or irrespective of time and place, and the formal exposition of the free trade argument in economic theory, with its careful assumptions, proofs and exceptions.[12] For another, the characterization of the success stories as economies which approximated to free trade and *laissez-faire* was partial if not caricature history, for their export orientation was not the equivalent of free trade, just as the visible hand of the State was more in evidence than the invisible hand of the market.[13]

In spite of these limitations, however, the neoclassical critique continued to gather momentum through the 1980s. The policy prescriptions derived from it became increasingly influential as these were adopted by the World Bank, to begin with in its research agenda and subsequently in its policy menu.[14] The process was reinforced by the reality that unfolded. The earlier success stories – South Korea, Hong Kong, Taiwan and Singapore – turned into the East Asian miracle, which spread to China, Malaysia, Thailand and even Indonesia. The debt-crisis which surfaced in Latin America moved to sub-Saharan Africa and ultimately caught up with South Asia. The collapse of the political system in East Europe, particularly in the former Soviet Union, represented the failure of planned economies. The disillusionment with the development consensus was complete. And, by the early 1990s, the Washington Consensus acquired a near-hegemonic status in thinking about development.

Economic policies and development strategies in much of the developing world and the erstwhile socialist bloc are now shaped by the Washington Consensus, in part because it provides the basis of policy reform advocated by the International Monetary Fund and the World Bank in their stabilization and structural adjustment programmes. In content, these adjustment and reform programmes are more elaborate than the earlier incarnation based on the neoclassical critique, but the logic is similar if not the same. The bottom line is more openness and less intervention. There is, however, more to openness than trade. It extends to investment flows, technology flows and financial flows. Similarly, reduced State intervention extends beyond deregulation and liberalization. It suggests rolling back the government in every sphere. Structural reform seeks to shift resources: (a) from the non-traded goods sector to the traded goods sector and within the latter from import-competing activities to export activities; and (b) from the government sector to the private sector. Apart from such resource allocation, structural reform seeks to improve resource utilization: (i) by increasing the degree of openness of an economy; and (ii) by changing the structure of incentives and institutions, which would reduce the role of the State to rely more on market forces and wind up the public sector to rely on the private sector.

It would mean too much of a digression to enter into a detailed discussion on the industrialization experience, its neoclassical critique and the neo-liberal prescription. There is an extensive literature on the subject, which is characterized by a diversity of views that range from the orthodox through the heterodox to the unorthodox. [...] Instead, I would simply like to highlight some of the analytical limitations of the new orthodoxy on trade and industrialization.

First, it is a simple fallacy in logic to claim that if something (State intervention or protection) does not work, its opposite (the free market or free trade) must work. This is true only in a dichotomous world of two alternatives. In the world of economic policies, where there are always more than two alternatives, such a view is obviously false. Thus, if A is wrong, it does not mean that the opposite of A (say B) must necessarily be right. If there are other alternatives, say C, D, E, or F, one of these rather than B may be right.

Second, the emphasis on trade liberalization, which assumes that international competition will force domestic firms to become more efficient, makes an elementary but commonplace error in the design of policies. It confuses *comparison* (of equilibrium positions) with *change* (from one equilibrium position to another). In the real world, economic policy must be concerned not merely with comparison but with how to direct the process of change. Thus, even if a reduction in protection can, in principle, lead to a more cost-efficient economy, the transition path is by no means clear. And the process of change should not be confused with the ultimate destination of an economy that is competitive in the world market.

Third, the analytical construct is narrow. Success at industrialization is not only about resource allocation and resource utilization at a micro-level. It is as much, if not more, about resource mobilization and resource creation at a macro-level. The excessive concern with resource allocation, in terms of static allocative efficiency criteria, is perhaps misplaced, while the strong emphasis on resource utilization, in terms of competition through deregulation and openness, is important but disproportionate. Significant new developments in the neoclassical tradition, whether in industrial economics or in trade theory, are almost ignored when such analysis is applied to problems of industrialization and development. Hence this approach, which is static rather than dynamic in conception, tends to ignore inter-temporal considerations and does not quite incorporate increasing returns, market structures, externalities or learning, which are inherent in any process of industrialization.

Fourth, there is a presumption that what is necessary is also sufficient. The management of incentives, motivated by the object of minimizing cost and maximizing efficiency at a micro-level, is based on a set of policies that is intended to increase competition between firms in the marketplace. Domestic competition is sought to be provided through deregulation in investment decisions, in the financial sector and in labour markets. Foreign competition is sought to be provided through openness in trade, investment and technology flows. It must, however, be recognized that policies may be necessary but not sufficient, for there is nothing automatic about competition. Policy regimes can allow things to happen but cannot cause things to happen. The creation of competitive markets that enforce efficiency may, in fact, require strategic intervention through industrial policy, trade policy and financial policy.

Fifth, the strong emphasis on allocative efficiency is matched by a conspicuous silence on technical efficiency. It is forgotten that low levels of productivity in most developing countries are attributable more to technical inefficiency than to allocative inefficiency. And inter-country differences, as also inter-firm differences, in technical efficiency are explained, in large part, by differences in technological (and managerial) capabilities at a micro-level. These capabilities determine not just efficiency in the short run but also competitiveness in the long run. But, given the nature of the learning process, such capabilities are both firm-specific and path-dependent.[15] The new orthodoxy simply ignores this critical dimension on the supply side. In contrast, the heterodox literature places the acquisition and development of technological capabilities centre-stage in the story of success at industrialization.[16] It also shows that the presumed relationship between trade liberalization and technical efficiency is dubious in terms of both theory and evidence.[17]

[…]

4. Globalization: the changed context

The preceding discussion suggests that the orthodox literature on trade and industrialization is narrow and selective in its focus. But that is not all. Subsequent development in the world economy, manifest in globalization, have led to far-reaching changes in the reality. The debate on trade and industrialization must now be situated in the changed international context if it is to retain its relevance.

Globalization means different things to different people. It can be defined simply as the expansion of economic activities across political boundaries of nation states. More important, perhaps, it refers to a process of increasing economic openness, growing economic interdependence and deepening economic integration between countries in the world economy. It is associated not only with a phenomenal spread and volume of cross-border economic transactions but also with an organization of economic activities which straddles national boundaries. This process is driven by the lure of profit and the threat of competition in the market.

The word *globalization* is used in two ways, which is a source of confusion and a cause of controversy. It is used in a *positive* sense to *describe* a process of increasing integration into the world economy: the characterization of this process is by no means uniform. It is used in a *normative* sense to *prescribe* a strategy of development based on a rapid integration with the world economy: some see this as salvation while others see it as damnation.

The world economy has experienced a progressive international economic integration since 1950. However, there has been a marked acceleration in this process of globalization during the last quarter of the twentieth century. The fundamental attribute of globalization is the increasing degree of openness in most countries. There are three dimensions of this phenomenon: international trade, international investment and international finance. It needs to be said that openness is not simply confined to trade flows, investment flows and financial flows. It also extends to flows of services, technology, information and ideas across national boundaries. But the cross-border movement of people is closely regulated and highly restricted. And, there can be no doubt that trade, investment and finance constitute the cutting edge of globalization.

The gathering momentum of globalization has already brought about profound changes in the world economy. It is worth highlighting the broad contours of these changes.[18] An increasing proportion of world output is entering into world trade, while an increasing proportion of world trade is made up of intra-firm trade (across national boundaries but between affiliates of the same firm). Between the early 1970s and the early 1990s, the share of world exports in world GDP rose from one-eighth to one-sixth, while the share of intra-firm trade in world trade rose from one-fifth to one-third. The significance of international investment flows has also registered a rapid increase. Between 1980 and 1992, the stock of direct foreign investment in the world as a proportion of world output rose from 4.8 per cent to 8.4 per cent, while world direct foreign investment flows as a proportion of world gross fixed capital formation rose from 2 per cent to 3.7 per cent. The growth in international finance has been explosive. So much so that in terms of magnitudes, trade and investment are now dwarfed by finance. The expansion of international banking is phenomenal. Between 1980 and 1991, net international bank loans increased from 51.1 per cent to 131.4 per cent of gross fixed domestic investment in the world economy. The international market for financial assets has experienced a similar growth. Between 1980 and 1993, gross sales and purchases of bonds and equities transacted between domestic and foreign residents rose from less than 10 per cent of GDP to more than

100 per cent of GDP in the major industrialized countries. Government debt has also become tradeable. Between 1980 and 1992, the proportion of government bonds held by foreigners rose from less than 10 per cent to more than 25 per cent in many industrialized countries. Global foreign exchange transactions have soared from $60 billion per day in 1983 to $900 billion per day in 1992. The size of international foreign exchange markets is staggering. This is apparent from the fact that, in 1992, world GDP was $64 billion per day and world exports were $10 billion per day, while the reserves of central banks put together were $693 billion.

The politics of hegemony or dominance is conducive to the economics of globalization. The process of globalization, beginning in the early 1970s, has coincided with the political dominance of the United States as the superpower. This political dominance has grown stronger with the collapse of communism and with the triumph of capitalism. And the political conjuncture has transformed the concept of globalization into a 'virtual ideology' of our times. Dominance in the realm of politics is associated with an important attribute in the sphere of economics. For globalization requires a dominant economic power with a national currency which is accepted as the equivalent of international money: as a unit of account, a medium of exchange and a store of value. In the late twentieth century, this role is being performed by the US dollar, ironically enough after the collapse of the Bretton Woods system when its statutory role as a reserve currency came to an end.

Economic theorizing often follows in the footsteps of political reality. It should come as no surprise, then, that recent years have witnessed the formulation of an intellectual rationale for globalization that is almost prescriptive. It is perceived as a means of ensuring not only efficiency and equity but also growth and development in the world economy. The analytical foundations of this world view are provided by the neo-liberal model. And it builds on the infrastructure of the Washington Consensus. Orthodox neoclassical economics suggests that intervention in markets is inefficient. Neo-liberal political economy argues that governments are incapable of intervening efficiently. The essence of the neo-liberal model, then, can be stated as follows. First, the government should be rolled back wherever possible so that it approximates to the ideal of a minimalist State. Second, the market is not only a substitute for the State but also the preferred alternative because it performs better. Third, resource allocation and resource utilization must be based on market prices which should conform as closely as possible to international prices. Fourth, national political objectives, domestic economic concerns or even national boundaries should not act as constraints.[19] In conformity with this world view, governments everywhere, particularly in the developing countries and the former communist, countries, are being urged or pushed into a comprehensive agenda of privatization (to minimize the role of the State) and liberalization (of trade flows, capital flows and financial flows). It is suggested that such policy regimes would provide the foundations for a global economic system characterized by free trade, unrestricted capital mobility, open markets and harmonized institutions. And the ideologues believe that such globalization promises economic prosperity for countries that join the system and economic deprivation for countries that do not.[20]

It needs to be stressed that this normative and prescriptive view of globalization is driven in part by ideology and in part by hope. It is not validated by history. The process of globalization during the period from 1870 to 1914, which provides a remarkable historical parallel, did not reproduce or replicate Britain everywhere.[21] Indeed, some of the most open economies in this earlier phase of globalization, such as India, China and Indonesia, experienced de-industrialization and under-development. The process of globalization was uneven then. It is so even now. There are less than a dozen developing countries which are an integral part of globalization in the late twentieth century: Argentina, Brazil and Mexico in Latin America; and South Korea, Hong Kong, Taiwan, Singapore, China, Indonesia, Malaysia and Thailand in Asia.[22] It would seem that globalization is most uneven in its spread. And, there is an exclusion in the process. Sub-Saharan Africa, West Asia, Central Asia and South Asia and many countries in Latin America and the Pacific are simply left out of the picture altogether. It is, then, plausible to suggest that globalization may lead to uneven development in the late twentieth century just as it did in the late nineteenth century.[23] But there can be no doubt that this process of globalization has profound implications for trade and industrialization everywhere in the developing world.

The process of globalization has placed new players centre-stage. There are two main sets of economic players in this game: transnational corporations, which dominate investment, production and trade in the world economy, and international banks or financial intermediaries, which control the world of finance. It would seem that the present conjuncture represents the final frontier in the global reach of capitalism to organize production, trade, investment and finance on a world scale without any fetters except, of course, for tight controls on labour mobility. Transnational corporations and international banks or financial inter-mediaries wish to set new rules of the game which would enable them to manage the risks associated with globalization. In this task, the nation states of the industrialized world provide the much needed political clout and support. The multilateral framework of the World Trade Organization, the International Monetary Fund and the World Bank is, perhaps, the most important medium.

The rules of the game for the international trading system are being pro-gressively set in the World Trade Organization. It would seem that this institutional framework for globalization is characterized by a striking asymmetry.[24] National boundaries should not matter for trade flows and capital flows but should be clearly demarcated for technology flows and labour flows. It follows that the developing countries would provide access to their markets without a corresponding access to technology and would accept capital mobility without a corresponding provision for labour mobility. This asymmetry, particularly that between the free movement of capital and the unfree movement of labour across national boundaries, lies at the heart of the inequality in the rules of the game for globalization in the late twenti-eth century. These new rules, which serve the interests of transnational corpora-tions as capital-exporters and technology-leaders in the world economy, are explicit as an integral part of a multilateral regime of discipline.

The rules of the game, which would serve the interests of the international banks or financial intermediaries in the process of globalization, are in part implicit and in part unwritten. Even here, there is an asymmetry as there are rules for some but not for other. There are no rules for surplus countries or even deficit countries in the industrialized world, which do not borrow from the multilateral financial institutions. But the IMF and the World Bank set rules for borrowers in the developing world and the erstwhile socialist bloc. The conditionality is meant in principle to ensure repayment but in practice it imposes conditions to serve the interests of international banks which lend to the same countries. The Bretton Woods institutions, then, act as watchdogs for moneylenders in international capital markets. This has been so for some time. But there is more to it now. IMF programmes of stabilization and World Bank programmes of structural adjustment in developing countries and in the erstwhile communist countries impose conditions that stipulate structural reform of policy regimes. The object is to increase the degree of openness of these economies and to reduce the role of the State, so that market forces shape economic decisions. In this manner, the Bretton Woods institutions seek to harmonize policies and institutions across countries, which is in consonance with the needs of globalization.

In a world of unequal partners it is not surprising that the rules of the game are asymmetrical, if not inequitable. But the process of globalization, combined with these rules, is bound to reduce significantly the autonomy of developing countries in the formulation of economic policies in their pursuit of industrialization and development. This is attributable, in part, to the asymmetrical rules and, in part, to the economic implications of globalization.

The existing (and prospective) rules of the WTO regime allow few exceptions and provide little flexibility to countries that are latecomers to industrialization. There was more room for manoeuvre in the erstwhile GATT, *inter alia*, because of special and differential treatment for developing countries. The new regime is much stricter in terms of the law and the implementation. The rules on market access, tariff binding, quantitative restrictions, subsidies, and so on, will make the selective protection or strategic promotion of domestic firms *vis-à-vis* foreign competition much more difficult. The tight system for the protection of intellectual property rights might pre-empt or stifle the development of domestic technological capabilities. The possible multilateral framework for investment, when it materializes, will almost certainly reduce the possibilities of strategic bargaining with transnational firms. Similarly, commitments on structural reform, an integral part of stabilization and adjustment programmes with the IMF and the World Bank, inevitably prescribe industrial deregulation, privatization, trade liberalization and financial deregulation. Taken together, such rules and conditions are bound to curb the use of industrial policy, technology policy, trade policy and financial policy as strategic forms of intervention to foster industrialization.

The constraints implicit in the economics of globalization are most easily explained with an example. Consider the vulnerability associated with rapid integration into international financial markets, which often begins with a reliance on portfolio investment to finance current account deficits in the balance of payments. An economy needs high interest rates together with a strong exchange rate regime to sustain portfolio investment flows in terms of both profitability and confidence. This erodes the competitiveness of exports over time and enlarges the trade deficit. It is important to recognize the macroeconomic implications. Larger trade deficits and current account deficits require larger portfolio investment inflows, which, beyond a point, undermine confidence and create adverse expectations, even if the government keeps the exchange rate pegged. But when a stifling of exports does ultimately force an exchange rate depreciation, confidence may simply collapse and lead to capital flight. These problems have indeed surfaced in several Latin American economies; most recently in Mexico.

The problem is, in fact, much deeper and larger. Exchange rates can no longer be used as a strategic device to provide an entry into the world market for manufactured goods, just as interest rates can no longer be used as a strategic instrument for guiding the allocation of scarce investible resources in a market economy. What is more, countries which are integrated into the world monetary system are constrained in using an autonomous management of demand to maintain levels of output and employment. Expansionary fiscal and monetary policies – large government deficits to stimulate aggregate demand or low interest rates to encourage domestic investment – can no longer be used because of an over-whelming fear that such measures could lead to speculative capital flight and a run on the national currency.

It is not surprising that the advent of international capital associated with globalization has meant significant political adjustment in the contemporary world. It has induced a strategic withdrawal on the part of the nation state in some important spheres. They remain the main political players but are no longer the main economic players. We live in an era where the old-fashioned autonomy of the nation state is being eroded by international industrial capital and international finance capital everywhere, both in the industrialized world and in the developing world. It needs to be stressed, however, that there is a qualitative difference in the relationship between international capital and the nation state when we compare the industrialized world with the developing world. The nation state in the former has far more room for manoeuvre than the nation state in the latter. In the industrialized countries, the political interests of the nation state often coincide with the economic interests of international capital. This is not so for developing countries, from which very few transnational corporations or international banks originate. In spite of the profound changes unleashed by the present phase of globalization, however, it would be naive to write off the nation state, for it remains a crucial player in political and strategic terms. Even today, only nation states have the authority to set the rules of the game. The nation states in the industrialized world provide international capital with the means to set new rules for the game of globalization. The nation states in the developing world provide these countries and their people with the means of finding degrees of freedom *vis-à-vis* international capital in the pursuit of development. [...]

5. Conclusion

This essay explores selected themes in trade and industrialization situated in the wider context of development. The stage is set by explaining the rationale of departures from free trade in economic theory and by setting out the orthodox critique of the experience with industrialization in developing countries. The latter highlights the sins of import substitution and State intervention to stress the virtues of openness and markets. However, the policy prescriptions derived are strong generalizations which do not match orthodox trade theory in terms of rigour and do not recognize recent theoretical developments in terms of insights. What is more, the neo-classical critique and the neo-liberal prescription are both characterized by analytical limitations. The discussion also reveals that the mainstream literature on trade and industrialization is narrow in its focus just as it is selective in its use of theory and experience. [...]

It is worth emphasizing an important conclusion that emerges. In spite of the shift in paradigm from the development consensus of the 1950s to the Washington Consensus of the 1990s, the degree of openness *vis-à-vis* the world economy and the degree of intervention by the State in the market have remained the critical issues in the debate on industrialization. This period during the second half of the twentieth century has, of course, witnessed a complete swing of the pendulum in thinking about these two issues. But the complexity of reality is not captured by either consensus: old or new.

The changed international context, attributable to globalization, has important implications for trade and industrialization in the developing world which must be recognized. An increase in the degree of openness of economies is inevitable, while the degrees of freedom for nation states are bound to be fewer. But it would be a mistake to consider this necessity as a virtue. Simplified prescriptions, which emphasize more openness and less intervention to advocate a rapid integration with the world economy combined with a minimalist state that vacates space for the market, are not validated either by theory or by history. Economic theory recognizes and economic history reveals the complexities of the industrialization process. The degree of openness and the nature of intervention are strategic choices in the pursuit of industrialization which cannot be defined (and should not be prescribed) once-and-for-all for they depend upon the stage of development and must change over time. And there can be no magic recipes in a world where economies are characterized by specificities in time and space. The irony is that, at the present juncture, when the disillusionment with the State is so widespread, given the reality of globalization, its role in the pursuit of industrialization and development is more critical than ever before. However, this does not mean, nor should it suggest, more of the same. Correcting for mistakes and learning from experience is vital. It is therefore essential to redefine the economic role of the State *vis-à-vis* the market, so that the two institutions complement each other and adapt to one another as circumstances or times change. That is what success at industrialization is about.

Notes

I am indebted to Amit Bhaduri for helpful discussion. I would also like to thank Satish Jain, Mrituinjoy Mohanty, Anjan Mukherji and Abhijit Sen for useful suggestions.

1   For a detailed discussion. see Nayyar (1996a).

2   This process started with Alfred Marshall and Francis Edgeworth in the late nineteenth century. It was taken to its logical conclusion by Eli Heckscher (1919), Bertil Ohlin (1933) and Paul Samuelson (1939) during the first half of the twentieth century.

3   The challenges to free trade are discussed, at some length, by Irwin (1991) and Bhagwati (1994). See also Nayyar (1996a).

4   The origin of the infant industry argument is associated with Alexander Hamilton, whose *Report on Manufactures* was published in the United States in 1791, and Friedrich List, whose *Das Nationale System der Politischen Okonomie* was published in Germany in 1841.

5   This generalization is attributable, among others, to Myrdal (1956). It was also in keeping with List's conception of an infant economy argument.

6   See, for example, Corden (1974), who provides a meticulous analysis of the condition under which the infant industry argument and the optimum tariff argument constitute valid arguments for protection.

7   Cf. Bhagwati and Ramaswami (1963) and Corden (1974). In this context, there are two points that are worth noting. First, an appropriately chosen trade policy intervention, even if it is second-best or third-best, may result in a level of welfare higher than would be attainable under free trade. Second, the tax-cum-subsidy alternative may not be first-best if the taxes levied involve large collection costs or impose sizeable distortions elsewhere and if the disbursement costs of subsidies are significant.

8   For an overview of new theories of international trade, see Dixit and Norman (1980), Helpman and Krugman (1985) and Krugman (1986).

9   It is no coincidence, however, that such theorizing has coincided with the resurgence of protectionism in the industrialized world. The analytical foundations of the new trade theories can be traced to the work of Edward Chamberlin and Joan Robinson, who explored the world of market structures other than perfect competition or pure monopoly. It become clear that, under conditions of imperfect competition, market prices did not reflect social costs. This undermined the basis of the free trade argument. But the question was not even posed. The ability of the new trade theories to question the optimality of free trade is, perhaps, attributable to the juncture in time.

10 For a lucid exposition of these arguments, which are associated with the work of several economists who have worked on the new trade theories, see Krugman (1987).

11 Cf. Helleiner (1992).

12 In an essay on the debate about trade and industrialization, this proposition was set out most succinctly by Carlos Diaz-Alejandro (1975, p. 96): 'In the trade and development literature, there has existed for a long time, going back at least to John Stuart Mill, a striking difference between the rigour of

formal proofs on the static advantages of free trade typically involving careful assumptions and caveats, and the impetuous euthusiasm with which most of the professional mainstream advocates free or freer trade policies, on both static and dynamic grounds, for all times and places.'

13 In the literature on the development experience of the East Asian success stories – Hong Kong, South Korea, Singapore and Taiwan – Lee (1981) was among the first to emphasize this limitation. It has come to be recognized far more widely with the subsequent work of Amsden (1989) and Wade (1991). See also Singh (1994). [The issue is discussed by Lall Chapter 10 of this volume.]

14 The research publications of the World Bank provide ample confirmation. See, for example, *World Development Report 1987* and World Bank (1993).

15 Cf. Rosenberg (1994).

16 See, for example, Lall (1997). See also Bell and Pavitt (1993), Dahlman et al. (1987) and Pack and Westphal (1986).

17 In an essay which analyses the relationship between trade policy and technical efficiency, based on theory and experience, Rodrik (1992, p. 172) reaches the following conclusion: 'If truth in advertising were to apply to policy advice, each prescription for trade liberalization would be accompanied with a disclaimer: Warning! Trade liberalization cannot be shown to enhance technical efficiency, nor has it been empirically demonstrated to do so.'

18 The figures cited in this paragraph draw upon earlier work by the author. For sources and details, see Nayyar (1995).

19 In this world, domestic economic concerns mesh with, and are subsumed in, the max-imization of international economic welfare, and national political objectives melt away in the bargain.

20 See, for example, Sachs and Warner (1995).

21 For an analysis of this historical parallel, between globalization in the late nineteenth century and in the late twentieth century, see Nayyar (1995).

22 These eleven countries accounted for 66 per cent of total exports from developing countries in 1992. The same countries, excluding South Korea, were also the main recipients of direct foreign investment in the developing world, accounting for 66 per cent of the average annual inflows during the period 1981–91 (Nayyar, 1995).

23 This argument is developed, at some length, in Nayyar (1995).

24 The asymmetry in the rules of the game for the international trading system, outlined here, is examined in Nayyar (1996a).

References

Amsden, A.H. (1989), *Asia's Next Giant: South Korea and Late Industrialization*, New York: Oxford University Press.

Bell, M. and Pavitt, K. (1993), 'Accumulating Technological Capability in Developing Countries', *Proceedings of the World Bank Annual Conference on Development Economics 1992*, 257–81.

Bhaduri, A. and Marglin, S. (1990), 'Unemployment and the Real Wage: The Economic Basis for Contesting Political Ideologies', *Cambridge Journal of Economics*, 14, 375–93.

Bhagwati, J. (1978), *Foreign Trade Regimes and Economic Development: Anatomy and Consequences of Exchange Control*, Mass.: Ballinger.

Bhagwati, J. (1994), 'Free Trade: Old and New Challenges', *Economic Journal*, 104(423): 231–45.

Bhagwati, J. and Ramaswami, V.K. (1963), 'Domestic Distortions, Tariffs and the Theory of Optimum Subsidy', *Journal of Political Economy*, 71(1): 44–50.

Bhagwati, J. and Desai, P. (1970), *India: Planning for Industrialization*. London: Oxford University Press.

Bhagwati, J. and Srinivasan, T.N. (1975), *Foreign Trade Regimes and Economic Development: India*, New York: Columbia University Press.

Corden, W.M. (1974), *Trade Policy and Economic Welfare*, Oxford: Clarendon Press.

Dahlman, C.J., Ross-Larson, B. and Westphal, L.E. (1987), 'Managing Technological Development: Lessons from the Newly Industrializing Countries', *World Development*, 15(6), 759–75.

Diaz-Alejandro, C.F. (ed.) (1975), 'Trade Policies and Economic Development', in P.B. Kenen (ed.), *International Trade and Finance: Frontiers for Research*, Cambridge: Cambridge University Press.

Dixit, A.K. and Norman, V. (1980), *International Trade*, Cambridge: Cambridge University Press.

Heckscher, E.F. (1919), 'The Effect of Foreign Trade on the Distribution of Income', *Economisk Tidskrift*, 495–512.

Helleiner, G.K. (1992), *Trade Policy, Industrialization and Development*, Oxford: Clarendon Press.

Helpman, E. and Krugman, P. (1985), *Market Structure and Foreign Trade: Increasing Returns, Imperfect Competition and the International Economy*, Cambridge, Mass.: MIT Press.

Irwin, D. (1991), 'Challenges to Free Trade', *Journal of Economic Perspectives*, 201–8.

Krueger, A.O. (1978), *Foreign Trade Regimes and Economic Development: Liberalization Attempts and Consequences*, New York: National Bureau of Economic Research.

Krugman, P. (1981), 'Trade, Accumulation and Uneven Development', *Journal of Development Economics*, 149–61.

Krugman, P. (ed.) (1986), *Strategic Trade Policy and the New International Economics*, Cambridge, Mass.: MIT Press.

Krugman, P. (1987), 'Is Free Trade Passé?', *Journal of Economic Perspectives*, 1(2): 131–44.

Lall, S. (1990), *Building Industrial Competitiveness in Developing Countries*, Paris: OECD Development Centre.

Lee, E. (ed.) (1981), *Export-Led Industrialization and Development*, Geneva: International Labour Organization.

Little, I.M.D., Scitovsky, T. and Scott, M. (1970), *Industry and Trade in Some Developing Countries: A Comparative Study*, London: Oxford University Press.

Mill, J.S. (1848), *Principles of Political Economy*, with an introduction by W.J. Ashley, London: Longman.

Myrdal, G. (1956), *An International Economy: Problems and Prospects*, London: Routledge and Kegan Paul.

Nayyar, D. (1989), 'Towards a Possible Multilateral Framework for Trade in Services: Some Issues and Concepts', in *Technology, Trade Policy and the Uruguay Round*, New York: United Nations.

Nayyar, D. (1994a), 'The Foreign Trade Sector, Planning and Industrialization in India', in T.J. Bytes (ed.), *The State and Development Planning in India*, Delhi: Oxford University Press.

Nayyar, D. (ed.) (1994b), *Industrial Growth and Stagnation: The Debate in India*, Bombay: Oxford University Press.

Nayyar, D. (1995), 'Globalization: The Past in Our Present', Presidential Address to the Indian Economic Association, 1995, reprinted in *Indian Economic Journal*, January 1996, 1–18.

Nayyar, D. (1996a), 'Free Trade: Why, When and for Whom?', *Banca Nazionale del Lavoro Quarterly Review*, 333–50.

Nayyar, D. (1996b), *Economic Liberalization in India: Analytics, Experience and Lessons*, Calcutta: Orient Longman.

Ohlin, B. (1933), *Interregional and International Trade*, Cambridge, Mass.: Harvard University Press.

Pack, H. and Westphal, L.E. (1986), 'Industrial Strategy and Technological Change: Theory versus Reality', *Journal of Development Economics*, 22(1), 87–128.

Ricardo, D. (1812), *Principles of Political Economy and Taxation*, with an introduction by Donald Winch, London: Dent.

Rodrik, D. (1992), 'Closing the Productivity Gap: Does Trade Liberalization really Help?', in G.K. Helleiner (ed.), *Trade Policy, Industrialization and Development*, Oxford: Clarendon Press.

Rosenberg, N. (1994), *Exploring the Black Box: Technology, Economics and History*, Cambridge: Cambridge University Press.

Sachs, J. and Warner, A. (1995), 'Economic Reform and the Process of Global Integration', *Brookings Papers on Economic Activity*, 1–118.

Samuelson, P. (1939), 'The Gains from International Trade', *Canadian Journal of Economics and Political Science*, 195–205.

Singh, A. (1994), 'Openness and the Market Friendly Approach to Development: Learning the Right Lessons from Development Experience', *World Development*, 1811–24.

Smith, A. (1776), *The Wealth of Nations*, with an introduction by Andrew Skinner, Harmondsworth: Pelican Books.

A Business Analytic Approach to Governments and Globalization

JOHN H. DUNNING*

Introduction

National governments can and do play a decisive role in affecting the competitiveness of the economic activities located within their borders. They do so both by providing the appropriate incentives for domestic firms to upgrade the quality of their ownership-specific assets; and by ensuring that the location-bound general-purpose inputs (including educational facilities and communications infrastructure) necessary for these assets to be fully and efficiently utilized are available. The advent of globalization does not materially alter this fact. But, in a variety of ways, globalization may require a reappraisal both by firms of their strategies to create and sustain core competencies, and by governments as they seek to make the best use of these competencies within their area of jurisdiction. This is the subject matter of this chapter.

Globalization and the strategy of firms

From the viewpoint of firms, one of the main consequences of globalization – or more correctly the forces leading to it – is that it is requiring them to reconsider not only the locational configuration of the home bases for their strategically distinct businesses, but how this configuration affects the rest of their foreign and domestic operations. The underlying idea is that, as world economic events and technological advances are deepening the structural interdependence between nations – and particularly that between advanced industrial nations – the diamonds of competitive advantages [see Chapter 9] of those nations become linked in such

* Oxford University Press for an extract from *Governments, Globalization and International Business* by John H. Dunning © John H. Dunning, 1997.

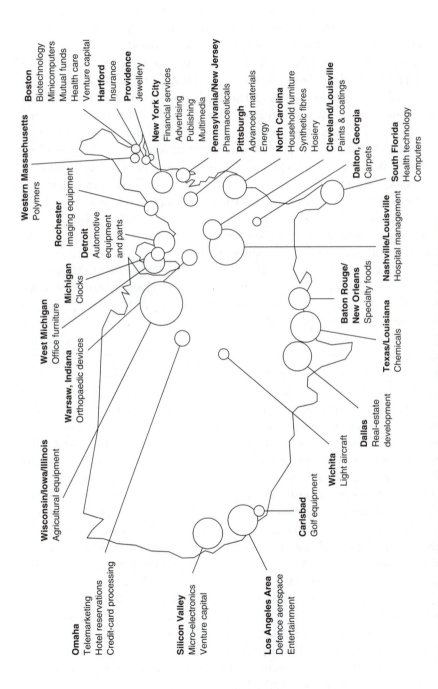

Figure 13.1 *Selected regional clusters in the USA of competitive industries*

a way that enterprises – and especially large MNEs – find it advantageous to disperse at least some of their home bases from their country of ownership to other countries. In the 1990s we see an increasing number of companies such as ABB, Philips of Eindhoven, IBM, 3M, and Nestlé establishing multiple home bases in countries other than that where their headquarters are situated.

What, then, determines the location of the home base of a particular business? Sometimes it is historical accident; yet, once embedded in a particular location, that business may take on a life of its own and attract 'virtuous' clusters of related activities. Sometimes it is (or was) determined by the availability of a particular natural resource or group of resources; and sometimes it is (or was) drawn by the presence of related firms, customers, or a pool of skilled labour. But, in today's innovation-led economy it is being increasingly influenced by the availability and quality of location-specific 'created' assets; and, most noticeably, the kind of infrastructure which fosters entrepreneurship and knowledge accumulation, and that helps to lower distance-related transaction costs. Often, too, by the policies they adopt to regional or urban development, sub-national governments may influence the locational competitiveness of different home bases.

The siting of the home bases of firms is, then, partly influenced by the presence of *national* agglomeration economies (e.g. an efficient telecommunications network), and partly by that of *micro-regional* clusters of economic activity. Although the advantages of regional clusters arise independently of the extent to which participating firms engage in international activities, they may well affect their ability to compete in the global market place. Figure 13.1 illustrates a selection of regional clusters in the USA. Most of these also house the 'domestic' home bases of the leading enterprises – including MNEs – in the sectors; and sometimes, too, the 'foreign' home bases of foreign-owned firms. Some reflect the presence of natural resources, or a favourable access to national or international transport networks; but many are based on a mixture of opportunism and the availability of immobile created assets and a supportive infrastructure. These latter advantages embrace both (Marshallian-type) agglomeration economies and the actions taken by local governments to foster cluster building.

While this figure is illustrative of the geography of concentration of economic activity, it tells us nothing about either the organizational structure or the economic viability of such clusters. But, as Anna Lee Saxenian (1994) has demonstrated in her comparison of the Silicon Valley and Route 128 (in Massachusetts) clusters of urban development, state governments may play a critical role in affecting the form, efficiency, and growth of these clusters.

Quite independently, then, of the role of national governments, the effect of globalization on the spatial distribution of the value-added activity is twofold. On the one hand, as a result of improved transport and communications facilities and lower artificial barriers to trade, it helps facilitate the movement of created assets, and with it the specialization of economic activity – including that normally associated with the home base of a particular business. On the other hand, it upgrades the capability of micro-regional spatial units to provide the complementary or support services necessary for these mobile assets to be properly assimilated and exploited; and it does so precisely as a means of minimizing the spatial transaction costs associated with the deployment of these location-bound assets.

The combined result of these forces is that the global strategy of firms is changed in two ways. First, it is no longer necessary for them to locate their home base for each of their distinct businesses in their country of origin. Though this may usually be the case – particularly for MNEs from the larger and more prosperous countries – in circumstances where the foreign diamonds of competitive advantage offer better resources and capabilities, such home bases are likely to be dispersed. In a globalizing economy, then, the need to locate the corporate headquarters of an MNE – and particularly one producing a wide range of products requiring different factor inputs or serving different markets – in its home country is likely to become less imperative than once it was. As a general principle, firms should locate new product-line bases in the country which offers the most favourable location-bound endowments for their innovation; and regional subsidiaries of MNEs should specialize in those activities in which they have a competitive advantage, and supply the output of these activities to regional or global markets.

As regards value-added activities other than those of the home base, globalization is likely to lead to a geographical dispersion of these – primarily via FDI and cross-border strategic alliances – whenever it is more efficient (i) to source basic factors (capital, raw materials, and generalized labour) from a foreign outlet, (ii) to secure or improve market access, and/or (iii) selectively to tap into particular skills, technologies, or learning experiences. While the location of the resource-based and market-seeking operations of MNEs is fairly self-evident, that of the third kind is primarily determined by the availability of the complementary created assets which the investing firms perceive they need if they are to make the best use of their own core competences. Sometimes these assets are, themselves, core competencies of related firms (e.g. suppliers); and sometimes they are part of the technological, educational, and legal infrastructure which provides the general (but no less essential) inputs to firms.

In a survey recently conducted by the author (Dunning 1996), it was found that the contribution of the foreign affiliates to the global competitiveness of 144 of the largest industrial MNEs[1] was perceived (by the senior executives participating in the survey) to be both substantial and growing. As might be expected, this contribution was closely related to the degree of multinationality of the investing firms. Thus, on a scale of 1 to 7 – 1 indicating that, in the opinion of the responding firm, all its competitive advantages were derived from its domestic operations, and 7 that all its advantages were derived as a result of foreign operations – MNEs whose foreign affiliates accounted for less than 15 per cent of their global assets or employment ranked the value of access of foreign-located natural resources and unskilled labour as 3.04, access to foreign-created assets as 2.30, and access to linkages with foreign-related firms (e.g. agglomeration economies) as 3.06. The corresponding values given by MNEs with 60 per cent or more of their assets or employment being accounted for by their foreign affiliates were 4.56, 3.73, and 4.87.

While the survey did not specifically concern itself with the location of multiple home bases, it was quite clear from the responses of firms that the foreign

Sourcing Factors

- Assembly in numerous countries to tap lower labour costs

Securing Market Access

- Manufacturing facilities in the USA to hedge against OMA and protectionism
- Joint venture with Rover in the UK, oriented towards the European market, including product development, marketing, and production

Selective Tapping into Foreign Diamonds

- Design studios in California and Germany
- Development of station wagon and all-terrain vehicle in the USA

Figure 13.2 *The dispersed activities of the Honda Motor Company*

Sourcing Factors

- Capital sourced worldwide
- Pancreases sourced from 20+ countries

Securing Market Access

- Created marketing joint ventures to reach local doctors and hospitals
- Established insulin-making and packaging facilities in France, South America, Japan, and the USA
- Located major enzyme production facilities in the USA to serve sophisticated customers, e.g. detergents and high-fructose corn syrup

Selective Tapping into Foreign Diamonds

- Acquired Zymotech in Seattle, Washington, for expertise in genetically engineered insulin
- Rapid approval in Japan relative to Denmark led to the establishment of a genetic engineering R&D facility in Japan

Genetic engineering capability was aggressively built up in Denmark

Figure 13.3 *The dispersed activities of the Novo Nordisk Group*

countries from which they were most likely to augment their competitive advantages comprised the triad of the USA, the EU, and Japan. Indeed, one or other of these was mentioned as the most important source of the base for exploiting or obtaining new technologies by 83 per cent of firms; and for exploiting or obtaining new technologies by 73 per cent of respondents (Dunning 1996).

As might be expected, the estimated significance of the foreign operations of MNEs was industry-, country-, and firm-specific. Further illustrations of the ways in which two companies – the Novo Nordisk Group, a Danish firm, and the Honda Motor Company – geographically disperse their value-added activities and, in so doing, tap into foreign diamonds are set out in Figures 13.2 and 13.3.

The changing roles of government

Some general remarks

In other writings, both Michael Porter and the present author have argued that the unique and critical role of modern democratic governments is to create and sustain an efficient economic system (Porter 1990 [see Chapter 9]; Dunning 1994). What exactly does this mean? From the viewpoint of upgrading the competitiveness of the resources and capabilities within their jurisdictions, we believe it means five things. First, governments must create and effectively communicate to their constituents a distinctive and challenging economic vision. This they will normally do after consulting with a broad range of their constituents. Secondly, they must ensure that the institutions responsible for translating that vision into reality are both willing and able to adjust to the changes required of them by a learning and innovation-driven economy.

Thirdly, it is the responsibility of national administrations to ensure that the availability, quality, and cost effectiveness of general-purpose inputs match up to the standards of their global competitors. By such inputs we mean location-bound societal assets which firms need to use jointly with their core advantages to produce goods and services. At one time, these assets mainly consisted of transport facilities and public utilities. Today they embrace all forms of educational and telecommunications infrastructure necessary to foster an efficient and modern innovation-led economy.

Fourthly, governments need to create and sustain an institutional framework and ethos that facilitates a continuous upgrading of the resources and capabilities within its jurisdiction. This not only means ensuring that markets for wealth-creating assets function efficiently, but that entrepreneurship is adequately motivated, consumers are persuaded to be more demanding of technical standards and product quality, and that there is a sufficient quality of inter-firm rivalry to promote learning and a continual improvement of asset usage. This last task of government serves to remind us that it is not only the kind of industries a nation or region competes in that matters, but how firms compete in these sectors. Finally, it encompasses the regular monitoring of various laws, regulations, and regimes (e.g. with respect to anti-trust, labour unions, and intellectual property rights) which help to lower the transaction and coordination costs of dynamic business activity.

Fifthly, governments should do everything to encourage, and nothing to impede, the formation of micro-regional clusters development, as it is becoming increasingly apparent that the competitiveness of a country's industries is dependent not only on the efforts of the constituent firms, but also on ways in which they interact with their suppliers, customers, and competitors.[2] Partly, as we have already noted, this kind of inter-firm cooperation is independent of spatial considerations;

- 'Balanced-development' policies across states and regions
- Incentives or requirements to locate in backward/distressed areas
- Poor transportation and communications infrastructrure
- Uniformity in vocational training and university curricula
- University research priorities set independently of local company needs
- Policies that encourage vertical integration (e.g. licensing requirements, reservation of sectors for small firms)
- Tolerance of monopolies/cartels

Figure 13.4 *Government impediments to cluster formation*

but partly, at least, it can be strengthened if the activities are in close proximity to each other. This is particularly the case where the transaction costs of doing business rise as the physical or psychic distance between the firms engaging in these activities increases. Such costs are likely to be more pronounced in the case of firms using pooled factor services, interdependent technologies, and idiosyncratic intermediate products; and where tacit knowledge, trust, and commitment are important intangible assets. The City of London is a classic example of a clustering of business services whose efficiency is dependent on their close physical proximity with other services which need to be jointly used with them.[3] A more recent example is the congregation of multi-media service providers in lower Manhattan, New York.

Because it is only recently that economists and business scholars have begun to give attention to the spatial 'stickiness' of some kinds of economic activity which exist, in spite of advantages of globalization earlier described, we will give a little more attention to this aspect of government involvement. How, if at all, is the role of government affected by the fact that some value activities are becoming location-bound, while others are becoming more footloose?

Governments and micro-regional clusters

In many respects, we believe that it is by avoiding inappropriate policies, rather than taking positive action, that governments can best promote an efficient intra-national distribution of economic activity. Such inappropriate policies arise through the understandable, but not necessarily judicious, intervention by governments to promote a locational strategy which aims at reducing the disparities in incomes and growth in the micro-regions within their jurisdictions. We set out some of these impediments in Figure 13.4. Of these, perhaps the first two are the ones most widely practised by governments and by regional authorities such as the European Commission.

Here, however, it is important to distinguish between two motives for government intervention. The first is to reduce the external *diseconomies* of industrial concentration,[4] and/or assist the spatial dispersal of both mobile and immobile

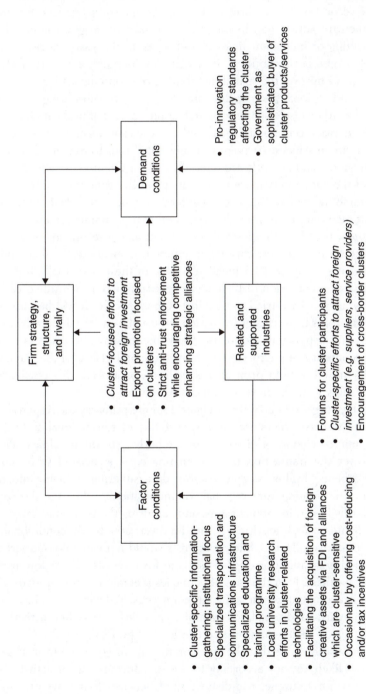

Figure 13.5 *Role of government in cluster-upgrading*

resources in a way that encourages new clusters. Such measures are essentially designed to reduce endemic market failure and to assist the efficient disposition of resources. The second motive is directed to helping micro-regions to offset their declining competitive advantages, in the same way as national governments have subsidized declining or inefficient firms or industries in the past. Policies of this kind, ostensibly aimed at promoting a 'balanced' development, are more likely to distort, rather than improve, the spatial distribution of economic activity.

National and regional governments are also prone to subsidizing economic activities in backward or distressed regions and, again, this is politically understandable, and, in some cases, economically justifiable. These cases include a conjunction of three sets of circumstances: (i) there is a substantial social investment at stake, (ii) the micro-region could be made economically viable again in a cost-effective way, and (iii) it costs the community more to relocate people outside the region than to relocate jobs inside the region. But, excepting these instances, if there is a rationale for government intervention, it has to be argued on non-economic grounds!

What, then, might be the positive role of national governments in cluster-upgrading or the creation of new clusters, using the framework of the diamond of competitive advantage? Figure 13.5 highlights some of these. Essentially, it can be seen that these are an extension of their more general functions identified earlier, although in this figure I have tried to be a little more specific. It will be observed that, although the gains from cluster formation are usually attributable to the presence of related and supporting industries, governments may affect access to the agglomeration economies of micro-regions through the other facets of the diamond. Those items identified in bold print arise specifically as a result of globalization, which we will deal with in the next section of this chapter.

Some of the suggested initiatives in Figure 13.5 are primarily the responsibility of national governments; others are the responsibility of sub-national authorities (e.g. of states, micro-regions, or cities). Most are fairly self-evident; almost all are intended to lower the transaction or coordinating costs associated with cluster formation or deepening by, for example, assisting data-gathering, reducing information asymmetries, facilitating intra-regional communications, aiding the absorptive capacity of spatially linked immobile assets, and capturing the economic and social externalities of interrelated activities. Some, however, are strictly conditional on particular circumstances. Thus, while economists would not generally support the subsidization of either natural or created assets to foster cluster formation, it may be appropriate, particularly in the case of countries seeking to catch up with their established foreign competitors, for some temporary cost-reducing or tax incentives to be offered to firms, conditional, for example, on their locating their activities in certain regions,[5] or on their achieving a certain level of performance.

We would also observe that the appropriate role of government in cluster-upgrading is also likely to vary according to the structure of cluster activity. Ann Markusen (1994), for example, has distinguished between four ways of organizing micro-regional business activity, each of which is likely to make a different contribution to the prosperity of the 'sticky' place of which it is a part.[6] These are

(i) the *flexible specialization* rubric, as typified by the Italian textile industry in Prato, North Italy, the watch industry of Switzerland, and the cork industry of Portugal, (ii) *hub-and-spoke* industrial districts where the pattern of economic activity is centred on a number of 'flagship' corporations or strategic centres (e.g. Toyota City in Japan and the Seattle industrial district), (iii) the *satellite industrial platform*, which is mainly made up of the affiliates of extra-regional firms (e.g. as export-processing and free trade zones in developing countries), and (iv) the *non-market-centred district*, where the local economy revolves around either a group of top-ranking educational institutions or a number of major government-owned administrative or research installations, as along Route 128 in the USA and the M4 corridor in the UK. Clearly, government action to promote type (iii) clusters, which tend to result in only a shallow integration of higher value activity, and type (i) or (ii) clusters, which could lead to more structural embeddedness, will be very different. Moreover, while most clusters of related activities tend to be somewhat vulnerable to economic fluctuations, types (i) and (ii), because they are reliant on a few large firms, or on specialized export markets, are likely to be especially so.

We would make one final point at this stage. [...] Even the most casual reading of the literature suggests that the influences of different governments on the four facets of the diamond of competitive advantage differ enormously. This is not to aver that there is one particular model of government intervention which is superior to all others; in any event, at least some of the assets of 'good' government are largely location-bound – that is, they cannot be transplanted to other countries. At the same time, it would be unusual if successful policies pursued by governments in one country (e.g. towards education and training, entrepreneurship and savings, raising environmental standards of quality, anti-trust legislation, and collecting and disseminating public information – to give just a few examples) did not contain at least some lessons for other governments. The ability to identify and judiciously adapt 'best-practice' techniques of governments from other countries[7] to one's own particular economic, institutional and cultural situation is, indeed, becoming a core competency in its own right![8]

Governments and globalization

Using, once again, the idea of linked diamonds as our unit of analysis, there are two ways in which national (or sub-national) governments may be affected by globalization. The first is directly by the changes it occasions in the interface between governments – and, in particular, those brought about by intergovernment rivalry. The second is by the way in which the four main facets of the diamond are affected by cross-border structural integration – and especially by FDI and the activities of MNEs; and on how this, in turn, may require modifications to the governance of governments, and to their systemic and operational roles.

INTERFACE BETWEEN GOVERNMENTS   [...] While globalization is only one of the factors making for 'competing' governments,[9] it is as a direct result of the increased mobility of many firm-specific assets, notably technology and organizational capacities, and some kinds of previously immobile assets (e.g. managerial and professional labour), that governments are required to consider the actions of other national administrations, who compete for these assets, when designing and implementing their own policies. For most of recent industrial history, nation states have been primarily linked by their trade and macro-economic policies, the latter in as much as interest rates may affect cross-border capital flows, and the exchange rates the real costs of production. But it is the growing mobility of created assets which is tending to bring about the deep integration between national government policies. While it is too early to identify a clear convergence or harmonization among such policies, there is little doubt that, in some areas – including, for example, those most affecting the cross-border location of activity such as FDI and competition policy – there is considerable pressure to do so. On the other hand, as long as there remain differences between countries – not only in their economic and market structures, but in their institutions, cultural mores, social priorities, and political ideologies – government policies are likely to remain differentiated from each other, just as the strategies of successful MNEs – even within the same sector – are distinct from one another.

GLOBALIZATION AND THE DIAMOND   There have been various attempts by scholars to explain the cross-border linkages between the diamond of one country and that of another. Alan Rugman, for example (Rugman and D'Cruz 1991; Rugman 1992, 1993), favours the concept of the double or multiple diamond. Elsewhere (Dunning 1992, 1993) the present author has introduced international business activity as an exogenous variable (like government) into the Porter model, and has sought to consider its influence on each of the four facets of the domestic diamond. Also, earlier in this chapter I acknowledged that, to advance their global strategies, diversified MNEs might wish to establish multiple home bases for at least some of their strategic distinct business.

While each of these various approaches attempts to identify and evaluate some of the effects of the geographical integration of economic activity, from either a sectoral or a country perspective, none gives much attention to the ways in which governments may influence the response of individuals, firms, and industries to their exposures to foreign diamonds. Yet the manner in which governments operationalize their various functions and responsibilities could critically determine both the speed and the ultimate success of the adjustment process. Let us explain what we mean by examining briefly each of the four facets of the diamond.

Factor endowments.   Through inward and outward FDI, cross-border alliances and trade in intermediate products, the competitiveness of a country's location-specific endowments is exposed to the actions of foreign economic agents. Where the value activities of an industry are confined to its national borders, this competitiveness (or lack of it) is revealed in its trade and payments balances with other countries. Where, however, its firms are free to produce in other countries, then it is the ability of that country – or, more specifically, the institutions of that country – to provide the location-based resources necessary to retain these footloose assets and attract those of foreign firms that is a better measure of its competitiveness.

What, then, should the government's reaction to globalization be? To some extent, this will depend on the type of factor endowments being considered. For natural assets, for example, there may be comparatively little that a government can do, except to ensure that the social infrastructure necessary for their efficient production and distribution is available. Yet even here, as is shown with many agricultural products, their value in global markets is derived not only from the physical properties of the products *per se*, but from the way they are processed and marketed.[10] However, in the case of created assets, governments may exercise a more decisive role. Some examples include helping to improve the quality of general inputs (e.g. via education and training policies), easing the flexibility of the labour market, ensuring that the capital market operates efficiently, implementing appropriate tax policies, supporting pre-competitive research, easing the access or acquisition of foreign skills and technologies, and facilitating the upgrading of domestic factor endowments by foreign firms. While we accept that most of these roles of government apply no less in a closed economy, globalization does impose a new urgency of action; and, perhaps, emphasizes the need for a closer complementarity of interests between the private and public sectors than existed previously.

Market structure and inter-firm rivalry.   Both technological advances and globalization have added several new dimensions to the competition between firms. Like many other aspects of structural integration, they have been ambivalent in their effects. On the one hand, in some instances, they have helped reduce the concentration of production within a country and intensified inter-firm rivalry – as, for example, in the automotive, pharmaceutical, and banking industries. On the other hand, they have led to a wave of cross-border M&As and strategic alliances which has made for a more pronounced oligopolistic competition.

While changes in market structure have not gone unnoticed by governments, by and large, they have taken little action to influence them. This is principally, one feels, because they believe that, on balance, globalization is leading to more, rather than less, competition; and that technological forces are compelling firms to engage in more M&As, and strategic alliances, in order to take full advantage of firm-level scale economies and speed up the process of innovation *vis-à-vis* their foreign competitors. Whether or not this view is correct remains to be seen; but, sooner or later, governments will have to articulate their competition policies better than they are currently doing, and, as Monty Graham points out these issues are also now on the agenda of international agencies, notably the WTO and the OECD.

Globalization is also compelling governments to take a more active stance in promoting an ethos, or mindset, of competitiveness. Margaret Thatcher's Conservative government of the 1980s is a classic example of the kind of influence a government can have on the attitude to wealth creation of both individuals and institutions; and also on entrepreneurship. Though many of the changes instituted during the Thatcher years were an attempt to resolve internal economic problems, there is little doubt that the threat to UK prosperity, brought about by relocation of UK investment and the possible loss of in-bound investment to other parts of the EU, was a major factor in promoting policies which not only deregulated and liberalized UK markets – including labour markets – but also initiated a whole range of fiscal and other incentives to motivate people and firms to upgrade their resources and capabilities and to become more aggressively competitive.[11]

Upgrading consumer expectations. Though it is not always necessary for superior-quality or low-price products to be produced where they are sold, there can be little doubt that the pressure of Japanese affiliates in the US and European automotive and consumer electronics industries has heightened the awareness of US consumers to the standards which are commonplace in Japan. At the same time, in their efforts to penetrate the Japanese market, foreign firms have had to take serious account of the particular demands of Japanese customers.

Deep structural integration is, then, leading to a convergence of consumer expectations and needs – at least as far as tradable goods and services are concerned. In the main, because firms are increasingly seeking new markets through continuous product improvement and innovations, this is resulting in a harmonization of consumer standards – at least among internationally traded branded goods – to the highest level – although sometimes the improvements may be cosmetic rather than substantive.

What, if anything, does this imply for national governments? First, it means that more attention is likely to be focused on the cross-border harmonization of technical and quality standards. Secondly, it means that governments need to study, and, where appropriate, adapt and implement, the 'first best' practices of other governments in respect of consumer protection, health and safety, and the environment.[12] While, in some cases, such intervention may add to the costs of production, in others, especially in the area of environmental regulations, there are suggestions that firms which pursue the most rigorous standards are, in fact, the most competitive (Lundan 1996). And, thirdly, it again emphasizes the role of government as a setter of an ethos, which encourages the consumers of both intermediate and final goods and services to be more rigorous and sophisticated in their demands of producers.[13]

Related and supporting industries. A previous section of this chapter has already analysed in some detail the ways in which national and sub-national governments may aid or inhibit the development of regional clusters. Referring back to Figure 13.5, I suggest that the response of governments may affect cluster formation in four main ways. First, in their cluster-focused efforts, they may wish to take into account the particular and special locational, and other, needs of foreign firms – as, indeed, they have done in the siting of free trade and export-processing zones. Secondly, they can, and do, reduce the social transaction costs, and particularly those to do with information inadequacies or asymmetries, as they affect both potential foreign investors and local firms seeking to establish partnerships with foreign firms. Most of the US states, for example, have offices in Europe and Japan specifically designed to promote the advantages of their own resources and capabilities; and most national commerce or trade departments help provide information – particularly to small and medium-sized firms – about the opportunities for licensing or other forms of cross-border licensing.

Thirdly, and more generally, in better recognizing the contribution of the affiliates of foreign firms to cluster development, sub-national governments may need not only to upgrade the locational attractiveness of the micro-regions for which they are responsible, but to do so in a way which also maximizes its spillover benefits (e.g. to suppliers, service providers, and so on).[14] This may require some reprioritization of the spatial distribution of the social capital of national governments; and also of the taxation and expenditure plans of sub-national governments.

Fourthly, as indicated earlier, technological forces and the liberalization of cross-border markets have changed not only the international and intra-national structure of economic activity, but also the competitive advantages of firms of different ownership. This creates certain tensions and dilemmas for national and regional governments. On the one hand, they wish to maximize the economic welfare of the constituents of the country or region they represent. On the other, they wish to avoid any marked spatial disparities of income and wealth; and any undue reliance on foreign ownership. We do not pretend to have a solution to these dilemmas, but we do believe that globalization is likely to sharpen the distinction between the options open to governments.

Conclusions

One of the features of globalization is that it is refocusing scholarly attention on the respective roles of firms and governments in advancing the competitiveness of a country or region within a country. In so doing, we are reminded of the distinction between locationally mobile and locationally bound created assets. In an innovation-driven economy, the competitiveness of firms increasingly depends on their ability to create and efficiently to organize the use of distinctive core competences in one or other lines of their business. Although, once produced, these assets, or their rights, are often transferable across national boundaries, their initial creation requires a strong home base. However, while the possession of these assets is a necessary condition for their success, it is not a sufficient condition. To be used effectively, the core competences of firms need to be combined with other assets which are sourced from *other* firms or from non-market institutions. Frequently, these complementary assets are location-bound; and frequently, too – as in the case of an educated labour force and an efficient transportation and communications network – their availability and quality are strongly influenced by the actions (or inactions) of national or sub-national governments. Indeed, since many mobile assets are becoming easier to access, it is the uniqueness and quality of location-bound assets, and the way firms are able to coordinate these with their own core advantages, that are, perhaps, the most important components of a country's competitive advantage.

This suggests that governments and firms are best considered as partners in the wealth-creating process. Although, in a market economy, it is the competitiveness of private corporations which determines a nation's prosperity, this competitiveness rests, too, on the five tasks of government described earlier being effectively implemented. If this is not done, then two things are likely to happen. First, where they are able, firms will 'vote with their feet' and relocate their value-added activities in countries which offer them more hospitable location-bound resources. Secondly, the capacity of the domestic economy – and particularly that of clusters of related firms – to absorb the benefits of inward direct investment and advance the home-base competences of MNEs will be reduced.

We have illustrated in this chapter the geographical widening of the home bases of MNEs. Where this is a result of market forces and consistent with the comparative dynamic advantages of both exporting and recipient countries, it is to be welcomed. Where it is a result of structurally distorting policies on the part of either the private or the public sector, it is to be deplored. Where it reflects the failure of governments to compete effectively, because of their inability to ensure the general purpose infrastructure necessary to create and absorb new wealth-creating assets, it is to be regretted.

We have also discussed the growing spatial interdependence between firms in innovation-led economies and the importance of cluster development. While acknowledging that there may be agglomeration diseconomies, current technological developments and the liberalization of many cross-border markets are increasing locational specificity or 'stickiness' as an asset in its own right. In my opinion, unless there are strong non-economic reasons for such intervention, governments should do nothing to hinder market-led concentrations of economic activity; indeed, where they perceive that the social net benefits of clusters exceed the net benefits to the participants in the cluster, they should encourage them. The nature and form of that action will depend on the types of clusters formed; but its aim should be to advance both the static and the dynamic comparative advantage both of the infrastructure of the region, and of the producing firms within it.

A final section of this chapter considered the ways in which the growing structural integration of the world economy links the diamonds of competitive advantage of countries' regions within economies. It again emphasized the interface between the export or import of mobile created assets by firms and the location-specific created assets of countries, and the role of governments in providing the institutional and enabling background for both sets of assets to respond efficiently to the challenges of economic change. It finally confirmed that, alongside the renaissance of market forces, there is the need for strong and wise government to ensure that these forces operate both to advance economic and social welfare, and to do so with the least amount of structural or endemic imperfections.

Notes

Based upon a presentation by Michael Porter at the Carnegie Bosch Conference in Washington. I am indebted to Professor Porter for permitting me to make full use of the material contained in his presentation. All the diagrams and exhibits have been produced by Professor Porter, although Figure 4 has been slightly modified by the author.

1 These firms accounted for about 40% of the global FDI stock of industrial MNEs in 1993.

2 As set out, e.g., in Porter (1990) [see Chapter 9] and in Alan Rugman and Joseph D'Cruz's five partners network model (Rugman and D'Cruz 1995). For analysis of the concept of alliance capitalism and its implications for the competitive advantages of firms, see Dunning (1995).

3 As documented in some detail by Dunning and Morgan (1971) over twenty years ago.

4 As, for example, occurred in the early post-war period, when the UK government tried to steer economic activity away from a congested London and towards the provinces.

5 As in the case of export-processing zones (McIntyre et al. forthcoming). For a review of the role of cost-reducing and fiscal incentives in attracting FDI, see UNCTAD (1995); for the actions taken by state governments in the USA to attract inward investment (be it from foreign or domestic firms), see Coughlin et al. (1991) and Donaghue (1997). The danger is, of course, that such locational tournaments may spark off 'beggar-my-neighbour' competitive bidding between states or regions, which is more cluster-distorting than cluster-facilitating. See also an interesting paper, Mytelka (1996).

6 For an alternative classification of the structure of regions, see Storper and Harrison (1991) and Miles and Snow (1992).

7 Again, the comparative advantage of governments varies according to the functions performed. For example, the policies of the Japanese government on education, savings, and corporate investment are worth close scrutiny, while their anti-trust policies and support of agriculture and some less competitive sectors leave much to be desired.

8 As, indeed, is the ability to adapt and utilize best-practice techniques from throughout the world an important competitive advantage of firms.

9 For example, no less important is the trend towards the convergence of economic structures among advanced nations and the growing significance of created assets, the quality and availability of which tend to be more influenced by governments than that of natural resources.

10 Ohmae (1990: 175) gives an illustration of the price of Blue Mountain coffee, which sells in Japan for four times the price of Brazilian coffee. 'Is it four times better?' he asks. 'Probably not,' he replies. 'Blind taste tests show little difference. What is different, however, is the clever and determined branding of the coffee. In other words, a managed effort to add value.' In his book, Ohmae goes on to cite other examples of branding creating large margins of value, including Kobe beef and Koshikari rice, both of which are produced in Japan.

11   The issue of governments influencing the ethos of competition is dealt with in Dunning (1991).
12   In some cases, these may be received as public goods: in others as affecting the design, contents, quality and usage of private goods.
13   Although we accept that there is nothing like inter-firm competition to ensure this!
14   The importance of related industries is particularly well seen in the case of the Portuguese cork industry, which is focused in two regions: Sante Maria de Feira and Sotubal. The efficiency of several hundred cork producers is aided by the presence of specialized cork processing machinery manufacturers, strong local wine and port producers, several large bottling companies, and a number of cork-related training and research institutes. I am indebted to Michael Porter for providing me with this example.

References

Coughlin, C.C., Terza, J.V., and Arromdee, V. (1991), 'State Characteristics and the Location of Foreign Direct Investment within the US', *Review of Economics and Statistics*, 73: 675–83.

Donaghue, J. (1997), *Disunited Governments*.

Dunning, J.H. (1991), 'Governments, Economic Organization and International Competitiveness', in L.G. Mattson and B. Stymne (eds), *Corporate and Industry Strategies for Europe* (Rotterdam: Elsevier Science Publishers), 41–74.

Dunning, J.H. (1992), 'The Competitive Advantage of Nations and TNC Activities', *Transnational Corporations*, 1 (February), 135–68.

Dunning, J.H. (1993), 'Internationalizing Porter's Diamond', *Management International Review*, 33/2 (special issue): 7–15.

Dunning, J.H. (1994), *Globalization: The Challenge for National Economic Regimes* (The Geary Lecture for 1993; Dublin: Economic and Social Research Institute).

Dunning, J.H. (1995), 'Reappraising the Eclectic Paradigm in the Age of Alliance Capitalism', *Journal of International Business Studies*, 26/3: 461–91.

Dunning, J.H. (1996), 'The Geographical Sources of the Competitiveness of Firms: Some Results of a New Survey', *Transnational Corporations*, 5/3.

Dunning, J.H., and Morgan, E.V. (1971), *An Economic Study of the City of London* (London: Allen and Unwin).

Lundun, S. (1996), 'Internationalization and Environmental Strategy in the Pulp and Paper Industry' (Ph.D. dissertation, Newark, NJ: Rutgers University).

McIntyre, J., Narula, R., and Trevino, L.J. (forthcoming), 'The Role of Export Processing Zones for Host Countries and Multinationals: A Mutually Beneficial Relationship', *International Trade Journal*, 10.

Markusen, A. (1994), *Sticky Places in Slippery Spaces: The Political Economy of Post-War Fast-Growth Regions* (Rutgers University Working Paper No. 79; New Brunswick Center for Urban Policy Research).

Miles, R.E., and Snow, C.C. (1992), 'Causes of Failure in Network Organization', *California Management Review*, 34: 53–72.

Mytelka, L.K. (1996), 'Locational Tournaments, Strategic Partnerships and the State' (mimeo; Ottawa: Carletion University).

Ohmae, K. (1990), *The Borderless World* (New York: Harper Business).

Peach, R. (ed.) (1994), *The ISO 9000 Handbook* (Fairfax, Va.: CEEM Information Services).

Porter, M.E. (1990), *The Competitive Advantage of Nations* (New York: Free Press).

Rugman, A.M. (1992), 'Porter Takes the Wrong Turn', *Business Quarterly*, 56/3 (Winter): 59–64.

Rugman, A.M. (ed.) (1993), *Management International Review*, 33/2 (special edition on Michael Porter's *Diamond of Competitive Advantage*).

Rugman, A.M., and D'Cruz, J.R. (1991), *Fast Forward: Improving Canada's International Competitiveness* (Toronto: Kodah Canada).

Rugman, A.M., and D'Cruz, J.R. (1995), 'The Five Partners Business Network Model' (mimeo; Toronto: University of Toronto).

Saxenian, A.L. (1994), *Regional Advantage: Culture and Competition in Silicon Valley and Route 128* (Cambridge, Mass.: Harvard University Press).

Storper, M., and Harrison, B. (1991), 'Flexibility, Hierarchy and Regional Development: The Changing Structure of Industrial Production Systems and their Forms of Governance in the 1990s', *Researcher Policy*, 20: 207–422.

UNCTAD (1995), United Nations Conference on Trade and Development, *Incentives and Foreign Direct Investment* (TD/B/ITNC/Misc 1; Geneva: United Nations).

Foreign Direct Investment and the Challenge of Development

WORLD INVESTMENT REPORT*

The new competitive context raises new challenges for governments and TNCs ...

The development priorities of developing countries include achieving sustained income growth for their economies by raising investment rates, strengthening technological capacities and skills, and improving the competitiveness of their exports in world markets; distributing the benefits of growth equitably by creating more and better employment opportunities; and protecting and conserving the physical environment for future generations. The new, more competitive, context of a liberalizing and globalizing world economy in which economic activity takes place imposes considerable pressures on developing countries to upgrade their resources and capabilities if they are to achieve these objectives. This new global context is characterized by rapid advances in knowledge, shrinking economic space and rapid changes in competitive conditions, evolving attitudes and policies, and more vocal (and influential) stakeholders.

A vital part of the new context is the need to improve competitiveness, defined as the ability to sustain income growth in an open setting. In a liberalizing and globalizing world, growth can be sustained only if countries can foster new, higher value-added activities, to produce goods and services that hold their own in open markets.

FDI and international production by TNCs can play an important role in complementing the efforts of national firms in this respect. However, the objectives of TNCs differ from those of host governments: governments seek to spur *national*

* UNCTAD/DITE, *World Investment Report 1999* for 'Foreign Direct Investment and the Challenge of Development' in *Transnational Corporations*, Vol 8, No 3 © UNCTAD/DITE, *World Investment Report 1999*.

developement, while TNCs seek to enhance their own competitiveness in an *international* context. In the new context, TNCs' ownership advantages are also changing. In particular, rapid innovation and deployment of new technologies, in line with logistic and market demands, are more important than ever before. Thus, TNCs have to change their relations with suppliers, buyers and competitors to manage better the processes of technical change and innovation. And they have to strike closer links with institutions dealing with science, technology, skills and information. The spread of technology to, and growth of skills in, different countries means that new TNCs are constantly entering the arena to challenge established ones.

A striking feature of the new environment is how TNCs shift their portfolios of mobile assets across the globe to find the best match with the immobile assets of different locations. In the process, they also shift some corporate functions to different locations within internationally integrated production and marketing systems (intensifying the process of 'deep integration'). The ability to provide the necessary immobile assets thus becomes a critical part of an FDI – and competitiveness – strategy for developing countries. While a large domestic market remains a powerful magnet for investors, TNCs serving global markets increasingly look for world-class infrastructure, skilled and productive labour, innovatory capacities and an agglomeration of efficient suppliers, competitors, support institutions and services. In addition, they may also seek to acquire created assets embodied in competitive host country firms, which may lead to a restructuring of these firms not necessarily beneficial for host countries. Low-cost labour remains a source of competitive advantage for countries, but its importance is diminishing; moreover, it does not provide a base for sustainable growth since rising incomes erode the edge it provides. The same applies to natural resources.

... and meeting them requires policy intervention

There is no conflict between exploiting static sources of comparative advantage and developing new, dynamic ones; existing advantages provide the means by which new advantages can be developed. A steady evolution from one to the other is the basis for sustained growth. What is needed is a policy framework to facilitate and accelerate the process: this is the essence of a competitiveness strategy. The need for such strategy does not disappear once growth accelerates, or economic development reaches a certain level; it merely changes its form and focus. This is why competitiveness remains a concern of governments in developing and developed countries alike. The starting point for this concern is that providing a level playing field and letting firms respond to market signals is sufficient only to the extent that markets work efficiently. The very existence of TNCs is a manifestation that this is not always the case. In the presence of market failures, for example when markets fail to exploit existing endowments fully, fail to develop new competitive advantages, or do not give the correct signals to economic agents so that they can make proper investment decisions, intervention is necessary – provided governments have the capabilities to design, monitor and implement policies that overcome market failures.

More specifically, government policies on FDI need to counter two sets of market failures. The first arises from information or coordination failures in the investment process, which can lead a country to attract insufficient FDI, or the wrong quality of FDI. The second arises when private interests of investors diverge from the economic interests of host countries. This can lead FDI to have negative effects on development, or it may lead to positive, but static benefits that are not sustainable over time. Private and social interests may, of course, diverge for any investment, local or foreign: policies are then needed to remove the divergence for all investors. However, some divergence may be specific to foreign investment. FDI may differ from local investment because the locus of decision-making and sources of competitiveness in the former lie abroad, because TNCs pursue regional or global competitiveness-enhancing strategies, or because foreign investors are less committed to host economies and are relatively mobile. Thus, the case for intervening with FDI policies may have a sound economic basis. In addition, countries consider that foreign ownership has to be controlled on non-economic grounds – for instance, to keep cultural or strategic activities in national hands.

The role of FDI in countries' processes and efforts to meet development objectives can differ greatly across countries, depending on the nature of the economy and the government. One vision – pursued, for example, by Malaysia, Singapore and Thailand – was to rely substantially on FDI, integrating the economy into TNC production networks and promoting competitiveness by upgrading within those networks. Another vision – pursued by the Republic of Korea and Taiwan Province of China – was to develop domestic enterprises and autonomous innovative capabilities, relying on TNCs mainly as sources of technology, primarily at arm's length. Yet another, that of the administration of Hong Kong (China), was to leave resource allocation largely to market forces, while providing infrastructure and governance. There is no ideal development strategy with respect to the use of FDI that is common for all countries at all times. Any good strategy must be context-specific, reflecting a country's level of economic development, the resource base, the specific technological context, the competitive setting and a government's capabilities to implement policies. [...]

FDI comprises a package of resources

Most developing countries today consider FDI an important channel for obtaining access to resources for development. However, the economic effects of FDI are almost impossible to measure with precision. Each TNC represents a complex package of firm-level attributes that are dispersed in varying quantities and quality from one host country to another. These attributes are difficult to separate and

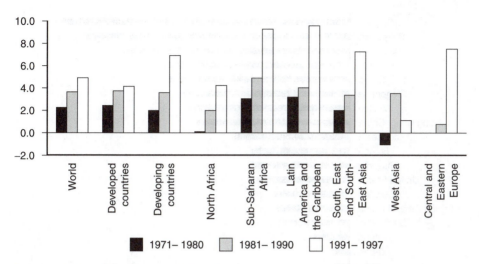

Figure 14.1 *The ratio of FDI inflows to gross fixed capital formation, by region, annual average, 1971–1980, 1981–1990 and 1991–1997 (percentage) (UNCTAD,* **World Investment Report 1999: Foreign Direct Investment and the Challenge of Development,** *Figure VI.1, p. 167)*

quantify. Where their presence has widespread effects, measurement is even more difficult. There is no precise method of specifying a counter-factual – what would have happened if a TNC had not made a particular investment. Thus, the assessment of the development effects of FDI has to resort either to an econometric analysis of the relationships between inward FDI and various measures of economic performance, the results of which are often inconclusive, or to a qualitative analysis of particular aspects of the contribution of TNCs to development, without any attempt at measuring costs and benefits quantitatively.

FDI comprises a bundle of assets, some proprietary to the investor. The proprietary assets, the 'ownership advantages' of TNCs, can be obtained only from the firms that create them. They can be copied or reproduced by others, but the cost of doing that can be very high, particularly in developing countries and where advanced technologies are involved. Non-proprietary assets – finance, many capital goods, intermediate inputs and the like – can usually be obtained from the market also.

The most prized proprietary asset is probably technology. Others are brand names, specialized skills and the ability to organize and integrate production across countries, to establish marketing networks, or to have privileged access to the market for non-proprietary assets (e.g. funds, equipment). Taken together, these advantages mean that TNCs can contribute significantly to economic development in host countries – if the host country can induce them to transfer their advantages in appropriate forms and has the capacity to make good use of them. The assets in the FDI bundle are:

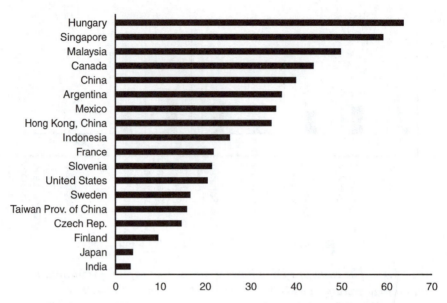

Figure 14.2 *Share of TNCs in primary and manufactured exports, latest available year[a] (percentage) (UNCTAD,* **World Investment Report 1999,** *Figure VIII.2, p. 245)*

- *Capital:* FDI brings in investible financial resources to host countries (Figure 14.1). FDI inflows are more stable and easier to service than commercial debt or portfolio investment. In distinction to other sources of capital, TNCs typically invest in long-term projects.

- *Technology:* TNCs can bring modern technologies, some of them not available in the absence of FDI, and they can raise the efficiency with which existing technologies are used. They can adapt technologies to local conditions, drawing upon their experience in other developing countries. They may, in some cases, set up local R&D facilities. They can upgrade technologies as innovations emerge and consumption patterns change. They can stimulate technical efficiency and technical change in local firms, suppliers, clients and competitors by providing assistance, by acting as role models and by intensifying competition.

- *Market access:* TNCs can provide access to export markets, both for goods (and some services) that are already produced in host countries, helping them switch from domestic to international markets; and for new activities that exploit a host economy's comparative advantages (Figure 14.2). The growth of exports itself offers benefits in terms of technological learning, realization of scale economies, competitive stimulus and market intelligence.

- *Skills and management techniques:* TNCs employ and have world-wide access to individuals with advanced skills and knowledge and can transfer such skills and knowledge to their foreign affiliates by bringing in experts and by setting up state-of-the-art training facilities. Improved and adaptable skills and new organizational practices and management techniques can yield competitive benefits for firms as well as help sustain employment as economic and technological conditions change.

- *Environment:* TNCs are in the lead in developing clean technologies and modern environmental management systems. They can use them in countries in which they operate. Spillovers of technologies and management methods can potentially enhance environmental management in local firms within the industries that host foreign affiliates.

While TNCs offer the potential for developing countries to access these assets in a package, this does not necessarily mean that simply opening up to FDI is the best way of obtaining or benefiting from them. The occurence of market failures mentioned above means that governments may have to intervene in the process of attracting FDI with measures to promote FDI generally or measures to promote specific types of FDI. Furthermore, the complexity of the FDI package means that governments face trade-offs between different benefits and objectives. For instance, they may have to choose between investments that offer short- as opposed to long-term benefits; the former may lead to static gains, but not necessarily to dynamic ones.

The principal issues to be addressed by governments fall into the following four groups:

- Information and coordination failures in the international investment process.

- Infant industry considerations in the development of local enterprises, which can be jeopardized when inward FDI crowds out those enterprises.

- The static nature of advantages transferred by TNCs where domestic capabilities are low and do not improve over time, or where TNCs fail to invest sufficiently in raising the relevant capabilities.

- Weak bargaining and regulatory capabilities on the part of host country governments, which can result in an unequal distribution of benefits or abuse of market power by TNCs.

... the benefits of which can be reaped through policy measures ...

While the ultimate attraction for FDI lies in the economic base of a host country and FDI-attracting efforts by themselves cannot compensate for the lack of such a base, there remains a strong case for proactive policies to attract FDI. Countries may not be able to attract FDI in the volume and quality that they desire and that their economic base merits, for one or more of the following principal reasons:

- *High transaction costs:* While most FDI regimes are converging on a similar set of rules and incentives, there remain large differences in how these rules are implemented. The FDI approval process can take several times longer, and entail costs many times greater in one country than in another with similar policies. After approval, the costs of setting up facilities, operating them, importing and exporting goods, paying taxes and generally dealing with the authorities can differ enormously.

- Such costs can, other things being equal, affect significantly the competitive position of a host economy. An important part of a competitiveness strategy thus consists of *reducing unnecessary, distorting and wasteful business costs*, including, among others, administrative and bureaucratic costs. This affects both local and foreign enterprises. However, foreign investors have a much wider set of options before them, and are able to compare transaction costs in different countries. Thus, attracting TNCs requires not just that transaction costs be lowered, but also, increasingly, that they be benchmarked against those of competing host countries. One important measure that many countries take to ensure that international investors face minimal costs is to set up one-stop promotion agencies able to guide and assist them in getting necessary approvals. However, unless the agencies have the authority needed to provide truly one-stop services, and unless the rules themselves are clear and straightforward, this may not help.

- Despite their size and international exposure, TNCs face *market failures in information.* Their information base is far from perfect, and the decision-making process can be subjective and biased. Taking economic fundamentals as given, it may be worthwhile for a country that receives lower FDI than desired to invest in establishing a distinct image of its own and, if necessary, attempt to alter perception of potential investors by providing more and better information. Such promotion efforts are highly skill-intensive and potentially expensive, and they need to be mounted carefully to maximize their impact. Investor targeting – general, industry-specific or company-specific – could be a cost-effective approach in some cases. Targeting or information provision is *not* the same as giving financial or fiscal incentives. In general, incentives play a relatively minor role in a good promotion programme, and good, long-term investors are not the ones most susceptible to short-term inducements. The experiences of Ireland, Singapore – and, more recently, Costa Rica – suggest that promotion and targeting can be quite effective in raising the inflow of investment and its quality.

Effective promotion should go beyond simply 'marketing a country', into coordinating the supply of a country's immobile assets with the specific needs of targeted investors. This addresses potential failures in markets and institutions – for skills, technical services or infrastructure – in relation to the specific needs of new activities targeted via FDI. A developing country may not be able to meet, without special effort, such needs, particularly in activities with advanced skill and technology requirements. The attraction of FDI into such industries can be greatly helped if a host government discovers the needs of TNCs and takes steps to cater to them. The information and skill needs of such coordination and targeting exceed those of investment promotion *per se*, requiring investment promotion agencies to have detailed knowledge of the technologies involved (skill, logistical, infrastructural, supply and institutional needs), as well as of the strategies of the relevant TNCs.

... that also minimize the adverse effects on domestic enterprise development

Domestic enterprise development is a priority for all developing countries. In this regard, the possible 'crowding out' of domestic firms by foreign affiliates is frequently an issue of concern. Crowding out due to FDI could occur in two ways: first, in the product market, by adversely affecting learning and growth by local firms in competing activities; second, in financial or other factor markets, by reducing the availability of finance or other factors, or raising costs for local firms, or both.

The first issue reflects 'infant industry' considerations, but without the usual connotation of protecting new activities against import competition. It concerns the fostering of learning in domestic firms *vis-à-vis* foreign firms. FDI can abort or distort the growth of domestic capabilities in competing firms when direct exposure to foreign competition prevents local enterprises from undertaking lengthy and costly learning processes. Foreign affiliates also undergo learning locally to master and adapt technologies and train employees in new skills. However, they have much greater resources to undertake this learning, and considerably more experience of how to go about learning in different conditions. In these cases, 'crowding out' can be said to occur if potentially competitive local firms cannot compete with affiliates at a given point in time.

The case for domestic enterprise protection differs from the infant industry argument for trade protection. When trade protection is eliminated, consumers benefit from cheaper imports and greater product variety; but some domestic production and employment can be lost. In contrast, in the case of local enterprise protection, the absence of such protection from FDI competition does not lead to loss of domestic production and employment in exchange for enhancing consumer benefits; but, indigenous entrepreneurial development may be hampered, particularly in sophisticated activities. The net cost of this is that linkages may be fewer and technological deepening may be inhibited. As with all infant industry arguments, crowding out is economically undesirable if three conditions are met. First, infant local enterprises are able to mature to full competitiveness if sheltered against foreign competition that takes place through (in this case) FDI. Second, the maturing process does not take so long that the discounted present social costs outweigh the social benefits. Third, even if there are social costs, there must be external benefits that outweigh them.

Crowding out can impose a long-term cost on the host economy if it holds back the development of domestic capabilities or retards the growth of a local innovative base. This can make technological upgrading and deepening dependent on decisions taken by TNCs, and in some cases hold back the host economy at lower technological levels than would otherwise be the case. However, it is important to distinguish between affiliates crowding out potentially efficient domestic enterprises and affiliates out-competing inefficient local firms that cannot achieve full competitiveness. One of the benefits of FDI can be the injection of new technologies and competition that leads to the exit of inefficient enterprises and the raising of efficiency in others. Without such a process, the economy can lack dynamism and flexibility, and can lose competitiveness over time, unless competition between local firms in the domestic market is intense, or they face international competition (say, in export markets).

TNCs, however, can also 'crowd in' local firms if they strike up strong linkages with domestic suppliers, subcontractors and institutions. Crowding in can take place when foreign entry increases business opportunities and local linkages, raises investible resources or makes factor markets more efficient. Such stimulating effects are most likely when FDI concentrates in industries that are undeveloped in (or new to) host countries. Where local firms are well developed, but still face difficulties in competing with foreign affiliates, there can be harmful crowding out. However, local firms can also become suppliers to TNCs, or be taken over by them, as discussed below.

A second variety of crowding out reflects an uneven playing field for domestic firms because of a segmentation in local factor markets: TNCs may have privileged access to factors such as finance (which may give them a special advantage especially *vis-à-vis* local firms) and skilled personnel because of their reputation and size. They can thus raise entry costs for local firms, or simply deprive them of the best factor inputs.

Both forms of crowding out raise policy concerns. Most governments wish to promote local enterprises, particularly in complex and dynamic industrial activities. Many feel that the deepening of capabilities in local firms yields greater benefits than receiving the same technologies from TNCs: linkages with local suppliers are stronger, there is more interaction with local institutions, and where innovatory activities take place, knowledge developed within firms is not 'exported' to parent companies and exploited abroad, and so on. The few developing economies that have developed advanced indigenous technological capabilities have restricted the entry of FDI (generally, or into specific activities). The possession of a strong indigenous technology base is vital not just for building the competitiveness of local enterprises – it is also important for attracting high-technology FDI and for R&D investments by TNCs.

At the same time, there are risks in restricting FDI *per se* to promote local enterprises. For one thing, it is very difficult in practice to draw the distinction between crowding out and legitimate competition. If policy makers cannot make this distinction, they may prop up uneconomic local firms for a long period, at heavy cost to domestic consumers and economic growth. The danger of technological lags if TNCs are kept out of sophisticated activities in a country is much greater now than, say, several decades ago. So is the risk of being unable to enter export markets for activities with high product differentiation and internationally integrated production processes. It is important, however, to strengthen the opportunities for domestic firms to crowd in after the entry of FDI by building up local capabilities and a strong group of small- and medium-sized domestic firms that could develop linkages with foreign affiliates.

The right balance of policies between regulating foreign entry and permitting competition depends on the context. Only a few developing countries have built impressive domestic capabilities and world-class innovative systems while restricting the access of TNCs. Some others have restricted foreign entry, but have not succeeded in promoting competitive domestic enterprises in high-technology manufacturing activities. Success clearly depends on many other things apart from sheltering learning, including the availability of complementary resources and inputs, the size of the domestic market and the competitive climate in which learning takes place. In sum, the infant enterprise argument remains valid, and can provide a case for policy intervention to promote local capability development, but interventions have to be carefully and selectively applied, monitored and reversed where necessary.

Similar consideration to those highlighted above apply to mergers and acquisitions (M&As) of local firms by TNCs, including privatization by sale of state enterprises to foreign investors, a common form of foreign entry into Latin America and Central and Eastern Europe, and more recently into developing Asian countries affected by the financial crisis. Some M&As that entail a simple change of ownership akin to portfolio investment can be of lesser developmental value. Some take-overs lead to asset stripping, and large M&A-related inflows can become large outflows when investments are liquidated, possibly giving rise to exchange rate volatility and discouraging productive investment. There may also be adverse effects on local innovatory capacity and competitiveness in trade, as illustrated by the acquisition of firms in the automotive and telecommunications industries of Brazil by TNCs. These resulted in a scaling down of R&D activities in the acquired firms. Reduced reliance by Brazilian firms acquired by TNCs on locally produced high-technology inputs also led to increased import penetration in areas such as in automobile parts and components, information technology and telecommunication products. Many countries, including developed ones, are also concerned about the adverse impact of M&As on employment. M&As can also have anti-competitive effects if they reduce substantially the number of competitors in a domestic market, especially for non-tradable products such as most services.

M&As may also yield economic benefits, however. Where the investor makes a long-term commitment to the acquired firm and invests in upgrading and restructuring its technology and management, the impact is very similar to a greenfield investment. In Thailand, for instance, in the context of the recent financial crisis, a number of M&As in the automobile industry are leading to restructuring and increased competitiveness, manifested by increases in commercial vehicle exports. FDI related to M&As can play an important role in modernizing privatized utilities such as telecommunications and public utilities, as is the case in some instances in Latin America. Foreign acquisitions can prevent viable assets of local firms from being wiped out; this can be particularly important in economies in transition and financially distressed developing countries.

The benefits of M&As (including in the context of privatization) depend on the circumstances of a country and the conditions under which enterprises are acquired and subsequently operated. However, there may be value in monitoring M&As, instituting effective competition policies, and placing limits on them when the macroeconomic situation justifies it.

This raises the question of the effects of FDI on market structure in host countries. There has been a long-standing concern that the entry of large TNCs raises concentration levels within an economy and can lead to the abuse of market power. TNCs tend to congregate in concentrated industries. Whether this leads to the abuse of market power is an empirical question requiring further research. If host economies have liberal trade regimes, the danger of anti-competitive behaviour in such structures is largely mitigated. However, it remains true that effective competition policy becomes more and more important in a world in which large TNCs can easily dominate an industry in a host country.

Positive dynamic FDI effects on host countries require appropriate skills and policies...

Many important issues concerning the benefits of FDI for technology acquisition and technological capacity-building, skills development and competitiveness revolve around its static versus dynamic effects. TNCs can be efficient vehicles for the transfer of technologies and skills suited to *existing* factor endowments in host economies. They provide technology at very different levels of scale and complexity in different locations, depending on market orientation and size, labour skills available, technical capabilities and supplier networks. Where the trade regime in host (and home) countries is conducive (and infrastructure is adequate), they can use local endowments effectively to expand exports from host countries. This can create new capabilities in the host economies and can have beneficial spillover effects. In low-technology assembly activities, the skills and linkage benefits may be low; in high-technology activities, however, they may be considerable. Unless they operate in highly protected regimes, pay particularly low wages (as in some export-processing zones in low-skill assembly) or benefit from expensive infrastructure

Table 14.1   *Collaboration of Indian research centres with TNCs: R&D contracts awarded by TNCs to Indian publicly funded R&D institutes in the early 1990s*

Institution	TNC involved	R&D area
IICT, Hyderabad	Du Pont, United States	Pesticide chemistry (by screening agro-chemical molecules)
IICT, Hyderabad	Abbot Laboratories, United States	Synthesis of organic molecules and advisory consultancy
IICT, Hyderabad	Parke Davis, United States	Supply of medicinal plants
IICT, Hyderabad	Smith Kline and Beecham, United States	Agrochemical and pharmaceutical R&D
NCL, Pune	Du Pont, United States	Reaction engineering, process modelling for new polymers, nylon research, catalysis, and a scouting programme
NCL, Pune	Akzo, Netherlands	Zeolite-based catalyst development
NCL, Pune	General Electric, United States	Processes for intermediates of polycarbonates

Source: UNCTAD, *World Investment Report 1999*, Table VII.3, p. 213

while paying no taxes, there is a strong presumption that FDI contributes positively to using host country resources efficiently and productively.

In this context one of the main benefits of TNCs to export growth is their ability to provide not simply the technology and skills to complement local resources, or labour to produce for export, but access to foreign markets. TNCs are increasingly important players in world trade. They have large internal (intra-firm) markets for some of the most dynamic and technology-intensive products, access to which is available only to affiliates. They have established brand names and distribution channels with supply facilities spread over several national locations. They can influence the granting of trade privileges in their home (or in third) markets. All these factors mean that they might offer considerable advantages in creating an initial export base for new entrants.

The development impact of FDI, however, also depends on the *dynamics* of the transfer of technology and skills by TNCs: how much upgrading of local capabilities takes place over time, how far local linkages deepen, and how closely affiliates integrate themselves in the local learning system (see, as an illustration, Table 14.1). TNCs may simply exploit the existing advantages of a host economy and move on as those advantages erode. Static advantages may not automatically transmute into dynamic advantages. This possibility looms particularly large where a host economy's main advantage is low-cost unskilled labour, and the main TNC export activity is low-technology assembly.

The extent to which TNCs dynamically upgrade their technology and skills transfer and raise local capabilities and linkages depends on the interaction of the trade and competition policy regime, government policies on the operations of foreign affiliates, the corporate strategies and resources of TNCs, and the state of development and responsiveness of local factor markets, firms and institutions.

- The *trade and competition policy regime* in a host economy may provide the encouragement for enterprises, local and foreign, to invest in developing local capabilities. In general, the more competitive and outward-oriented a regime, the more dynamic is the upgrading process. A highly protected regime, or a regime with stringent constraints on local entry and exit, discourages technological upgrading, isolating the economy from international trends. This is not to say that completely free trade is the best setting. Infant industry considerations suggest that some protection of new activities can promote technological learning and deepening. However, even protected infants must be subjected to the rigours of international competition fairly quickly – otherwise they will never grow up. This applies to foreign affiliates, as well as to local firms. A strongly export-oriented setting with appropriate incentives provides the best setting for rapid technological upgrading.

- The second factor concerns *policies regarding the operations of foreign affiliates,* including local-content requirements, incentives for local training or R&D, and pressures to diffuse technologies. The results of the use of such policies have often been poor when they were not integrated into a wider strategy for upgrading capabilities. However, where countries have used them as part of a coherent strategy, as in the mature newly industrializing economies, the results have often been quite beneficial: foreign affiliates enhanced the technology content of their activities and of their linkages to local firms, which were supported in raising their efficiency and competitiveness. Much of the effort by foreign affiliates to upgrade local capabilities involves extra cost, and affiliates will not necessarily undertake this effort unless it is cost-effective and suits their long-term objectives. For the host economy, it is worth doing so only if it leads to efficient outcomes. If upgrading is forced beyond a country's capabilities, it will not survive in a competitive and open environment.

- The third factor involves *TNC strategies*. Corporate strategies differ in the extent to which they assign responsibility to different affiliates and decide their position in the corporate network. TNCs are changing their strategies in response to technological change and policy liberalization, and much of this is outside the scope of influence of developing host countries. Nevertheless, host country governments can influence aspects of TNC location decisions by measures such as targeting investors, inducing upgrading by specific tools and incentives and improving local factors and institutions. This requires them to have a clear understanding of TNC strategies and their evolution.

- The fourth factor, the state and responsiveness of *local factor markets, firms and institutions*, is probably the most important one. TNCs upgrade their affiliates where it is cost-efficient to do so. Moreover, since firms in most industries prefer their suppliers to be nearby, they will deepen local linkages if local suppliers can respond to new demands efficiently. Both depend upon the efficacy and development of local skills and technological capabilities, supplier networks and support institutions. Without improvements in factor markets, TNCs can improve the skills and capabilities of their employees only to a limited extent. They do not compensate for weaknesses in the local education, training and technology system. In the absence of rising skills and capabilities generally, it would be too costly for them to import advanced technologies and complex, linkage-intensive operations.

At the same time, there are risks that the presence of TNCs inhibits technological development in a host economy. TNCs are highly efficient in transferring the results of innovation performed in developed countries, but less so in transferring the innovation process itself. While there are some notable exceptions, foreign affiliates tend to do relatively little R&D. This may be acceptable for a while in the case of countries at low levels of industrial development, but can soon become a constraint on capability building as countries need to develop autonomous innovative capabilities. Once host countries build strong local capabilities, TNCs can contribute positively by setting up R&D facilities. However, at the intermediate stage, the entry of large TNCs with ready-made technologies can inhibit local technology development, especially when local competitors are too far behind to gain from their presence. Where a host economy adopts a proactive strategy to develop local skills and technology institutions, it may be able to induce TNCs to invest in local R&D even if there is little research capability in local firms. The appropriate policy response is not to rule out FDI, but to channel it selectively so that local learning is protected and promoted. In countries that do not restrict FDI, it is possible to induce advanced TNC technological activity by building skills and institutions.

... as well as strong bargaining capabilities, regulatory regimes and policy-making capacity

In some cases, the outcome of FDI depends significantly on how well a host economy bargains with international investors. However, the capacity of developing host countries to negotiate with TNCs is often limited. The negotiating skills and information available to TNCs tend to be of better quality. With growing competition for TNC resources, the need of many developing countries for the assets TNCs possess is often more acute than the need of TNCs for the locational advantages offered by a specific country. In many cases, particularly in export-oriented investment projects where natural resources are not a prime consideration, TNCs have several alternative locations. Host countries may also have alternative foreign investors, but they are often unaware of them. Where the outcome of an FDI project depends on astute bargaining, developing host countries may sometimes do rather poorly compared to TNCs. The risk is particularly great for major resource-extraction projects or the privatization of large public utilities and other companies. Considerable bargaining also takes place in large manufacturing projects where incentives, grants, and so on, are negotiated on a case-by-case basis. Though the general trend is towards non-discretionary incentives, considerable scope for bargaining still exists, and developing countries tend to be at a disadvantage in this respect.

To strengthen developing countries' bargaining capabilities, legal advice is often required, but the costs of obtaining such advice are usually prohibitive, especially for least developed countries. Establishing a pilot facility that would help ensure that expert advice in contract negotiations is more readily available to developing countries is worth considering. Such a facility would benefit not only developing host countries, but also TNCs by reducing specific transaction costs in the process of negotiations (for instance, by reducing the risk of delays) and, more generally, by leading to more stable and lasting contracts.

To return to the regulatory framework: with liberalization and globalization, there are fewer policy tools available to countries left to influence the conduct of foreign and local firms. The capacities of host developing countries to regulate enterprises in terms of competition policy and environment policy are emerging as the most active policy-making areas. An effective competition policy is therefore an absolute necessity. However, most developing countries lack such policy. Mounting a competition policy is a complex task requiring specialized skills and expertise that are often scarce in developing countries. It is important for host countries to start the process of developing these skills and expertise, especially if large TNCs with significant market power are attracted to their markets.

Similar concerns arise with respect to the environment. Many developing host countries have only limited regulations on the environment, and often lack the capacity to enforce them effectively. TNCs are often accused of exploiting these in order to evade tougher controls in the developed world. Some host developing countries are accused of using lax enforcement to attract FDI in pollution-intensive activities. The evidence on the propensity of TNCs to locate their investments in order to evade environmental regulations is, however, not conclusive. TNCs are usually under growing pressure to conform to high environmental standards from home country environmental regulations, consumers, environment groups and other 'drivers' in the developed and developing world. Many see environment management not only as necessary, but also as commercially desirable. However, it is up to host governments to ensure that all TNCs and domestic firms follow the examples set by the 'green' TNCs.

Another important regulatory problem is that of transfer pricing to evade taxes or restrictions on profit remission. TNCs can use transfer pricing over large volumes of trade and service transactions. The problem is not restricted to dealings between affiliates; it may also arise in joint ventures. However, it may well be that the deliberate abuse of transfer pricing has declined as tax rates have fallen and full profit remittances are allowed in much of the developing world. Double-taxation treaties between host and home countries have also lowered the risk of transfer-pricing abuses. However, this problem still remains a widespread concern among developed and developing countries. Tackling it needs considerable expertise and information. Developing country tax authorities are generally poorly equipped to do this, and can benefit greatly from technical assistance and information from developed country governments in this area.

Managing FDI policy effectively in the context of a broader competitiveness strategy is a demanding task. A passive, *laissez faire* approach is unlikely to be sufficient because of failures in markets and deficiencies in existing institutions. Such an approach may not attract sufficient FDI, extract all the potential benefits that FDI offers, or induce TNCs to operate by best-practices standards. However, a *laissez faire* FDI strategy may yield benefits in host countries that have under-performed in terms of competitiveness and investment attraction because of past policies. Such a strategy sends a strong signal to the investment community that the economy is open for business. FDI will be attracted into areas of existing comparative advantage. However, there are two problems. First, if attractive locational assets are limited, or their use is held back by poor infrastructure or non-economic risk, there will be little FDI response. Second, even if FDI enters, its benefits are likely to be static and will run out when existing advantages are used up. To ensure that FDI is sustained over time and enters new activities requires policy intervention, both to target investors and to raise the quality of local factors. Needless to say, for the great majority of countries the form of intervention has to be different from traditional patterns of heavy inward-orientation and market-unfriendly policies – it has to be aimed at competitiveness.

What all this suggests is that there is no ideal universal strategy on FDI. Any strategy has to suit the particular conditions of a country at any particular time, and evolve as the country's needs and its competitive position in the world change. Increasingly, it also has to take into account the fact that international investment agreements set parameters for domestic policy making. Governments of developing countries need to ensure, therefore, that such agreements do leave them the policy space they require to pursue their development strategies. Formulating and implementing an effective strategy requires above all a development vision, coherence and coordination. It also requires the ability to decide on trade-offs between different objectives of development. In a typical structure of policy making, this requires the FDI strategy-making body to be placed near the head of government so that a strategic view of national needs and priorities can be formed and enforced.

* * *

In conclusion, TNCs are principal drivers of the globalization process, which defines the new context for development. In this context, there is more space for firms to pursue their corporate strategies, and enjoy more rights than before. The obvious question is: should these increased rights be complemented by firms' assuming greater social responsibility? The notion of social responsibility of TNCs encompasses a broad range of issues of which environmental, human and labour rights have attracted most attention in recent years. In a liberalizing and globalizing world economy, this question is likely to be asked with increasing frequency and insistence. In his Davos speech in January 1999, the Secretary-General of the United Nations initiated the discussions on this question by proposing a global compact. Perhaps they could be intensified in the framework of a more structured dialogue between all parties concerned. Development would have to be central to this dialogue, as this is the overriding concern of the majority of humankind and because it is, in any event, intimately linked to the social, environmental and human rights objectives that lead the agenda in this area. The dialogue could build on the proposal of a global compact made by the Secretary-General, with a view towards examining how, concretely, the core principles already identified, as well as development considerations, could be translated into corporate practices. After all, companies can best promote their social responsibilities by the way they conduct their own businesses and by the spread of good corporate practices.

The world today is more closely knit, using different means of organization, communication and production, and is more subject to rapid change than ever before. At the same time, the past 30 years show striking – and growing – differences between countries in their ability to compete and grow. They also show how markets by themselves are not enough to promote sustained and rapid growth: policies matter, as do the institutions that formulate and implement them. There is an important role for government policies, but not in the earlier mould of widespread intervention behind protective barriers. Rather, in a globalizing world economy, governments increasingly need to address the challenge of development in an open environment. FDI can play a role in meeting this challenge. Indeed, expectations are high, perhaps too high, as to what FDI can do. But it seems clear that if TNCs contribute to development – and do so significantly and visibly – the relationship that has emerged between host country governments, particularly in developing countries, and TNCs over the past 15–20 years can develop further with potential benefits for all concerned.

Information Technology and Global Capitalism

MANUEL CASTELLS*

The global, networked economy

In the last two decades of the twentieth century, a new economy has emerged around the world. It is certainly capitalist. Indeed, for the first time in history, the whole planet is either capitalist or highly dependent on capitalist economic processes. But it is a new brand of capitalism, characterised by three fundamental features.

Productivity and competitiveness are, by and large, a function of knowledge generation and information processing; firms and territories are organised in networks of production, management and distribution; the core economic activities are global – that is, they have the capacity to work as a unit in real time, or chosen time, on a planetary scale. Not everything is global. In fact, most employment is local or regional. Yet the strategically crucial activities and economic factors are networked around a globalised system of inputs and outputs, which conditions the fate of all economies and most jobs. By 'strategically crucial economic activities' I mean, primarily, capital markets, science and technology, information, specialised labour, affluent consumer markets, multinational networks of production and management in manufacturing (including industrialised farming), and advanced services, media communication (including the internet), entertainment (including sports) and – not to forget – global crime.

New information and communication technologies, based on microelectronics, telecommunications and network-oriented computer software, have provided the infrastructure for this new economy. While the internationalisation of economic activities is certainly not new, this technological infrastructure is.

---

* The Random House Group Ltd for an extract from *On the Edge* by W. Hutton and A. Giddens, published by Jonathan Cape © M. Castells, 2000.

Network-oriented information and communication technologies allow for unprecedented speed and complexity in the management of the economy. Thus economic transactions and production are able to increase their size dramatically without hampering their connectivity. They can operate in real time or in chosen time, and, furthermore, the flexibility of the new technological system makes it possible for this new economy to select its components around the planet, in an endlessly variable geometry of value searching. This implies bypassing economically valueless or devalued territories and people. So, the global economy is at the same time extraordinarily inclusive of what is valued in the networks of business interaction, and highly exclusive of what has little or no interest in a given time and space. There is no value judgement in the electronic networks, except for assessing value – which is increasingly measured in terms of prospective capital growth rather than profit rates. Indeed, short-term profit-making is not the correct indicator of value any longer, as shown by the high value of stocks for money-losing internet firms.

The versatility and dynamism of this networked, global/informational capitalism, powered by the most extraordinary technological revolution in history, seems to enable its expansion without limits, and without challenges. Or does it?

The Automaton: global financial markets

If globalisation is widely acknowledged as a fundamental feature of our time, it is essentially because of the emergence of global financial markets. Indeed, to say that capital is globalised (or, more accurately, globally interconnected) in real time is not an incidental remark in a capitalist economy. While the process of financial globalisation has long historical roots and has gradually expanded over the past quarter of a century, its acceleration can be traced back to the late 1980s. To select, rather arbitrarily, a symbolic event, I would suggest the beginning of this new era was signalled by the City of London's 'Big Bang' on 27 October 1987, when the deregulation of capital and securities markets occurred. This is to emphasise that deregulation and liberalisation of financial trading were the crucial factors in spurring globalisation, allowing capital mobility between different segments of the financial industry and around the world, with fewer restrictions and a global view of investment opportunities. New technology was crucial both in allowing quasi-instantaneous trading world-wide, and in managing the new complexity brought in by deregulation and financial ingenuity. Mutual funds, a household appliance these days in the homes of the rich world, were the direct result of new rules and new financial models, powered by computer technology. As another example, take derivatives, that catch-all word for all manner of new, synthetic securities.

Derivatives may combine underlying values of stocks, bonds, options, commodities, currencies or, for that matter, any other support of any monetary value, actual or potential. By recombining value across space (markets around the world) and through time (futures markets), derivatives extraordinarily increase the possibility of trading on value. In so doing, they create market capitalisation value out of market capitalisation value. How much? Some estimates put the market value of derivatives traded in 1997 at US $360 trillion. If this figure would stand scrutiny, it would represent something in the vicinity of twelve times the size of global gross domestic product (GDP) – not a very useful calculation, but a powerful image.

This extraordinary growth of tradable financial value is possible only because of the use of advanced mathematical models, made operational by powerful computer systems, fed with and constantly adjusted by information transmitted electronically from all over the world. Domestic deregulation, liberalisation of trans-border transactions, financial wizardry and new information technology have succeeded in mobilising potential sources for investment from everywhere to everywhere, and from whatever to whenever. In 1995, in the USA, investment by mutual funds, pension funds, and institutional investors in general, accounted for US $20 trillion, a tenfold increase since 1980 – and the trend has accelerated since then. In 1997, for the first time, a higher proportion of US households' assets were in securities than in real estate. As a result, the ratio between stock market capitalisation and GDP in the USA reached a record 140 per cent in 1998. Cross-border transactions of bonds and equities between 1970 and 1996, measured as a percentage of domestic GDP, increased by a factor of about 54 for the USA, of 55 for Japan, and of almost 60 for Germany. This financial investment frenzy went global, seizing in particular the opportunities offered by two different kinds of situation. One lay in the rapidly growing economies of the Asian Pacific, where investment appreciation could be anticipated. The other was generated by bargain prices in newly industrialising countries, particularly in Latin America (Argentina, Chile, Mexico, Peru, Brazil), but also in Russia in the mid-1990s, in spite of the economic uncertainty there. In the USA overseas investment by pension funds increased from less than 1 per cent of their assets in 1980 to 17 per cent in 1997. Between 1983 and 1995, calculating in average annual rates of change, while the world's real GDP grew by 3.4 per cent, and world exports volume increased by 6 per cent, total issues of loans and bonds grew by 8.2 per cent, and total stocks of outstanding bonds and loans increased by 9.8 per cent. As a result, in 1998, stocks of outstanding loans and bonds amounted to about US $7.6 trillion, or about 5.5 times the GDP of the UK in 1998. Global investors took advantage of loose financial and banking regulations in the emerging markets, which enabled speculative manoeuvres. Investors also counted on the expected support from governments in case of financial crisis. The factors that are blamed for the 1997–8 financial crisis in emerging markets (government interference, lack of financial transparency) are thus among the key elements that attracted global financial investment in the first place. Under these conditions, acquisitions of overseas stocks by investors from industrialised countries increased by a factor of 197 between 1970 and 1997, inextricably linking financial markets around the planet. Currency markets exploded, becoming a critical element in the inability of any government to control economic policy, given that the value of the national currency, and thus interest rates, became largely determined by financial markets. In 1998, on average, global currency markets exchanged every day the equivalent of US $1.5 trillion – that is, about 110 per cent of the UK's GDP in 1998. This represented an increase in the value of global currency trading by a factor of 8 between 1986 and 1998. Financial markets have become interconnected in several ways. First of all, online transactions and computer-based information systems allow for very fast movements of capital between financial products, currencies and countries – often in a matter of seconds. Second, new financial products have appeared, mixing valuables from various countries to be traded in other countries. When one component of these products is affected by a sudden change in value in one market, it affects the product as a whole, in a range of markets. This was particularly the case of derivatives in Asian financial markets in 1997. Third, speculative investors looking for high financial rewards move swiftly from one market to another, trying to anticipate price movements of different products in different currencies, using forecasting models.

An important source of these speculative movements is hedge funds, another catch-all term covering non-conventional investment funds which don't rely on bonds, equities and money market funds. Hedge funds are, by and large, unregulated, and have extraordinarily increased in number and capital power in the 1990s: between 1990 and 1997 hedge funds assets increased by a factor of 12, and now there are about 3,500 hedge funds managing US $200 billion. To this sum must be added all they can borrow on the basis of these funds. Hedge funds manage the money of large investors, including banks, pension funds and institutional investors who circumvent their regulatory limits by the intermediation of hedge funds. To a large extent, we all are the speculators – willingly (through our pension funds), or unwillingly (through placing our savings, like most small investors, in mutual funds or retirement accounts). Besides hedge funds, investors of all kinds (large and small), equipped with networked computers, fed with information in real time, buy, sell and redistribute financial tradables of all kinds, of all origins and in most markets, inducing turbulences and reacting to them. A fourth major factor of interconnection must be emphasised: information-providers and opinion-makers. Market valuation firms, such as Standard&Poor or Moody's, business financial gurus and leading central bankers may induce market appreciation or depreciation for securities, currencies, or even whole national economies, by upgrading/downgrading their value (and thus the values of companies in the rated countries, according to the 'sovereign ceiling doctrine', which provides a benchmark for lenders, to give a range of key indicators of national financial distress). While it is debatable how objective these evaluations are, it is not the case that they are proved statements. If we add the impact of political events and of statements by influential decision-makers on financial markets, we can conclude that largely uncontrolled information turbulences are as important as supply and demand in setting prices and trends in global financial markets. Finally, international financial institutions, and particularly the International Monetary Fund (IMF), intervene as lenders of last resort in economies in crisis. The IMF's criteria, which are, by and large, uniformly applied as a standard recipe in its fundamentals, tend to unify the rules of the game in financial markets around the world. This is precisely the pre-condition for capital flows to move unfettered, thus further integrating global finance. The outcome of this process of financial globalisation may be that we have created an Automaton, at the core of our economies, decisively conditioning our lives. Humankind's nightmare of seeing our machines taking control of our world seems on the edge of becoming reality – not in the form of robots that eliminate jobs or government computers that police our lives, but as an electronically based system of financial transactions. The system overwhelms controls and regulations put in place by governments, international institutions and private financial firms, let alone the considerations of individual investors, consumers and citizens. Since income from all sources finds its way into financial markets, where the highest capital growth takes place, this network of electronic transactions, enacting global/local capital flows, has established itself as a collective capitalist. Its logic is not controlled by any individual capitalist or corporation – nor, for that matter, by any public insti-tution. While capitalists, and capitalist managers, still exist, they are all determined by the Automaton. And this Automaton is not the market. It does not follow market rules – at least, not the kind of rules based on supply and demand which we learned from our economics primers. Movements in financial markets are induced by a mixture of market rules, business and political strategies, crowd psy-chology, rational expectations, irrational behaviour, speculative manoeuvres and information turbulences of all sorts. All these elements are recombined in increas-ingly unpredictable patterns whose frantic modelling occupies would-be Nobel Prize recipients and addicted financial gamblers (sometimes embodied in the same persons). Yet, how automatic is this Automaton? After all, new financial regulations were set in the New York Stock Exchange after automated trading by computer programs amplified market trends which helped to induce the crash of October 1987. There are few instances of fully automated transactions without the inter-vention of human decision-makers, apart from routine operations. Anthropologist Caitlin Zaloom, observing trading in the pits of the Chicago Board of Trade in 1998, reported that personal interaction, business savvy and company intermedia-tion were alive and well in a critically important market. Technology backs up and implements human decision, but traditional securities trading does not disappear and regulations remain in place. However, there are major changes under way: Eurex, an electronic exchange system, now controls the major German bond futures marker; MATIF, the French futures exchange, moved entirely to an elec-tronic system in 1998; and London's LIFFE was planning to do so too.

In September 1998, New York's Cantor Fitzgerald Brokerage, the world's largest bond broker, started Cantor Exchange, an electronic exchange to trade future contracts on US Treasury bonds. The major change in stocks trading is related to the development of electronic communication networks (ECNs) which grew as an offshoot of Nasdaq transactions. Nasdaq, a non-profit association like the New York Stock Exchange (however ironical that may sound), does not have a central trading floor. It is an electronic market-place built on computer networks.

New rules designed to encourage electronic trading allowed ECNs to post orders from their clients on Nasdaq's system and receive a commission when the order was filled. Lured by potential profits, a number of firms, including some large Wall Street brokers, set up private electronic trading networks, the largest being Instinet, a subsidiary of Reuters Group plc. These networks are not subjected to the same strict regulations that hem in Nasdaq or the New York Stock Exchange. For instance, investors may trade anonymously. This could prompt the established trading markets to do the same, even further obscuring stocks transactions. Indeed, in 1999, the New York Stock Exchange was studying how it might set up its own electronic trading system, and with Nasdaq was exploring the possibility of their association, which would dramatically enhance the role of electronic trading in the future. Changes in financial trading have been accelerated by internet brokers since 1997. Day-traders, most of them individual investors, often investing in internet-related stocks, started the trend. In 1999, in the USA, electronic trading was used in about 25 per cent of transactions by individual investors. Major broker-age companies entered this trade, led by Charles Schwab & Co (with 27 per cent of the online trading market). In 1998, 14 per cent of all equity trades in the USA were online, a 50 per cent increase on 1997. The online brokerage industry in 1998, in the USA, doubled accounts to 7.3 million and doubled customers' assets to US $420 billion. It is important to retain this last figure, because US $420 billion represented the equivalent of 35 per cent of total value of German stocks in December 1998. Given the foreseeable rate of growth for online investment and the current value of its assets, this is clearly a formidable source of capital to reckon with in the near future.

What are the implications? Why does the technology of investment matter? First, it considerably reduces transaction costs associated with active trading (online trading commissions declined by 50 per cent in 1997 in the USA), thus attracting a much broader pull of individual investors. Second, it opens up investment opportunities to millions of individual investors, assessing value and opportunities on the basis of computerised information. It follows, on the one hand, that information turbulences, amplified by massive direct inputs from individual investors, may increase their role in affecting movements of capital. On the other hand, volatility of investments increases, since investment patterns become highly decentralised, investors go in and out of securities, and market trends trigger quasi-immediate reactions. Moreover, the decline of central market-places, and the looser regulation of electronic trading, make it much more difficult to track capital movements. The growing secrecy of investment attracts large pools of capital but it also leaves small investors in the dark. There follows greater decentralisation of investment and broader participation of individual investors in stocks trading, but decreasing levels of information for them, because of the secrecy and anonymity allowed by looser regulations. These trends add uncertainty, on both grounds, to the overall investment pattern: more people invest, and more do so without having key information on their computer screens. The net result is greater complexity and greater volatility. Most electronic trading is taking place in the USA, for the time being, but it is rapidly expanding in Europe. Moreover, given the interdependence between US financial markets and global financial markets, movements in US markets (for instance, the irresistible ascension – and fall? – of internet stocks) deeply affect financial markets around the world. In sum, globally interdependent financial markets are not on automatic pilot – in fact, we have witnessed the opposite trend, as millions of investors, besides the competitive efforts of large institutional investors, and the guerrilla tactics of hedge funds and other speculative investors jam market circuits with conflicting signals. This complex network of transactions, resulting from interactive, contradictory bets on market values in different space and time frames, is, as a whole, beyond the control of governments, financial institutions and specific business groups – regardless of their size and wealth.

Random movements rather than economic calculations seem to be the primary forces shaping market trends. So the random Automaton thrives, simultaneously inducing growth and wealth, and triggering disinvestment and crisis. However, financial markets are only one element, albeit extremely important, of the dynamics of global capitalism which are reshaping our world.

Productivity, technology and the new economy

Volatility and the interdependence in global financial markets were at the roots of the crisis of emerging markets in 1997–9 – a crisis that, coming after the Mexican crisis of 1994, rocked the Asian Pacific (1997), Russia (1998) and Brazil (1999), and sent shock waves around the world. The global economy absorbed the shock. Most foreign banks that were in trouble because of their investments in emerging markets were bailed out by IMF-led policies. Capital flows simply reversed course, heading towards European and US markets: for instance, in 1996 private capital flows into Malaysia, the Philippines, South Korea, Thailand and Indonesia amounted to US $93 billion. In 1997 there was an outflow of US $12 billion, and in 1998 an additional outflow of US $9 billion. This swing of US $114 billion in capital flows devalued the currencies of these countries and induced a severe recession in most of the Asian Pacific economies, as I have analysed elsewhere – yet capital investment world-wide has continued to grow, and stock market values in the USA reached a historic height in 1999, going over the 11,000 level on the Dow Jones index. European stock markets were also performing at a high level in mid-1999. The flexibility of the new techno-economic system allows for this geographic redistribution of investment so that, while economies suffer, most global investments do not. Some global investors may in fact benefit from devaluations, if they time their movements well, or simply get lucky. When crisis strikes in emerging markets or in advanced but shaky economies such as Japan, investment flows find new opportunities in the advanced Western economies. In 1997–8, while stock markets in Asian economies, including Japan, and in Russia and in Brazil were substantially devalued, the US stock market rose by 31 per cent and the German stock market by 54 per cent. While European Union economies performed well during the emerging markets' crisis, helped by the smooth transition to the euro, it is the performance of the US economy which keeps growth and dynamic stability in the global economy, by absorbing investment and exports from around the world. In a showcase of the bright side of the new economy, led by domestic consumption and stocks revaluation, the USA was able in 1998 to grow at 3.9 per cent (including a stunning 6.1 per cent in the last quarter of 1998), with low inflation, quasi-full employment (with the unemployment rate at 4.2 per cent in August 1999) and a surplus in the federal budget, albeit at the price of a significant increase in the current account trade deficit. This is why the rest of the world did not sink into global recession. Indeed, in 1999, most Asian economies were bouncing back, helped by their renewed exports competitiveness, and the return of foreign investment attracted by bargain prices of stocks and assets.

At the heart of the resilience of the global economy we find the performance of the US economy, which induces a virtuous circle by attracting foreign investment, both directly and in stocks acquisition.

European companies, which spent US $58.5 billion in acquiring US companies in 1996, and another US $48.4 billion in 1997, stepped up their cross-Atlantic investment, with a spending spree of US $280 billion in 1998 and the first two months of 1999, including the acquisition of Chrysler by Daimler-Benz, of Amoco by British Petroleum, and of Airtouch Communications by Vodafone. Since American companies did their own business in Europe (Ford, for instance, bought Volvo's automobile business), a renewed Atlantic connection seems to have established itself as the axis of the global economy, as Lester Thurow predicted.

However, the new system is somewhat more complex. Geographical metaphors cannot account for the complexity and speed of global flows of capital and trade. Networks, rather than countries or economic areas, are the true architectures of the new global economy. In this way recession in Asia offered tremendous investment opportunities to European and US companies. And they seized them, from Thailand, to South Korea, to Japan. The Japanese financial market is finally being cracked through the acquisition of, or participation in, Japanese banks and savings associations by US and European financial firms. This may represent global access to a gigantic and largely untapped savings market, in hundreds of billions of dollars – enough to refuel capital investment in the global economy, as long as there are investment opportunities. But are there? The answer lies, on the one hand, in how we assess the new US economy; on the other hand, it depends on the ability of the European Union to enter this 'new economy' on its own terms, preserving its social model. Without this, Europeans will simply resist the move. What is the secret behind the performance of the US economy? And what is this 'new economy'? How can it grow, as it did in 1998, adding 225,000 jobs per month (and 310,000 in July 1999), and increasing hourly wages by about an annual 4 per cent, with 1.6 per cent inflation? The usual suspect, in these cases, is productivity. With the exception of a few, if notorious, economists, such as Paul Krugman, many of us thought that new information technology and major organisational changes (networking in the first place) were about to induce a surge in productivity growth. I argued in my book *The Rise of the Network Society* (2000 [1996]) that the reasons we could not observe substantial productivity increases were twofold: the absolute inadequacy of our statistical categories to measure the new informational/global economy; and the necessary time-lag between technological innovation and organisational change for productivity potential to be realised. The first obstacle continues to exist, and it is a major hindrance in understanding our new world. But even with statistical measures that underestimate actual productivity growth, productivity is finally showing up, not only in the high-tech and advanced business services sectors, but in the US economy as a whole. In testimony before the US Congress, on 23 February 1999, Alan Greenspan reported that productivity growth in non-financial corporations averaged 2.2 per cent in this business cycle, compared with 1.5 per cent in the late 1980s. Overall, productivity growth averaged 2 per cent in 1995–8, twice the growth rate between 1973 and 1995. Greenspan traced the origins of productivity increases back to 1993, when capital investment, particularly in information technology equipment, rose sharply.

Business spending on new equipment in the USA increased 60 per cent in 1994–8. Growth is led by information-based industries (such as software, communication and consulting), which add well-paying jobs at an annual rate of 3.7 per cent, twice the rate of the rest of the economy. These trends were not slowing down in 1998/9: overall work productivity growth in the fourth quarter of 1998 reached 4.6 per cent, the fastest growth in six years, and GDP growth for 1999 was projected to be around 3 per cent. In September 1999, Macroeconomic Advisers, a leading US economic forecasting firm, issued a report predicting productivity growth at annual rates around 2.3 per cent, as long as the investment boom in information technology would continue. Indeed, information technology is at the heart of this new economy in several ways. It provides the technology for business restructuring around networks. It reduces the prices of both equipment and consumer goods, from computers and VCRs to a whole range of household appliances. It is creating a whole new generation of products and processes by shifting from Operating System technologies, centred on the PC, to information-sharing technologies, decentred on electronic networks powered by co-operative servers. It is creating jobs and generating earnings at an unprecedented pace. And it is leading the growth of the stock market, as internet stocks skyrocket. This is partly because internet technology allows small investors to trade electronically following their own strategies, thus pushing up stock prices regardless of rational expectations based on previous trends. There is widespread belief that internet stocks will crash one day, and they may have crashed by the time you read this. But since investors continue to believe that it will be tomorrow, not today, they keep delaying the day of reckoning. Even when or if that day does happen, the huge amount of capital attracted to the internet industry in the meantime will have modified the realm of information technology and of business as a whole. Market capitalisation of internet companies, most of which still do not make profits, has reached extraordinary levels, as compared with giant companies of the industrial age. In January 1999, America OnLine, employing 10,000 peoples, was valued at US $66.4 billion. This can be contrasted to General Motors, employing 600,000 workers, whose market value was US $52.4 billion. In another telling example, Yahoo!, employing 673 people, was worth US $33.9 billion. Pure speculation? Unreal economy? In fact this is anticipation of trends. The S&P top five growth stocks for 1995–9 are Dell Computer (9,402 per cent increase in five years), Cisco Systems (2,356 per cent), Sun Microsystems (2,304 per cent), Qualcomm (1,646 per cent) and Charles Schwab (1,634 per cent), all firms making their business in/around the internet. Internet stock frenzy is in fact an indicator of the decisive shift of the economy to the new sources of value and growth.

Is info-growth sustainable?

There is no scarcity of paradoxes in this brave new economic world. In early 1999, at the time the network economy was spurring growth in the USA, with stock markets' values rising on both sides of the Atlantic, there were widespread fears of a world-wide deflation that would crush the high hopes of information-based global capitalism at the very moment of take-off. According to calculations by *The Economist*, in 1998 producer prices fell in fourteen out of fifteen rich economies monitored. In February 1999, consumer price inflation was dropping to an average of 1 per cent in the rich economies. In the euro zone, in 1998, consumer prices increased by 0.8 per cent: French annual inflation rate was 0.3 per cent, German rate was 0.5 per cent. China's consumer prices fell by 1.2 per cent, and producer prices by 8 per cent, so that the Chinese government was establishing price controls to keep them up. In 1998, with most emerging economies stalled by austerity policies set up to defend their currencies, with investment down because of capital outflows, and with the Japanese economy in recession, over-capacity built up in standard chips, cars, steel, textiles, ships, chemicals and a long series of manufacturing industries. Even in the high-growth USA, 337,000 manufacturing jobs were lost between March 1998 and March 1999. The automobile industry, world-wide, had 30 per cent unused capacity. The extraordinary addition of manufacturing plants in the world during the 1990s, particularly in Asia, seemed to be leading to a glut of manufactured goods, thus lowering prices, sometimes below production costs. Furthermore, commodity prices fell by 30 per cent in 1997–8, according to *The Economist* index, which reached its lowest level in 150 years. Oil prices were down to their pre-1973 level. With emerging market economies reeling from the crisis, Japan politically paralysed in its economic restructuring and the European Central Bank still putting the brakes on European economies through interest rates, which, in early 1999, were not low in real terms (considering inflation rates were between 0.3 per cent and 1 per cent), global capitalism was dependent on the performance of the US economy. Deflation is like cholesterol in the human system:

there are good and bad kinds. It is bad, very bad, when it reflects depressed demand, as a result of stagnant economy. It is good, very good, when it reflects gains in productivity (mainly because of technological innovation) and greater efficiency of economic management, both at the level of the firms (owing to networking and flexibility) and in macroeconomic terms (because of market integration and lower transactions costs, as with the advent of the euro).

All indications are that global capitalism at the end of the twentieth century features both kinds of deflationary trends – good and bad. But they do not cancel each other, because they are unevenly distributed across the regions of the global economy. By and large the US economy, fuelled by technology and networking, is sustaining a fast pace of info-growth. In contrast, many emerging economies, particularly in Latin America, plus the submerged economies of Africa, the ex-Soviet Union and many regions in other countries around the world, are stagnant, and suffering because of lower commodity prices, and austerity policies. However, in the summer of 1999, Japan seemed to be recovering from the recession, and the Asian Pacific economies, particularly in South Korea, resumed growth. The main European economies also started to grow again, after a period of stagnation in the first half of the year. They were helped by their exports performance, largely based on the weakness of the euro *vis-à-vis* the dollar. However, European and Asian recoveries seemed to be fragile, as they were partly induced by strong demand from the USA and, in Japan and South-East Asia, by new government spending. For this growth to be sustained the critical issue is if the sources of US productivity increase and economic growth can be adapted or adopted by Europe, and subsequently by Japan. In this case, the leading economies will become closely connected in a new pattern of info-growth. If this happens, global capitalism will thrive at its core and will reconnect again, in a much more selective and cautious way, the economies of emerging markets, articulating a self-expanding network of wealth creation and appropriation. However, it is not clear that Europe and Japan could join the info-growth model. If the institutional Automaton created by European countries (meaning Wim Duisenberg and his team of 'retro' inflation fighters in the European Central Bank) or the IMF's neo-classical globetrotters remain fixed on the terrors of the inflation age (actually a blip in economic history), they can wreck the capitalist ship simply out of bad management. It has happened before. Furthermore, if networking flexibility and technological innovation are perceived, in Japan and Europe, as being tantamount to dismantling the welfare state and curtailing workers' rights, there will be a backlash of social struggles and political reactions that will simply block reform and innovation. If this stalemate is long enough it will exhaust the growth capacity of the US economy, which is now interdependent on global performance. The USA cannot go on producing and consuming an increasing share of the world's output by itself (currently standing at over a quarter of the world's GDP) – mainly because domestic consumption remains the principal factor accounting for economic growth, and households' savings are reaching dangerously low levels. Productivity gains, after all, have to be realised by sale of output to someone with money to spend. Either Europe and Japan will join the expansion, or the US machine will stall and start spiralling downwards. Devaluation of stocks will erode the wealth accumulated on paper by both firms and households, and technology-led productivity potential will mutate into over-capacity, spilling into the morass of bad deflation on a global scale. Do not worry. Yet. It could still be worse.

A world of Silicon Valleys?

Let's imagine that Gerhard Schröder finds a way to seduce, convince or blackmail Duisenberg, and the European Central Bank finally agrees in letting low-inflation growth happen in the European Union. By a stretch of imagination, let's consider the chance that British Labour's 'third way' approach to info-capitalism with a human face (which amounts to social democracy with an enhanced brain) succeeds in convincing European citizens that they can still live in a network society without becoming Yankees or, worse, Californians. Then, in the apotheosis of fictional political economics, let us hope the IMF/World Bank starts lending for growth instead of imposing retrenchment. Global capitalism will blossom, in a virtuous circle encompassing technologically led productivity, financially fuelled growth and socio-institutional engineering. We will be truly in the new Information Age – albeit, certainly, its capitalist incarnation. But all we have considered to this point still excludes a considerable proportion of humankind. The favourable hypothesis of weathering *fin-de-siècle* storms of global capitalism assumes a growing, dynamic integration between the USA–NAFTA bloc, the European Union and Japan. It further assumes a selective integration of emerging markets, though no longer with the carelessness that characterised global investment flows in the 1990s – not because governments will do much about it, but because investors will be more careful, knowing they cannot count on being bailed out by national governments and international institutions. While so-called 'speculative investments' will continue to take place, because that is the nature of the beast, quick reaction systems will develop among the main financial players to minimise capital losses. Some regulatory procedures are already being put into place to limit destructive contagion into the core of global financial markets. This new and relatively cautious strategy by global investors (which is the fundamental lesson learned from the 1997–8 crisis) implies a much more limited penetration of emerging economies, creaming off the best opportunities in both stocks and direct investment, and letting the bulk of people and territories go about by themselves, until they find a way to make themselves valuable without being unreasonably risky for global investors. This leaves a substantial number of bodies out of the dynamic networks of global capitalism, for the time being. So-called 'emerging markets' represented, in 1998, only about 7 per cent of global value in market capitalisation, but comprised about 85 per cent of humankind. Grant, generously, that 20 per cent of people in emerging economies will directly benefit from economic growth in these dynamic networks, and this will still leave over two-thirds of humankind living under the influence of global capitalism but largely excluded from most of its benefits. If we add the considerable numbers of people who are socially excluded in advanced countries, the critical mass of disposable people – through the binary logic of being either in or out of the networks – expands significantly. In the USA, in the midst of this most extraordinary boom, other strata persist: about 15 per cent of the population living below poverty level (including 25 per cent of all children), and 5.5 million people in the criminal justice system (including almost 2 million in prisons). I have argued elsewhere that there is a systemic relationship between current features of global capitalism and the new technological system, because of the amplifying effects of information technologies on inequality and exclusion through disparities in education and networking capabilities. Nothing is wrong fundamentally with the technology – it could be the source of a sym-metrically opposite effect, used (but by whom?) in a deliberate effort to create a more egalitarian society.

But educational possibilities are not the focus of my argument here. My question is this: is the trend sustainable? My answer is no. The illusion of a world made of Silicon Valley-like societies driven by technological ingenuity, financial adventurism and cultural individualism, high-tech archipelagos surrounded by areas of poverty and subsistence around most of the planet, is not only ethically ques-tionable but, more important for our purpose, politically and socially unsustainable. The rise of fundamentalism, the spread of new epidemics, the expansion of the global criminal economy – with its corrosive effects on governments and societies around the world – the threat of biological/nuclear terrorism, the irreversible destruction of the environment (that is, of our natural capital, the most important legacy for our grandchildren), and the destruction of our own sense of humanity, all are potential consequences (many already under way) of this dynamic, yet exclusionary, model of global capitalism.

In sum, there are three different, although inter-related, sources of unsus-tainability for info-capitalism:

- the dangers of implosion of global financial markets;

- the stagnation caused by relative shrinkage of solvent demand in proportion to the extraordinary productive capacity created by technological innova-tion, organisational networking and mobilisation of capital resources;

- the social, cultural and political rejection by large numbers of people around the world of an Automaton whose logic either ignores or devalues their humanity.

Taming the Automaton?

The Asian crisis of 1997 and its aftermath (Russia, Brazil and beyond) has shaken the self-assurance of global capitalists, and their experts. The ugly sight of African massacres, of Aids epidemics, of global trade in children and women, of the fast-paced destruction of the planet's forests and of criminal networks taking over public institutions prompted well-meaning philanthropists to imagine a less disruptive path to informational, global capitalism. The 1999 World Economic Forum meeting at Davos rang with discussions about various schemes to regulate and control global capital flows, and to avoid speculative movements that would disrupt markets. Proposals abounded, both there and in other forums closer to the decision-makers. There are major technical obstacles to their implementation. Given the global electronic connection between financial markets, it becomes extremely difficult to avoid the massive movement of capital, which can be achieved in seconds by a computer instruction. Financial firms have growing numbers of offshore bases in countries where there exist few regulations or none at all, and the internet enables investments to be moved around while obscuring their origin and destination, if desired. Because many financial products are synthetic combinations of values from different markets, the impact of their fluctuations affects markets around the world, independent of the actual movement of capital. Furthermore, unless regulations are internationally agreed upon and internationally enforced, countries imposing strict limits on capital movements on a continuing basis are or will be bypassed by capital flows. This is the main feature of the network economy, epitomised in its financial dimension: the ability to extend or retrench its geometry without excessive disruption simply by reconforming the networks of investment and trade. This occurs in instants, in an endless flow of circulation. Recurrent examples of governments that have effectively implemented capital controls are proposed in every debate – a popular example is Chile's requirement for one year's deposit of 30 per cent of short-term capital invested in the country. It was successful and useful, as long as Chile had a considerable capital inflow, but it was eliminated in 1998 as soon as the foreign capital crunch started to be felt in Latin America. Another example commonly cited is Malaysia's effort to make inconvertible its unit of currency, the ringgit, and to impose strict controls on financial transaction by foreign capital, which it suspected of being a part of a Jewish global conspiracy. By mid-1999, thinking the worst of the crisis was over, Malaysia lifted most restrictions, while keeping the anti-Jewish and anti-Soros rhetoric, partly because the government was facing a serious domestic political challenge. China, the most important exception to the Asian crisis, at least until 1999, was showing the benefits of the non-convertibility of the People's Currency, the renminbi, and of the domestic insulation of its very troubled banking system. However, critics argue that this was China's good luck, simply as a consequence of its still limited integration into the global economy. Should China aim at becoming a full-fledged global player, it would need resumption of the extraordinary capital inflow it enjoyed in the 1990s, and this would be hardly compatible with strict government controls, particularly in matters of currency exchange and re-export of profits.

All in all, objections to capital controls derive from three main arguments. The first is a market fundamentalist argument about capital's fundamental right to unfettered freedom. This is losing ground in the face of widespread evidence about the damage caused by free-wheeling capitalism, something that our forebears understood in the 1930s and 1940s. That damage is now amplified by network technologies and global contagion. The second argument refers to the need for a concerted international action, at least among the G7 countries and their ancillary networks, to set up a new regulatory framework. [...] Third is the question of the technical feasibility of such controls in the age of electronic networks. My colleagues who are computer scientists voice the opinion that a global regulatory environment can be enforced technologically, precisely because of the extraordinary versatility and accuracy of new electronic technologies. For instance, if a financial tax (or mandatory deposit in the mode of Chile) were imposed on short-term transactions, all electronic financial networks could be programmed to include automatically such tax, rerouting the amount to a different account. In fact, you already have in your Windows 98 an individualised code that marks automatically all your computer documents in their trips around electronic networks (Microsoft just forgot to tell you). Book-keeping is now performed electronically, so a global financial inspection could have access to all accounts legally susceptible to inspection by using a virtually unbreakable password (it exists, and takes a code of a mere 4,096 bits). Speed and complexity can work both ways in the new technological environment. The Automaton could be dotted with electronic codes and instructions that would keep him (it's certainly not female) active but on a leash. All this discussion, and by extension the discussion about financial regulation in various forums, is entirely academic for the time being: it faces the opposition of the US government (represented lately by Robert Rubin and Larry Summers, but do not bet on the chances of a change of mind-set in the near future) and of its ancillary, the International Monetary Fund (officially presided over by a respectable French technocrat, as a guarantee of its independence, but actually managed by Stanley Fisher, a brilliant MIT product). Without US co-operation, there is no chance of global financial regulation, beyond what Rubin and his alma mater, Wall Street, propose – better global information systems and more transparency in accounting procedures and book-keeping, for governments, banks and corporations, plus more secure, and expeditious, bankruptcy laws. And more money for the IMF, so that, as lender of last resort (or financial rapid deployment force), it can intervene or lead pre-emptive strikes in countries in danger of financial turmoil – in exchange for assuming economic control in those countries until the conditions for safe global investment have been restored. Why has the USA so adamantly opposed global financial regulation, and why will it do so in the foreseeable future? Simple: the current system, at least in the short term, is working to the great advantage of the US economy and US firms, particulary those financial firms which are channelling a growing proportion of global investments. As for government officials, their mantra remains, 'It's the economy, stupid!' With its tremendous competitive advantage in technology, networking, information and management, the US economy is thriving. There is evidence that the US government, particularly during the Clinton administration, spearheaded the effort to expand global capitalism by opening up emerging markets, demanding the dismantling of regulations and government controls around the world.

And it worked, since the pain inflicted by the reversal of financial flows was suffered by other countries. Because such crises do not trigger immediate geo-political dangers, given the military superiority of the USA and Nato, they can be contained within the economic sphere. The US economy cannot grow by itself in a globally interdependent economy, which is why the US government and the IMF are pressuring Japan and Europe for reflation, while trying to stabilise those emerging markets such as Brazil which could jeopardise global financial equili-brium. The belief is that with pragmatic attention to financial crises when and where they occur, everything will be all right and global capitalism will continue to blossom, with US capitalism as its renewed core – even if the core is now a node of a global network. As for the poor of the world, they ought to be taken care of by a combination of trickled-down economic benefits, targeted programmes led by the World Bank, grass-roots survival efforts helped by inter-national charities, and a new round of family planning to stabilise population growth. Do not hold your breath as you wait for a serious attempt at global finan-cial regulation. It will happen only if dramatic financial crisis or social upheaval hit info-capitalism.

The Great Disconnection?

The naive illusion of a comprehensive, integrated global economy, enacted by capi-tal flows and computer networks, and reaching out to most people in the planet, was shattered on 2 July 1997 as economic crisis struck Asia. At the turn of the millen-nium, we find instead that most people, and most areas of the world, are suffering from, but not sharing in, the growth of global info-capitalism. Major economies, such as China and India (accounting for over one-third of humankind), remain relatively autonomous in terms of global capital flows. Countries that suffered the shocks of financial volatility, such as Indonesia or Russia, are shrinking the market sector of their economies. Indonesia is witnessing a significant return to rural areas, as people fight for survival and leave crumbling megacities. The total value of Russian stocks in December 1998 was about half of the value of market capitalisation for the online book-trader Amazon (Russia's US $12 billion versus Amazon's US $25.4 billion). But life goes on, because about 50 per cent of the Russian economy works on a barter system, and because the inability to import foreign goods has stimulated Russian domestic production – an interesting revival of import substitution as a development strategy. In March 1999, Brazil yielded to the IMF's pressure to impose a state of austerity, in order to save its last currency reserves and avoid further devalu-ation and subsequent inflation. But the social and political cost was very high, threatening to destabilise society, with a consequently disruptive impact on the economy. Japan is stubbornly trying to rebuild its economy in its own terms, actually proposing an Asian zone and an Asian investment fund, dissociated from the IMF and the USA. Even the essential Atlantic integration between the European Union and the United States was clouded in March 1999 with threats of a trade war – over bananas, with the EU representing the interests of French Caribbean colonies and the USA representing the interests of its former colonial companies, harvesting bananas in Ecuador and Central America, in a new paradox of twisted globalisation. At the same time the European Commission came under suspicion of corruption, leading to the resignation of all the Commissioners. The fragility of this unevenly connected global system is such that a new round of financial instability, perhaps induced by the collapse of internet stocks or by a sudden panic around electronic trading networks, could trigger another stampede towards the exits. This time, there could be governments and whole societies, or significant segments of societies, opting out of global capitalism – not necessarily to build an alternative system, but just to recover some degree of control over their lives, specific interests and values. For instance, in August 1999, Venezuela (the main oil supplier to the United States) engaged in a democratic process of nationalist reform, making clear it would not accept IMF-style imposition of austerity policies. The Great Disconnection is not mere political fiction. Its embroys are already planted in the social fabric of global capitalism. They may grow or not, depending upon the course of upcoming history. We know the probable response to such trends, from observing the currently dominant countries and firms. Networks of capital, technology, information and trade will be reconfigured, keeping what can be saved and discarding dead wood or spoiled human flesh. I am not sure it will work so easily next time.

And yet, the Information Age could be different. We do not have to choose between unfettered info-global capitalism and communal retrenchment. New information technologies (including ethically controlled genetic engineering) could yield their promise of a virtuous interaction between the power of mind and the well-being of society. No need to look into the future: just look around at courageous efforts such as those taking place in Finland. The Finns have quietly established themselves as the first true information society, with one website per person, internet access in 100 per cent of schools, a computer literacy campaign for adults, the largest diffusion of computer power and mobile telephony in the world, and a globally competitive information technology industry, spearheaded by Nokia. At the same time they have kept in place, with some fine-tuning, the welfare state. Finnish society fosters citizen participation and safeguards civility. It is probably not an accident that Linus Torvalds is a Finn. Torvalds is the software innovator who, as a 21-year-old student at the University of Helsinki, created Linux, a much better operating system than Microsoft's, and released it free on the internet. By so doing, he contributed to a growing open-access software code movement, with thousands of Linux users contributing online to improve the code. Its users – currently about ten million – consider it far superior to any other Unix software, precisely because it is continuously improved by the work of their collective mind. Open information technology contributes to much better information technology empowering minds around the world to use technology for living. That includes making money, without equating their lives to their stocks.

The catch is that Linus Torvalds now lives in Silicon Valley.

Notes

Data used in this chapter are in the public domain and have been reported by newspapers and business magazines, such as *The New York Times*, *Wall Street Journal*, *Financial Times*, *El Pais*, *Le Monde*, *Business Week*, *The Economist* and *Fortune*. Thus, I do not consider it necessary to burden the chapter with precise references to sources. The best synthesis of data and analyses on globalisation is Held et al. (1999). Global data on social exclusion and social inequality can be found in the United Nations' *Human Development Report* (1997, 1998 and 1999). This note should serve as generic reference to data sources.

I am citing a selected bibliography, limited to a few books that have been directly helpful in the analysis presented in this chapter. I refer the reader to these books for further elaboration on the issues discussed here. However, I consider it unnecessary to attach each reference to a specific paragraph in the text. This note should serve as generic reference to background sources.

Bibliography

Arthur, Brian (1998) *The New Economy*, Ann Arbor: University of Michigan Press.

Canals, Jordi (1997) *Universal Banking: International Comparisons and Theoretical Perspectives*, Oxford: Oxford University Press.

Carnoy, Martin (forthcoming) *Sustaining Flexibility: Work, Family and Community in the Information Age*, New York: Russell Sage Foundation.

Castells, Manuel (1998) 'Globalization and Social Inequality', paper for United Nations Research Institute for Social Development's conference, Geneva, 22 June.

Castells, Manuel (2000 [1996]) *The Rise of the Network Society* (revised edition), Oxford: Blackwell.

Castells, Manuel (2000 [1998]) *End of Millennium* (revised edition), Oxford: Blackwell.

Eichengreen, Barry (1999) *Toward a New International Financial Architecture: A Practical Post-Asia Agenda*, Washington, DC: Institute for International Economics.

Held, David, McGrew, Anthony, Goldblatt, David, and Perraton, Jonathan (1999) *Global Transformations*, Stanford, CA: Stanford University Press.

Hoogvelt, Ankie (1997) *Globalisation and the Post-colonial World*, London: Macmillan.

Kelly, Kevin (1998) *New Rules for the New Economy*, New York: Viking/Penguin.

Sachs, Jeffrey (1998a) 'International Economics: Unlocking the Mysteries of Globalization', *Foreign Affairs*, Spring: 97–111.

Sachs, Jeffrey (1998b) 'The IMF and the Asian Flu', *The American Prospect*, March–April: 16–21.

Scott, Allen (1998) *Regions and the World Economy*, Oxford: Oxford University Press.

Shapiro, Carl, and Varian, Hal, R. (1998) *Information Rules: A Strategic Guide to the Network Economy*, Cambridge, MA: Harvard Business School Publishing.

Tapscott, Don (ed.) (1998) *Blueprint to the Digital Economy: Wealth Creation in the Era of E-business*, New York: McGraw Hill.

Touraine, Alain (1999) *Comment sortir du liberalisme?*, Paris: Fayard.

Zaloom, Caitlin, 'Information Technology and Global Finance: the View from the Pits', Berkeley: University of California, PhD Dissertation in Anthropology (in progress).

Acknowledgements

I wish to thank, for their insightful comments to this chapter, my students at two graduate seminars (CS 290, and CP 229) at the University of California, Berkeley, in the Spring Semester, 1999. I particularly thank Caitlin Zaloom. I also want to acknowledge comments from my colleagues Jerry Feldman, Martin Carnoy and Vilmar Faria.

Regional Policy

D oes the growing globalization of economic activity imply that geography no longer matters? This section argues against such a presumption. Even as advances in technology and the operations of multinational firms are bringing the world closer, forces are at work that are increasing rather than diminishing the distinctiveness of geographic regions. This calls for due attention to be paid to the role of regional policies at the sub-national level.

Chapter 16, by Lawson, extends competence theory from the firm to the region. Lawson explains why regions might come to acquire distinctive clusters of resources and capabilities. Several factors may contribute to this phenomenon, which include externalities associated with information, knowledge and technology, inter-firm mobility in the labour market and the importance of high-trust relationships. Proximity in geographic space may reduce communication costs and cultural distance and facilitate relational contracting and interdependence. It may also lead to an evolution of a common business language, norms and culture that is conducive to co-ordination of economic activity. Firms may thereby be able to develop new competencies by sharing complementary capabilities with their suppliers, customers and each other. Agglomeration in geographic space may also lead to a creation of a number of 'untraded interdependencies': not all exchanges can be conducted through the market. Lawson illustrates his notion of development of regional competencies by discussing how the Cambridge region in the UK has come to be characterized by a high-tech cluster of industries centred on the University of Cambridge.

Chapter 17, by Belussi, builds upon the discussion in the previous chapter and explores how regional policy may facilitate regional development. Belussi draws upon the experience of industrial districts in Italy to illustrate how policy may help to promote the growth of knowledge-intensive local production systems. Belussi discusses the various routes through which regional policies may support and complement information- and knowledge-generating market institutions. Belussi also claims that the Italian experience demonstrates that regional policies need to be flexible and responsive to local needs and circumstances: grand 'top-down' policies may not always work. Regional policies, however, are in some ways being constrained by the growing integration of the world economy. Some of the Italian regional clusters of economic activity have recently been threatened by the relocation of certain kinds of economic activity to low-wage nations. This development poses new challenges for regional policy.

Towards a Competence Theory of the Region

CLIVE LAWSON*

Introduction

Recent years have witnessed a growing number of attempts to re-conceptualise both the region and the firm in economic research. The focus on the region has revolved around various (overlapping) themes. Some contributions have been concerned with identifying the reasons for the economic success of certain regions: for example, the districts of NEC Italy, Toyota City, Silicon Valley, Baden Württemberg. Others have responded to the realisation that an increasing amount of international trade and investment flows have actually increased regional speciali-sation, rather than uniformity. Perhaps the most discussed of all has been the observation that, despite falling transport and communication costs, there has been an increase in the importance of firm clustering, especially in high-technology, information-intensive sectors – sectors which, given the enormous recent develop-ments in information technologies, one might have expected to be the least sensitive to the need for geographical proximity. In attempting to explain these phenomena, attention has shifted away from a focus upon individual firms to a concern with the productive system within which firms operate,[1] with particular atten-tion being paid to the region-specific qualities of the linkages and relations that exist between firms. This strategy has not, however, been a unified or systematic one. One result of this is that there now exists a relative plethora of new terminology, including terms such as 'industrial district', 'technological district', 'technology district', 'techno-logical complex', 'innovative milieu', and 'nexus of untraded interdependencies', and it is not clear to what extent these terms, or the literatures generating them, share commonalities at either the substantive or the methodological level.

The literature on the firm has similarly been concerned with linkages and rela-tions: opening up the 'black-box' conception of the firm dominant in mainstream

* Oxford University Press for C. Lawson, 'Towards a Competence Theory of the Region', *Cambridge Journal of Economics*, 1999, Vol 23, No 2.

economics and focusing upon the internal organisational make-up of firms. It is fair to say that this literature on the firm is rather more coherent and less dispersed than that on the region. Certainly, the firm literature exhibits a greater uniformity of terminology and general orientation. This coherence, it has been argued, follows from a shared underlying *competence perspective* or, more specifically, a 'competence theory of the firm' (see especially Foss and Knudsen, 1996). The central thesis of the present chapter is that there is much value in extending this competence perspective to the analysis of the region or, more correctly, regional productive system. In arguing this, I shall endeavour to clarify what is essential to the competence perspective and show that there are good reasons for extending this perspective beyond the scope of the firm to that of the region; that is, the competence perspective is just as appropriate to analysis of the region. I shall also outline recent points of convergence in the regional literature and indicate that the factors focused upon in these accounts are particularly suitable for conceptualisation in terms of competences.

The rest of this chapter is as follows. The next section reviews the main ideas of the competence theory of the firm literature, and investigates the reasons for its popularity or 'resonance' within both academic and business communities. I argue that the main benefit of this literature is that it draws attention to a layered or structured notion of causality and identifies capabilities and competences as different types of things to the events and states of affairs that they generate and explain. I also argue that as the concept of competence is developed, to avoid existing tensions in the competence literature, it becomes increasingly arbitrary not to extend the concept to productive systems in general. These ideas are related in the third section to the study of regional productive systems in particular by considering what appear to be growing points of convergence in the regional literature, especially in those contributions which focus upon the importance of learning and inter-firm linkages in explaining particular spatial patterns of economic behaviour. A final section provides further illustration of the potential fruitfulness of a conception of regional competences, and, in particular, how a conception of firm and regional competences can be usefully combined, by focusing upon one particular, geographically defined productive system, the cluster of high-technology firms in the Cambridge region of the UK.

The competence perspective

Although terms such as 'competence' (Burgelman and Rosenbloom, 1989; Prahalad and Hamel, 1990) and 'capabilities' (Teece et al., 1992; Grant, 1991; Teece and Pisano, 1994) are not always used in precisely the same way, a significant number of recent contributions have focused upon (core) competences, capacities or capabilities of firms which share sufficient 'family resemblances' and key ideas to be regarded as indicative of a distinct, and currently very influential, approach to the study of firm behaviour. Indeed, several volumes now exist which are given over, more or less completely, to the task of clarifying the history of, and connections between, such terms as 'competences' and 'capabilities' and to drawing out implications for current research (e.g. Hamel and Heene, 1994; Montgomery, 1996; Foss and Knudsen, 1996). The most recent of these volumes even begins with the contention that 'the competence perspective is – in its various guises – the dominant perspective on firms and firm behaviour today' (Foss, 1996, p. 1). In order to distinguish the main features and advantages of this general *perspective*, a contrast can usefully be drawn with two other research approaches traditions. In particular, the competence perspective can be contrasted with contractual theories of the firm and with the portfolio-based management strategy literature.

Contractarian perspectives emanate from the work of Coase (1937) and include such contributions as Williamson (1975, 1985) and Alchian and Demsetz (1972). These accounts focus upon the cost of making and monitoring transactions, and the reduction of these costs by the organisational hierarchies that constitute the firm. Exchange is primary and the main concerns are problems of forming and maintaining (monitoring/policing) contracts between input owners. In contrast, competence theories focus more upon production, viewing the firm as a 'repository of productive knowledge' (Foss, 1996) rather than as a 'nexus of contracts'. Hodgson (1998) pursues these differences, emphasising the methodological weaknesses of contractarian approaches. In particular, contractarian approaches are criticised for their neglect not only of production but of dynamic features of firm behaviour more generally, and also for the treatment of individual agents as atomistic and as given. On the one hand, this view of agents deflects attention from the importance of non-contractual relations, such as trust, loyalty, cooperation, etc., and from the ability of individuals to learn and develop. On the other hand, contractarian approaches, as typified by Williamson and Coase, are preoccupied with comparative statics. In fact, advocates of the contractarian approach often state explicitly that their approach is unsuitable for the more dynamic processes central to innovation and technical change (Williamson, 1985, pp. 143–4). For competence theories, in contrast, learning is centre stage, as are the relationships (of trust, etc.) which surround and facilitate different types of learning and the dynamic processes of change which follow. Although contractarian approaches are often portrayed as attempts to open the 'black box' of mainstream conceptions of the firm, in relation to competence theories at least, such attempts do not go very far, either substantively or methodologically. In short, the competence perspective is much more concerned with a realistic conception of what a firm is and does.

The portfolio approach has emerged from the management strategy literature and is concerned with the particular risks involved in managing some portfolio of businesses. Strategic decision-making is related to the allocation of capital across business units, with success depending ultimately upon the market position occupied by a corporation. The competence perspective is instead concerned with the abilities of business units to do certain things – to learn, produce, occupy certain market positions, etc. At the heart of the contrast, although rarely explicitly drawn out, is the idea of a 'deeper' level of analysis. Specifically, the portfolio approach concentrates on the surface phenomena of everyday experience, such as turnover, profits, products, etc., while the competence approach is concerned with factors which lie below the surface but condition these everyday phenomena. The following example is illustrative. Rumelt (1994), in attempting to explain the 'resonance' among corporate managers and academics created by Prahalad and Hamel's 1990 article on core competences, cites the following features of their account as central:

1. *Corporate span*. Core competences span businesses and products within a corporation. Put differently, powerful core competences support several products or businesses.

2. *Temporal dominance*. Products are but the momentary expression of a corporation's core competences. Competences are more stable and evolve more slowly than do products.

3. *Learning by doing*. Competences are gained and enhanced by work. Prahalad and Hamel (1990, p. 82) say that 'core competences are the collective learning in the organisation, especially how to co-ordinate diverse production skills and integrate multiple streams of technologies. ... Core competence does not diminish with use ... competences are enhanced as they are applied and shared.'

4. *Competitive locus*. Product-market competition is merely the superficial expression of a deeper competition over competences. Hamel (1991, p. 83) says that 'conceiving of the firms as a portfolio of core competences and disciplines suggests that inter-firm competition, as opposed to inter-product competition, is essentially concerned with the acquisition of skills'. (Rumelt, 1994, p. xvi)

Each point contains the idea that competences exist at some 'deeper' level giving rise to and explaining the basic phenomena of portfolio accounts, such as products, market positions and, especially, sustained competitive advantages or disadvantages. In some accounts, this distinction is made (implicitly) in terms of 'persistent difference': the concept of competence being invoked to explain persistent differences in (surface phenomena such as) competitive position, profitability, company practices, etc. (e.g. Dosi and Marengo, 1994). The more superficial focus of the portfolio approach ('attention was focused on products, profits were measured and tracked with precision' [Rumelt, 1994, p. xviii]) is replaced in the competence perspective by a concern with phenomena which underlie and govern. Although other accounts do not use the same terminology (core vs. non-core, etc.), a pervasive feature of all these accounts is an acceptance of, and focus upon, the *structured nature of the explananda of firm performance*.

Contrasting the competence approach to the portfolio and (in particular) to the contractarian approaches highlights the concern in the former with the internal workings of the firm. Highlighting such concerns as the main distinguishing feature of the competence perspective raises the issue of the relation of the competence perspective to another collection of contributions that has traditionally been associated with the concern to illuminate the internal workings of the firm, that is, the resource-based tradition. The resource-based view emanates from the work of both management strategists, such as Andrews (1980) and Chandler (1962), and economists, such as Penrose (1959) and Wernerfelt (1984). Similarities between the two traditions are regularly drawn out, and the resource-based contributions are even presented as precursors of the competence perspective (Montgomery, 1996). However, various accounts have been criticised for not being aware of important differences – these criticisms usually involving the idea that the basic categories of competences and resources have not been sufficiently distinguished. For example, various criticisms of the classic Prahalad and Hamel (1990) contribution take the form that the notion of competence itself is left unacceptably vague because of a failure to distinguish between competences and resources (see Eriksen and Mikkelsen, 1996). Prahalad and Hamel's definition of core competences is the 'collective learning in the organisation, especially how to co-ordinate diverse production skills and integrate multiple streams of techno-logies' (Prahalad and Hamel, 1990, p. 82). Both the Eriksen and Mikkelsen (1996) and Stalk et al. (1992) contributions point out that Prahalad and Hamel's examples focus upon 'pools of functionally specific skills' and make no significant distinction between pools of skills that can be drawn upon by the firm and what the firm actually is, its competences.[2] However, and this is the main point of referring to these issues here, even in accounts that attempt to distinguish resources and competences explicitly (Dierickx and Cool, 1989; Teece et al., 1990), there is significant ambiguity. The primary distinction made is that whereas resources are both tangible (physical capital) and intangible (human capital), competences are always intangible. But this distinction still does not help, since the focus of attention (for the critics noted above) is the failure to distinguish intangible resources from intangible competences.[3] In some of the more sophisticated accounts, the idea of a competence is linked to that of emergent properties (e.g. see Foss and Eriksen, 1996). But the notion of emergence employed is left undeveloped. Specifically, there is little explicit consideration of how the idea of emergent properties relates to other ideas such as the 'deep' character of competences or even of the conception of social system (in this case the firm) which these properties constitute. However, it is possible (and necessary given the concerns of this chapter) to reconstruct a more precise account of the nature of competences, especially in regard to the relevance of a notion of competences to the conceptualisation of social systems other than firms. In so doing, I am drawing here upon existing accounts in social theory which have been exclusively concerned with the nature of social being or ontology (especially Giddens, 1984; Bhaskar, 1989; T. Lawson, 1997).[4]

System competences and social interaction

The idea of a competence or capability presupposes a structure of some kind or a structured 'thing'. Cups (have the power to) hold tea, bicycles transport their riders, violins can be used to play music (or table tennis) because of their internal structures. For example, it is the structure of the violin which allows it to vibrate and create sounds in certain ways (or to hit ping-pong balls!). Certain events or outcomes are explained in terms of other kinds of things – structures. This insight is underpinned by recent contributions to the philosophy of science and social theory. It is recognised that an essential feature of scientific inquiry is a movement in levels, this movement being termed, following Peirce (1967) and Hanson (1965), as 'retroduction'. In the context of specifically social inquiry, there has been much attention given to the nature of social structures and, especially, their qualities as underlying and generative of outcomes and states of affairs. More specifically, social structure is understood to consist in rules, relations and positions. Taking these in turn (social) rules are conceptualised as something other than the patterned behaviour they govern. The motorist who does not stop at a red light does not lead us to doubt our understanding of the rule 'when at traffic lights stop if the light is red'. Neither does it force us to consider such a rule as an 'average' or 'normal' description of what people do, even though most people may indeed stop at red lights. The rule is not, and cannot be evaluated as, a prediction of actual behaviour; it is something different in kind. Next, while there is general agreement that the social world is highly rule-governed, the existence of social relations is more often contested. However, once it is accepted that different rules, rights, obligations, etc., are not equally applicable to all, it is difficult to avoid some notion of relations and positions. The sorts of activity allowed or constrained for a foreman are different to those of a manager or employee. Each has different responsibilities and rights in virtue of the position he or she occupies.

The activities constrained or enabled tend to be oriented towards some other group, thus indicating a causal role for certain forms of relationship. Of particular importance are internal relations, where two objects are what they are by virtue of the relationship in which they stand to each other. For example, with a wife and husband, landlord and tenant, it is not possible to have one without the other. For each couple, the relation defines what each is and does. Thus the basic building-blocks of society are positions which depend upon, or are constituted by, social rules, rights and obligations defined in relation to other positions which are also occupied and open to change by individuals.

On this conception, social systems (such as firms, trade unions, national and regional economies, etc.) can be understood as an 'ensemble of networked, internally related positions with their associated rules and practices' (T. Lawson, 1997, p. 165). This conception, among other things, avoids the frequently noted problem of conceptualising such systems as either some simple aggregation of individuals or individuals 'writ large'. Of particular significance, in this context, is the advantage that the elements of structure (rules, relations and positions) are elaborated in such a way as to avoid their collapse into the actions, practices, etc., that they explain. The distinction between events and underlying mechanisms is maintained, with competences being located at the latter level. 'Retroducing' the capabilities of material 'things' like pieces of copper is essentially the same as retroducing the capabilities of firms, regions or nations. For example, the structure of copper (identified as an element of the deep) can explain various (events) activities of electrical appliances. In a similar way, the ability of firms to learn, produce or distribute (deep) can be used to explain (events such as) the existence of particular products, the occupancy of particular market positions, levels of unemployment, etc. In short, social systems such as firms, regions and economies have competences and capabilities because of the manner in which they are structured.

If, however, such systems as regions and firms can both be usefully conceptualised in terms of competences, how can differences between them be understood? Two distinct paradigms for 'the structured' are often distinguished, the first relating to the powers of a thing or particular kind, the second relating to co-determining relations, relations between elements of a system (Bhaskar, 1986, pp. 131–2). Something like this distinction appears to underlie many of the attempts to distinguish firms and regions.[5] This may explain much of the hesitation of commentators on the firm to extend competence ideas beyond the boundaries of the firm – the firm is a clearly identified 'thing', whereas the region is (at best) a system of relations. However, I want to suggest that in this context it is better to think of both (firms and regions) as particular structures (within structures) and, in keeping with the explicit realist orientation of those noted above, focus upon the different *modes* of existence – that is, the ways in which the different structures concerned are reproduced or transformed. The different structures which account for the capabilities of humans, cups or trade unions may be reproduced at the biological, physical or social level, and accordingly need to be studied in different ways. Systems (such as trade unions, firms or regions) have capabilities in the same way (and to the extent) that the relations between the elements are indeed really existing things. The distinguishing feature of social systems is that they only exist in virtue of the activities they govern or facilitate. This is the sense in which competences can be understood as the *emergent* properties of social activity. Some level of organisation can be said to be emergent if there is a sense in which it has arisen out of some lower level but is not reducible to it or predictable from it. Two features of this conception need to be emphasised: that the higher level is not independent of the lower level out of which it has arisen, and indeed is conditioned and 'rooted in' this lower level, and that the highest level cannot be predicted from the lower if it really is emergent in any real sense.[6] On this account, firms and regions consist of capabilities that are the emergent properties of social activity, and both take the form of structures within structures (rather than structured things).

To distinguish between firms and regions is, then, a more substantive issue which rests on identifying the manner in which interaction, constitutive of the competence in question, is reproduced or transformed. In this, a crucial difference between the two (which other differences may often reduce to in practice) will be the relevance of contractual/legal rights and obligations. Firm competences are crucially constituted by interaction confined (or defined, along with membership, identity, etc., of those within the firm) by such contractual/legal considerations (the main insight of the contractarian tradition). However, these are not likely to have much direct bearing upon interaction constitutive of regional competences. Thus, in the case of regional competences, there is a particular onus to account for any coherence (reproduction) of relationships observed. Furthermore, the relevant interaction will tend to take place between organisations and between different types of organisation. As such, the different means by which relationships emerge and are sustained between organisations becomes a central concern. Processes such as labour mobility between organisations, birth and death rates (spin-offs, vertical disintegration, etc.), which are typically considerations that fall outside the purview of competence theories of the firm, become central to the analysis of regional competences as initiating all manner of relationships. A common feature to all these types of interaction is that spatial proximity is likely to be important in a way which is not relevant to the interaction constitutive of a firm (or nation or international community). Taking all these factors together, the region, as a productive system, may be differentiated as an ensemble of competences that 'stretches' both through space and across organisations, and contains a degree of coherence in virtue of the nature of (localised) interaction constitutive of it.

Various implications follow from the general conception of system competences argued for here. First, at this level of analysis at least, it is not clear that there is a meaningful distinction to be made between resources and competences, once a clear distinction between a 'thing' (which can draw upon external resources and be constituted by competences) and a 'system' becomes less clear. Second, distinguishing between such systems as firms and regions must involve investigation of the manner in which the relevant social interaction (from which their competences emerge) is reproduced or transformed. Accordingly, a focus upon relationships, which are not reducible to the events and states of affairs that they generate, becomes an explicit and central focus of analysis. Third, and most important, it appears that the more attempts are made to clarify exactly what is meant by the term 'competence', the more relevant the resulting conception appears to be to the region. In other words, although firms and regions are not the same things, both are ensembles of competences that emerge from social interaction and so there appears to be no reason at all why the competence perspective should not be as relevant to the study of the region as to the study of the firm.

Regional competences and some recent points of convergence

Not only does it appear rather arbitrary not to extend the idea of competences to the analysis of regions, but there are some timely reasons for considering such an extension. I suggested above that the fruitfulness of a conception of regional competences can also be argued for by indicating that recent shifts of focus in a variety of accounts concerned with regional issues are (independently) converging upon factors which can themselves be most usefully conceived of as regional competences. Although there are significant differences between the contributions considered, the main focus here is upon similarities. In particular, I shall focus upon points of convergence in these contributions that (i) have not been made explicit,

(ii) emphasise the importance of the elements of a competence perspective noted above, and (iii) provide examples of the forms that regional competences may actually take in practice.

The first of these strands can be termed the Californian school of economic geography (e.g. Scott, 1986; Scott and Storper, 1987). The main shift in emphasis identifiable within these accounts is from a focus upon *traded* to *untraded* inter-dependencies. In the early contributions of this school, regional business clustering is theorised in terms of the relationship between the division of labour, transaction costs and agglomeration. The (vertical) disintegration of production leads to increased transaction costs, which leads to agglomeration as agents attempt to reduce extra transaction costs arising from geographical distance. However, the focus in these early contributions is predominately on 'traded' relations, typically conceptu-alised as input–output relations. More recently, Storper, drawing upon ideas from the technological trajectories literature (see Dosi, 1987; Dosi and Orsenigo, 1985; Arthur, 1989) and the technological learning literature (Lundvall, 1992), has argued that it is *untraded* interdependencies that explain the observed spatial patterns, and that these 'cannot be easily accommodated within transactions-cost based theories' (Storper, 1995, p. 207). These untraded interdependencies cannot be captured by reference to input–output transactions or contract exchanges, but involve technological spillovers. conventions, rules and languages for developing, communicating and interpreting knowledge, etc. A central point is that these untraded interdependencies give rise to or generate observed input–output rela-tions but are more enduring. Storper explicitly makes the argument that Silicon Valley shows no sign of weakening as an agglomeration because 'geographically-constrained untraded interdependencies outlive geographically-constrained input–output linkages' (Storper, 1995, p. 209).

A similar shift in focus can be discerned in the literature on industrial districts inspired by the work of Marshall. In this literature, a firm's survival is taken to depend upon increased differentiation and more complex or sophisticated coordination (see You and Wilkinson, 1994, p. 261). Two elements can be discerned in this move to increased interdependence which have clearly been brought out in the literature influenced by Marshall, especially that concerned with the industrial districts of north-east and central Italy. There is much concentration, in the litera-ture, on transactions between firms in sequential stages in supply chains: frequent sharing of equipment, the possibility of jointly taking on larger orders, large pools of appropriately skilled labour, etc. Moreover, there is a special emphasis upon the importance of particular forms of cooperation which take place in these districts, for example sharing technical information, subcontracting out to other (often less successful) competitors, refraining from wage competition and labour poaching (Brusco and Sabel, 1981; Sabel and Zeitlin, 1985, pp. 146–9; Lorenz, 1992). However, in explaining these linkages, or in elaborating them in more detail, two different emphases are evident. The first simply relates to the existence of external economies (economies of scale which, although external to a particular firm, are internal to the productive system, e.g. industrial district, as a whole). The second relates to a general climate or 'industrial atmosphere' (see especially, Bellandi, 1989; Becattini, 1990). In Marshall's work, this aspect is most clearly brought out in his famous discussion of special and hereditary skills – where 'the mysteries of the trade become no mysteries; but are ... in the air'. Here, however, the emphasis is upon the network of conventions, rules, common understanding, etc., which make up the cultural, socio-economic 'industrial atmosphere' (Bellandi, 1989).

A third example is to be found within the GREMI literature (Aydalot, 1986; Aydalot and Keeble, 1988; Camagni, 1991). In this literature it is the local environment or *milieu* which is seen as the relevant unit of analysis, the focus being especially on the ability of the milieu to foster or facilitate *innovation*. In particular, the emphasis is upon a complex network of mainly informal social relationships (Camagni, 1991). Innovations result from 'collective interactions' linking a system of production to a particular technical culture (Crevoisier and Maillat, 1991). In attempting to distinguish the GREMI approach from others which emphasise the role of socio-cultural relationships, Camagni isolates what he terms 'static' and 'dynamic' approaches to the interpretation of economic space (both of which are aspects of the GREMI approach). Among the former, Camagni includes both transaction costs and Marshallian external economies approaches. When discussing the 'dynamic' aspects of the GREMI approach, Camagni points to the milieu as, on one hand, facilitating 'collective learning' and, on the other hand, reducing 'dynamic uncertainty'. The term 'collective learning', although not always used consistently within the GREMI literature, may be defined as the creation and further development of a base of common or shared knowledge among the individuals within a productive system. This allows both the coordination of action and the resolution of problems (see Lazaric and Lorenz, 1997). Essentially, collective learning refers to that learning which is made possible through membership of some particular milieu (set of relationships making up a productive system [see C. Lawson, 1997]). Shared knowledge results from (and adds to) the establishment of a common language, technical know-how and organisational conventions. Uncertainty, particularly that faced by small firms, is also understood to be reduced by membership of the milieu. Various forms of uncertainty are considered, for example following from: the complexity of information (requiring a *search* function); the problem of inspecting, *ex ante*, qualitative features of inputs, equipment etc. (requiring *screening*); the problem of processing available information (*transcoding*); and assessing the outcomes of one's own actions and the actions of others. A distinction is then made between the types of linkage that serve to reduce uncertainty in each case. Collective information-gathering and screening takes place through informal interchange of information between firms signalling, for example, various successful decisions or reputation. Skilled labour mobility within the local labour market, customer–supplier technical and organisational interchange, imitation, application to local needs or general-purpose technologies and informal cafeteria effects enable the transcoding function. A collective process of selecting decision routines results from managerial mobility, imitation, cooperative decision-making through local associations etc. Finally, it is argued that an informal process of decision coordination is achieved via interpersonal linkages through families, clubs, associations, etc., which has the advantage of easier and faster information circulation and similar cultural backgrounds. None of these factors is likely to be captured by any kind of input–output analysis, or study of simple (material) transactions.

To take stock, there are clear common developments in each of these approaches. Given an environment of organisational (vertical) disintegration, the links between smaller units have increasingly become the major focus of attention. However, a concern with such linkages has increasingly been accompanied by a movement in focus away from simple input–output, or more superficial, linkages to a consideration of underlying relations which are somehow more enduring, but less 'concrete' in some sense – factors which are 'in the air' or 'untraded'. Now, although these points of convergence are nowhere discussed in such terms, the convergence is upon sets of relationships which emerge from social interaction and exist at a different level to the events, such as practices, products, etc., that they explain. And it is precisely these factors that I am suggesting underlie, or constitute, the region's competences or capabilities.[7] In particular, I am arguing that our understanding of such factors can benefit from reference to a growing literature on the nature and importance of firm-based competences and capabilities, but they are not simply 'in the air' or 'untraded'. They are real factors which emerge from, and are reproduced through, the interaction of agents where some systems of interaction are better, more competent, at facilitating some kinds of outcome than are others.

By way of illustration,[8] let me recast Rumelt's four points in terms of regional as well as firm competences. First, *(regional/corporate) span*: competences span not only products but firms themselves at any point in time. Competences support not only many products or businesses within a corporation, but also many corporations. Second, *temporal dominance*: competences may not only be more stable and evolve more slowly than products, but may be more stable and evolve more slowly than firms themselves. Thus firms, like products, may be only the temporary expression of a region's competences. However, this idea is not intended to encourage a view of firms as simply events. It is likely that some regionally defined productive system may only be the temporary manifestation of firm competences also (e.g. where multinationals move into a region for a short time to exploit natural resources, cheap labour, etc.). Both firms and regions consist of bundles of competences; which set is more enduring, explanatorily dominant, etc., at any moment in time is an open question. Third, *learning by doing*: competences are gained or enhanced not only by work but also by trade and other inter-firm interaction. How such interaction is structured, how diverse skills are integrated with multiple technologies, is learned through such interaction. Again, competences, as with learning, are not diminished with use and are enhanced as they are applied and shared. However, this now involves not only the activity of some established firm, but also (often repeated) attempts to set up firms and form all manner of links to other organisations. Fourth, *competitive locus*: the relative performance of regions as well as the relative performance of firms is merely the superficial expression of a deeper competition over competences. Thus regions may maintain their comparative position, even though firms or sectors may come and go, in much the same way that a firm may maintain its competitive position while at the same time significantly changing the nature of its product.

Combining firm and regional competences – an illustration

In order to illustrate these ideas further, it is useful to focus upon one particular region and its competences. However, in so doing, it is important to spell out what I am trying to illustrate. The last section, in focusing on the nature of regionally significant relationships not reducible to actual events and states of affairs, provides an indication of the kinds of things regional competences are likely to involve. However, the problem remains that of combining firm and regional competences, especially in terms of the explanatory primacy given to either firm or regional competences. As such it is illustrative to consider the case of the Cambridge high-technology cluster. This is, in part, because thc Cambridge region provides an example of a quite clearly defined/bounded (and investigated) productive system and because it provides an example of a system in which regional competences are particularly deeply embedded, enduring and relatively easily identifiable, thus providing an example of a situation in which regional competences can easily be compared to and combined with firm competences in some explanatory account.

The Cambridge region's high-technology firms have generated significant interest among academics and policy-makers since the 1970s. It has even been claimed that Cambridge is the country's 'undisputed centre for R&D' (Shirreff, 1991). The region's success, in R&D especially, appears to have been a major spur to all the main political parties in establishing support for 'enterprise development' (Garnsey and Cannon-Brookes, 1993). The county recorded the largest volume of high-technology employment growth of all the UK counties between 1980 and 1990, with a further growth of 4,800 jobs, or 17%, between 1991 and 1995 (Keeble, 1989, 1994). By 1996, the county contained over 1,000 firms, overwhelmingly small and medium-sized firms, in high-technology sectors (Cambridge County Council Research Group, 1996). However, there is general acceptance that early optimistic forecasts of rapid growth by the Cambridge region's firms, especially as generated by the 1985 Segal Quince Wicksteed report, *The Cambridge Phenomenon*, have not been realised in practice. Cambridge has failed to produce large multinational firms to rival those of Silicon Valley. Firms tend to remain small. Furthermore, where growth has occurred, this has often been accompanied by firm takeover by an external source. This state of affairs is often attributed to the region's lack of 'real' networks, either between Cambridge University and firms spun out from the University or between the region's firms. Certainly, the Segal et al. report commented on the lack of hard evidence. Saxenian (1988) went on to argue that the early comparisons between Cambridge and Silicon Valley were simply misplaced. Although observers often cite social networks among local entrepreneurs as a sign of the region's growing potential, Saxenian found no evidence of such interaction – 'tenants of the Cambridge Science Park complain repeatedly that there is no interaction – social or technical – among firms there' (Saxenian, 1988, p. 74).

I would argue, however, that reconciling these apparently contrasting accounts is relatively straightforward once a regional competence view is adopted. To pursue this, it is useful to distinguish three main forms of link, the first of these being between local firms and the University.[9] Apart from providing a highly skilled pool of labour, the University acts as a very important source of ideas and knowledge. Formal knowledge-transfer relationships between the University and local firms exist in the form of consultancy, collaborations, etc. A crucial form of transfer, although often neglected, is the significant spin-off activity in the region, where individuals, encouraged by, among other things, a conducive attitude towards intellectual property rights in the University, set up their own firms to realise their ideas, innovations, etc., directly in the market. More often this transfer takes informal channels, as personal relationships are maintained between people in both the University and firms, encouraged by a particular college system that enables the maintenance of close relationships through the occupancy of college fellowships. Although a significant amount of firm–University relations are concerned with the flow of ideas, there are other benefits. For example, informal personal relationships act to transfer information about prospective employees, equipment can be borrowed or hired, etc. Less tangibly, but of increasing importance, the University's presence helps to create an academic-type culture and atmosphere in terms of the kinds of local amenities offered, such as certain types of cinemas, restaurants, etc., as well as the more direct possibilities for interaction. The second type of relation is between the firms themselves. This is clearly crucial given the small firm size, and often the more important links reflect the fact that a considerable number of tasks must be performed externally. However, many more horizontal, research and knowledge transfer-oriented links also exist between firms in the region. This collaboration is encouraged by the small-scale niche orientation of many firms, allowing substantial overlap in activities without direct competition. Many firm links also arise because of corporate spin-out activity. One particularly important example of this process is the activity of the region's technical consultancies. At risk of oversimplification, the (core) consultancy part of the firm concentrates upon solving problems for customers. This serves both as a source of revenue in itself and as a way of discovering what general needs exist at some point in time. If, in the course of finding a solution, the consultancy feels there is the potential to develop ideas into a more generally sellable product, a firm is spun out to develop the product itself. Again, links with the (consultant) parent persist in many forms, such as financial aid, advice (often from members on the board) use of equipment, contacts. etc., as much because of shared language, experiences and personal trust as technology or economic objectives. Lastly, the third type of link operates through the functioning of the local labour market. Apart from providing access to a vast range of technical skills, the frequent movement of employees between firms, and from the University to firms, has served to facilitate knowledge flows. This has been so not only because employees take a 'once and for all' stock of knowledge with them but, by maintaining (often personal) relationships with personnel in previous firms or the University, an ongoing link is established with 'ready-made' history, trust and mutual understanding.

Taking these factors together, Cambridge, as a region, has a significant capability for taking new ideas to market, especially via the process of new start-ups centred on a research-based idea or innovation. Both the organisational structure of Cambridge University and local firms act to encourage spin-off activity. The small size of the region's firms means that many employees are very 'close' to management decision-making, providing the motivation and know-how for these employees to start up new firms. Extensive networks exist, which, although often taken for granted, are drawn upon and which facilitate the workings of firms often with few material resources. With these firms, the distinction between products and the firms themselves is in practice quite fine. In competence terms, the firm itself is 'thin'. Now, although conceptualising such firms as 'thin' in competence terms should not encourage the idea that firms can be conceptualised in the same way as products (as noted above in the recasting of Rumelt's points – any firm, however small or specialised, is, of course, always capable of producing far more than it does), so doing can easily explain why many firms fail or are taken over by other firms, and why such a dense network of interconnections is generally needed (although not always directly observable). However, this 'failure' of individual firms to develop 'thick competences' does not have to be seen as a 'regional bad' in any sense. Ideas do come to market, employees do gain experience and training, and form all manner of personal relations which facilitate productive activity; new types of firms (and whole sectors) are likely to emerge relatively quickly and easily (an obvious example is the recent growth of the telecoms sector in Cambridge). To focus upon the success or failure of particular firms ignores the features of the wider context in which the conditions for significant technology creation and transfer are reproduced. The firm-based competence perspective correctly identifies factors other than events and states of affairs (products, market positions, etc.) in explaining economic phenomena. The distinction between firms that are 'thin' or 'deep' in terms of competences is clearly relevant in accounting for the experience of Cambridge firms. But what is missing in the firm-based competence perspective, in this case, is the regional set of competences within which the firms' activities need to be understood and assessed.

Conclusion

The basic thesis of this chapter is that grounds exist for extending the competence perspective from the study of firms to the study of social systems more generally, and in particular to the study of geographically defined productive systems. I have argued that much of the popularity or 'resonance' of the competence perspective follows from its focus upon 'deeper' levels of analysis – understood in terms of a layered causality. On this account, competences of productive systems can be understood to exist at this 'deeper' level and are best conceived of as emergent properties of social interaction. As such, the idea of competences is as relevant to the region as it is to the firm. Moreover, a competence perspective or competence theory of the region of this sort seems especially suited to accommodating ideas to which important strands of the regional literature are converging. This has, at the very least, the advantage of bringing together work that has until now proceeded in relative isolation and been rather loosely conceptualised as 'in the air' or as 'untraded'. Lastly, although neither firm nor regional competences are *a priori* explanatorily primary (in the same sense that competences occupy a more significant explanatory role in relation to events and states and affairs), firms as structured processes of interaction always exist within other such processes, including geographically defined productive systems. Thus even in circumstances where the focus is explicitly upon the firm, for example where the aim of analysis is the provision of management 'advice', restriction of the competence perspective to the internal capabilities of firms would appear to be not only unnecessary but unhelpful.

Notes

1 The term 'productive system' (Wilkinson, 1983) is used in preference to the more widely used 'production system' in order to avoid the bias towards input–output linkages implicit in the latter.

2 Eriksen and Mikkelsen (1996) take these arguments further and argue that a failure to distinguish resources and competences leads not only to vagueness but also to an inability to understand 'processes of competence development and relationships between competences and sustained competitive advantage'.

3 What appears to lie at the heart of these ambiguities is a notion of resource as somehow 'external' and 'drawn upon', which can then be distinguished from a competence, which is 'internal' and 'constitutive'. Such a hard distinction, however, only really makes sense where there is some 'thing' such as (and perhaps only in the case of) a human being that is clearly distinguishable from external resources that can be drawn upon. But this is plainly not the case here, where the main focus is upon systems of competences.

4 Only a brief reference to these accounts can be made here, but see especially T. Lawson (1997) for a detailed account of the implications of adopting such an account for the undertaking of actual research, and Bhaskar (1989) and C. Lawson (1994) for an account of the transformational model of social activity, in which a (complementary) account is given that focuses upon the emergence of coherent social forms through time, rather than, as here, through space.

5 The slippage from the latter to the former paradigm appears to underlie the rather unconvincing attempts to distinguish resources from competences noted above.

6 Neglect of the former feature leads to an omission of the human-dependent nature of social structures; neglect of the latter leads to no real notion of social structure at all (as witnessed by even the more sophisticated methodological individualist accounts).

7 I am not suggesting, however, that existing terminology adequately captures the idea of competence. For example, the distinction between traded and untraded does not correspond directly to the distinction between (deep) competence and (surface) event. I am arguing that the sort of factor Storper is concerned with is *better* (more adequately) conceptualised as a regional competence.

8 It should be emphasised that these points are intended to be illustrative of the manner in which existing ideas about firm competences can be extended. They are not intended as an exhaustive list of 'regional competence' considerations or template for a general regional competence perspective.

9 This discussion draws upon the findings in Lawson et al., 1997 and Keeble et al., 1998.

References

Alchian, A. and Demsetz, H. (1972), Production, information costs and economic organisation, *American Economic Review*, Vol. 62, 777–95.

Andrews, K. (1980), *The Concept of Corporate Strategy*, Homewood, Ill., Richard D. Irwin.

Arthur, W. (1989), Competing technologies, increasing returns and lock-in by historical events, *The Economic Journal*, Vol. 99, 116–31.

Aydalot, P. (ed.) (1986), *Milieux Innovators en Europe*, Paris, GREMI.

Aydalot, P. and Keeble, D. (ed.) (1988), *High Technology Industry and Innovative Environments: the European Experience*. London, Routledge.

Becattini, G. (1990), The Marshallian industrial district as a socio-economic notion, pp. 37–51 in F. Pyke, G. Becattini and W. Sengenberger (eds), *Industrial Districts and Inter-firm Co-operation in Italy*, Geneva, International Institute for Labour Studies.

Bellandi, M. (1989), The industrial district in Marshall, pp. 136–52 in E.A. Goodman (ed.), *Small Firms and Industrial Districts in Italy*, London, Routledge.

Bhaskar, R. (1986), *Scientific Realism and Human Emancipation*, London, Verso.

Bhaskar, R. (1989), *The Possibility of Naturalism*, Brighton, Harvester.

Brusco, S. and Sabel, C. (1981), Artisan production and economic growth, pp. 99–114 in F. Wilkinson (ed.), *Dynamics of Labour Market Segmentation*, London, Academic Press.

Burgelman, R. and Rosenbloom, R. (1989), Technology strategy: an evolutionary process perspective, *Research on Technological Innovation, Management and Policy*, Vol. 4, 1–23.

Camagni, R. (1991), Local milieu, uncertainty and innovation networks: towards a new dynamic theory of economic space, in R. Camagni (ed.), *Innovation Networks: Spatial Perspectives*, London, Belhaven Press.

Cambridge County Council Research Group (1996), *The Hi-Tech 'Community' in Cambridgeshire*, Cambridgeshire County Council.

Chandler, A. (1962), *Strategy and Structure: Chapters in the History of the American Industrial Enterprise*, Cambridge, MA, MIT Press.

Coase, R. (1937), The nature of the firm, *Economica*, Vol. 4, 386–405.

Crevoisier, O. and Maillat, D. (1991), Milieu, industrial organisation and territorial production systems: towards a new theory of spatial development, in R. Camagni (ed.), *Innovation Networks: Spatial Perspectives*, London, Belhaven Press.

Dierickx, I. and Cool, K. (1989), Asset stock accumulation and sustainability of competitive advantage, *Management Science*, Vol. 35, 1504–11.

Dosi, G. (1987), 'Institutions and Markets in a Dynamic World', SPRU Discussion Paper no. 32.

Dosi, G. and Marengo, L. (1994), Some elements of an evolutionary theory of organisational competences, in R.W. England (ed.), *Evolutionary Concepts in Contemporary Economics*, Ann Arbor, University of Michigan Press.

Dosi, G. and Orsenigo, L. (1985), 'Order and Change: An Exploration of Markets, Institutions and Technology in Industrial Dynamics', SPRU Discussion Paper No. 22.

Eriksen, B. and Mikkelsen, J. (1996), Competitive advantage and the concept of core competence, pp. 54–74 in N. Foss and C. Knudsen (eds), *Towards a Competence Theory of the Firm*, London, Routledge.

Foss, N. (1996), The emerging competence perspective, in N. Foss and C. Knudsen (eds), *Towards a Competence Theory of the Firm*, London, Routledge.

Foss, N. and Eriksen, B. (1996), Competitive advantage and industry capabilities, in C.A. Montgomery (ed.), *Resource-based and Evolutionary Theories of the Firm*, Boston, Kluwer.

Foss, N. and Knudsen, C. (eds) (1996), *Towards a Competence Theory of the Firm*, London, Routledge.

Garnsey, E. and Cannon-Brookes, A. (1993), The Cambridge phenomenon revisited: aggregate change among Cambridge high technology companies since 1989, *Entrepreneurship and Regional Development*, Vol. 5, No. 1, 179–207.

Giddens, A. (1984), *The Constitution of Society: Outline of the Theory of Structuration*, Cambridge, Polity Press.

Grant, R. (1991), The resource-based theory of competitive advantage: implications for strategy formulation, *California Management Review*, Vol. 33, 114–35.

Hamel, G. (1991), Competition for competence and inter-partner learning within international strategic alliances, *Strategic Management Journal*, Vol. 12, 83–103.

Hamel, G. and Heene, A. (eds) (1994), *Competence-based Competition*, New York, John Wiley.

Hanson, N. (1965), *Patterns of Discovery*, Cambridge, Cambridge University Press.

Hodgson, G. (1998), Evolutionary and competence-based theories of the firm, *Journal of Economic Studies*, Vol. 25, 25–56.

Keeble, D. (1989), High-technology industry and regional development in Britain: the case of the Cambridge phenomenon, *Environment and Planning C, Government and Policy*, Vol. 7, No. 2, 153–72.

Keeble, D. (1994), Regional influences and policy in new technology-based firm creation and growth, pp. 204–18 in R. Oakey (ed.), *New Technology-based Firms in the 1990s I*, London, Paul Chapman.

Keeble, D., Lawson, C., Lawton Smith, H., Moore, B. and Wilkinson, F. (1998), 'Collective Learning Processes and Inter-firm Networking in Innovative, High-technology Regions', ESRC Centre for Business Research Working Paper, WP86, Dept. of Applied Economics, University of Cambridge.

Lawson, C. (1994), The transformational model of social activity and economic analysis: a reinterpretation of the work of J.R. Commons, *Review of Political Economy*, Vol. 6. No. 2, April, 186–204.

Lawson, C. (1997), 'Territorial Clustering and High Technology Innovation: From Industrial Districts to Innovative Milieux', ESRC Centre for Business Research Working Paper 54.

Lawson, C., Moore, B., Keeble. D., Lawton Smith, H. and Wilkinson, F. (1997), Inter-firm links between regionally clustered high-tech SMEs: a comparison of Cambridge and Oxford innovation networks, in R. Oakey and W. During (eds), *New Technology-based Firms in the 1990s IV*, London, Paul Chapman.

Lawson, T. (1997), *Economics and Reality*, London, Routledge.

Lazaric, N. and Lorenz, E. (1997), Trust and organisational learning during inter-firm co-operation, in N. Lazaric and N. Lorenz (eds), *The Economics of Trust and Learning*, London, Edward Elgar.

Lorenz, E. 1992. Trust, community and co-operation: towards a theory of industrial districts, pp. 195–204 in M. Storper and A. Scott (eds), *Pathways to Industrialisation and Regional Development*, London, Routledge.

Lundvall, B. (1992), *National Systems of Innovation: Toward a Theory of Innovation and Interactive Learning*, London, Frances Pinter.

Montgomery, C. (1996), *Resource-based and Evolutionary Theories of the Firm: Towards a Synthesis*, Boston, Kluwer.

Peirce, C. (1967), *Collected Papers of Charles Sanders Peirce, 1931–35*, Vols. 1–6, edited by C. Hartshorne and P. Weiss, Cambridge, MA, Harvard University Press.

Penrose, E. (1959), *The Theory of the Growth of the Firm*, London, Basil Blackwell.

Prahalad, C. and Hamel, G. (1990), The core competence of the corporation, *Harvard Business Review*, Vol. 68, No. 3, 79–91.

Rumelt, R. (1994), Foreword, pp. xv–xix in G. Hamel and A. Heene (eds), *Competence-based Competition*, New York, John Wiley.

Sabel, C. and Zeitlin, J. (1985), Historical alternatives to mass production: politics, markets and technology in nineteenth-century industrialization, *Past and Present*, Vol. 108, 133–76.

Saxenian, A. (1988), The Cheshire cat's grin: innovation and regional development in England, *Technology Review*, February/March, 67–76.

Scott, A. (1986), High technology industry and territorial development: the rise of the Orange county complex, *Urban Geography*, Vol. 7, 3–45.

Scott, A. and Storper, M. (1987), High technology industry and regional development: a theoretical critique and reconstruction, *International Social Science Journal*, Vol. 112, 215–32.

Segal Quince Wicksteed (1985), *The Cambridge Phenomenon: The Growth of High, Technology Industry in a University Town.*

Shirreff, D. (1991), The business guide, *Cambridge Business Magazine*, February, 89–101.

Stalk, G., Evans, P. and Schulman, L. (1992), Comment, *Harvard Business School*, May–June.

Storper, M. (1995), The resurgence of regional economies, ten years later: the region as a nexus of untraded interdependencies, *European Urban and Regional Studies*, Vol. 2, No. 3, 191–221.

Teece, D. and Pisano, G. (1994), The dynamic capabilities of firms: an introduction, *Industrial and Corporate Changes*, Vol. 3, No. 3, 537–56.

Teece, D., Pisano, G. and Shuen, A. (1990), 'Firm Capabilities, Resources and the Concept of Strategy', CCC Working Paper, No. 90–8, University of California, Berkeley.

Teece, D., Pisano, G. and Shuen, A. 1992. 'Dynamic Capabilities and Strategic Management', University of California Working Paper.

Wernerfelt, B. (1984), A resource-based view of the firm, *Strategic Management Journal*, Vol. 5, 171–80.

Wilkinson, F. (1983), Productive systems, *Cambridge Journal of Economics*, Vol. 7, 413–29.

Williamson, O. (1975), *Markets and Hierarchies: Analysis and Antitrust Implications*, New York, Free Press.

Williamson, O. (1985), *The Economic Institutions of Capitalism: Firms, Markets, Relational Contracting*, New York, Free Press.

You, J. and Wilkinson, F. (1994), Competition and co-operation: toward understanding industrial districts, *Review of Political Economy*, Vol. 6, No. 3. 259–78.

Policies for the Development of Knowledge-Intensive Local Production Systems

FIORENZA BELUSSI*

1. Introduction

For many years now, experts in Italy have focused their attention on the increasing importance of local production systems within the performance of regional economies. This can be demonstrated by the wealth of research conducted into the development of industrial districts,[1] peripheral regions based on small enterprises,[2] and local production *networks*.[3] Increasing importance has been attached to the phenomenon of spatial agglomeration[4] and the uneven territorial distribution of innovative activities.[5]

Analyses of local production systems have highlighted a great diversity in terms of morphology (with more or less concentrated industrial structures), levels of competitiveness, innovative capabilities and, above all, evolutionary tendencies.[6] Moreover, institutional, cultural and social factors have been highlighted as contributing to the generation and consolidation of these structures.[7]

This chapter focuses on the importance of industrial policies in supporting the local production system within the 'spontaneous' working of the market. The aim is to propose a conceptual framework for the formulation of public policies that stresses the importance of collective learning. This is the local 'value' of industrial policies that favour the adoption of innovation and the intensification of technological learning. In the.next section, the structure and evolution of the Italian local production systems are examined in detail. In Section 3, the market-driven process of cumulative growth of the local production system is explained using a conceptual framework in which institutions play an important

* Oxford University Press for F. Belussi, 'Policies for the Development of Knowledge-Intensive Local Production Systems', *Cambridge Journal of Economics*, 1999, Vol 23, No 6.

role in channelling markets and in supporting positive firm strategies (cooperation, technology adoption, collective learning). In Section 4, the influence of policies in determining the performance of local production systems is discussed. Despite some inconclusive results on the linear relationship between institution and performance, the Italian case proves rich in examples which allow the development of a prescriptive framework.

2. Structure and evolution of local production systems

Italian local production systems are defined by the existence of a specific sectoral specialisation of the local economy (in a relatively limited part of the territory, which usually includes only a few municipalities). This implies the presence of a multitude of firms belonging to the same sector. Firms are often very small and production is mainly coordinated by the market, in a horizontal manner. In other words, there are many similar producers with an identical hierarchical relationship with the market, and numerous subcontracting firms that work for one or several producers. A central characteristic of this type of development over time has been the creation of new, related sectors both in services and in manufacturing (downstream and upstream in the productive *filière*) or loosely connected with the original nucleus of industrialisation. So these areas have become attractive for the localisation of producers of machinery and the suppliers of specialised goods.

It is not sufficient, in identifying an instance of a 'local system', simply to make the trivial observation that some firms belonging to the same sector are located in the same area, and possess the practical know-how to produce a particular product (whether tiles, clothes, chairs or tourist services). A local production system can be defined only when one can observe historically its reproductive capability. This is linked to the principles that govern its self-organisation: (a) the generation of new firms; (b) the expansion of existing firms, the economic and social determinants of the matrix that gives rise to entrepreneurship (Belussi and Pozzana, 1995); (c) the socialisation of knowledge among blue-collar workers; (d) the role played by collective actors (e.g. the institutional model that regulates the working of the system and the regulation model of local industrial relations); (e) the degree of openness towards the outside, and so on.

In Italy, we can find a vast range of different local production systems. Strictly speaking, they can be classified as industrial districts only if they are formed exclusively of an isolated aggregation of small firms belonging to a specific sector (as in the famous case of Prato, an industrial district of nearly 50,000 employees, specialising in textile production). In all other cases, we have to use more general terms, such as system areas, localised clusters, local production networks, etc. The degree of inter-firm coordination may vary according to the particular production system considered. In terms of governance structure, Italian

Table 17.1   *Map of the evolution of Italian local production systems*

Decline in the industrial structure because of a loss of competitiveness.	Vigevano (footwear) Casarano (footwear) Carpi (clothes) Lumezzane (cutlery) Busto Arsizio (textile mobilisation) Prato (textile)
Partial de-localisation of activities towards lower labour-cost areas.	Barletta (footwear) Benetton system (clothes) Riviera del Brenta (footwear)
Increase in production re-centralisation with the expansion of the role of medium-sized firms. More hierarchisation of the industrial structure.	Mirandola (bio-medical) Langhirano (food) Castel Goffredo (hosiery) Pesaro (furniture) Arzignano (tanning) Cittadella (area mechanics) Murano (glass) Cadore (spectacles) Sassuolo (ceramics) Biella (textile) Como (silk) Vigevano (machinery for footwear) Marche (footwear) Montebelluna (footwear) Bologna (packaging machinery) Varese (anti-theft alarms)
Production diversification.	Cantú (furniture) Reggio Emilia (machinery for agriculture) Milanese hinterland (logistics)

Sources: Censis (1995), Onida et al. (1992), Crestanello (1995), Camagni and Rabellotti (1994), Franchi (1994), Bozzi and Bramanti (1994), Creti (1994), Cento Bull (1992), Da Canal (1993), Belussi (1994, 1995)

local production systems are characterised by the presence of a great many types of productive organisation: artisanal firms; small autonomous producers; pure subcontracting firms; medium-sized firms that sell their product both in the final markets and in subcontracting; medium–large firms or groups of firms with significant market power; large productive entities: verticalised firms, network firms, conglomerates. Often present within local production systems are hierarchical enterprises or leading enterprises that have direct access to the market and which control internally the more strategic functions (R&D, marketing, logistics, quality control, and so on). They may activate quasi-stable 'production networks'. So, very often, local production systems are crossed by overlapping networks of enterprises, and the institutional architecture of the system can be constituted, in various ways, by stable and 'durable' relations. During the 1990s, an evolutionary shift towards hierarchically organised 'districts', with dominant core/ring structures centred on one or more leading firms, appears to have been a structural feature. In addition, many local production systems are now specialised in more than one sector (see Anastasia et al., 1995). In the Italian case, an examination of local production systems highlights the possible co-evolution of differentiated structures rather than suggesting epochal shifts towards small (Piore and Sabel, 1984) or large enterprises (Harrison, 1994).

The evolution of local production systems offers a rich subject for analysis. Some empirical research has clearly highlighted the general outlines of a development towards a state 'of maturity' (Scarpitti, 1991). Bianchi (1992) has questioned the capacity of the district model to face the complex competitive pressure emerging from the globalisation of markets, but, in general, the hypothesis of their substantial stability has prevailed among Italian economists (Brusco, 1993).

The absence of a systematic and comparable body of research makes it difficult to evaluate the entire range of evolutionary paths. The picture that emerges from the variety of research available (see Table 17.1), even though it is incomplete, allows us to underline the impressive resistance of these economic areas. Turning our attention to individual cases highlights the important changes that have occurred within the local milieu. These changes can be summarized by four characteristic evolutionary paths: (i) a tendency towards a general decline in output, employment and number of firms because of a general loss in competitiveness; (ii) a partial de-localisation of activities to low labour-cost countries; (iii) a strong internal restructuring with more hierarchisation among enterprises; (iv) a shift of the local system towards new production.

2.1 The decline of the local industrial structure

This tendency seems to have affected at least five local systems in the north of Italy specialising in traditional production (such as footwear, clothing and textiles). Loss of competitiveness is attributed to the entry into European markets of products from East Asian countries. For firms within the local production systems that were analysed, risks were higher in the low-quality segments of the market, characterised by standardised items sold at very cheap prices. In the case of Lumezzane (a cutlery district less well known than Sheffield, but sharing the same ancient origins), the most dynamic firms, in recent years, have tried to regain their former market position through the improvement of product quality. In this way, traditional European markets have gradually been reconquered. A certain decline in output share has been registered in the footwear systems of Vigevano and Casarano. However, in the case of Vigevano the productive specialisation of the area is shifting upwards, towards the production of specialised footwear machinery. In contrast, firms in Casarano are suffering from the contraction of the internal market. The big fall in orders which these firms have experienced has increased price competition, forcing the smallest to cut costs further through the use of informal and irregular labour.

2.2 Productive de-localisation

In this respect, better economic performance has been displayed by the specialised footwear districts that followed the route of productive delocalisation towards Eastern European or North African countries (Albania, Morocco and Tunisia), as in the case of the Riviera del Brenta (Ve) or Barletta (Ba). However, the extension of the subcontracting chain has created many organisational problems for firms, especially the smallest ones.[8] The final phases of production are, in any case, still performed within the local production system by skilled workers: in fact, local entrepreneurs are not willing to lose the strategic and tacit knowledge owned and accumulated in the past. International outsourcing is not just a factor for a few local systems, but rather a general trend affecting all large corporate *networks*. It is interesting to note, for instance, the case of Benetton, a famous textile-clothing firm. In the past, its development was based on an accentuated 'localism': its entire production network, formed by nearly 500 firms, was located almost entirely in the Veneto region, near its headquarters. However, by the beginning of the 1990s, the group had decentralised to the Newly Industrialising Countries (NICS) the production of nearly 10 million items per annum (about 18% of all items produced). And if we add the value of production manufactured with TFP (traffic of tax-free products for perfecting), this number goes up to 22.4% (Da Canal, 1993).

2.3 The development of groups of enterprise

The radical change in relations between small and large enterprises is the most widespread evolutionary pattern registered so far. The creation of both formal and informal economic groups around successful enterprises has, in recent years, radically changed the distribution of entrepreneurial power within the existing industrial structure. Economic recentralisation has also occurred through mergers and acquisitions. In many old Italian industrial districts, a few leading firms now account for nearly 50%–60% of the total output of local firms (Marazzi for the ceramic district in Sassuolo;[9] Luxottica for the spectacles area of Cadore; some dominant foreign multinationals in the case of the bio-medical sector in Mirandola in the province of Modena; Rossi for the footwear district of Brenta; Nordica for the footwear district of Montebelluna; and Ratti for the silk sector based around Como). This process is the result of at least two factors: first, the increase of the minimum (organisational) threshold necessary to compete effectively in international markets; and, second, the reduction of coordination costs connected to the application of new information and telecommunication technologies (this has caused a re-centralisation of some production phases previously removed from the firms' internal cycle).

2.4 Productive diversification

By analysing Table 17.1, it can be noted that strategies putting emphasis on radical product diversification have seldom been followed. On the whole, in Cantú, firms of the local furniture district have focused their activity on a more artisanal type of production and on 'made to measure' pieces, while, in Reggio Emilia, enterprises producing agricultural machinery have re-engineered production to cater for a more lucrative and expanding sector: gardening machinery. Another interesting case is that of the area around the Milanese hinterland (including Varese and Como), analysed by the regional Unioncamere Observatory of the Lombardia region. Here we have witnessed the transformation of transport firms into logistics operators (the most important innovation that has changed the specialisation of the local production system has been the introduction of methods for the *time to market*).

To conclude, the empirical results of a good deal of research appear to show a remarkable resilience in Italian local production systems. However, the pure 'industrial district' form no longer seems to be dominant.

3. A partially spontaneous and market-driven process of collective learning

In Italy, the growing interest in the industrial district has been particularly influenced by Beccatini's writings. In contrast to the neoclassical approach, Beccatini re-evaluated Marshall's contribution to the study of industrial organisation. It was Marshall who introduced the category of 'industrial district' as a new unit of analysis, relating to the spatial clustering of firms producing similar products. Marshall wanted to explain the localisation of specific segments of industry, going beyond the classical approach based on the location of natural resources, closeness of demand scale economies and costs of transportation. He proposed an analytical framework within which he included factors such as the 'industrial atmosphere', the application of more general economic themes like externalities (which stem from factors external to each individual firm but internal to the district), and sociological issues, such as the economic impact of loyalty in enhancing exchange among the producers within the district area. However, while Marshall stressed the free exchange of given information and knowledge among agents located in geographical proximity, the more recent literature on innovation and technology stresses instead the importance of closeness and interaction among agents as the means to create new pieces of knowledge, and for the successful development of incremental innovations. In particular, great importance is assigned to the mechanisms of use and transformation of tacit knowledge, mechanisms related to various forms of learning (by using, by doing, by interacting, by searching) that lead to dynamic efficiency (as opposed to allocative efficiency). Thus, the growth of localised clusters of firms is based mainly on rents, which are the returns from collective learning, the consequence of the development of new technological capabilities among firms belonging to the district.

Empirical research has highlighted the existence of a multitude of factors that have contributed to the consolidation of local production systems. These issues, relating to the diffusion of technical change and know-how within local production systems, allow us to speculate as to how a mechanism for endogenous growth might have emerged.

(1) The knowledge of the agents is sunk in nature (workers and entrepreneurs) operating within a specific context (spatially delimited and focused on a specific sector).[10] This type of knowledge, acquired through direct experience and observation, and very often practical and tacit in nature, cannot be conceived *in toto* as a public good (especially where traditional methods of production are still important, as in clothing, ceramics, chair production, furniture or machinery). This knowledge, which characterises the specific competences[11] or even specific and latent resources (Colletis-Wahl, 1995) of the enterprises that are a part of a given local context, is embodied in individuals and in the collective learning of organisations, and is freely socialised and spread only among citizens/workers within that specific context, remaining fairly inaccessible to people coming from outside. This type of knowledge is in some sense territorially embedded, characterising the productive culture of each local production system and growing cumulatively over time. For instance, Calzabini and Bosco (1996) have categorised the diverse and complex skills of workers from the pottery district of Civita Castellana in terms of: (i) manual skills: rapidity and precision of actions (in the touching phase), attentive eye (to pinpoint the imperfections), perceptive hearing (to recognise from the sound if a dish has imperfections), etc.; (ii) knowledge of ceramic mixture (its visual characteristics and consistency) and its variation with respect to the external (dampness of the air) and internal (extent of dampness of chalk stamps) environment; and (iii) autonomy: on the basis of knowledge of mixture and humidity gradient, which can vary from one day to the next, evaluating and deciding on the time of 'withdrawal' (solidification) of the mix. In the case of the Matera leather-sofa district, in the south of Italy, the ability of upholsterers is the key factor for success. It is a matter of knowing specific phases of the productive process, of mastering manual skills, of knowing where to cut the pieces of the leather mantel to eliminate the natural defects, and so on. All this tacit knowledge is embedded in the population of the district, and has grown in parallel with the expansion of firms. Local knowledge has been nourished by the experiments of the leading firm of the area, the Natuzzi group, now an international leader in upholstery, covering alone a share of 5% of the US market.

(2) The spatial and social proximity of agents produced by the aggregation of firms and workers, and thus the spatial (and social) proximity of the agents, forms an integrated system within which interactions are more fluid, and within which many (informal and institutionalised) channels are built up through which information can quickly circulate. Thus, all subjects increase their possibility of *learning* and *knowing* (Bellandi, 1992; Gottardi, 1996).

(3) The formation of local production systems allows a reduction of the transaction costs associated with dealing with uncertainty. Subjects sharing the same local traditions, production culture, community regulations and communication codes have a lower propensity towards opportunism and free-riding behaviours.[12]

(4) Even more important, within these systems, higher levels of inter-firm cooperation[13] tend to be found. This makes it realistically possible to implement a greater and more efficient[14] inter-firm division of labour. Therefore, in the long term, a local system made up of many small-sized firms that has developed an increasing specialisation of activities can achieve better performance (because of the dynamic efficiency of the increasing divisibility and improvement of all the various productive phases) than other organisational models[15] where the organisation of the activities is coordinated by large, firm-like organisations.

(5) Within local production systems an acceleration of technological learning can happen thanks to the number of agents experimenting with given technologies. This encourages the frequent diffusion of incremental innovations; so, generally speaking, the introduction of exogenous radical innovations merges with the sequential overlapping of marginal improvements (Belussi, 1988).

(6) Very often these systems are characterised by the inability to defend an industrial secret (given the closeness of firms and the inter-firm mobility of skilled workers). This is certainly a 'market failure' in a stationary world where irreversible barriers to the acquisition of new knowledge are assumed. But, in a dynamic world, the rapid diffusion and adoption of innovations (generated by leading firms in the area), or the acquisition of the best available-on-the-shelf technology, becomes a positive feature of hyper-competition that strengthens the incentives' for continuous innovation. Competition among firms is determined by the implementation of dynamic mechanisms, which include *lead time*, accelerated product variation and continuous product innovation.[16]

(7) Furthermore, a local productive system stimulates its enterprises to adopt innovation processes more rapidly. Because there is a considerable (and concentrated) market for technology, suppliers of machinery tend to target their marketing strategies on *all* the firms belonging to the most important local production system, whatever their size. Even the smallest enterprises may quickly have access to up-to-date technological innovations. Over time in these areas, a 'pool' of enterprises/firm advisers/advanced service centres is created. In the most dynamic production systems, these tendencies have allowed for a continuous *up-grading* of technologies in use and for the diffusion of the organisational best practice among enterprises.

Italian local production systems can be viewed as experimental laboratories in which the so-called 'spontaneous' working of the market has been channelled, limited and/or stimulated by the role of institutions, here conceived as collective actors capable of providing economically valuable public goods or of setting institutional models, rules and regulations, which enable certain types of interaction among the various agents operating in the local context (mainly cooperative behaviours). Thus pure market process outcomes have been regulated by extra-economic factors.

However, the genesis of local production systems stems not only from 'policy'. The mechanisms of start-up and growth must be evaluated on the basis of the mobilisation of 'local' knowledge and collective learning, where local policies, widely speaking, have played an important – but not exclusive – part.

In Belussi (1996), the 'laws' of motion of local production systems are discussed, focusing on three factors which influence local development patterns: (a) the processes of inter-firm division of labour,[17] (b) the specialisation[18] of economic agents, and (c) the accumulation of knowledge in firms. A recursive sequence of a cumulative growth-inducing mechanism can be illustrated, modelling the various stages of growth of a typical local production system. Demand growth increases the division of labour among firms. Specialisation increases scale economies and the generation of new knowledge (in a Smithian sense). In turn, this renders the local production system more competitive. Its (national or international) market share increases. The higher volume of production allows for a further division of labour among enterprises, and the sequence starts again. Local production systems, where firms are dynamic enough, are thus characterised by greater innovation incentives, and by more efficiency.[19]

4. Local policies as an induced mechanism for collective learning

In the case of Italy, the influence of policy in determining the performance of local production systems has been largely indirect. This is not to say that at a local level there has been no action. Rather, there has been no substitution of policy action for the spontaneous work of the market, but the slow yet constant process of growth of these productive systems has been accompanied from time to time by forms of intervention that regulated or complemented the way in which resources were allocated in the market. If we assume this theoretical viewpoint, we can trace a divergence from the prevailing explanation for public intervention in the economy, where it is the lack of private incentives for investment (the Arrow 'market failures' theory) which provides the theoretical foundation that justifies, in certain specific situations, the intervention of government (as opposed to market).[20]

The functioning of Italian institutions and the focus of the local policies that were activated were typically set in a context in which they were supporting the technological dynamics of firms, through specific legislation (for instance, credit facilities for small firms), by encouraging cooperation among firms, by being directly involved in the creation of positive externalities and, sometimes, by providing directly quasi-public goods for the industrial environment (the so-called 'policy of *servizi reali alle imprese*').

Thus, both institutions and markets have a role to play in determining the performance of the systems. But a genuine interpretation of these policies must stress the fact that the Italian local production systems are not simply the result of a 'grand up–down planned policy'.

In the view put forward in this chapter, traceable back to the institutional school, and to 'evolutionary' thought (a typically evolutionary approach has been recently adopted in the works of Gerybadze, 1992, and Bellet, 1993), institutions and market may converge in an effort that can substantially improve the organisation of a given industrial sector, or the quality of human capital utilised by firms – or may not, depending on *ad hoc* circumstances.

To give a clear example: in the case of Italy, the implementation of similar policies (for instance, the Law 696, which during the 1980s provided significant incentives to investment in new machinery, incorporating automated technologies) has been of great utility for the small firms in the regions of Third Italy (i.e. Venteto, Friuli-Venetio-Giulia, Emilia Romagna and Tuscany), where it was widely utilised, while in the Mezzogiorno, the southern and less-developed part of the country, it has produced less than nothing.

In the past, all the significant interventions promoted by the Cassa del Mezzogiorno (an Italian development agency) or by the state-owned firm, the holding Iri, were related to the creation of new firms in the petrochemical industry or in iron metallurgy. The large firms established never acted as poles of development, and the experiment failed. The policy was unsuccessful in terms of resolving the long-standing problems of unemployment, and in some cases it aggravated the situation, because it pushed out of the market many pre-existing small, backward firms. In Italy this became known as a policy of 'cathedrals in the desert'. Thus, we can see that development policies are not always able to ensure fast-growing firms. In Basilicata, a region of the south of Italy, there are actually more than 20 industrial sites, financed over the last decade through Law 64, that are now empty, abandoned by unsuccessful firms (many were cases of de-localisation from firms based in the north of Italy). Ironically, the fastest-growing district of the region, the above-mentioned sofa district, is indigenous, and it has grown up quite independently of state aid. Firms are located in inappropriate areas, within industrial estates that developed spontaneously, and where the municipality has been not able to provide even elementary services such as water, electricity, roads, etc.

It seems unquestionable that impact depends on the social nature of the development, and that this is a process of social mobilisation led by the central actor, the entrepreneur. The positive actions of institutions count for nothing if markets lack strategic actors able to respond adequately to the right market signals.

Again, quoting the Italian case, policies that could produce substantial efficiency have not always been selected. Within local production systems, institutions and firms (or collective actors) can hold conflicting strategies, so an incapacity to coordinate an effective regulative policy may be experienced. At other times, the abstract nature of the problem-solving solution chosen by the strategic decision-making actor (public institution or private association) has blocked its possible adoption. Parri (1993) has studied several unsuccessful attempts to set up local policies concerning the establishment of real services for small firms. In his research, he paid attention to three dynamic local production systems based in north Italy, Veneto and Lombardy where 'policy failure' had occurred. This shows the procedural complexity linked to the activation of desirable *ad hoc* policies.

However, the Italian case can also be used to claim that slightly different local policies have accounted for similar results in terms of economic dynamics. Freschi

(1994), in a recent survey[21] has described, using a comparative methodology, the adoption of local policies in Tuscany, Emilia-Romagna and the Veneto region. While in the Emilia case the modality *servizi reali alle imrrese* was widely chosen (the creation of these centres was organised by Ervet, an independent institution for regional policies), this type of intervention in Tuscany was minimal, and totally absent in the Veneto region. In other words, the three most typical regions of the Third Italy model, accounting for the major presence of 'industrial districts' and 'local production systems', have in fact been doing things quite differently. The inconclusive evidence relating to the causal relationship of institutions–(policies adopted)–performance does not obviously undermine the efficacy of the Emilia model in terms of local policies.

The institutional dimension appears to be a central issue in the view of many economists.[22] In an evolutionary perspective, institutions are endogenous (at least in the long term) to the context in which collective actors operate. More than one alternative can survive by market selection. Variation in institutional forms increases over time. However, this chapter argues that the essential lesson in the Italian case is that the real influence and importance of policies linked to the provision of 'real services' (as opposed to financial services) to firms has probably been exaggerated, while the positive impact of vocational training institutes as locally based institutions centred on the development of collective learning has until now been absolutely underestimated. Such institutions, specialising in whichever sector dominates the local industrial structure, are scattered across Italy. Where they exist, they have supported the diffusion of practical and technical knowledge among skilled workers and potential new entrepreneurs, through teaching and experimentation with new types of machinery. An interesting example is the Aldini Valeriani school in Bologna (Capecchi, 1997). This vocational training institute is at the centre of the success of the surrounding industry of the packaging district. A recent analysis of the district (Belussi and Tolomelli, 1997) has shown that 70% of all students find a job as qualified technicians in firms of the packaging district. The school was founded by the municipality, by the association of entrepreneurs and by the region. One estimate of the expenditure devoted to investment in human capital has been calculated: an annual investment of 17 billion liras, and a total expenditure for each student (during the five-year course) of nearly half a billion. Lipparini (1995, p. 103), in his empirical work, has stressed the importance of the school in terms of incentives to entrepreneurship. Of the 40 most successful entrepreneurs interviewed by him, 25 had attended the Aldini Valeriani school.

The existence of such institutions, which are able to create the right conditions for a good matching between the development of technology and the existing economic and social structure, is of extreme importance, and certainly constitutes a desirable element for the construction of the relative advantages of a local production system. However, in using an 'evolutionary' conceptual frame, we have also to recognise the limits of the range of possibilities left open to the working of institutions and policies.

Table 17.2   *Local policies and mechanisms for collective learning*

Levels of conceptual intervention	Concepts and processes	Outline of specific options
Mobilisation of knowledge and creation of new knowledge.	1. Focusing on various interventions to maintain the elevated level of knowledge acquired in the past (accumulated knowledge) in the specific sectors of specialisation. 2. Reinforcement of empirical learning (practical knowledge acquired through direct experience and observation). 3. Development of imitative (vicarious) learning through access to second-hand experience. 4. Favouring new connections in the local productive context: by pushing acquisitions or joint-ventures of external firms of strategic interest, or by attracting to the area innovative enterprises, or highly specialised personnel. 5. Promoting specific research projects (R&D activity for the implementation of innovative solutions.	1. Promotion of specific training activity to diffuse 'technological knowledge' accumulated in depository organisations. 2. Promotion of unintentional and unsystematic learning opportunities (e.g. participation of local firms in fairs, conferences, debates on technology, and on other economic issues). 3. Promotion of reverse engineering and benchmarking practices. 4. Establishing institutional channels for imitation practices: using consultants, promoting meetings between technicians. 5. Shortening of learning curves of firms (financing the experimentation of new technologies (e.g. Sabatini law ([L. 696] or French videotel). 6. Establishment of centres for providing services to advanced functions of firms. 7. Predisposition of specific initiatives focused on themes relating to the competitiveness of local firms to improve working methods, standards, and environmental themes.
Coordination and distribution of information.	1. Using specific structures and collective actors to intensify the distribution of information.	1. Increasing the number of information offices. 2. Wide publicity to the initiatives organised by local institutions. 3. Favouring access to international data banks and to the global communication networks.
Production of codes and languages to interpret knowledge. Reinforcing local identities and production culture.	1. Construction of communication channels for inducing more cooperation among collective agents and among the most important firms of the area. 2. Reinforcement of progressive coalitions.	1. Systematic control of economic and social performance of the local system. 2. Activation of local development projects open to foreign partnerships. 3. Promotion of social dialogue with collective actors.

(contd.)

Table 17.2   (*contd.*)

Levels of conceptual intervention	Concepts and processes	Outline of specific options
Actions to store the accumulated specific knowledge.		1. Financing specific cultural 'deposits' (e.g. the boot museum in Montebelluna). 2. Promoting the setting up of archives on local history. 3. Promoting research on local development.

In Italy, the case of the industrial district of Prato is of great significance. In the last decade considerable economic resources have been mobilised in order to develop an information system suitable for connecting the small firms operating in the district (the project was organised by Enea – *Ente nazionale per l'energia* – in Rome). The resulting system has not been much used by local entrepreneurs, who remain proud of their autonomy. And in any case, none of the planned interventions has been able to counter an incipient decline, as shown in Table 17.1. Generally speaking, then, the question of how (and if) local policies have influenced the growth of Italian local production systems remains largely unanswered. According to the framework proposed above, the main evolutionary paths followed by Italian local production systems during the last decade seem to have been quite uncorrelated with the policies adopted. Clearly, in the same manner, one could also have argued that without certain types of policies, the decline of Carpi, for instance, would have been more consistent.

Competition as a discovery process remains the driving force of the system. And this must be enacted by markets and by dynamic entrepreneurs. So, in relation to local policies, there are no general recipes that can be widely applied in less developed countries to transfer or replicate the 'beauty' of the Italian model of competitive local production systems. Policy and institutions cannot work as a substitute for the market (in an Arrowian sense). And what has proved good under some conditions, and in a given context, may not work in others. The essential claim of this chapter is that institutions can set the rules, channel and mobilise knowledge, and increase the transferability of knowledge from one individual to another, but they cannot re-create or develop markets if they lack the productive capacity. The 'endogenisation' of local institutions, and their involvement as external actors in the market, is the most obvious consequence of this statement.[23]

The argument set out in Table 17.2 seeks to develop an operational and positive approach to the normative setting of local policies. It illustrates a scheme of connected interventions and actions related to increasing and intensifying collective learning. The process of accumulation and transmission of knowledge can be viewed as collective not only because it is dispersed among many individuals. It is collective in the sense that the storage of knowledge and experience is made largely by collective entities (firms and institutions) and in the productive cultural traditions of each local system (tacit skills, customs and habits developed locally). Four principal classes are identified:

(i)   the process of mobilisation of knowledge and the creation of new knowledge;

(ii) the process of coordination and distribution of information;

(iii) the reinforcement of the local institutional setting with the emphasis on the creation of specific identities, where common rules, loyalties and behaviours can emerge, also creating a good match between innovation (often exogenous) and the local structure;

(iv) the storage of the knowledge in the collective memory.

Technology policies at the local level must be based on the existing pool of knowledge embodied in firms and in specific entities (leading enterprises, training organisations, research centres, groups of experts and scientists employed in the public structures and company consultants). Projects for upgrading must be placed at the centre of interest of local authorities. Public policies can reinforce the diffusion of practical knowledge (acquired through experience) by favouring the localisation of research laboratories and technical training centres. It also seems important to support other types of informal learning by promoting participation in fairs, conferences, etc. Important elements of the learning process are reverse engineering methods and benchmarking of best practices.

Let us take the case of the Emilia-Romagna region. This region and its local associations of entrepreneurs are good at sponsoring the participation of firms in international exhibitions. This is not only important for the establishment of commercial relationships, but is also a tool for upgrading and spreading knowledge. A striking example came from an entrepreneur interviewed in the packaging district of Bologna. The interviewee's firm is now one of the most successful in the area of those providing logistic and packaging systems to the firms producing packaging machinery (the transportation of heavy and large lines of machinery has always been a problem in the area). His take-off started when he was able to introduce new concepts and materials in the packaging phase. This all began when he got support to visit the Frankfurt exhibition of packaging machinery. He went there two days before the official opening of the fair so he could observe the unpacking of the new kinds of machinery presented. In particular, he admitted to having learned a lot from the new techniques applied by the Japanese firms (although, despite their efforts, Japanese firms are not so strong in packaging machinery, and international leadership rests with German and Italian firms).

In this context, actions must generate incentives for the transfer of knowledge from the more advanced contexts. Linsu (1997) has described the Korean approach to the long-term development of indigenous capabilities in the car industry. For the development of Korean cars, Hyundai approached 26 firms in five countries for various technologies: ten in Japan and Italy for style design, four in Japan and the United States for equipment in a stamping shop, five in the United Kingdom and

Germany for casting and forging plants, two in Japan and the United Kingdom for engines, and five in the United Kingdom and United States for integrated parts and components. These firms were visited by Hyundai engineers, whose work was to assimilate the literature related to the various aspects of car design and manufacture, thus accumulating tacit knowledge. How Hyundai assimilated style-design technology is informative. Engineers were sent to Italy for a year and a half. The highly motivated team shared a flat near Italdesign, in Turin, keeping a record of what they had learned during the day, and conducting group reviews every evening. These engineers later became the core of the design department in Korea.

Local policies may also be socially targeted to select specific research that can be partly sponsored in order to improve production methods used by local enterprises or working methods.[24] Obviously, the problem of diffusion of information must be taken into consideration (for instance, access to databanks, construction of local networks, etc.). Markets are good in price signalling, but they do not work so well with other forms of dispersed knowledge.

Local policies must be developed in the context of actions supportive to the functioning of the market (with incentives also directed at the firm level). In Italy, during the 1980s, industrial policy in favour of local production systems was mainly applied at a local level, without a clear distinction of roles and division of functions between central government and regional institutions. The vast majority of initiatives has been developed at regional (or sub-regional) level. The Italian approach was mainly a bottom-up approach along the following lines: (a) to promote and reinforce collective learning; (b) to increase the opportunity for an improvement of the technological capabilities of firms; and (c) to develop centres linked to the 'tertiary' functions (logistics, planning, quality control, marketing) as discussed in Bianchi (1992), Brusco (1993) and Tolomelli (1992).

In many contexts, specific local policies were useful but not necessities. The development of local production systems was above all an unplanned phenomenon, and a spontaneous outcome of market forces. The planning of industrial sites has been systematically pursued in Emilia-Romagna, whereas in the Veneto region all intervention was focused on credit facilities for small firms. In the south, intervention through the planning of industrial sites proved relatively unsuccessful.

5. Conclusion

This chapter has analysed the structure and the evolution of local production systems in Italy. An evolutionary pattern of growth occurred during the 1970s and 1980s in many areas of the Third Italy. The accumulation of knowledge in founder firms gave rise to local systems. Entrepreneurs were the agents of development, possessing the relevant knowledge of the productive process and of market opportunities. By means of a gemmation process (new firms created by former employees of an existing established firm), firms proliferated, and each local system became a complex architecture of differentiated production networks of cooperation and competition. The picture which emerges from the variety of research available has stressed four characteristic evolutionary paths: a tendency towards a general decline; a partial de-localisation of activities to low labour-cost countries; a strong internal restructuring with more hierarchisation among enterprises; and a shift of the local system into new products. However, the dominant tendency has been a generalised hierarchisation. In fact, a remarkable resilience has been observed. The Italian local production systems can be viewed as experimental laboratories where the spontaneous working of the market has been channelled by the role of institutions. Local institutions have played an important role in the setting of some general rules embodied in the local context. This has favoured creative cooperation among firms and has enabled the spontaneous aggregation of firms into systems. They have also influenced the process of new firms' start-up, lowering entry barriers, and providing quasi-public goods (real services) to firms. Another important feature has been the accumulation and mobilisation of knowledge, supporting collective learning, a process in which both markets and institutions have played a crucial role. Using the Italian experience, the last part of this chapter has sought to define an analytical framework in which the open outcome of markets and institutions can logically be articulated by prescriptive local policies focused on the mobilisation of knowledge among collective actors and on the creation of new knowledge.

Notes

1   In Italy there is a vast range of literature on the argument. See, for example, work by Becattini (1979, 1987, 1989), Gandolfi (1988), Gobbo (1989), Pyke et al. (1990), Sforzi (1990), Pyke and Sengenberger (1992), Moussanet and Paolazzi (1992), Falzoni et al. (1992), Amin and Robins (1990), Amin (1991, 1993), Schmitz (1992), Capecchi (1990), Hirst and Zeitlin (1992), Nuti (1992), Harrison (1990), Lombardi (1994), Bellandi and Russo (1994), Gottardi (1996) and Cossentino et al. (1996).

2   See Bagnasco and Trigilia (1984, 1985), Garofoli (1978, 1983, 1992, 1995), Bianchi (1992), and, in an international context, Sabel and Zeitlin (1982), Sabel (1989), Williams et al. (1987) and Benko and Lipietz (1992).

3   For a theoretical viewpoint, see Best (1990) and Camagni (1989). For an analysis of important production networks, see, for instance, Sako (1989) and Belussi (1992).

4   Studies in regional economics are essentially based on the work of Krugman on the notion of increasing returns. The contributions that appeared in the *Revue d'Economie Régionale et Urbaine*, no. 3 (1993) are relatively interesting in relation to the issue of the 'economy of proximity'.

5   From this perspective, see the various contributions presented by Antonelli (1986, 1994), or the comparisons of different regional innovative systems: Longhi and Quere (1994), Gordon (1992) and Audretsch and Feldman (1994).

6   See Falzoni et al. (1992), Anastasia (1995), Sforzi (1995), Franchi (1994), Dei Ottati (1995), Crestanello (1993), Bellandi (1993), Bramanti and Senn (1994) and Carminucci and Casucci (1995).

7   See Brusco (1982), Becattini and Rullani (1996), Dei Ottati (1987, 1994) and Bartolozzi and Garibaldo (1995).

8   The thinning out of the central core of the enterprise has been at the heart of the debate about the hollow corporation (*Business Week*, 1986). For an insight into the impact of the networking economy on enterprise models, see Belussi and Arcangeli (1998).

9   This production system was also analysed in detail by Russo (1990) and Porter (1990).

10   On the notion of sunk costs, see also Sutton (1991) and Stiglitz (1987).

11   The specific nature of the resources used by the enterprises is a theme that has been widely discussed in economic literature. See Carlsson and Eliasson (1994) and Pavitt (1984, 1986).

12   The market is here viewed as a network of social relations, more or less regulated by the collective actors, and as the place where trust is established. An interesting contribution related to the analysis of Italian industrial districts is represented by the work of Mutti (1987) and Dei Ottati (1994). For a general framework, see the work by Dore (1983, 1987) and Sako (1991).

13   This aspect has been developed by Dore (1987) and Sako (1991).

14   As demonstrated by Rosenberg (1976) and Chandler (1990), the process of inter-firm division of work is an element that should be assumed in an historical perspective.

15   A local production system based on small enterprises may not be characterised by high levels of inter-firm division of labour and by enterprises that cooperate with each other in a technologically dynamic context. For example, Bull et al. (1991), by studying three cases of textile industrial districts in Italy, UK and France, based essentially on small-sized firms, demonstrated that only the Italian district corresponded to these characteristics.

16   The visibility of firm investment policy makes the speed of the adoption of technologies incorporated in new machinery quite uniform. Innovation in product design is, on the contrary, a less even process because it depends on the differentiated capability of firms.

17   See the arguments put forward by Rullani (1993): 'If the small specialised enterprise belongs to a quite large system, the relevant scope economies … should be measured according to the size of the value-chain of the whole territorial system … In other words, what is important for the generation of value and competitive advantages is not the size of the enterprise but … the level of the efficiency of the local system' (p. 35).

18   On this topic, see Metcalfe and De Liso (1995), Robertson and Langlois (1995) and, on the notion of scope economies, Di Bernardo (1991).

19   Note that, in the Italian case, the prevailing small size has also allowed a high reduction in internal organisational costs (You, 1995). The introduction of technological innovations was favoured, given the small scale of the investment needed for the modernisation of plants.

20   This is a typical neoclassical way of reasoning, presupposing the resolution of an allocative type of problem. Arrow has shown that the market for the development of new scientific knowledge, if left to act spontaneously, would produce a situation of under-investment, deviating from Paretian equilibrium. The most recent economic discussion has also highlighted the limitations of public intervention, introducing the theme of 'government' failures (see Wolf, 1993).

21   On the same issue, see Bellini et al. (1991), Cooke (1994), and the legislative analysis proposed by Bartolozzi (1993).

22 This is a theme that has been examined by Nelson and Winter (1982), Freeman (1987), Foray and Freeman (1993), Lundvall (1992, 1994), Bellet (1993) and Leoni and Mazzini (1993).

23 On this aspect, see also Vanberg (1992), Gilly and Grossetti (1993) and Kirat (1993).

24 There is room here for regulative policies. One considers, for instance, the German case where regulative policies pushed by the Green movement were quite successful in the area of promoting energy-saving processes (with the development of new industries focusing on material recycling: glass, paper, electric household and cars) or in the creation of environmental-friendly new products (for instance, new types of glues without toxic components).

References

Amin, A. (1991), These are not Marshallian times, in R. Camagni (ed.), *Innovation Networks: Spatial Perspectives*, London, Belhaven Press.

Amin, A. (1993), 'The Difficult Transition from Informal to Marshallian District', University of Newcastle upon Tyne, mimeo.

Amin, A. and Robins, K. (1990), Industrial districts and regional development: limits and possibilities, in F. Pyke, F. Becattini and W. Sengenberger (eds), *Industrial Districts and Inter-firm Cooperation in Italy*, Geneva, ILO.

Anastasia, B. (1995), Flussi di esportazione e processi di internazionalizzazione: il contributo dei distretti industriali veneti, *Olter il ponte*, No. 50.

Anastasia, B., Corò, G. and Crestanello, P. (1995), Problemi di individuazione dei distretti industriali, *Olter il ponte*, No. 52.

Antonelli, C. (1986), Technological districts and regional innovation capacity, *Revue d'Economie Régionale et Urbaine*, No. 5.

Antonelli, C. (1987), Dall'economia industriale all'organizzazione industriale, *Economia Politica*, No. 2.

Antonelli, C. (1994), Technological districts, localised spillovers, and productivity growth: the Italian evidence on technological externalities in the core regions, *International Review of Applied Economics*, Vol. 8, No. 1.

Audretsch, D. and Feldman, M. (1994), R&D spillover and the geography of innovation production, Discussion Paper, FS IV 94–2, Wissenshaftszentrum, Berlin.

Bagnasco, A. and Trigilia, C. (eds) (1984), *Società e Politica nelle Aree di Piccola Impresa, Il Caso di Bassano*, Venice, Arsenale Editrice.

Bagnasco, A. and Trigilia, C. (ed.) (1985), *Società e Politica nelle Aree di Piccola Impresa: Il Caso della Valdelsa*, Milan, Angeli.

Bartolozzi, P. (1993), 'Le Politiche Industriali e di Sostegno all'impresa PM-Artigianato delle Autorità Regionali in Emilia Romagna, Marche, Toscana, Veneto, Friuli', Bologna; Ires Emilia Romagna memeo.

Bartolozzi, P. and Garibaldo, F. (eds) (1995), *Lavoro Creativo e Impresa Efficiente: Ricerca sulle Piccole e Medie Imprese*, Rome, Esi.

Becattini, G. (1979), Dal settore industriale al distretto industriale: Alcune considerazioni sull' unità di indagine in economia industriale, *Economia e Politica Industriale*, No. 1.

Becattini, G. (ed.) (1987), *Mercato e Forze Locali: Il Distretto Industriale*, Bologna, Il Mulino.

Becattini, G. (1989), *Modelli Locali di Sviluppo*, Bologna, Il Mulino.

Becattini, G. and Rullani, E. (1996), Local systems and global connections: the role of knowledge, in F. Cossentino, F. Pyke and W. Sengenberger (eds), *Local Regional Response to Global Pressure: The Case of Italy*, Geneva, ILO.

Bellandi, M. (1992), The incentives to decentralised industrial creativity in local systems of small firms, *Revue d'Economie Industrielle*, No. 59.

Bellandi, M. (1993), 'Structure and Change in the Industrial District', *Studi e discussioni*, no. 85, Dipartimento di Scienze Economiche, Università di Firenze.

Bellandi, M. and Russo, M. (eds) (1994), *Distretti Industriali e Cambiamento Economico Locale*, Turin, Rosenberg e Sellier.

Bellet, M. (1993), Evolution de la politique technologique, et role de la proximite: repères sur le cas français, *Revue d'Economie Régionale et Urbaine*, No. 3.

Bellini, N., Giordani, M., Magatti, P. and Pasquini, F. (1991), Il livello locale e la politica industriale, in Nomisma, *Strategie e Valuatzione nella Politica Industriale*, Milan, Angeli.

Bellon, B. (1994), L'etat et l'entreprise, in B. Bellon et al. (eds), *L'Etat et le Marché*, Paris, Economica.

Belussi, F. (ed.) (1988), *Innovazione Technologica ed Economie Locali*, Milan, Angeli.

Belussi, F. (ed.) (1992), *Nuovi Modelli di Impresa, Gerarchie Organizzative ed Imprese Rete*, Milan, Angeli.

Belussi, F. (1994), 'Industrial Innovation and Firm Development in Italy: The Veneto Case', SPRU, University of Sussex, Ph.D. thesis.

Belussi, F. (1995), L'evoluzione dei comparti produttivi nella provincia di Reggio Emilia, in Economie locali e politiche per lo sviluppo, *Ires Materiali* No. 1.

Belussi, F. (1996), Local systems, industrial districts and institutional networks: towards a new evolutionary paradigm of industrial economics?, *European Planning Studies*, Vol. 4, No. 3.

Belussi, F. and Arcangeli, F. (1998), A typology of networks: flexible and evolutionary firms, *Research Policy*, Vol. 27.

Belussi, F. and Pozzana, R. (1995), *Natalità e Mortalità delle Imprese e Determinanti dell'Imprenditorialità*, Milan, Angeli.

Benko, G. and Lipietz, A. (eds) (1992), *Les Régions Qui Gagnent*, Paris, Presses Universitaires de France.

Best, H.B. (1990), *The New Competition*, Cambridge, Polity Press.

Bianchi, P. (1992), Sentieri di industrializzazione e sviluppo regionale negli anni '90: strategie politiche di intervento pubblico nella nuova fase competititiva post-fordista, in F. Belussi (ed.), *Nuovi Modelli di Impresa, Gerarchie Organizzative ed Imprese Rete*, Milan, Angeli.

Bozzi, C. and Bramanti, A. (1994), Struttura ed evoluzione di un settore dinamico: il caso degli antifurti nella provincia di Varese, *Quaderno* no. 2, Collana Osservatiorio, Milan, Università Bocconi.

Bramanti, A. and Senn, L. (1994), Cambiamenti strutturali, connessioni locali e strutture di governo in tre sitemi locali dell lombardia del nord-ovest, *Quaderno Opes*, no. 5, Milan, Università Bocconi.

Brusco, S. (1982), The Emilian model: productive disintegration and social integration, *Cambridge Journal of Economics*, Vol. 6, No. 2.

Brusco, S. (1993), II modello emiliano rivisita il distretto, *Politica ed Economia*, Luglio.

Bull, A., Pitt, M. and Szarka, J. (1991), Small firms and industrial districts: structural explanation of small firms' viability in three countries, *Entrepreneurship and Regional Development*, Vol. 3.

Business Week (1986), The hollow corporation, March, No. 3.

Calzabini, P. and Bosco, M.C. (1996), 'The socialisation of competence in the development of human resources in the small enterprise district, paper presented at the Udine Conference on the Italian district, December 1995, revised version.

Camagni, R. (1989), Accordi di cooperazione, e alleanze strategiche: motivazioni, fattori di successo ed elementi di rischio, *Rassegna Economica Ibm*, supp. to No. 4, December.

Camagni, R. and Rabellotti, R. (1994), 'Footwear production systems in Italy: a dynamic comparative analysis', paper presented at IV meeting Gremi, Grenoble, 11 June.

Capecchi, V. (1990), A history of flexible specialisation of industrial districts in Emilia Romagna, in F. Pyke, F. Becattini and W. Sengenberger (eds), *Industrial District and Inter-firm Cooperation in Italy*, Geneva, ILO.

Capecchi, V. (1997), La ricerca della flessibilità: l'industria meccanica Bolognese dal 1900 al 1992, *Sviluppo Locale*, Vol. 4, No. 4.

Carlsson, B. and Eliasson, G. (1994), The nature and importance of economic competence, *Industry and Corporate Change*, Vol. 3, No. 3.

Carminucci, C. and Casucci, S. (1995), 'Il Ciclo di Vita dei Distretti Industriali. Ipotesi Teoriche ed Evidenze Empiriche', Censis, mimeo.

Chandler, A.D. (1990), *Scale and Scope: The Dynamics of Capitalism*, Cambridge, MA, Belknap Press.

Colletis-Wahl, K. (1995), L'hypothèse des facteurs de concurrence spatiale, quels fondamants?, *Cahiers de Recherche Adis*, no. 32, Université de Paris Sud.

Cooke, P. (1994), 'Building a 21st-century regional economy in Emilia Romagna', paper presented at conference on 'Industrial districts and local development in Italy: challenges and policy perspectives', Bologna, 2–3 May.

Cossentino, F., Pyke, F. and Sengenberger, W. (eds) (1996), *Local Regional Response to Global Pressure: The Case of Italy*, Geneva, ILO.

Crestenello, P. (1993), 'Le trasformazioni dei sistemi produttivi locali durante gli anni '80 attraverso l'analisi di dieci casi', relazione al seminario di Prato, 1–2 July.

Crestanello, P. (1995), L'industria del vetro artistico di Murano, *Oltre il Ponte*, No. 49.

Creti, A. (1994), La logistica industriale-distributiva: la globalizzazione di un *milieu*, *Quaderno,* no. 4, Collana Osservatorio, Università Bocconi.

Da Canal, P. (1993), 'La Nuova Geografia delle Imprese-rete e la Globalizzazione dei Sistemi Produttivi: le Nuove Forme Spaziali della Gerarchizzazione', Università di Venezia, unpublished thesis.

Dei Ottati, G. (1987), Il mercato comunitario, in F. Becattini (ed.), *Mercato e Forze Locali: Il Distretto Industriale,* Bologna, Il Mulino.

Dei Ottati, G. (1994), Trust, interlinking transactions, and credit in industrial districts, *Cambridge Journal of Economics*, Vol. 18, No. 6.

Dei Ottati, G. (1995), Economic changes in the district of Prato in the 1980s: towards a more conscious and organised industrial district, *European Planning Studies*, Vol. 4, No.3.

Di Bernardo, B. (1991), *La Dimensione di Impresa: Scala, Scopo, Varietà*, Milan, Angeli.

Dore, R. (1983), Goodwill and the spirit of market capitalism, *British Journal of Sociology*, Vol. 34, No. 4.

Dore, R. (1987), *Taking Japon Seriously: A Confucian Perspective on Leading Economic Issues*, London, Athlone.

Falzoni, A., Onida, F. and Viesti, G. (eds) (1992), *I Distretti Industriali: Crisi o Evoluzione?*, Milan, Egea.

Foray, D. and Freeman, C. (eds) (1993), *Technology and the Wealth of Nations*, London, Pinter.

Franchi, M. (1994), 'Developments in the districts of Emilia-Romagna', paper presented at the conference of 'Industrial districts and local developments in Italy: challenges and political perspectives', Bologna, 2–3 May.

Freeman, C. (1982), *The Economics of Industrial Innovation*, London, Pinter.

Freeman, C. (1987), *Technology Policy and Economic Performance: Lessons from Japan*, London, Pinter.

Freschi, A.C. (1994), Istituzioni politiche e sviluppo locale nella Terza Italia, *Sviluppo Locale*, Vol. 1, No. 1.

Gandolfi, V. (1988), *Aree Sistema: Internazionalizzazione e Reti Telematiche*, Milan, Angeli.

Garofoli, G. (ed.) (1978), *Ristrutturazione Industriale e Territorio*, Milan, Angeli.

Garofoli, G. (1983), Le aree-sistema in Italia, *Politica ed Economia*, Vol. 11.

Garofoli, G. (1992), Les systèmes de petites entreprises: un cas paradigmatique de dèveloppement endogène, in G. Benko and A. Lipietz (eds), *Les Régions Qui Gagnent*, Paris, Presses Universitates de France.

Garofoli, G. (ed.) (1995), *Industrializzazione Diffusa in Lombardia*, Pavia, Iuculano Editore.

Gerybadze, A. (1992), The implementation of industrial policy in an evolutionary perspective, in U. Witt (ed.), *Explaining Process and Change*, Ann Arbor, University of Michigan Press.

Gilly, J.P. and Grossetti, M. (1993), 'Organisations, Individus et territoires: le cas des systèmes locaux d'innovation, *Revue d'Economie Régionale et Urbaine*, No. 3.

Gobbo, F. (ed.) (1989), *Distretti e Sistemi Produttivi alla Soglia degli Anni '90*, Milan, Angeli.

Gordon, R. (1992), 'State, Milieu, Network: Systems of Innovation in Silicon Valley', paper presented at workshop on Systems of Innovations, 5–6 October, Bologna.

Gottardi, G. (1996), Strategie technologiche, innovazione senza R&D, e generazione di conoscenza nei distretti e nei sistemi locali, *Quaderni del Dipartimento di Scienze Eonomiche Marco Fanno*, No. 63.

Harrison, B. (1990), 'Industrial Districts: Old Vine in New Bottles?', Working paper no. 90, Carnegie Mellon University, Pittsburg.

Harrison, B. (1994), *The Lean and the Mean*, New York, Basic Books.

Hirst, P. and Zeitlin, J. (1992), Specializzazione flessibile e post-fordismo: realtà e implicazioni politiche, in F. Belussi (ed.), *Nuovi Modell: di Impresa, Gerarchie Organizzative ed Imprese Rete*, Milan, Angeli.

Kirat, T. (1993), Innovation technologique et apprentissage institutionnel: institutions et proximité dans la dynamique des systèmes d'innovation territoriales, *Revue d'Economie Régionale et Urbaine*, No. 3.

Leoni, R. and Mazzini, M. (1993), Processi di innovazione tecnologica e istituzioni di sostegno a livello locale, *Quaderni del Dipartimento di Scienze Economiche*, No. 14.

Linsu, K. (1997), *Imitation to Innovation: the Dynamics of Korea's Technological Learning*, Boston, Harvard University Press.

Lipparini, A. (1995), *Imprese, Relazioni tra Imprese e Posizionamento Competitivo*, Milan, Etas Libri.

Lombardi, M. (1994), Meccanismi evolutivi nella dinamica dei sistemi di imprese, Ricerca di Base, *Quaderni dell'Universitô Bocconi*, No. 3.

Longhi, C. and Quere, M. (1994), 'Europe as a Mosaic of Local Systems of Innovation', Eunetic Conference, 6–8 October, Strasburg.

Lundvall, B. (ed.) (1992), *National Systems of Innovations*, London, Pinter.

Lundvall, B. (1994), Learning Economics, *Industry Studies*, No. 2.

Metcalfe, J. and De Liso, N. (1995), 'Innovation, Capabilities, and Knowledge: the Epistemic Connection', University of Manchester, mimeo.

Moussanet, M. and Paolazzi, L. (eds) (1992), *Gioielli, Bombole, Coltelli. Viaggio nei Distretti Produttivi Italiani*, Milan, II Sole 24-Ore.

Mutti, A. (1987), La Fiducia un concetto fragile, une solida realtà, *Rassegna Italiana di Sociologia*, Vol. 2.

Nelson, R. and Winter, S. (1992), *An Evolutionary Theory of Economic Change*, Cambridge, MA, Belknap.

Nuti, F. (ed.) (1992), *I Distretti dell'Industria Manifatturiera in Italia*, Vols 1 and 2, Milan, Angeli.

Parri, L. (1993), 'I dilemmi dell'azione collettiva nell'evoluzione dei distretti industriali Italiani: i casi di Cantù, Carpi ed Arzignano', *Oltre il Ponte*, No. 41.

Pavitt, K. (1984), Sectoral patterns of technical change: towards a taxonomy and a theory, *Research Policy*, Vol. 13, No. 6.

Pavitt, K. (1986), Chips and 'trajectories': how does the semiconductor influence the sources and directions of technical change?, in R. Maclean (ed.), *Technology and the Human Prospect*, London, Pinter.

Piore, M.J. and Sabel, C.F. (1984), *The Second Industrial Divide: Possibilities for Prosperity*, New York, Basic Books.

Porter, M. (1990), *The Competitive Advantage of Nations*, Cambridge, MA, MIT Press.

Pyke, F. and Sengenberger, W. (eds) (1992), *Industrial Districts and Local Economic Regeneration*, Geneva, ILO.

Pyke, F., Becattini, F. and Sengenberger, W. (eds) (1990), *Industrial Districts and Inter-firm Cooperation in Italy*, Geneva, ILO.

Revue d'Economie Régionale et Urbaine (1993), Numéro spécial, 'Economie de Proximités', No. 3.

Robertson, P. and Langlois, R. (1995), Innovation, networks and integration, *Research Policy*, Vol. 24.

Rosenberg, N. (1976), *Perspectives on Technology*, Cambridge, Cambridge University Press.

Rullani, E. (1993), L'impresa minore nella teoria economica e nelle osservazioni empiriche, *Rivista Italiana di Economia, Demografia e Statistica*, Vol. 47, No. 3–4.

Russo, M. (1990), 'Cambiamento Tecnico e Distretto Industriale: Una Verifica Empirica', Materiali di discussione, No. 70, Università degli studi di Modena.

Sabel, C. (1989), Flexible specialization and the reemergence of regional economics, *Economy and Society*, Vol. 18, No. 4.

Sabel, C. and Zeitlin, J. (1982), Alternative storiche alla produzione di massa, *Stato e Mercato*, Vol. 5.

Sako, M. (1989), 'Neither Markets Nor Hierarchies: a Comparative Study of the Printed Circuit Board Industry in Britain and Japan', paper presented at conference on 'Comparing Capitalist Economies', Bellagio, May.

Sako, M. (1991), The role of 'trust' in Japanese buyer–supplier relationships, *Ricerche Economiche*, No. 2–3.

Scarpitti, L. (1991), Ambiti e metodi d'intervento a livello locale, in Nomisma (ed.), *Strategie e Valuatzione nella Politica Industriale*, Milan, Angeli.

Schmitz, H. (1992), Industrial districts: models and reality in Baden-Wurttemberg Germany, in F. Pyke and W. Sengenberger (eds), *Industrial Districts and Local Economic Regeneration*, Geneva, ILO.

Sforzi, F. (1990), The quantitative importance of Marshallian industrial districts in the Italian economy, in F. Pyke, F. Becattini and W. Sengenberger (eds), *Industrial Districts and Inter-firm Cooperation in Italy*, Geneva, ILO.

Sforzi, F. (1995), 'Elenco dei Sistemi Locali di Piccola e Media Impresa 1991', paper presented at the meeting on 'Lo sviluppo locale', 11 September.

Stiglitz, J. (1987), Technological change, sunk costs, and competition, *Brookings Papers on Economic Activity*, No. 3.

Sutton, J. (1991), *Sunk Costs and Market Structure*, Cambridge, MA, MIT Press.

Tolomelli, C. (ed.) (1992), *Le Politiche Industriali Regionali: Esperienze, Soggetti, Modelli*, Bologna, Clueb.

Vanberg, V. (1992), Innovation, cultural evolution, and economic growth, in U. Witt (ed.), *Explaining Process and Change*.

Williams, K. et al. (1987), The end of mass production?, *Economy and Society*, Vol. 6, No. 3.

Witt, U. (ed.) (1992), *Explaining Process and Change*, Ann Arbor, University of Michigan Press.

Wolf, C. (1993), *Markets or Governments. Choosing between Imperfect Alternatives*, Cambridge, MA, MIT Press.

You, J. (1995), Small firms in economic theory, *Cambridge Journal of Economics*, Vol. 19, No. 3.

Environmental policy

Deforestation, pollution, global warming, the ozone hole, extinction of species of flora and fauna – all of us are familiar with the range of problems with which we are faced with respect to our natural environment. But why cannot the market take care of these issues? Why do we need to have policies with respect to the natural environment? How are we to agree on and implement an environment policy that commands collective consent? Why is it proving so difficult to agree on policy in this area?

Chapter 18 explores a range of environmental policy issues. For its author, Atkinson, sustainable development refers to development that generates current human well-being without imposing significant costs on future generations. The definition is subjective, and he discusses why this needs to be so. Owing to the existence of multiple sources of market failure, the market cannot generate optimal results with respect to the production and consumption of natural resources. Markets simply do not exist whereby future generations can transact with the current generation over the consumption of natural resources. If current generations are to care about the consequences of their actions for future generations, this concern can only be based on altruism or a sense of responsibility, not on narrow and exclusively material notions of self-interest. There are analysts, whom Atkinson calls the 'technology optimists', who claim that we need not really worry since resource scarcity and environmental degradation will induce appropriate technological progress to counter these adverse developments. However, given the irreversible nature of much environmental damage and some of the possible catastrophic consequences of environmental degradation, would it be wise to rely on the hope that technological progress will occur in time to combat these changes? Atkinson also discusses the market failures relating to intra-generation issues in addition to the inter-generation ones. Pollution is, for example, a classic externality that cannot be adequately dealt with through the market. An equally pressing issue is the global distribution of income. While the vast bulk of the world's population still lives in poverty, a small proportion of the world's population consumes a highly disproportionate share of the world's natural resources. Moreover, this picture has grown worse in recent years, as the distribution of global income has become more unequal. With economic growth now occurring in the developing world, it may no longer be sustainable to have ever-increasing levels of consumption in the developed world, and a more egalitarian structure of global economic activity may be required. But would the privileged in the developed and developing countries be prepared to make sacrifices for the sake of the less privileged? In the final analysis, the survival of our planet may turn out to rest on our capacity to look and care beyond our narrow and material self-interest.

Sustainable Development

GILES ATKINSON*

1. Introduction

In June 1992, the world's politicians descended on Rio de Janeiro, Brazil, to attend the United Nations Conference on Environment and Development, known as the Earth Summit. They were joined by thousands of other delegates eager to exert an influence on the proceedings. The Earth Summit had been over-dramatically hailed by some as 'the last chance to save the Earth'. But even allowing for the hype, the environmental problems debated in Rio do have global ramifications for the way in which human populations intend to use the environment to meet their economic development goals in the future. The wide range of concerns can be summarized as the need for *sustainable development* – development that generates current human well-being without imposing significant costs on future generations.

The objectives of this chapter are threefold. The first is to convey the scale of environmental change, or more accurately global environmental degradation, and to introduce the concept of sustainable development as a response to it (Section 2). I will illustrate the problem by focusing on deforestation and its consequences – such as global warming and biodiversity loss.

The second objective is to show that economics is at the heart of discussions regarding sustainable development (Section 3). The environment is seen by economists as a form of capital: environmental capital. Our decision to degrade the environment erodes our ability to satisfy the well-being of future generations, so that it has been proposed that sustainable development requires the maintaining

* The Open University (1995) D216 *Economics and Changing Economics*, Book 4, Chapter 27 'Sustainable Development' © The Open University.
Table 18.1: Kogan Page for *Blueprint 3* by David Pearce, et al., published by Earthscan Publications, Ltd. Table 18.2: Oxford University Press for *World Without End* by David Pearce and Jeremy Warford.

Table 18.1   *Relative forest cover in EU countries, 1992*

	Total land area (million hectares)	Forest cover (%)
Portugal	9.2	40
Spain	49.9	31
Germany	34.9	30
France	55.0	27
Italy	29.4	23
Belgium/Luxembourg	3.3	21
Greece	13.1	20
Denmark	4.2	12
UK	24.1	10
Netherlands	3.4	9
Ireland	6.9	5
European Union	233.4	25

Source: Moran, 1994

of environmental capital. Economics also helps us to look for the most efficient way to meet this constraint whilst ensuring that the current generation can still meet its own needs as far as possible.

The final objective is to examine the prospects for policy to promote sustainable development (Section 4). Global problems require global solutions, and the role of international co-operation is crucial. Unfortunately, it would be naive to think that such co-operation is the inevitable result of an appeal for the global good. Countries with large amounts of environmental capital tend to be those that are not in a position to conserve. Conversely, those countries that are in a better position to shoulder the burdens of sustainable development are those with less environmental capital. Solutions must be politically feasible, reconciling conflicting economic interests.

2. Sustainable development

2.1 Deforestation

Deforestation, the *permanent* clearing of forest lands by human populations, is not a new phenomenon. It is reckoned that when the Romans landed in Britain nearly 2000 years ago most of the land was covered by broad-leaved forests (Gradwohl and Greenberg, 1988). By 1992, total forest cover was about 10 per cent of land area in what is now the UK, which represents an increase in forest cover from those levels which prevailed at the beginning of the twentieth century. This experience is common to many industrialized countries. In the European Union, forest cover was on average 25 per cent of land area in 1992. As Table 18.1 shows, this masks country variations, from Portugal, where 40 per cent of total area was under forest cover, to Ireland, where forest cover was only 5 per cent.

Table 18.2   *Estimates of tropical forest area and rate of deforestation for 87 countries*

Region or sub-region	Countries in region	Forest area (thousand hectares)		Deforestation (% per year)
		1980	1990	
Latin America	32	923 000	839 900	0.9
Central America and Mexico	7	77 000	63 500	1.8
Caribbean sub-region	18	48 800	47 100	0.4
Tropical South America	7	797 100	729 300	0.8
Asia	15	310 800	274 900	1.2
South Asia	6	70 600	66 200	0.6
Continental south-east Asia	5	83 200	69 700	1.6
Insular south-east Asia	4	157 000	138 900	1.2
Africa	40	650 300	600 100	0.8
West Sahelian Africa	8	41 900	38 000	0.9
East Sahelian Africa	6	92 300	85 300	0.8
West Africa	8	55 200	43 400	2.1
Central Africa	7	230 100	215 400	0.6
Tropical Southern Africa	10	217 700	206 300	0.5
Insular Africa	1	13 200	11 700	1.2
Total	87	1 884 100	1 714 800	0.9

Source: World Resources Institute, 1992; adapted from Pearce and Warford, 1993, Table 5.7

However, current concerns about deforestation have shifted to other types of forests – in particular to tropical broad-leaved (hardwood) forest, of which 80 per cent is tropical rain forest. By and large these tend to be located in so-called 'developing' countries or regions, particularly Amazonia, central Africa and south-east Asia. Tropical rain forests are defined by ecologist Norman Myers as 'evergreen/ partly evergreen forests in areas receiving over 100 mm rain in any six months for two out of three years, with a mean annual temperature of over 24°C' (Myers, 1990). Other important characteristics of forests are determined by the degree to which the forest has been disturbed by human activity. *Primary forest* is forest which has not been disturbed by humans. In such forest, growth has reached a climax where tree death will equal tree growth. *Secondary forest*, on the other hand, is forest which has been disturbed by human activity, but has the ability to exhibit net growth.

Where rates of cutting are persistently greater than the ability of the forest to grow back, an ever-decreasing forest area will result. Table 18.2 shows some measurements of deforestation, surveying 87 countries in the tropics. Column 3 gives an 'opening balance' for land area under forest in units of 1000 hectares in 1980.

Column 4 gives the 'closing balance' in 1990. The final column translates these data into an average annual rate of deforestation. As the column shows, although deforestation is occurring throughout the tropics, the pressures tend to be concentrated in particular regions or continents. [...]

Scanning the final column, it is clear that if we are interested in relative rates of deforestation then the most marked losses are in Central America and Mexico, insular and west Africa and Asia. However, Latin America has the largest absolute deforestation rate in terms of hectares lost. If these rates of deforestation are continued, forests in these regions are set to dwindle almost to exhaustion.

Why, then, does deforestation matter? Tropical forests provide a rich array of functions, which will be lost when forest land is permanently cleared of trees. Such losses have implications for areas within tropical countries but also affect the well-being of the world as a whole. I will focus on the two global issues: the role of forests as a habitat for flora and fauna; and forests as stores of carbon dioxide and as fixers (or sequestrators) of carbon.

2.1.1 WHY DEFORESTATION MATTERS: BIODIVERSITY

Forests provide an important habitat for plants and animals collectively known as biological diversity or biodiversity. Tropical deforestation is a proximate cause of the mass extinction of species. I use the term 'proximate cause' because there are forces driving the deforestation itself, including unequal land tenure and poverty.

Biological diversity can be defined in several ways. The best known is *species diversity*, the number and variety of species. There are other definitions such as *genetic diversity*, which refers to the genetic information contained not only in each different species but also within individual members of each particular species. In addition, there is *ecosystem diversity*, which refers to the variety of habitats, communities and ecological processes. Tropical forests represent one type of ecosystem within which resides a myriad of different species, each containing its own unique genetic information. In fact, as Swanson (1990) reports, about half the world's species live in the world's tropical forests. Countries which contain a relatively large proportion of the world's species diversity are sometimes referred to as 'megadiversity countries' and include Brazil, Zaïre [the Democratic Republic of Congo], Mexico, Indonesia, Colombia and Madagascar. Table 18.3 indicates the extent of deforestation in these countries during the 1980s. Tables 18.4 and 18.5 provide an indication of threatened animal and plant species relative to known species in these countries. [...]

Deforestation matters because biodiversity is lost as a result. It seems reasonable to ask why the loss of biodiversity matters. The answer is not easy but many would agree that biodiversity provides important economic, social and ecological services. For example, plant diversity is an important source of genes for the development of new crop species that are integral to productive agricultural systems. Another benefit of biodiversity is that cures for fatal diseases such as AIDS might lie in the genetic information of plants indigenous to tropical forests. To take one example, the World Resources Institute (1992) reports that in the USA, an effective anti-cancer drug was developed from the bark of the yew trees found in the

Table 18.3 *Deforestation in 'megadiversity countries' as a percentage of forest land*

Country	Forest area (thousand hectares)		Deforestation (% per year, 1981–90)
	1980	1990	
Brazil	514 480	489 330	0.5
Colombia	51 700	43 550	1.7
Indonesia	116 900	111 180	0.5
Madagascar	13 200	11 700	1.2
Mexico	43 350	38 000	1.3
Zaïre	177 590	174 070	0.2

Source: World Resources Institute, 1992

Table 18.4 *Known and threatened[a] animal species, number, 1990*

Country	Mammals		Birds		Reptiles		Amphibians		Freshwater fish	
	Known species	Threatened species	Known species	Threatened species	Known species	Threatened species	Known species	Threatened species	Known species	Threatened species
Brazil	394	24	1567	123	467	11	487	0	–	9
Colombia	358	25	1665	69	383	10	375	0	–	0
Indonesia	479	50	1500	135	–	13	–	0	–	29
Madagascar	105	53	250	28	259	10	144	0	–	0
Mexico	439	26	961	35	717	16	284	4	–	98
Zaïre	409	22	1086	27	–	2	–	0	700	1

[a]Threatened species are either endangered, vulnerable, rare or indeterminate.
– not available.

Source: World Resources Institute, 1992

Table 18.5 *Known and threatened plant taxa,[a] 1991*

Country	No. of plant taxa	No. of rare and threatened plant taxa	Rare and threatened plant taxa per 1000 existing taxa
Brazil	55 000	240	4
Colombia	45 000	316	7
Indonesia	–	–	–
Madagascar	10 000–12 000	193	16–19
Mexico	20 000	1111	56
Zaïre	11 000	3	0

[a]Threatened species are either endangered, vulnerable, rare or indeterminate.
Taxa: native plant species found in the country.
– not available.

Source: World Resources Institute, 1992

ancient forests of the Pacific Northwest. In Madagascar, a plant called the rosy periwinkle has also been proven to have anti-cancer medicinal properties. Indeed, in 1985 plant-derived drugs had an estimated retail value of $43 billion. Loss of plant species could translate into significant economic costs.

Possibly as important, but less clearly established, is the suggestion that biodiversity may help to maintain the stability and resilience of ecosystems after shocks and stresses. Yet it would be inaccurate to portray the state of knowledge concerning the functions of biodiversity as anything but incomplete. Nevertheless, the uncertainty surrounding the consequences of biodiversity loss is seen by many as a source of global concern in itself. While there is no consensus estimate of species loss, many biologists believe that a process of mass extinction is being experienced. Some estimates suggest that at least 27 000 species per annum are being lost in tropical forests alone (Myers, 1992). This does not include species lost in other ecosystems such as coral reefs, wetlands and islands (which may push the annual species loss beyond 30 000). If these trends continue, as much as 20 per cent of all species could be lost by the second decade of the twenty-first century.

A counter-argument is that the developed countries of the north have depleted much of their diversity without any catastrophic or serious effects. Perhaps the developing nations in the south could follow the same model of development. However, this would be a strategy with highly uncertain pay-offs because the globalized costs of successive conversions of land and loss of diversity are probably increasing. While early conversions and extinctions left plenty of diversity and thus had little impact, this is not true of later conversions, which are eating into an ever-decreasing stock of diversity. What is clear is that species extinction is an irreversible process – lost species cannot be recreated. Even if it were possible to restore biodiversity eventually, the time frame for this reversal would be millions of years (Wilson, 1992).

2.1.2 WHY DEFORESTATION MATTERS: CLIMATE CHANGE   Forests serve important climatic functions. By assimilating carbon dioxide through the process of photosynthesis, trees (and vegetative matter) help to stabilize the climate. Forests therefore provide a sink for the emissions of carbon dioxide (the most significant greenhouse gas in the atmosphere in terms of volume), and hence play their part in slowing global warming. Moreover, when forests are cleared, the trees are often burnt, releasing additional carbon dioxide into the atmosphere. Yet the economic activities that usually replace forestry, such as permanent agriculture or pasture, do not replace these carbon-fixing functions.

Global warming refers to an increase in mean global temperature as a result of the 'greenhouse effect'. The greenhouse effect is a natural process by which energy from the sun passes through the atmosphere. Heat is radiated back from the earth but is partially blocked by atmospheric gases, usually called 'greenhouse gases' (GHGs) because they cause the atmosphere to warm. Global warming is not caused solely by deforestation. Indeed, deforestation probably contributes only 15–20 per cent of GHGs (carbon dioxide, ozone, water vapour, chlorofluorocarbons

[CFCs], methane and nitrous oxide) in the atmosphere. Carbon dioxide is more usually emitted from the burning of fossil fuels such as oil and coal to meet our energy needs. At the moment these emissions occur predominantly in the industrialized north.

The atmosphere can assimilate (absorb and process) some but not all of these GHGs. Competing human activities 'use up' the earth's capacity to absorb carbon dioxide and other GHGs. This intensifies the 'greenhouse effect' and global temperature may rise. It has been estimated that, if nothing is done to stop the trend of emissions, global mean temperature will rise by between 0.2 per cent and 0.5 per cent a decade. However, there are many scientific uncertainties in this field. While there is evidence that the climate has changed since the industrial revolution, this slight warming is consistent with natural variations rather than being induced by humans. The uncertainty surrounding the predicted rate of warming leaves plenty of scope for fierce debate concerning the gravity of effects that may (or may not) take place. In fact, some scientists have reasoned that global warming is a myth or at least is so uncertain that we are not under any obligation to take remedial action.

Pearce and Warford (1993) outline some of the possible effects of climate change.

- Increases in regional temperature may have an effect on crops through reductions of soil moisture and the risk of summer drought. Changes in regional rainfall might occur; for example, arid zones might become even more arid.

- Increases in temperature could cause the oceans to expand and ice sheets to melt. This may cause sea levels to rise by 3 to 10 centimetres a decade if no action is taken to prevent climate change. Low-lying land by the sea is put at risk. In the UK, one of the areas at risk is around the Wash in East Anglia. [. . .]

While some ecologists claim that global environmental change is potentially life-threatening to humans, such apocalyptic visions are not required in order to argue that significant costs are entailed by allowing this change to proceed unhindered. The implication can be drawn that further economic development should be undertaken only if it is sustainable.

2.2 Sustainable development and time preference

The term 'sustainable development' has become something of a buzz phrase, but what does it actually mean? In this section I discuss the definition of sustainable development and some of the philosophical issues it raises.

A definition of 'sustainable' is not hard to agree on; it means long-lasting or enduring. Development is slightly harder to define for it means different things to different people. It might generally be agreed that development refers to an increase in human well-being. However, human well-being cannot be directly measured, and in practice, development is often narrowly defined as increasing real gross national product per head of the population. This definition is sometimes broadened to consider improvements in other aspects of the 'quality of life' such as those embodied in social indicators which reflect, for example, the education and health of people within a country.

The most commonly cited public definition of sustainable development emanated from the World Commission on Environment and Development (WCED, or the 'Brundtland Commission') in 1987. Sustainable development is development that 'meets the needs of the present without compromising the ability of future generations to meet their own needs' (WCED, 1987, p. 8). So sustainable development is development that generates current human well-being without imposing significant costs on the future. For the Brundtland Commission, significant costs are translated into the inability to meet future development needs. For Pearce and Warford (1993), sustainable development is development that secures an increase in the well-being of the current generation provided that future well-being does not decrease. This effectively takes the same form as the Brundtland definition but substitutes 'welfare' for 'needs'. What it implies is that we should not trade off well-being now for a loss of well-being in the future.

If accepted as a worthwhile social goal, sustainable development implies that development should be evenly distributed across generations. This does not mean that economic progress is sacrificed so that each generation is guaranteed equal levels of well-being. What it means is that progress must not be reversed at a future date. The way in which the current generation is using the environment may represent one way in which potentially large costs are being passed on to the future. In this sense, we may be buying our development at the expense of our descendants. The suggestion that this is not an acceptable trade-off raises philosophical issues concerning fairness or justice which are not easy to resolve.

Sustainable development is therefore based on the concept of *intergenerational justice*, which refers to distribution across generations. This is distinct from distribution within a generation, or intragenerational justice. It is worth noting that environmental problems also impose significant costs on the present generation, which does raise questions of intragenerational justice. For example, pollutants emitted from power stations such as sulphur dioxide generate significant current costs in terms of adverse effects on human health and in some cases death from respiratory problems.[...] Possible connections between current inequalities and the problems of achieving sustainability are discussed towards the end of this chapter.

The concept of intergenerational justice has been debated at length by philosophers, political scientists, economists and environmentalists. The basic problem, as the economist and philosopher John Broome (1992) points out, is how to weigh up against each other goods and bads that occur at different times. In assessing environmental projects, one common approach discussed further in Section 3 is to add up the costs and the benefits of the project over time and to compare the two. But this is not a satisfactory decision rule if the benefits largely accrue to the current generation and the costs fall on the future. How can we value benefits and costs which have yet to occur?

We are all familiar with the sort of decisions individuals make in this regard. An individual may, for example, compare the costs of doing a degree with the future benefits. *Discounting* is a technique for comparing the worth of goods and bads which occur at different times by expressing future benefits and costs in terms of an estimate of their *present value*. One of the basic principles on which discounting is based is positive time preference. This means that, other things being equal, you would probably prefer £100 cash now to £100 cash in a year's time. In other words, £100 in a year's time is worth less to you than £100 now. So positive time preference means that current benefits are preferred to future benefits which are, at the time they occur, of the same magnitude. This is not the sole reason for discounting but it is the rationale that often receives the most attention in analyses of sustainable development. This is because it deals with impatience on the part of individuals or society: a preference for the present over the future.

Discounting

Discounting provides a technique for measuring the degree to which future benefits are worth less than current benefits. Positive time preference, for example, underlies the payment of interest on loans. Suppose that you are willing to postpone spending £100 if someone pays you 10 per cent interest in return for borrowing the money for a year. The rate of interest you are willing to accept represents the rate at which you are discounting the benefits of spending £100 because they are postponed for one year.

We can measure the effects of discounting using a formula derived from the concept of compounding. Discounting can be thought of as compounding in reverse: the longer the postponement the less you value the future benefits.

The present value, *PV*, of a future benefit, *FB*, is given by the formula

$$PV = \frac{FB}{(1 + r)^t}$$

where *r* is the discount rate (in this example the interest rate) and *t* stands for the number of years which elapse before the benefit becomes available (in this example the duration of the loan). The discount rate is expressed as a decimal rather than a percentage — in this example, 0.1 for 10 per cent. So the present value of £100 in a year's time is:

$$PV = \frac{£100}{1.1} = £90.91$$

[…] Let us apply the discounting formula to a hypothetical case involving environmental costs and benefits. A golf club wishes to extend its course and one option is to buy a small copse and fell the trees. The landowner is offered £12 000 and is told that refusal would lead the club to adopt an alternative plan leaving no prospect of a future sale of the copse. An ornithological trust which wishes to preserve the habitat of a rare bird offers the landowner a grant of £3000 a year for 5 years. The landowner is on the point of accepting the grant, for £15 000 easily outbids the golf club's £12 000. However, his daughter is an economist and, home for the week-end, explains discounting.

The present value of £3000 a year for 5 years, assuming once again a discount rate of 10 per cent, is calculated as follows. The formula is:

$$PV = \frac{FB}{(1 + r)^t}$$

We can calculate the present value of each separate £3000 payment. So after one year ($t = 1$):

$$PV = \frac{£3000}{(1 + 0.1)} = £2727$$

The second payment, after two years ($t = 2$) has a present value:

$$PV = \frac{£3000}{(1 + 0.1)^2} = £2479$$

Over the five years, the total present value of the grant to the landowner is:

$$PV = \frac{£3000}{1.1} + \frac{£3000}{(1.1)^2} + \frac{£3000}{(1.1)^3} + \frac{£3000}{(1.1)^4} + \frac{£3000}{(1.1)^5}$$
$$= £2727 + £2479 + £2254 + £2049 + £1863 = £11\,372$$

Assuming the landowner wants to maximize his income and has positive time preference and a 10 per cent discount rate, he sells the copse to the golf club.

The limitations of discounting are discussed below but one problem is worth mentioning here. A discount rate of 10 per cent is fine for the purposes of a hypothetical example. But how should we choose a discount rate when discounting a real environmental project? This is a crucial question. For example, if the landowner applied a discount rate of 5 per cent, the present value of £3000 a year for 5 years is £12 990 and he would therefore accept the grant from the ornithological trust.

The rate of interest you are willing to accept in return for postponing spending indicates the rate at which you are discounting future spending compared with current spending. In deciding on a rate at which to discount the future benefits of a conservation project, for example, it is therefore reasonable to take an interest rate as a starting point. But should we think of the benefits of the project as postponed consumption and choose an interest rate households might expect to receive from a bank or building society? Or should we regard the benefits as the return on an investment (in the resources of production used in the project) and take an interest rate firms might face in borrowing to finance the investment? And how should a society's discount rate differ from our individual time preference rates? There are no easy answers. The choice of discount rate remains controversial, and is discussed further in the next section. […]

The use of discounting has received significant criticism from environmentalists because it biases decision making towards policies and projects that yield immediate benefits. In contrast, policies or projects that yield benefits which only occur relatively far into the future rather than providing quick returns will be judged in an unfavourable light. For example, the extent of deforestation and the losses entailed might suggest that a project to reforest areas that have been cleared might be desirable. However, trees take a long time to grow. Under a regime of discounting a programme of afforestation would not fare very well relative to an alternative project that yielded its benefits sooner. The opportunity costs of afforestation – the loss of immediate benefits from the alternative project – would appear too high.

The implication of this line of thought is that there is a tension between the concept of intergenerational justice, and hence sustainable development, and the use of discounting in evaluating future benefits. Discounting favours the present over the future. But we may feel that, morally, the well-being of future generations should be given equal consideration to that of the current generation. We might derive such a principle from a concept of fairness: either fairness in outcomes, or fairness in what is intrinsically right. John Rawls' concept of social justice has been discussed in terms of impartiality between individuals (see Rawls, 1972). We could extend this impartiality across time, in arguing that the well-being of each generation should be equally valued. This implies, as Broome (1992, Chapter 3) notes, that the rate of discount applied by society to future well-being – the social rate of discount – should be zero.

Concepts of intergenerational justice underpin the argument for sustainable development. Against these arguments for an equal consideration of future welfare some commentators have raised the problem of uncertainty. We, the current generation, do not know what future generations will want, so perhaps discounting future benefits is a reasonable response to this uncertainty.

Uncertainty is discussed further in Section 3, but two points may be made here. First, it is reasonable to assume that basic needs will probably remain the same. For example, if the environment does provide unique life-support functions, then it is reasonable to make the assumption that future generations will value these functions and therefore value their preservation. Second, we can conceptualize concern for future generations, even though we do not know what they will want, by thinking in terms of the choices left available to them. Development that is not sustainable indicates that the current generation is 'closing off' choices that future generations would otherwise be free to make, thus narrowing their opportunities.

We can now turn to the question of how the current generation can secure sustainable development. We have already seen that one way to achieve this might be to use a zero social discount rate in making decisions that affect the future. There are, however, other ways by which we can assess the obligations of this generation towards the future. Can it, for example, compensate the future for imposing costs? The current generation holds a stock of environmental capital which can be used to derive well-being now and into the future. However, using up this capital by degrading environments erodes the opportunities of future generations. Is it feasible to compensate them for this loss?

3. An economic framework for environmental policy

3.1 The environment as 'capital'

This section explores some of the implications of the concept of sustainable development within a framework of economic analysis. Much of economics is concerned with a search for scientific objectivity. Yet, as our earlier discussion revealed, development is a value term concerning the well-being of individuals and society. Sustainable development also embodies a value judgement regarding how we should treat future generations. Such value judgements are inevitable, and rather than being avoided, they should instead be explicitly recognized. Let us begin from a familiar value judgement in economics, the concept of Pareto efficiency or the Pareto principle. In this framework each individual starts off with an initial endowment of inputs of productive resources which determines his or her well-being. Any change in economic activity is judged in relation to this initial well-being. The Pareto principle states that society is better off if a change in the allocation of inputs or outputs of economic activity leaves at least one person better off *without* making someone else worse off. This gain is known as a Pareto improvement, and when all such gains have been exhausted, then Pareto efficiency is achieved.

When the Pareto principle is used to analyse the efficiency with which resources are allocated between current and future generations, it can generate implications which are somewhat similar to those of sustainable development. In order to think about intergenerational concerns, the definition of endowments needs to be expanded so that it includes environmental resources. In particular, it is the time path of environmental resources that is of interest. Where these resources are being used up, then this particular endowment will be decreasing.

Consequently, there is less to be passed on to future generations, which decreases the economic opportunities open to them to meet their development goals. This violates the requirement for sustainability as laid out in the Brundtland Commission's report. It also contradicts the Pareto principle extended to consider future generations. No gain in current well-being can be achieved at the expense of future well-being.

What this amounts to is a requirement that an increase in well-being today does not lead to a reduction in well-being tomorrow. The endowments we have tomorrow must generate at least as much well-being as our current endowments. A large part of these endowments consists of various forms of productive capital.

The most common example of capital is manufactured capital such as machines. However, when capital is defined in this way, knowledge is also capital – human capital. Environmental resources are capital, too. When available, these resources provide flows of ecological services that contribute to human well-being over time. Environmental capital takes many forms, including tropical forests, which provide a habitat for an abundance of living things. Thus biodiversity preservation can be viewed as a service flow from the forest, which is in turn seen as a capital asset.

An economic approach to sustainable development therefore couches the main requirement for sustainability in terms of non-declining endowments, or capital, over time. An important issue is whether or not the composition of the total stock of capital can be permitted to change. If so, then sustainability might be promoted in other ways than by preserving environmental capital. However, even if this is possible, future generations must still be compensated for loss of environmental capital with some other form of capital, i.e. gains must compensate losses. As the following sections show, it is far from clear that we are in a position to determine the appropriate level of compensation for the loss of environmental resources.

3.2 Compensating the future

Capital provides a stream of benefits over time. Thus, capital provides a return and it is from this return that current and future generations are believed to derive well-being. The production function specifies the way in which inputs such as raw materials and manufactured capital are transformed into outputs through production processes:

$$Q = f(F_1, F_2, \ldots, F_N)$$

The same principle could apply here. However, this time Q is human well-being and the Fs are forms of environmental and manufactured capital. The basic idea is that if we have less of one particular capital component, then, other things being equal, we would expect to generate less well-being. A simple rule for sustainability suggested in Section 3.1 is that capital should be left intact, that is, productive capacity should not be eroded. This might be achieved via capital bequests: the current generation must pass on a capital stock that in terms of its productive capacity is at least as large as it inherited.

But does this mean that the composition of the capital stock must remain unchanged? Must we have as much of each *F*, or can the *F*s be substituted for each other? [...] Economists tend to assume that inputs or productive resources – the *F*s – are easily substitutable one for another. It is not unusual for a firm to substitute new technology for labour. However, it may in practice be very hard to replace the loss of environmental capital (raw materials) with human capital (skill and knowledge). The extent to which human and manufactured capital can be substituted for environmental capital is a highly contentious issue.

Tropical deforestation represents the loss of environmental capital. The current generation is passing on a physically smaller stock of tropical forests than it inherited. However, this does not necessarily imply unsustainable development. Whether it does so will ultimately depend on whether or not future generations can be compensated for this loss of capacity. This in turn depends on whether the 'productive capacity' of tropical forests can be substituted by alternative forms of capital (such as machines and knowledge). The legitimacy of development based on replacing environmental capital with 'produced' capital is a major source of disagreement between (some) economists and environmentalists. The former argue that the loss of one particular capital asset does not matter insofar as its services can be provided by a substitute asset. Environmentalists, on the other hand, stress the uniqueness of environmental capital.

This debate has its roots in an interchange that occurred in the early 1970s, between the 'Club of Rome' (an international non-governmental organization) and economists studying the use of natural resources. The argument presented by the 'Club of Rome' in *The Limits to Growth* (Meadows et al., 1972) was that development could not be sustained indefinitely because the world's supply of non-renewable resources, such as oil, gas and metals, is finite. The ultimate exhaustion of these resources implied a physical limit to economic growth. This pessimistic vision of the future led to a flurry of research intended to reassess the human plight, which was given further stimulus in 1973 by the four-fold increase in the international price of oil.

Oil is a non-renewable resource, which means that the extraction of one unit today means there is one less unit of oil to extract tomorrow. The question was how to use this valuable energy source without depriving future generations of a means of generating well-being. The answer, according to economist John Hartwick, was that 'oil economies' should invest a certain portion of oil revenues in alternative forms of capital. 'Hartwick's rule', as this principle has become known, works on the assumption that future generations can produce as much well-being without oil provided that the current generation passes on the means to achieve this (Hartwick and Olewiler, 1986). An increasing quantity of manufactured capital can replace the decreasing amounts of environmental capital represented by oil. Extended to our tropical forests example, then, deforestation could be condoned if the proceeds are reinvested in other forms of capital. The largest proximate cause of deforestation is the clearing of land for use in agriculture. Agricultural production might form the basis of the compensation that is required for sustainable development. Another example is associated with the cutting of forests for sale as timber. If part of the proceeds of timber sales are reinvested, then development might be sustainable without tropical forests.

Does this sound plausible? If so, then most environmentalists and many scientists would appear to be unduly pessimistic concerning the ability to compensate the future for deforestation. Instead, a radically changing environment might be viewed as an inevitable outcome of the development process. Yet the view that it is possible to compensate future generations for the loss of environmental capital by bequeathing greater quantities of other forms of capital is a debatable assumption, not an established fact. I will proceed here, however, by accepting that assumption for the sake of argument.

The next step is to try to assess the level of compensation that is required when environmental capital such as tropical forest is depleted. Cost–benefit analysis is a technique which can be used to evaluate the economic implications of cutting down tropical forests. This in turn requires a method of measuring economic values which is explained in Section 3.3. However, this method is not without its critics and so, in Section 3.4, I will consider an alternative view which holds that there is too much uncertainty surrounding exactly what it is we lose when tropical rain forests are destroyed for cost–benefit analysis to be an appropriate technique.

3.3 Measuring economic values

In the previous section I discussed the issue of compensating future generations for the loss of environmental capital. It seems that justice requires that we make such compensation and, if we assume that there is some substitutability between forms of capital, it is possible, at least in principle, to do so. However, it might turn out in practice that the scale of compensation entails a sacrifice of living standards which the current generation would be unwilling to make. The problem is then to decide whether it is worth investing in the manufactured capital designed to replace the environmental capital which has been degraded. Will the rate of return – the stream of future benefits from the new capital – be sufficient to offset the losses in future well-being incurred through the degradation of environments? It is the social rate of return that is relevant here, that is, the stream of benefits (net of costs) to society as a whole.

In order to assess the social rate of return from preserving environments such as tropical forests, some measure of their economic value is needed. How, you might ask, can the value of a forest be measured? There are no markets for forests; no auction rooms in which the forces of demand and supply work out the market price. In the absence of such mechanisms environmental economists have developed their own methods of measuring environmental values.

There are three main classifications of environmental values. The first concerns the direct use values associated with the environment. In the case of tropical forests these *direct use values* include the harvest of forest produce, fuelwood and timber. Use values are also related to tourism ('ecotourism'), where sites of out-standing natural beauty can be visited by tourists. Also many people derive pleasure from watching wildlife films. Although they may never actually visit the area filmed, this pleasure can also be regarded as a use value.

The second type of environmental value is that of indirect use values. Examples would be the storing of carbon in forests, and providing a habitat for bio-diversity. The evaluation of these functions is sometimes conceptualized in terms of the damage done by losing the service. In the case of carbon storage, the damage would be the contribution to global warming that may occur as a consequence of the increase in carbon emissions into the atmosphere.

The third class of values are non-use values. These are based on the ethical views which people may hold in connection with the environment. The main non-use value is existence value: the valuing of something in and of itself rather than for its uses. People clearly value the existence of species such as elephants, mountain gorillas or humpback whales, or they value whole ecosystems such as rain forests. Donations to environmental groups represent one mechanism by which existence values are revealed in people's behaviour. It is hard to separate existence value in practice from use value, since it is human preferences which are being expressed in both cases. However, the very remoteness of some environments for which pledges are made might justify the idea of 'existence value' as a separate category.

These different measures of environmental values provide the basis for cost–benefit analysis, a widely used economic framework which may be applied to evaluate environmental issues. In simple terms cost–benefit analysis involves the comparison of the costs and benefits of an environmentally sensitive activity. The concept of opportunity cost is relevant here. The opportunity cost of an economic activity is the benefit which would have been gained from the activity forgone. In the case of deforestation, for example, the opportunity costs of conserving the forest are the benefits of an alternative use of the land, such as agriculture. If those benefits are greater than the assessed value of the forest, there is a net gain associated with cutting down trees and developing the land for agriculture. Losers can be compensated for the loss of forests and there is still a net gain to human well-being. However, the discussion of environmental values, above, implies that the calculation must include the non-market values just outlined: it must be a full *social* cost–benefit analysis.

An example of how social cost–benefit analysis can be applied is provided by the case of the Amazonian tropical forest. Amazonia is a vast area of tropical forests in South America extending into six countries: Brazil, Colombia, Peru, Venezuela, Ecuador and Bolivia. Brazil accounts for two-thirds of the Amazonian forest (which also corresponds to a significant proportion of global tropical forests). In assessing the economic value of this forest there are two dimensions to be considered. First there are the domestic benefits associated with the forest. Within Brazil policy makers will try to maximize the net domestic benefits of policy towards forests. These domestic benefits are those which a sovereign country can 'capture' for its own development. There will be domestic benefits associated with both conservation and development. However, if we assume that these two benefit streams will be mutually exclusive, each land-use policy will involve forgone domestic benefits. So Brazil will seek to choose the option yielding the greater net benefits.

What are the domestic benefits of conservation? These will vary depending on the conception of conservation that is adopted. 'Strict' conservation or preservation leaves environments as wilderness. This rules out many direct uses of these areas, such as ecotourism, or sustainable harvest of timber. However, these benefits are exactly the kind of value that the country can appropriate. Indirect uses might also include domestic benefits, such as flood protection functions. The scientific evidence is disputed, but one argument is that forests, by preventing soils from washing away after severe rainfall, thereby prevent the sedimentation of rivers and flooding. The domestic benefits of development are perhaps easier to assess. These refer to the benefits derived from a change in land use to some other activity. Typically, this may involve clear cutting forest (as opposed to sustainable harvesting), and either selling this once and for all timber harvest, or burning it and then using the land for agricultural production.

The consideration of indirect use values is a required step in the full evaluation of the benefits of conservation. Matters are even further complicated when we turn to the second dimension: global costs and benefits. The environmental effects of conservation or deforestation do not respect national boundaries. The whole world benefits from, for example, carbon storage. Global benefits may also be derived from the pure existence of a unique ecosystem such as a forest.

In order to weigh up the costs and benefits of the conservation of tropical forests a common unit of analysis must be found. One way to achieve this is to put monetary values on costs and benefits. Pearce (1992) undertook just such an exercise in Amazonia. First, he estimated the monetary value of this tropical forest as a carbon sink – a receptacle for storing carbon. The annual global benefit is described in terms of the damage that would have been caused by carbon dioxide emissions if the forest did not exist. This he calculated to be $3.9 billion per annum. The second part of his calculation looked at Amazonia as a unique natural asset. Amazonia is a true focal point for global environmental concerns. There may be non-use value associated with the knowledge that this forest is conserved. Estimates of non-use value are not easy to obtain but, working from a number of studies that are available, Pearce derives a 'very conservative' estimate of $8 per adult per annum. The next step is to estimate how many individuals hold this value, which Pearce assumes to be 400 million (corresponding to the adult population of the richest nations of the world). This yields a non-use value of $3.2 billion per annum.

These values should be compared with the revenues (net of costs of production) that farmers in the Amazon now obtain from forestry. On the basis that these revenues are about 20 per cent of gross output in the forestry sector in Amazonia, an annual figure of $3.2 billion is obtained. This provides an estimate of the net benefit from preservation of the Amazonian forests in the region of some $3.9 billion per year. This estimate is based only on carbon sink value and non-use value. If the value of biodiversity were also considered then this would consolidate Pearce's findings. Note, however, that there is nothing 'concrete' in the numbers discussed here. What they illustrate is the possible magnitude of monetary values of tropical forests relative to those values we customarily think of as relevant to economics: e.g. those that pass through markets (such as timber and agricultural production).

This example can be restated in more general terms. Global benefits associated with conservation can be written B_g. The 'host' country will consider the domestic costs of conservation C_h. These are the forgone development benefits associated with forestry or agriculture (in other words the opportunity cost of forest conservation). C_h will be weighed up against the domestic benefits of conservation, B_h. Deforestation occurs because within the host country:

$$C_h > B_h$$

so that the host country would have incurred net costs, $C_h - B_h > 0$, had it decided to conserve and forgo the benefits of changing land uses. In Pearce's example the net costs of conservation C_h were \$3.2 billion (the value of forestry activity in Amazonia). Pearce assumed that $B_h = 0$. There are no domestic benefits from conservation in his model.

Where the environmental resource is unique, as in the case of Amazonia, we would expect the global benefits B_g to be large. What Pearce found was that global benefits actually might exceed the net domestic costs of conservation.

$$B_g > C_h - B_h$$

where $B_g = \$3.9 \text{ billion} + \$3.2 \text{ billion}$.

We know that

$$C_h - B_h = \$3.2 \text{ billion}$$

since B_h is assumed to be zero.

So there is a global net benefit of conservation:

$$B_g - (C_h - B_h) > 0$$

How can it be ensured that this global net benefit is achieved? This problem is complicated by the inherent conflict between the developing country (the 'host' to the forest) and the population of richer countries benefiting from conservation, implied by the model just set out.

In contrast to the case of the global commons which includes the atmosphere and the world's oceans, the forest, as we have seen, is slightly different. Forests provide global benefits but are within the sovereignty of particular countries (although within countries ownership will probably be poorly defined). While the world benefits from the conservation of tropical forests, it is unlikely that a country facing a choice regarding its land-use policy will attach much weight to these values. Conserving the environment is more likely to be regarded as a luxury that simply cannot be afforded. So, individuals and countries in the relatively low-income developing world may not value the services of environmental resources. Rather, at low levels of income, people may be willing to trade off environmental quality for increased income. However, at some higher level of income people are less willing to accept the trade-off, and wish to use their increased incomes to improve environmental quality. Hence, the demand for environmental benefits is biased towards the rich.

In the face of this conflict of interest, one way of achieving the net global benefits identified by the model is for richer countries to compensate the host country interests for the loss of domestic revenues that occur due to conservation. The compensation principle is based on *incremental cost*. The aim of the principle of incremental cost is to compensate host countries for the benefits that they cannot appropriate and hence to ensure a shift in host country decision making to reflect global well-being. In the formula set out above these benefits are designated C_h because, as the forgone benefits of developing the forest, they are the opportunity cost to the host country of its conservation. The amount of compensation is determined by $C_h - B_h$, that is, the cost to the host country of forest conservation net of any benefits that conservation might bring it. In Pearce's model the figure of $3.2 billion is further described as gross incremental cost because B_h is set at zero. Net incremental cost subtracts from the compensation a positive estimate of the domestic benefits of conservation. These might consist of tourism revenue from visitors to the forest.

Another adjustment to net incremental cost might be made for the distortions introduced by host country governments. These distortions help to stack the odds in favour of projects that involve forest clearing. In this way unsustainable practices are actively subsidized by government policy. For example, during the 1970s and part of the 1980s, the Brazilian government granted subsidized credit to projects that involved forest clearance, in particular claiming land for the ranching of livestock. The credit subsidy lowered the (private) rate of return that a project needed to earn in order for it to be profitable. Many of these subsidy schemes are now being dismantled, but significant losses have already been incurred. [...]

The Pearce example and the subsequent discussion of incremental cost provided a powerful rationale for conservation of tropical forests. However, it was one which recognized that a trade-off between conservation and deforestation might be possible and desirable. In cases where the costs of conservation outweigh the benefits, this analysis would suggest that society is better off pursuing a more general objective of sustainability. Deforestation could be permitted but the proceeds would be reinvested elsewhere. While some environmentalists would find this suggestion of a potential trade-off unacceptable on, say, moral grounds, another line of reasoning highlights the degree of error associated with the estimates of benefits. This position, which is often based on the lack of unequivocal scientific evidence surrounding the precise losses associated with the destruction of ecosystems, will be discussed in the next sub-section. A possible way of reconciling the two approaches, based on the idea of safe minimum standards, will then be considered.

3.4 Uncertainty and safe minimum standards

In undertaking a cost–benefit analysis of a conservation project, economists attempt to weigh up the costs and benefits of two scenarios, destroying or degrading some piece of environmental capital and conserving it, on the assumption of other things being equal. In other words, we try to predict two possible future courses of the world by assuming that the only difference between them is that in one the environmental capital is destroyed and in the other it is conserved. In reality, other things will change but, since we are concerned with the future, we cannot possibly know for certain what those changes will be. In this section I want to examine four main sources of this uncertainty: the life-support functions of ecosystems; the irreversibility of some environmental processes; technological progress; and population growth. I will then discuss a possible policy response to uncertainty: safe minimum standards.

3.4.1 LIFE SUPPORT FUNCTIONS OF ECOSYSTEMS In the previous section, it was suggested that the economist's concept of indirect use benefits encapsulates the so-called 'life-support functions' of ecosystems. In principle, the importance of ecosystems in regulating life could be evaluated alongside more traditional economic variables such as those market-traded services provided by ecosystems. In reality, however, knowledge of the natural world is seriously incomplete. So, while it is believed that biodiversity plays a critical role in preserving ecosystems from shocks and stresses, little is known about the role of particular species or groups of species over time in the provision of these services (Barbier et al., 1994). In fact, out of a possible 30–50 million species in the world, only about 1.4 million have actually been identified.

A suspicion also remains that there is more to the total value of an ecosystem than the sum of the values of individual functions. The economist's taxonomy of values, set out in Section 3.3, is regarded by ecologists as a set of secondary values. Ecologists describe the forest ecosystem as the primary value, where the 'component parts of an ecosystem are contingent on the existence and functioning of the whole' (Turner, 1993). This might not seem too far removed from an analysis of a tropical rain forest as a capital asset that supplies numerous service flows. The difference is that ecologists stress that the total value is more than just the sum of the parts. The 'extra' bit represents the 'glue' value of an ecosystem: in other words, the ecosystem is holding the functions together, and that is a function in itself. There is therefore, some disagreement between economists and ecologists over the scope of cost–benefit analysis in measuring the value of ecosystems: economists need to consider whether they accept the concept of a primary value and can recognize it within their calculations.

3.4.2 IRREVERSIBILITY Tropical deforestation is an irreversible process, in that this valuable asset cannot simply be built up again later. For example, outside the realms of science fiction species extinction cannot be reversed. In effect, biological diversity is non-renewable and its loss is therefore technically irreversible. Not all environmental resources are characterized by irreversibility. Air quality can be improved through the control of emissions of pollutants from, for example, power stations. Water quality can also be improved. However, there may come a threshold point where damage becomes irreversible. Such threshold effects imply that continued environmental degradation beyond the threshold level renders damage costs infinite.

Irreversibility can also refer to the feasibility of imposing a technically reversible solution. Global warming is very likely to be feasibly irreversible, because of the pressures of growing population and economic growth. An expansion of human numbers caused by population growth increases the pressure on natural resources, while economic growth may increase resource requirements per head of population. Both result in increased energy use and, as more fossil fuels are burnt, emissions of GHGs are increased. Even if countries commit themselves to reducing emissions of GHGs, concentrations of these gases in the atmosphere would still increase for some time to come (although this will vary with the degree of commitment). Some warming of global temperatures may already be inevitable even if action were to be taken now. Global warming might also be feasibly irreversible simply because current generations may find the adjustments required unpalatable in terms of current sacrifice. Because of the uncertainty of outcome associated with environmental change, they may prefer to carry on 'business as usual'.

However, uncertainty may be a reason for action rather than inertia, a view which is the basis of a decision-making rule known as the *precautionary principle*. This principle argues on the grounds of uncertainty for the conservation of environmental resources such as biodiversity and tropical forest habitats even if cost–benefit analysis suggests that development would be beneficial. This is especially urgent where the degradation of resources is irreversible.

3.4.3 TECHNOLOGICAL PROGRESS Sustainable development, as we saw in Section 2.2, is connected to the notion that the current generation should aim to bequeath to the future at least as much capital as it inherited. Two schools of thought were identified: one believes that it does not matter what form this bequest takes, while the other believes that particular components of environmental capital must form part of this bequest. The assumption behind the second view is that these resources are unique and their contribution to development cannot be replaced by substitutes. I now want to explore this debate further by examining the possibility of technological progress. Technological optimists (or 'cornucopians') claim that improved technology will always look after the interests of future generations. They regard the concept of sustainable development as irrelevant, because technological progress ensures the current generation is always poorer than those that follow.

Technological progress expands the opportunities open to the future, enhancing the production and consumption possibilities of an economy by raising the productivity of capital. One way to think of this is that greater output can be obtained for the same level of inputs; this implies the same Qs for fewer Fs in Section 3.2. This reduces the onus on the current generation to pass on to the future as much capital as it inherited and hence constitutes an argument in favour of discounting. It also raises another possibility. Environmental capital which is currently thought to be the unique provider of certain benefits may not be seen in this light in the future, because of the development of substitute goods or substitute processes made possible through technological breakthroughs. The technological optimists would argue that history is full of such instances.

Fuel use in the developing world provides an example. The burning of biomass such as fuelwood is an essential source of energy in many developing countries, mostly in rural and poorer urban communities. It is estimated that fuelwood provides 62 per cent of energy requirements in Africa and 34 per cent in Asia. In some sub-Saharan African countries it accounts for up to 90 per cent of total energy consumption. Natural forests and woodlands provide the bulk of fuelwood needs, and although fuelwood and charcoal production accounts for only 10 per cent of total forest depletion, it is a powerful erosive force at the forest edge. The size of this threat in terms of energy use will depend upon the availability of substitute fuels (e.g. kerosene) but also on technological measures, such as fuel-efficient stoves that increase the productivity of the scarce resources. When more efficient stoves are introduced into the household, more energy is produced from a given amount of fuelwood. Forest depletion falls, and labour is released for other economic activity.

While technological optimists are convinced of the pervasiveness of improved technologies in overcoming constraints on development, surprisingly little is known about how such changes actually come about. According to the theory of induced innovation, the development of new technologies is a response to pressing problems. For example, population pressures, it is argued, have a 'forcing effect' on agricultural productivity increases. So farming systems changed from 'shifting cultivation' to 'long fallow periods', to 'short fallow farming and cropping rotations with organic manuring', to 'modern intensive monocultures' based on high-yield crops and the application of irrigation, fertilizers, insecticides and pesticides (Pearce, 1990). This latter structural change is characteristic of what has become known as the 'Green Revolution'. Increasing demand increases the price of agricultural products, and so farmers respond to this change in incentives by adapting their farming techniques.

Can technological change mitigate the potentially serious effects from the loss of tropical rain forests and other ecosystems by replacing, for example, critical life-support functions? Some technological optimists argue that it can, although it is largely a question of faith. In fact, environmental resources have in the past provided the key for technological change. Section 2.1 indicated the role of plant diversity in providing the genetic information needed to develop new types of grains.

Technical solutions to the global warming process have been put forward. One suggestion is the emission of particles such as dust into the atmosphere, which would have a cooling effect on climate by reflecting back the sun's radioactive rays. However, most scientists regard with suspicion any attempt to deliberately control the global climate. Similarly, sulphur dioxide from the burning of fossil fuels may help to mitigate the global warming process by reflecting radiation from the sun. Sulphur dioxide is transformed in the atmosphere by chemical reactions to form sulphate aerosols, which reflect radiation in the same way as dust particles but are probably more powerful coolants. However, sulphur dioxide is a pollutant, both in its own right and as a precursor to acid rain, which is a significant source of damage to human health, buildings, materials and ecosystems. In addition, sulphate aerosols contribute to visibility loss (such as at the US Grand Canyon).

The benefits of technological change are themselves uncertain. Chlorofluorocarbons (CFCs) were hailed as a technological breakthrough when discovered in the 1930s and were found to have multiple uses in foam packaging, refrigerators and aerosol sprays. What could not have been anticipated at the time of discovery was that CFCs would play the major role in the depletion of the ozone layer, which blocks the sun's radiation. Depletion of the ozone layer increases the risk of skin cancers and cataracts due to increased exposure to the sun's ultraviolet rays. CFCs are also a powerful greenhouse gas.

3.4.4 POPULATION GROWTH   Technological progress can play an important role in relieving human pressure on environmental resources. Population growth has the opposite effect. Other things being equal, population growth increases the human pressure on environmental resources. An expanding human population requires habitat and resources. In the case of agriculture, only if the effects of technological progress offset the effects of population will pressure on land be relieved. [...]

Table 18.6 shows that world population levels more than doubled from 1950 to 1990. Between 1990 and 2025 world population is estimated to increase by just over 60 per cent. Stabilization in world population at around the 10–12 billion mark may only occur by the middle of the twenty-first century.

In contrast to the technological optimists, the 'neo-Malthusians' are pessimistic regarding our prospects. In the early nineteenth century, Thomas Malthus argued that the population of England was limited by the availability of food. Populations expanded so long as food supplies allowed. It follows that any progress that could be made by improving agricultural practices would induce further population growth. Human populations were doomed to live at the biological minimum, the standard of living consistent with human survival and adequate functioning but no more. With the benefit of hindsight it is clear that Malthus underestimated the capacity for improvements in technology to outstrip the increased demand for food that population growth brought.

The neo-Malthusians are so called because they have reintroduced the idea of absolute limits on population and economic growth in terms of increased environmental pressures. An increase in economic activity, it is argued, increases the amount of resources that are dragged through the economic system, so that, for example, a greater absolute amount of energy is required although energy per unit

Table 18.6   *World population size and growth: actual and future*

Region	Population size (millions)				Average annual population change (%)		
	1950	1990	1995	2025	1975–80	1985–90	1995–2000
World	2516	5292	5770	8504	1.73	1.74	1.63
Africa	222	642	747	1597	2.88	2.99	2.98
North and Central America	220	427	453	596	1.47	1.29	1.09
South America	112	297	326	494	2.28	2.01	1.71
Asia	1377	3113	3413	4912	1.86	1.87	1.68
Europe	392	498	504	515	0.45	0.25	0.23
USSR (former)	180	289	299	352	0.85	0.78	0.64
Oceania	13	26	28	38	1.49	1.48	1.24

Source: World Resources Institute, 1992

of GNP might stay constant. The idea of upper limits to population levels and levels of economic activity is still central to the claims of some ecologists and neo-Malthusians. Humans compete for resources on a finite planet. The pressure is determined both by the scale of economic activity and the number of humans. If economic activity or population are to expand, they may do so at the expense of ecosystems such as tropical forests. Ecologists argue that there is an upper limit to this process whereby the 'integrity' or quality of ecosystem functions are seriously compromised.

It has been calculated that the global human population directly or indirectly appropriates about 25–40 per cent of the global ecosystem (Vitousek et al., 1986). As indicated in Table 18.6, the natural world will have to accommodate multiples of present population pressure within several decades. The proposed upper limit to this process is sometimes linked to the ecological notion of 'saturation points'. A saturation point is the maximum population that a given area can sustain. At low levels of population, food and space are relatively abundant, allowing rapid increases in population. At higher levels of population, the rate of growth begins to taper off and population approaches the saturation point. This ecological concept is commonly applied to animal and plant species where the only constraint is that the population survives indefinitely. Biologist Paul Ehrlich has claimed that a sustainable global population at the current average living standard in the developed world would be as low as 2 billion, a fraction of the actual world population. Any estimate of sustainable population is highly sensitive to the degree of optimism that is adopted with respect to technological progress. Ehrlich's claims err on the side of extreme caution.

The idea of an upper bound to economic activity and population size is anathema to technological optimists. They would argue such reasoning falls into the same traps as Malthus's original hypothesis and is based on a static, unchanging view of the world. Of course both views are caricatures of the world in which we live. So while history informs us of many instances where human pressures on the environment have been eased by technological progress, population growth is nonetheless implicated in the deforestation process. However, the past is not necessarily a good guide to the future. Some would argue that maintaining environmental capital, as embodied in tropical forests, in fact represents a cautious view of the ability of improved technology to absolve us of our responsibilities towards the future. On the other hand it is usually argued that forest loss and biodiversiy loss are not susceptible to technological fixes.

I will go on to investigate appropriate policy responses to the conservation of environmental capital. While I have stated that population pressures have been suggested as one reason for deforestation it is less clear what this implies for public policy. It can be wrongly interpreted as a rationale for control over household fertility decisions, although more usually policy prescriptions have focused on increasing the flow of information concerning birth control, and the role of female rights and access to education. However, in Section 4 I will effectively by-pass these particular controversies and take population growth as given in order to look at alternative policies that have been suggested for the maintenance of environmental capital. The purpose of this sub-section has been to highlight the central role attributed to population pressures by some environmentalists and ecologists. [...]

3.4.5 SAFE MINIMUM STANDARDS   So what is an appropriate policy response to the levels of uncertainty just outlined? One approach is the development of safe minimum standards (SMS), a concept proposed by Ciriacy-Wantrup (1952) as a guiding rule for nature conservation. In this framework, sustainable development, defined in terms of the conservation of environmental capital, is placed beyond the reach of routine trade-offs with other social goals such as higher living standards. The basic idea is that we should avoid irreversible damage to the environment unless the social costs — the loss of the benefits of development — are intolerably large.

A policy rule from safe minimum standards

Pearce (1992) provided an example where the benefits of clearing land for an alternative activity are known, along with the benefits of conservation. Normally, it might be expected that while the benefits of development may be known with some reasonable degree of certainty, conservation benefits will be uncertain. Fortunately, it is not required that the magnitude of these conservation benefits is known in order to draw conclusions for policy. The only information that we do require is that yes (Y) benefits do exist or no (N) benefits do not exist for both conservation and development. Let us label conservation benefits P and development benefits D. So development benefits, which are known, are written B_D. B_D can be interpreted as the costs of conservation.

B_P is now the benefits of conservation which are not known. Pearce et al. (1990) have analysed the decision-making rule which can be drawn out of this available information in terms of the following matrix:

	Y	N	Maximum loss
Develop (D)	B_P	0	B_P
Conserve (P)	$B_D - B_P$	B_D	B_D

The matrix describes a combination of four possible choices. Each is characterized by its own loss, that is, its opportunity cost. These are:

- (D,Y) develop the land when there are benefits of conservation. This entails losses of B_P.

- (D, N) develop the land when there are no benefits of conservation. This entails no losses, hence the entry of 0.

- (P,Y) conserve when there are benefits of conservation. The loss here is equivalent to the forgone development benefits minus the benefits of conservation.

- (P, N) conserve when there are no benefits of conservation. Losses are the forgone development benefits.

In the face of uncertainty and irreversibility the decision rule to follow is to minimize the maximum loss, a procedure known as the minimax solution. This means that developing the land can only be justified where B_D is extremely large, outweighing high estimates of the unknown conservation benefits.

Bishop (1993) conceives of SMS along similar lines to Pearce's analysis set out above. Bishop's example is that 90 pence worth of biodiversity cannot be given up for a pound's (£) worth of coffee. If we were rigidly sticking to the rules of cost–benefit analysis then we would not reach the same conclusion, because there would be a net gain of 10 pence from growing coffee. Hence, the SMS decision rule demands caution when assessing the benefits of conservation relative to the benefits of development.

The effect of SMS is to reverse the bias in environmental decision making. Instead of assuming that environmental resources are there to be developed unless there is some strong reason for believing the development to be unsustainable, the approach is to make conservation the preferred option unless the forgone development benefits are intolerably large. However, what is meant by 'intolerable' is left unclear, though Bishop would intend it to reflect substantial costs. The SMS rule still requires conservation and hence sustainable development to compete for funding with other worthwhile social objectives. The magnitude of 'intolerable' costs is still determined by the current generation. Hence in the extreme, if the present generation does not care about the future, any current sacrifice for conservation may seem intolerable. The SMS approach still implies some system of weighting, so perhaps we are back where we started. There is no escaping value judgements about the well-being of different generations.

4. The need for international co-operation

If preserving environmental capital is required for sustainable development, then this requires that countries which have run down their natural capital compensate countries which still retain natural capital. The former can be thought of as countries in the 'developed north' with relatively high levels of other forms of capital, while the latter are countries in the 'developing south' with relatively little other capital. The richest 20 per cent of the world's population, most of whom live in the north, have 82.7 per cent of global income (United Nations Development Programme, UNDP, 1992). In contrast, the poorest 20 per cent have only 1.4 per cent. In 1960–70 these respective shares were 70.2 per cent and 2.3 per cent, indicating that economic disparities have increased.

4.1 Aid and the environment

4.1.1 EXISTING AID FLOWS   What are the implications of existing north–south aid flows for sustainable development? About 70 per cent of overseas development assistance (ODA) is bilateral, that is, given directly from one country to another. These transfers are not intended to secure sustainable development. They derive from a mixture of humanitarian motivations, historical ties with developing countries, and sometimes the objective of securing benefits (Thirlwall, 1994). Much of total aid flows to the richest 40 per cent of developing countries, who are relatively high military spenders and have relatively low provision for priority programmes that aim to supply basic needs (UNDP, 1992). It would seem that ODA is often poorly targeted, if our objective for assistance is to foster development amongst the poorest citizens of the world. The United Nations sets a uniform target for ODA of 0.7 per cent of GNP. [...]

Table 18.7 indicates that few developed countries donate anything approaching this target. However, a more equitable basis for determining the magnitude of transfers would be to allocate the burden of the 0.7 per cent ODA requirement on the basis of GNP weightings (UNDP, 1992). This would mean that economies with relatively large GNP per capita would contribute a correspondingly greater proportion of total GNP as aid. The adjusted target column of Table 18.7 shows how this would alter the structure of allocations.

A critique of ODA can also be made on environmental grounds. Not only do funds often end up financing a project with dubious development and economic

Table 18.7   *Total ODA as a percentage of GNP: selected countries and regions*

Country or region	As % of GNP		
	1970 actual	1990 actual	Adjusted target[a]
Canada	0.41	0.44	0.69
Japan	0.23	0.31	0.87
USA	0.31	0.19	0.76
European Union	0.36	0.41	—
France	0.46	0.52	0.65
Germany	0.33	0.42	0.74
Netherlands	0.60	0.93	0.58
UK	0.42	0.27	0.53
Nordic countries	0.34	0.90	0.80
OECD countries	0.33	0.33	0.70

[a]Adjusted target is 0.7 multiplied by one plus the percentage difference between the donor's 1989 GNP per capita and the average GNP per capita of all donors.

Source: UNDP, 1992

benefits, but they also appear to work against sustainable development. One of the most conspicuous examples of this are some large-scale hydroelectric dam projects which have contributed to deforestation, changes in downstream water quality, the flooding of forested land and the displacing of rural populations.

Turner (1990) suggests that poverty is the enemy of sustainable development. By encouraging short-term decision making in order to ensure immediate survivability, poverty forces people away from actions that would ensure sustainable livelihoods. For example, poverty tends to encourage subsistence farming on marginal lands with poor soil productivity. The soil quickly erodes and is exhausted of nutrients so that farming activity soon has to switch to other land, creating a vicious spiral of poverty and environmental degradation. In so far as aid packages raise incomes and alleviate poverty, environments may benefit.

There are now pressures to ensure that the environmental sensitivity of aid projects is taken into account. An alternative to traditional projects is to give developing countries technological know-how as aid. The technological gap that exists between the developed and developing world is seen as a major cause of wealth and income disparities between the two regions. The encouragement of soil conservation methods and improved farming technologies is one way in which this gap could be closed. However, some have voiced concern that developing countries do not have the technical or the institutional capacity to absorb the potentially large resource transfers that are proposed as part of 'sustainability packages'.

4.1.2 THE ENVIRONMENT-INDEBTEDNESS LINK   In 1990, the total external debt of developing countries stood at $1350 billion in contrast to a mere $100 billion in 1970 (UNDP, 1992). The major impact of this debt is in Latin America and sub-Saharan Africa, where debt is respectively 50 per cent and

100 per cent of GNP. Servicing debt has become a severe problem in these regions. Environmentalists have argued that the crisis of international debt is deepening environmental problems, which in turn worsens the debt problem. For example, in order to earn foreign exchange with which to repay external debt, indebted countries will seek to increase exports of natural resources such as timber. Yet, although the timber industry is implicated in deforestation, the international trade of timber is probably only responsible for 10 per cent of deforestation. There is in fact little evidence for a positive relationship between debt and environmental degradation. Deforestation is caused by more fundamental driving forces, such as land tenure arrangements, population pressures and the mismatch between domestic and global benefits. Other mechanisms whereby debt can *indirectly* contribute to environmental degradation have been proposed. For example, where the obligation to service debts lowers the standard of living and competes with other uses of a country's GNP, environmental objectives may be downgraded (Pearce et al., 1995).

'*Debt-for-nature*' swaps might be seen as one mechanism for tackling the compensation issue. A debt-for-nature swap reduces the debt obligations of a developing country to a developed country in return for the conservation of certain environmental resources. A creditor purchases the protection of a rain forest (or some other environmental asset) in return for retiring part of the country's debt. The emphasis in countries such as Costa Rica, Ecuador, Zambia and Madagascar where debt-for-nature swaps have been initiated has been on achieving a particular conservation goal. The policy is not intended to resolve the problem of indebtedness itself.

4.2 Problems of international co-operation

It is clear that any international agreement for sustainable development must be mutually beneficial in order for a sufficient number of countries to sign up. Yet such international co-operation is intensely problematic in a very unequal world. First, the compensation might not be forthcoming, or at least donors might not be willing to give sufficient quantities of compensation. Second, the potential recipients may not be willing in principle to give up what they see as a right to use their environments how they see fit.

An international strategy to conserve environmental capital therefore requires the creation of new and additional transfers specifically designed as environmental aid or environmental compensation. An example of an international agency designed to facilitate environmental 'aid' flows is the Global Environmental Facility (GEF), which was set up in 1990 by the World Bank, the United Nations Environment Programme (UNEP) and the United Nations Development Programme (UNDP). The aim of the GEF is to shift the emphasis of decision making on to the consideration of global benefits in addition to local benefits. Specifically the GEF was established in order to:

- protect the ozone layer;

- protect international water resources;

- protect biodiversity; and

- ensure a decrease in GHG emissions.

International attention has also shifted to the negotiation of global agreements to promote the conservation of environmental capital. Four major agreements emerged from the Earth Summit. One was a huge document called *Agenda 21* described as a global 'masterplan for sustainable development' (Grubb et al., 1993). Individual governments carry the responsibility to implement the requirements set out in this document. Overseeing the progress of each is a new international body set up during the Earth Summit: the Commission for Sustainable Development (CSD). However, although each sovereign government must report to the CSD, this body has no international legal status and therefore cannot actually *force* countries to comply with *Agenda 21*.

The other agreements reached at the Earth Summit covered climate change (the Framework Convention on Climate Change, FCCC), biodiversity conservation (the Convention on Biodiversity, CBD) and deforestation (the Forest Principles). It is important not only for developing countries to sign up to these conventions (which for the most part they have done) but also for the developed world to share the burden of implementation. Any agreement will be worthless if the developing countries do not find it in their interests to comply. Rapid population growth and economic growth will conspire against any attempts by the developed world to bring into effect a unilateral agreement. For example, increasing emissions of GHGs would negate the actions of countries attempting to decrease their own emissions. I want now to look more closely at the Convention on Biodiversity in order to illustrate some of the conflicts that might arise in attempting to implement international agreements to secure sustainable development.

4.2.1 THE CONVENTION ON BIODIVERSITY The CBD committed countries to the conservation and sustainable use of biological resources. However, biodiversity conservation was designated as an issue of national sovereignty to be determined within national boundaries, which raises doubts as to the actual commitment to conservation that will result. National governments may decide that maximizing domestic or host country benefits requires reneging on the sustainability constraint. Ensuring compliance may necessitate changing the economic incentives that key decision makers face. In particular, it will require the creation of new and additional funds to finance compensation in accordance with the principle of incremental cost.

However, there is no mention of global benefits in the convention. The CBD states that compensation is the difference between how much a country spends on biodiversity preservation *without the* CBD and what it would have to spend *with the* CBD. The sustainability constraint operates without any reference to the magnitude of global benefits. In a sense, this fits in with an approach based on positive but uncertain benefits, perhaps based on a notion of SMS. The absence of specific reference to global benefits was, however, largely a concession to political conflicts between the developed countries and the developing countries.

The developing nations of the south regard an emphasis on global benefits to be against their interests, implying an obligation to provide stores of biodiversity in forests and other ecosystems for the global good rather than to develop these resources for their own domestic benefit. An illustration of this is the furore that surrounded the convention on the protection of the world's forests. This was due, in the main, to the protestations of India and Malaysia, who were implacably opposed to the idea that their forests should be preserved as a sink for the GHG emissions of the developed world (Grubb et al., 1993). The developed countries had already threatened the capacity of the globe to absorb GHGs by increasing their own emissions in the past and had largely depleted their forests. Agarwal and Narain (1992) argue that the thinking behind various suggested international environmental conventions, which would include the FCCC and the CBD, is a form of 'environmental colonialism'. They argue that the problem of sustainable development as the conservation of environmental capital originated in the 'excessive' consumption of the developed world and in particular the USA. Developing countries have their own environmental priorities based on preventing desertification, land and water degradation and declining prices of the natural resources that they trade on international markets. Although some of these concerns are not unrelated to concerns surrounding deforestation, the critique indicates that international agreements are not necessarily easily achieved even if new and additional funds are made available.

The political will of the developed world to provide adequate compensation and therefore to share the burden of implementation of international conventions can also be questioned. No actual magnitudes for compensation were agreed at the Earth Summit. The signing of the CBD was almost scuttled by the reluctance of three key signatories – the USA, UK and Japanese governments – to commit themselves to an agreement that left open-ended the monetary sums that might be required to save the world's biodiversity. Japan and the UK wavered but eventually signed the CBD during the summit. It took just over a year and a change of President for the USA to sign. The Earth Summit coincided with the US presidential elections and a serious downturn in global and US economic activity. Short-term economic concerns are often in conflict with policies that require sacrifice on the part of current generations, and this is a major obstacle to the achievement of sustainable development.

Although many figures have been bandied about, the true magnitude of the sums ultimately required is simply not known. Credible estimates have looked at the costs of improving the monitoring and conservation of remaining wildernesses (of which closed tropical forests form part), the costs of decreasing emissions of GHGs, particularly carbon dioxide (by switching to less-polluting fuels or reducing energy use), and additional ODA for conventional development needs. Pearce et al. (1993) suggest a figure of about $50 billion per annum. At the time of the Earth

Summit a figure of $100 billion per annum was considered as a reference level. The Global Environmental Facility has an annual budget of $2 billion.

Given the ambiguous legal status of these new international agreements, countries may either renege altogether on compensation by not ratifying the conventions in their own parliaments or use ambiguities in the conventions to their own advantage. The fact that countries often prefer to allocate blame for global environmental change to other countries does not augur well for the success of international co-operation. The classic example is the emphasis of the developed world on future projected rates of economic growth and population growth in the developing world. Conversely, the developing world focuses on 'over-consumption' in the developed world. The real danger is that these conflicts will lead countries to let environmental events simply unfold in front of them. If the global costs of environmental degradation are increasing, then solutions will become more expensive. These increasing costs will be passed on to future generations, contrary to the notion of sustainable development. [...]

5. Conclusion

Sustainable development has been defined as human well-being generated now that is not reversed in the future. I have devoted most attention to the view that the way to achieve this social goal is to maintain environmental capital, using as an example tropical deforestation and its implications for biodiversity loss and global warming. One approach to conserving such environmental capital focuses on the role of discount rates in decisions that affect future generations. I have concentrated on analysing the most efficient ways to maintain capital, illustrating this with the global and national costs and benefits of tropical forest conservation. This led me to a compensation rule based on incremental cost, which in turn is based on the principle that the victim pays. A key factor in the implementation of such strategies is the political will required to fund these solutions and the role of international institutions to broker such trades.

Perhaps the most persistent theme of this chapter has been uncertainty. At the scientific level, the effects of biodiversity loss and the likelihood of global warming are hard to predict. At the philosophical level considerable uncertainty surrounds the concept of intergenerational justice: the problem of how to strike the right balance between the needs of the current generation and those of future generations. At the political level, the self-interest of nations threatens to disrupt efforts at international policy co-operation to secure sustainable development. I have tried to show how economics can help to guide policy in the context of uncertainty by making the concept of sustainable development as precise as possible, by devising ways of evaluating the costs and benefits of alternative courses of action, by identifying key aspects of uncertainty and by drawing out policy rules such as safe minimum standards from alternative assumptions.

References

Agarwal, A. and Narain, S. (1992), *Global Warming in an Unequal World: a Case of Environmental Colonialism*, New Delhi, Centre for Science and Environment.

Barbier, E.B., Burgess, J.C. and Folke, C. (1994), *Paradise Lost: the Ecological Economics of Biodiversity*, London, Earthscan.

Bishop, R. (1993), 'Economics, efficiency, sustainability and biodiversity', *Ambio*, Vol. 22, no. 2–3, pp. 69–73.

Broome, J. (1992), *Counting the Costs of Global Warming*, Cambridge, White Horse Press.

Ciriacy-Wantrup, S.V. (1952), *Resource Conservation: Economics and Policy*, Berkeley, University of California Press.

Gradwohl, J. and Greenberg, R. (1988), *Saving the Tropical Forests*, London, Earthscan.

Grubb, M. et al. (1993) *The Earth Summit Agreements*, London, Earthscan.

Hartwick, J.M. and Olewiler, N.D. (1986), *The Economics of Natural Resource Use*, New York, Harper and Row.

Meadows, D.H., Meadows, D.L., Randers, J. and Behrens, W. (1972), The 'Club of Rome', *The Limits to Growth*, London, Earth Island.

Moran, D. (1994), 'Forestry', in D.W. Pearce et al., *Blueprint 3: Measuring Sustainable Development*, London, Earthscan.

Myers, N. (1990), 'Tropical forests', in J. Leggett (ed.), *Global Warming: the Greenpeace Report*, Oxford, Oxford University Press.

Myers, N. (1992), 'Biodiversity preservation and the precautionary principle', *Ambio,* Vol. 22, No. 2–3, pp. 74–9.

Pearce, D.W. (1990), 'Population growth', in D.W. Pearce (ed.), *Blueprint 2: Greening the World Economy*, London, Earthscan.

Pearce, D.W. (1992), 'Deforesting the Amazon: toward an economic solution', *Ecodecision*, Vol. 1, pp. 40–50.

Pearce, D.W. and Warford, J.J. (1993), *World Without End: Economics, Environment and Sustainable Development*, New York, Oxford University Press.

Pearce, D.W., Barbier, E. and Markandya, A. (1990), *Sustainable Development*, London, Earthscan.

Pearce, D.W., Moran, D., Maddison, D. and Adger, W.N. (1995), 'Debt and environment', *Scientific American*, Vol. 272, No. 6, pp. 8–32.

Rawls, J. (1972), *A Theory of Justice*, Oxford, Oxford University Press.

Swanson, T. (1990), 'Biodiversity', in D.W. Pearce (ed.), *Blueprint 2: Greening the World Economy*, London, Earthscan.

Thirlwall, A.P. (1994), *Growth and Development*, 5th edn, London, Macmillan.

Turner, R.K (1990), 'Environmentally sensitive aid', in D.W. Pearce (ed.), *Blueprint 2: Greening the World Economy*, London, Earthscan.

Turner, R.K. (1993), 'Speculations on weak and strong sustainability', in R.K. Turner (ed.), *Sustainable Environmental Economics and Management: Principles and Practice*, 2nd edn, London, Belhaven.

United Nations Development Programme (1992), *Human Development Report* 1992, New York, UNDP.

Vitousek, P.M., Erlich, P.R., Erlich, A.H. and Matson, P.A. (1986), 'Human appropriation of the products of photosynthesis', *Bioscience*, Vol. 36, No. 6, pp. 68–73.

Wilson, E.O. (1992), *The Diversity of Life*, London, Penguin.

World Commission on Environment and Development (WCED) (1987), *Our Common Future*, Oxford, Oxford University Press.

World Resources Institute (1992), *World Resources 1992–93*, Washington, DC, World Resources Institute.

INDEX